Hopewell Settlement Patterns, Subsistence, and Symbolic Landscapes

UNIVERSITY PRESS OF FLORIDA

Florida A&M University, Tallahassee
Florida Atlantic University, Boca Raton
Florida Gulf Coast University, Ft. Myers
Florida International University, Miami
Florida State University, Tallahassee
New College of Florida, Sarasota
University of Central Florida, Orlando
University of Florida, Gainesville
University of North Florida, Jacksonville
University of South Florida, Tampa
University of West Florida, Pensacola

HOPEWELL SETTLEMENT PATTERNS, SUBSISTENCE, AND SYMBOLIC LANDSCAPES

Edited by

A. Martin Byers and DeeAnne Wymer

University Press of Florida
Gainesville/Tallahassee/Tampa/Boca Raton
Pensacola/Orlando/Miami/Jacksonville/Ft. Myers/Sarasota

First cloth printing, 2010
First paperback printing, 2024

29 28 27 26 25 24   6 5 4 3 2 1

Library of Congress Cataloging-in-Publication Data
Hopewell settlement patterns, subsistence, and symbolic landscapes /
edited by A. Martin Byers and DeeAnne Wymer.
p. cm.
Papers from the Society for American Archaeology's 2004 symposium.
Includes bibliographical references and index.
ISBN 978-0-8130-3455-3 (cloth) | ISBN 978-0-8130-8059-8 (pbk.)
1. Hopewell culture—Ohio—Congresses. 2. Land settlement patterns—
Ohio—History—Congresses. 3. Subsistence economy—Ohio—History—
Congresses. 4. Landscape—Symbolic aspects—Ohio—History—
Congresses. 5. Landscape—Social aspects—Ohio—History—Congresses.
6. Earthworks (Archaeology)—Ohio—Congresses. 7. Ohio—
Antiquities—Congresses. I. Byers, A. Martin, 1937– II. Wymer, DeeAnne.
III. Society for American Archaeology.
E99.H69H674 2010
977.1'01—dc22 2009044787

The University Press of Florida is the scholarly publishing agency for the State University
System of Florida, comprising Florida A&M University, Florida Atlantic University,
Florida Gulf Coast University, Florida International University, Florida State University,
New College of Florida, University of Central Florida, University of Florida, University
of North Florida, University of South Florida, and University of West Florida.

University Press of Florida
2046 NE Waldo Road
Suite 2100
Gainesville, FL 32609
http://upress.ufl.edu

Contents

Figures

Tables

Acknowledgments

Many hours of dedicated work on the part of numerous individuals have gone into making this unique volume a success. We would like to sincerely thank all of our volume authors for their patience and for taking time out of their very busy schedules to not only draft and rewrite their original contributions but also, with extra dedication to the theme of the volume, to read and comment on the contributions by their fellow section authors. We also want to thank Dr. N'omi B. Greber and Dr. Robert Hall, who participated as discussants for the Society for American Archaeology 2004 symposium from which this book emerged, and a special thanks for N'omi B. Greber, who also agreed to write the final chapter of this book. We gratefully acknowledge all of the help and hard work on the part of University Press of Florida editors and personnel in helping to craft this book—and a special thank-you must go to John Byram at UPF for his dedication, his help, and his willingness to take a chance on the unusual format of our volume.

Finally, we would like to thank the outside reviewers for their insightful comments and suggestions on the manuscript.

Introduction

A. Martin Byers and DeeAnne Wymer

The cognitive-normative stance that has been developing in archaeology in the last several decades seems to be aggravating rather than resolving the materialist-idealist dichotomy. This is ironic since the promotion of this cognitive-normative approach has been greatly facilitated by the postprocessualist critique. This critique was initially directed to rebalancing archaeological interpretation by arguing that the focus on the materialist pursuit of survival promoted by Binfordian processualism has led to treating the cognitive-normative dimension of human experience as either epiphenomenal, at worst, or, at best, as merely an afterthought of human existence.

The materialist-idealist dualism has been particularly detrimental by creating what is virtually a two-world approach within the domain of archaeology—in essence, a two solitudes among archaeologists. Although not exclusive to Middle Woodland studies, this problem has been particularly apparent in Hopewellian studies because of the rich and varied material cultural assemblage that characterizes much of the Middle Woodland period across the Eastern Woodlands. Furthermore, the Middle Woodland archaeological record of the Eastern Woodlands, especially in Ohio, is strongly dichotomized between the material residue of ceremonialism, often in the form of monumental earthworks and mortuary facilities, on the one hand, and, on the other, the material residue of everyday domestic life, hardly visible archaeologically in many cases. It is almost as if two different social systems existed in the same time and place, one in which symbolism, ritual, and the esoteric played a central role and the other in which the nitty-gritty of the pursuit of survival played the dominant role.

Because this symbol/function, ceremony/survival duality so strongly dichotomizes the material record, it also has tended to divide archaeologists themselves into two camps, such that, in some cases, they do not have much to say to each other. The "monumental earthworks and mortuary/ceremonial" idealist camp is caught up in the nature of the cognitive-normative sphere, which seems so central to their focus of study; the other, the "pursuit of survival" materialist camp, is equally caught up on the minutiae of midden analysis, lithic-wear analysis, and the reconstruction of the Middle Woodland diet. Those of the materialist camp often carry out their fieldwork next to monumental earthworks while apparently oblivious to their presence, whereas those of the cognitive-normative camp, busily measuring the earthworks and eliciting any patterning that their azimuth alignments might have had, are equally oblivious to the excavations being carried out by their archaeological colleagues in the next field over.

Although, obviously, we are exaggerating the situation, it seems to us that Hopewellian studies in particular and, for that matter, archaeological studies in general cannot allow the two solitudes to continue. We now know that the two cultural spheres of symbolic ceremonialism and practical survival entailed the same population and that this population constituted only one, albeit complex, social system. For this very reason, the archaeologists who focus on the great earthworks and the complex mortuary residue so often associated with them and who attempt to make sense of these in symbolic and cognitive-normative terms cannot forget that this ceremonial sphere was the product of the same people who had to adapt effectively to the material imperatives of everyday survival. Equally, those archaeologists focusing on the practical tools and residue of the ongoing day-by-day pursuit of survival must be mindful that this complex record was the skilled outcome of the very same people who devoted significant labor and time building and using the earthworks and filling them with their dead. It is obvious that, for the Hopewell, feeding the spiritual world through ritual and ceremony was as vital to them as feeding themselves. What appears to us as two contrasting ways of life to these people actually constituted a single, highly intelligible, indeed, sensible, way of life. Thus the activities performed by the communities in the ceremonial sphere would have been evaluated by them in terms of how they believed these tasks enhanced or possibly repressed the success of their everyday pursuit of survival and, recursively, how their performances in the latter sphere either enhanced or limited the success of their ritual activities. When we see the problem in this light, it is our archaeological collective task and duty, whether one is of the materialist camp or the cognitive-normative camp, to develop and integrate both the theoretical frameworks and the methodological tools that will allow us to better understand and interpret this complex archaeological record.

A growing awareness of a need to bring researchers together to focus on such issues led to our planning a special symposium on this topic for the Society for American Archaeology meeting of 2004. The theme was sacred landscapes and settlement patterns. Through the symposium we hoped to stimulate Hopewell researchers to present papers that would address these two aspects, especially encouraging individuals to "think through the issues" in a rational, integrated manner. Our ultimate goal was to pull these papers together to create a coherent overview of the problem and make some tentative advances toward a solution. We hope this book is a step in that direction because, as the editors, we are firmly convinced that only if archaeology can treat the symbolic-ideational and material-instrumental in a coherent and integrated manner can we make real advances in our understanding of the cultures that were responsible for the creation of the archaeological record.

We are aware of some pitfalls, of course. Foremost is the epistemological problem of demonstrating and validating our claims concerning the nature of the cognitive-normative sphere. It is almost axiomatic in the view of many archaeologists that, since symbolic meaning is abstract and conventional, there is no realistic manner by which we can confirm the hypotheses that we make concerning this domain. Can we ever, for example, demonstrate that the multiple azimuth alignments of the great Ohio Hopewell embankment earthworks of Newark, High Bank, and others, or even the long-distance intersite alignments that some of the authors of chapters to this book propose, were the outcome of ancient ideological strategies that had among their goals the construction of such alignments and interconnections? In plain words, can we demonstrate this to be deliberate or are we doomed to remaining forever in the grip of "mere speculation"?

In stark contrast to this epistemic or methodological quandary would seem to be verifying the claims about the much more concrete nature of the pursuit of survival. This is made up of a complex of tangible rather than abstract practices that are directly manifested in the material residue, in the stones and bones and seeds. Therefore, are we not—by the very nature of symbolic/instrumental dichotomy and our methodological limitations—fated to emphasize the instrumental and objective at the expense of the cognitive-normative and symbolic? Indeed, since it is clear that the Hopewell were very successful in resolving their pursuit of survival (otherwise they would not have had the labor or energy to devote to earthwork ritual) should we not simply accept the symbolic sphere as a given in order to focus our scientific energies and resources on what we can most concretely establish? Furthermore, some might be inclined to argue that the symbolic can never hold the balance of significance in understanding the archaeological record since, in the long term, if it were to dominate, it would waste the limited labor resources of a society and, inevitably, its communities would be doomed to perish. Taking such a position would thus seem to imply not only that we can safely ignore the symbolic and cognitive-normative but that we might need to in order to focus on what really moves history by reconstructing the practicalities of the social system, a focus that will be well rewarded by its very direct relating of nonconventional, that is, instrumental activity as necessarily being realized in the material residue that the activity generated.

This is a critically important comment. What it highlights is the prevailing interest of archaeology on focusing upon the material activities of the past. While never denying that thought and morality were also part of the past, it seems to be the case that the latter tend to be abstract and leave little in the way of material residue while human activity and its modification were largely tied into the development of tools—and we have plenty of these in great variety. While tools also presuppose cognition, they do not entail the type of abstract cognition that we have come to identify with symbolism. We typically assume that the cognitive aspect that material tools manifest is that of practical design and function, the very cognition that is needed in the pursuit of survival. This tight integration of practical tools and practical cognition is basic to processualism, of course, and it is manifested in Binford's well-known tripartite technomic, socio-technic, and ideo-technic typology of artifacts (Binford 1962). However, the way these categories are theoretically defined and methodologically identified reveals a strong bias for practical cognition since artifacts are fitted into the technomic category if they are identified by the absence of any properties that would promote nonpractical or noninstrumental purposes. Therefore, socio-technic and ideo-technic artifact categories are identified by the addition of properties that, it is assumed, could only serve such noninstrumental purposes or, at the extreme, were characterized by the complete absence of any such practical properties. Indeed, this means that only technomic artifacts had real action-mediation capacity and the less the practical nature of the tangible properties of the artifact (in our archaeological eyes, that is), the less its real action-mediation nature.

The great benefit of this tripartite typology is that it gave the archaeologist a methodological tool for moving from the statics of the archaeological deposit to the dynamics of the prehistoric activity. However, the implicit assumption here is that the less technomic-like and the more socio-technic-like and/or ideo-technic-like artifacts appeared to us, the less such items were designed to mediate action and the more they were designed for abstract ritual-like and passive, nonpractical cognitive mediation. This also meant that the technomic artifacts could be rather directly used to explore the range of real practical activities for which they had been made such that not only was their purpose and use made accessible to the archaeologist but also, as analytic refinement occurred, the complexity and variation among the practical activities this instrumental assemblage mediated became more accessible. At the same time, however, the socio-technic and ideo-technic artifact categories, while becoming more elaborate and complex, nevertheless were also a measure of the absence of "real" action and, instead, a measure of abstract "pseudo" action (e.g., ritual) or of social posturing (e.g., displaying elite status). Hence this typology promoted a strong instrumental/sociosymbolic dichotomy and enhanced the former as being dynamic and varied, manifesting cognitive design capacities that were more or less carefully attuned to the imperatives of survival. The latter, then, was treated as abstract and passive, the epitome of the absence of action, and keyed to an abstract and intangible sphere of social relations and esoteric ideas.

This privileging of the instrumental during the maturing phase of the New Archaeology was well illustrated when Robert Dunnell proposed that the advancement of archaeology was best served through an evolutionary theoretical approach and that much of what he, and many other scholars struggled with, lay in the arena of how archaeologists treated the concept of "style":

> *Style denotes those forms that do not have detectable selective values.*
> *Function is manifest as those forms that directly affect the Darwinian*
> *fitness of the populations in which they occur.* . . . A profitable direction
> may lie in identifying stylistic elements by their random behavior. . . . A
> more detailed examination of the nature of style shows that the behavior
> of style is fundamentally stochastic. This observation explains its success
> in chronological matters and illuminates the nature of culture histori-
> cal "explanatory" processes like diffusion. . . . This observation explains
> why evolutionary processes such as natural selection have not been ef-
> fectively employed. (Dunnell 1978: 199–200)

It seems apparent that Dunnell saw what archaeologists traditionally thought of as design/symbolic elements (style) as measuring stochastic processes, while artifacts (or elements of a culture) involved in survival activities were more directly influenced or impacted by Darwinian selection, implying, of course, the nonimportance of style to survival.

This typology and the framework of assumptions that presupposes it has promoted the view that the technomic artifact category most directly ties the present to the past and views the upper stratum of the "cultural pyramid" (socio-technic/ideo-technic) as intangible and a static abstract ideational realm that might be better ignored. The operationalization of the actions of the past through the interpretation of the properties of technomic artifacts has been the primary methodological anchor of the processualist program and, of course, has advanced the discipline's traditional focus on treating activity as tangible and therefore real while treating the abstract cultural reality realized in thought and cognition as intangible and therefore somewhat less than real.

Promoting this focus on action, in our opinion, is the strength of this tripartite typology and its theoretical framework. However, it also has entrenched the separation of the more abstract cognitive-normative aspect of culture and of the intangible but causally real social structural aspect of community from the technological aspect, thereby promoting the *fallacy* of the sociosymbolic/ instrumental dichotomy. Arising from this tripartite typology, therefore, has been a series of contrasting dichotomies, with the left hand side of each consistently privileged over the right hand side: Functional/symbolic, Concrete/ abstract, Action/thought, Dynamic/passive, Real/imaginary, and so on. The result has been to entrench the two solitudes. Further, it is perhaps not surprising that we speak in privilege/underprivileged dualities, in asymmetrical sets of two, since the very theoretical foundation of postprocessualist theory (such as structuralism, cognitive archaeology, among others) necessarily presupposes a world embedded within a conflict of duality, the Marxist "have versus have-nots," if you will (see, for example, Hodder 1986, 1992; Leone 1986, 1995; Shanks and Tilley 1987b, 1989). After all, as Tilley so boldly put it, "The move recommended here is not from science to the creation of fairy tales of the past, but from a pseudo-science to a dialectically conceived science. . . . A self-critical archaeology should be especially concerned to examine the ways in which material culture is and can be used to legitimate power strategies and ideological practices both in the past and the present" (1998: 321–325). Even the opposition of the titles "processualism" versus "postprocessualism" reveals all too clearly our own cultural inclination to fall into the trap of casting the world in inherent and asymmetrically charged dualities.

Hopewellian studies, however, clearly demonstrate that these dichotomies must be overcome. There was nothing passive or abstract about the practices that Hopewell ritual promoted; they required major labor. We take the position that Binford was correct in insisting that archaeologists must tie their interpretations to the archaeological data and that the most effective manner to do this is to take the action-mediation approach. That is, artifacts, features, and facilities are the media of action, and their forms and variations in forms can track the variation and transformation of prehistoric material action. However, the behaviorist conceptualization of action that this tripartite typology promotes and even presupposes must be eschewed. The tripartite technomic, socio-technic, and ideo-technic typology is firmly grounded on the separation of action from social structure and belief. As noted above, this typology defines technomic artifacts as the material media of practical action, socio-technic artifacts as the material media of intangible social status, and ideo-technic artifacts as the material media and expression of intangible as well as abstract beliefs.

The problem with this typology is that even technomic artifacts have social structural and cognitive-normative meaning. The very existence of a category of practical tools for hunting presupposes the beliefs in the existence of the animals that would be the targets of the hunter, and of course no hunter could produce hunting tools without having the requisite knowledge of the habits of the animals of prey. Indeed, the concept "hunter" may seem straightforward and obviously practical, but the full social and cultural meaning of this concept must be appreciated in order to understand the form of the instrumental tools that a hunter in a given social system typically uses. That is, the items we as archaeologists identify as technomic artifacts cannot be cognitively or normatively separated from their users since they necessarily define their users *as* hunters within their communities, and as such these practical devices are also socio-technomic devices. Further, there may be special artifacts that are imbued with specific social meaning (i.e., socio-technic items) that are possessed by only a few people (and perhaps these folks in addition do not possess or use such technomic items as hunting tools). If so, defining the exclusive possessors of these socio-technic artifacts as elite immediately defines the possessors of the hunting tools as non-elite, possibly commoners. The same "bleeding" of these three categories applies to the cognitive-normative sphere since no typical preindustrial society separates the practical beliefs and know-how of the hunter and hunting, for example, from the religious beliefs that are paramount about the very animals that are exploited. Hence the hunting tool may necessarily implicate its user as having strong religious convictions tied into and realized in hunting protocol.

In short, these three categories of technomic, socio-technic, and ideo-technic artifacts express an inadequate and, indeed, seriously misleading methodology and implicate an equally misleading social theoretical background. A more positive way of putting this is to say that all technomic artifacts have social and ideological meaning and implication and all socio-technic and ideo-technic artifacts have some action meaning. Ironically, Binford in his seminal publication "Archaeology as Anthropology" clearly implicated this inadequacy of his tripartite categorization when he noted, "It has often been suggested that we cannot dig up a social system or ideology. Granted we cannot excavate a kinship terminology or a philosophy, but we can and do excavate the material items which functioned together with these more behavioral elements within the appropriate cultural subsystems" (1962: 217).

Therefore it is not surprising that although there was an initial rush of theoretical and methodological ingenuity to push the limits beyond merely stating the artifactually obvious (this item functioned as a spear point; this sherd came from a cooking vessel [see Longacre 1964, 1970]), eventually frustration in breaking through the barriers of meaning led to a dismissal of this cognitive-normative aspect of culture as "archaeological pseudo-psychology." Clearly, what is incumbent on us is to reexamine precisely the nature of action such that we can say that not only do practical tools mediate action but so do so-called nonpractical tools. If this can be done, then the traditional action-oriented focus of archaeology can be used to enter into the social structural and cognitive-normative spheres of prehistoric societies. The trick is, then, to once again create a more refined theoretical perspective, and to push the limits of "methodological ingenuity" and Hopewell archaeology, perhaps like no other archaeology, is a perfect beginning point.

If the focus on the action-mediated nature of the material cultural record is to be preserved and advanced, which we think it must be in order to overcome the instrumental/symbolic dualism, what is required is a different characterization of the nature of material culture. Rather than privileging instrumental tools over symbolic artifacts because the former mediate material action and mark the users as dynamic interveners in the material world while the latter mediate thought and display a passive orientation to this world, we believe that it is necessary to recognize that all *regularized forms of human material action, here termed material practices*, are simultaneously materially composed and symbolically constituted. In other words, the real problem underwriting the tripartite artifact typology is the behaviorist conflating of "behavior" and "action." Archaeologists tend to either treat these two terms as largely synonymous or, if there is a difference in meaning, privelege the term "behavior" over "action," the latter employed as simply referring to behavior in terms of observable, tangible outcomes. In stark contrast to this behaviorist perspective, we treat action as an emergent social phenomenon. This means that *by means of symbolic mediation* the behavioral interventions by which humans engage with the real world are constituted as the social actions (practices). Of course, as the actions are symbolically constituted, each society will have a range of formal types specific to it. This view treats symbols in the standard way, as items used as signs to represent something more than their tangible properties and, therefore, as having conventional meaning. This meaning resides in the mind of the active users. Since symbols are conventional, the meanings that symbols have are collective or shared meanings that are constituted as a code that presupposes and invokes a set of collective beliefs, values, and intentions.

Both Wobst (1977) and Wiessner's (1983) initial work with symbolism mediated through a population's practical perspective (this spear point is different from ours!) clearly illustrated that design and manufacture held meaning for their study populations. We certainly agree with Wobst and Weissner in this regard, namely, that practical devices held meaning; however, the problem with their treatment is that they both emphasize reference over expression. To say that the symbolic moment of material things is used to refer to the social identity of the user is quite different than to say it is used to express the social identity of the user. The reason this is the case is that a referential use of a symbol is a conventional form of substituting. As we say, a symbol "stands for" its referent. Therefore it cannot be identical with what it "points at." But a symbol used expressively is always part of the expressive use and, therefore, it can be identified with the user. Hence the user of style is constituted in his or her social identity by that usage. It is precisely this referential/expressive distinction that makes Wobst and Wiessner's construing of the nature and meaning of style different from ours. That is, the approach we promote claims that humans do not use either practical tools or even nonpractical items to mediate reference but to mediate expression. Through expressing action intentions and the social position of the user, the users constitute the action-nature of their behaviors. In this case, therefore, artifacts (and features such as earthworks) not only act as physical levers to assist users to make tangible changes they intend but also express and, thereby, manifest the intentions and social positions of their users.

Thus manifesting (that is, expressing) intentions and social positions by means of conventional signs (material cultural style) makes a critical difference in the human social world. For example, hunting and poaching may entail the same killing behaviors but the terms define different social actions. Similarly, gathering and pilfering, storing and hoarding, residing and squatting: Each pair can be performed with the same basic behaviors. However, they are experienced by the knowledgeable members of the community as different social actions. Any number of pairings (or triplings and quadruplings, and so on) can be done in which the behaviors and/or the behavioral outcomes are objectively the same while the participants in a given society recognize and experience the common behaviors as different social actions, for example, manslaughter, murder, assassination, execution, sacrificing, and various other symbolically constituted refinements of one human set killing another. Such differential recognition constitutes real and different practices performed with the same basic behavioral interventions since, of course, in any given community the person who is seen to be behaving in a manner that counts as, for example, poaching will be treated quite differently from the person who is seen as, for example, hunting, even though the predatory component of the two behaviors may be identical.

We insist that the difference that makes the difference in socially situated human perception is the symbolic expressive moment. Understood in these terms, the material cultural artifacts as symbols, whether behaviorally treated as technomic, socio-technic, or ideo-technic artifacts, are not so much conventional modes of reference as they are *conventional modes of expression* and what they express conventionally is the action intentions and social standing of the users. This expressive moment, typically mediated by "style," is almost always taken for granted by all relevant parties. Yet this expressivity is critically important because it is by expressing or manifesting the user's social standing and intentions in the very moment of the behavior the user's artifactual kit is mediating that her or his interventions are experientially or phenomenologically transformed. Transformed, that is, in the collective understanding and perception of both the user and all relevant parties to count as and be the types of social actions they were intended to be. It is this symbolically mediated transformative moment that constitutes action as emergent from the tangible, visible behavioral interventions themselves. And it is a real phenomenon since, in fact, it makes a critical difference in the social world.

Hence the instrumental tool that archaeologists might identify as a projectile point used for hunting will have a form that makes it distinctive, although probably without reducing its killing-enabling properties, compared to the different forms of equivalent tools of more distant neighbors, while simultaneously transforming the killing behavior it mediates so that it counts as an (emergent) hunting action as defined in the users' society. The distinctiveness of its form, one that the archaeologist uses as a diagnostic of the culture, is usually referred to by archaeologists as its "style," and this style is the symbolic medium. The different instrumental tool properties of length, width, shape, resource type, and size might be analyzed without residue or remainder, so that there is no surplus that might identify it as "symbolic," implying that the total form is instrumental. Nevertheless, to the users not to use that form of tool for killing an animal would constitute the killing as "poaching." That is, style must be treated as a gestalt pattern, and while, as illustrated by Wiessner (1983, 269) in the case of the different San arrow styles, people materially adapted to the very same environment can generate different tool forms, each of which consists of material properties that can be exhaustively analyzed in instrumental terms, the overall patterning of the arrows of different San groups makes it rather easy to sort them into the different styles, each associated with a different San community. While Wiessner interprets this gestalt-like stylistic differentiation as a mode of symbolic referencing of ethnicity, we treat it in symbolic expressive terms, as a culturally specific means of constituting the exploitation of the animals that the users' regularly kill as hunting and themselves as hunters, thereby as a legitimate form of appropriation of the lives of the animals whereby, as hunters, the users can discharge their ongoing communal duties.

Different styles could probably come to be used to identify different communities of users, but this would not be the reason the users developed the forms they did. Or to put it another way, since the San do not differentiate among themselves in terms approaching what we mean by ethnicity, then making an arrow in a certain form could not include the need or intention to identify one's ethnicity as among the conditions of satisfaction of the producers. The ethnicity argument is the imposition of the anthropologist's methodological needs onto the intentionality of the San. Wiessner's analogy of the B-grade western movie in which the Indian scout proudly identifies an arrow as "Cheyenne" or "Sioux" does indeed say it all.

Byers has elaborated on this view of the symbolic moment of material culture, referring to it as the "expressive warranting moment," and he has argued that it is the outcome of a universal characteristic of social human beings. Individuals must manifest their intentions and the social positions they are occupying in the moment of material cultural usage (whether artifacts, features, facilities, or combinations) in order to constitute their behaviors that this usage mediates as the type of social action or practice intended. He has termed it the "symbolic pragmatic" model of style (Byers 1999, 2004). The critical role it plays is that it dissolves the series of theoretical dichotomies listed above of Instrumental/symbolic, Concrete/abstract, Action/thought, Dynamic/passive, Real/imaginary, and so on, and this means, therefore, not that Hopewell earthworks are symbolic while the dispersed hamlets are in some sense less symbolic or not symbolic at all, but that they are both symbolic and instrumental simultaneously but differently so.

Thus earthworks mediate and represent a complex of action practices that the hamlets cannot mediate while the latter, the hamlets, mediate a range of activities that cannot be performed in the ceremonial context of the earthworks—even though in many cases the behaviors might be identical (e.g., subsistence butchering in the hamlets or ceremonial butchering for a feast in the earthworks). Seen in these terms the symbolism of the earthworks no longer can be treated as passively reflecting thought but as the dynamic medium of the action nature of the behaviors being regularly performed in their context. Given the material labor investment, it is reasonable to claim that this earthwork-mediated action would have been no less critical in the users' collective or shared understandings and experiences of what would count as a proper life as would be the practical activity of gardening, hunting, and gathering. Indeed, in terms of a symbolic pragmatic perspective, both the hamlet and the earthwork practices would be (differently) symbolic in nature, and through the complementary nature of their symbolism, they may and likely were perceived as intrinsically related. Hence the activities mediated by the earthworks and the activities mediated by the domestic hamlets, while quite different in profound ways, would probably be related in consequence.

In dissolving the instrumental/symbolic dichotomy while sustaining the behavior/action duality as a property of human social existence, this treatment of the symbolic moment of material culture as action-constitutive necessarily opens a portal to dissolving the puzzle of the earthwork/domestic dichotomy. This symbolic pragmatic perspective is presented here as the way people perceive and constitute one another's activities, and we claim, therefore, that the peoples responsible for the dichotomy would not be puzzled. The archaeologists studying it should strive to develop theory and methods that recognize this dichotomy as the outcome of real differences, not in the instrumental/symbolic way but in the nature of the symbolism of the two spheres.

The Organizing Structure of This Volume

It should be noted that this book is the outcome of a more interactive approach than the standard edited volume. We consider critical debate to be a crucial component of archaeological methodology and the growth of the discipline. This is because we take a realist approach to our subject matter, arguing that what we are studying exists independently of our understanding of it and, at the same time, that as archaeologists we can develop theoretical and methodological perspectives that can allow us to rationally choose from among a range of possible characterizations and explanations of the archaeological record. This means that we recognize that we must critically draw on our preexisting general theoretical and substantive knowledge of the subject in order to develop models by which to interpret the archaeological data. In this view, all models are fallible and, therefore, corrigible, and correcting models is done by criticizing the theoretical backgrounds and the degree of empirical fit they make of the data. While we accept that all our models should be amenable to change so that none should be assumed to be a "final" account, we must still make rational choices among these alternatives. The critical method is what makes our choices rational and avoids the accusation of relativism while, at the same time, recognizing that all knowledge claims are fallible but not necessarily equally fallible. In the end, we must not only develop ideas (whether model or theory) that explicate the archaeological record, from artifact to earthwork, but also develop methods to evaluate the validity of those ideas.

Thus we believe that it is crucial to promote critical debate in archaeology and that the debate can be most effective when all the parties are addressing the same empirical data. We hope a synergistic cycle develops that leads to an upward spiraling of model correction and transformation resulting in better approximations that, at the same time, open new questions and research directions that, in all likelihood, will force a reexamination of the very models that enabled these new questions. To facilitate this cycle, all the authors of this book have written critical commentaries of one other's chapters as well as reaffirming the claims of their own chapters by giving reasoned rejoinders and even, where they see the criticisms as well founded, modifying their original positions. Clearly we can only promote and not fully explore this critical cycling of interpretation and knowledge enhancement in the context of this book, simply because space and the reader's patience are limited properties. Therefore the authors have agreed to limit their commentary to the section level. Only the participants whose contributions are in the same section will comment on one another's chapters, and they limit their rejoinders to these commentaries. To ensure that the editors are part of the critical process, however, all participants were encouraged to respond critically in their individual rebuttals to any commentary that the editors have made, in this introductory chapter and/or in the penultimate closing overview chapter by DeeAnne Wymer. Furthermore, the editors have agreed that, having had their say, they waive any right to rebuttal of this and the overview chapter. But all participants in this project also have agreed that the closing chapter of the book by our discussant, N'omi Greber, will be immune to this critical exchange. In this way we hope to avoid an "infinite" regress of critical commentary.

In organizing these commentaries and rebuttals, we followed the *Current Anthropology* format by placing the authors' commentaries of a particular chapter at the end of the relevant section, and these are immediately followed by the response of the author(s). This is also the place where the author(s) can respond to any of the editors' commentary in this introductory chapter and in Wymer's penultimate overview chapter. Following this introductory chapter, we have organized the book into five sections. Sections 1 through 4 address substantive questions of settlement and landscape. These sections are grouped by either regional focus, parallels in theoretical orientation, or approach (or in come cases, by different theoretical assessment of the same suite of problems or data). Section 5 serves as the opportunity to reflect on issues raised by the overall perspective and empirical constraints that Hopewell settlement and landscape present.

Finally, our concluding chapter has been penned by one of the original participants in the 2004 Society for American Archaeology symposium that was the genesis for this book—Dr. N'omi Greber. Her contribution brings a gratifying close to the volume in which she "[muses] a bit about concepts of theory and data" and touches upon what she terms "frameworks for thinking." A perfect ending, we believe, to this rather unusual and, we hope, thought-provoking volume.

SECTION 1

Symbolic and Practical
Settlement Interaction

The three chapters that make up section 1 delineate some of the central themes of this volume. Chapter 1 by Douglas K. Charles is particularly appropriate because his dual objective and cultural characterization of the lower Illinois River valley landscape during the Middle Woodland period articulates the major concern expressed in the introduction: How can Hopewellian archaeology synthesize the objective perspective that is almost second nature in North American archaeology, based on the view that no matter what kind of symbolic articulation a people might make of the world around them, their biological and social survival entails ensuring that this symbolic construction affords them an adequate flow of material energy in the form of food and shelter? He fully accomplishes this by elucidating a parallel scheme of structuring, an objective scheme in which riverine and upland resource availability is shown to be objectively constrained and generated by the particular linearity of the temperate climatic regime of this local "riverworld." He then postulates a meaningful structuring of this same environment in terms that would not be unfamiliar to the prehistoric occupants themselves, given what we currently understand of the cultural traditions of their descendants (the historic Native American peoples of the Eastern Woodlands). This dual perspective nicely encapsulates and lays out the sort of interpretive approach to Hopewell that this book advocates.

Paul J. Pacheco's contribution acts as an excellent cautionary comment to Charles's chapter, the very type of caution that we must maintain in all our interpretations. While Charles points out that the objective environmental constraints found in the lower Illinois Valley were generally similar to those under which most regional Hopewellian manifestations developed across much of the Eastern Woodland, he notes there was a significant difference to the Illinois Valley region that might make the meaningful interpretation that we can apply to it somewhat unique. Indeed, the north-south linearity and almost "too neat" low floodplain to higher upland/prairie sequential development of the topography that characterizes the lower Illinois Valley and that almost invites the type of interpretation that Charles makes of it does not so clearly characterize the Ohio Hopewell landscape. It is this difference that may lend particular weight to Pacheco's focus on the objective material conditions and how these may account for what may be a unique combination of sedentary domestic settlement, large-scale ceremonial centers, and a rather expedient, albeit strictly organized, system of lithic technology. Pacheco's contribution is an important addition to the question of how we can enhance our understanding of the actual nature of the settlement system: Did the domestic and ceremonial settlement practices contrast as sedentary and transient, respectively, as he argues, or were they both essentially transient, the result of a highly mobile logistical regime, as he claims Frank Cowan characterizes them? The definitive answer is not given in this chapter, but it does highlight the importance of more adequately resolving this question.

Finally, Lauren Sieg and Jarrod Burks present an overall material-symbolic framework of the Ohio Hopewell landscape that echoes the approach presented by Charles for the lower Illinois Valley Hopewell. In this case, they explore the possibility that the underlying conceptual duality structuring Ohio Hopewell ceramic and nonceramic artifactual assemblages might be discernible as equivalently generating the structuring of the mortuary and related features with which they were associated. Indeed, their chapter focuses on extending this duality to the landscape itself, arguing that much like the Ohio Hopewell artifact stylistics being based on a form of "yin-yang" duality of negative/positive space, this same duality of structuring may be immanent in the complementary contrast of the monumental earthworks and the near-archaeological invisibility of the domestic sphere. They suggest referring to the great embankment earthworks as the "positive" structural aspect of this holistic landscape and the land between these earthworks in which the domestic settlements were widely dispersed as the "negative" structural aspect. These terms, "positive" and "negative," are not used to privilege the former and underprivilege the latter; rather, they simply highlight that the two may have existed in a complementary meaningful relational mode of proscribing and prescribing the forms of activity appropriate in each zone. Clearly, this ties into the possibility that the intelligibility of the ritual activity performed in the great earthwork locales, the "positive spaces," would be dependent on the performance of proper domestic and ecological activity carried out in the "negative spaces," and vice versa. This view—that there were two complementary forms of space associated with equally complementary forms of activity for each—nicely captures a central theme of this book.

Riverworld

Life and Meaning in the Illinois Valley

Douglas K. Charles

The initial inspiration for this chapter was a series of science fiction novels written by Philip José Farmer beginning in the 1970s. The novels' plots and most of their content are irrelevant for our purposes but are summarized as follows in a blurb from *LUNA Monthly* printed inside the front cover of the Berkley paperback edition (Farmer 1984) of the first book in the series, *To Your Scattered Bodies Go*: "The premise here is that an unknown but highly advanced group of beings have used their formidable scientific abilities to resurrect every human being who ever lived, on the shores of a multi-million mile long river. . . . The plot involves the quest of Sir Richard Burton and assorted others, ranging from a Neanderthal man Kazz to Hermann Goring, to find the source of the river and the base of the secret masters of the Riverworld."

While the phrase "highly advanced group of beings . . . [using] their formidable scientific abilities to resurrect every human being who ever lived" might be a description of archaeological practice or at least hubris, it is rather the notion of the world arrayed along a great river that I wish to pursue in this chapter. Archaeologists' maps of the Hopewellian world (c. 2000–1600 B.P.) generally show a bounded area, limited more or less by the Great Lakes to the north, the Appalachian Mountains to the east, the Gulf of Mexico to the south, and the Great Plains to the west, projected onto a two-dimensional Cartesian grid or a modified version, such as a Mercator projection, that takes account of our conception of the world as a sphere (Figure 1.1). We sense, however, that the major and minor rivers of the American Midwest provided the spatial framework for the Hopewellians themselves. For example, settlement systems and polities seem contained within the Scioto, Little Miami, or Muskingum river valleys in Ohio (Greber 2006); systematic surveys have documented the burial mounds lining the Illinois River valley (Charles 1992b); and the Tennessee Valley Authority flooded the core of the Copena region when it dammed

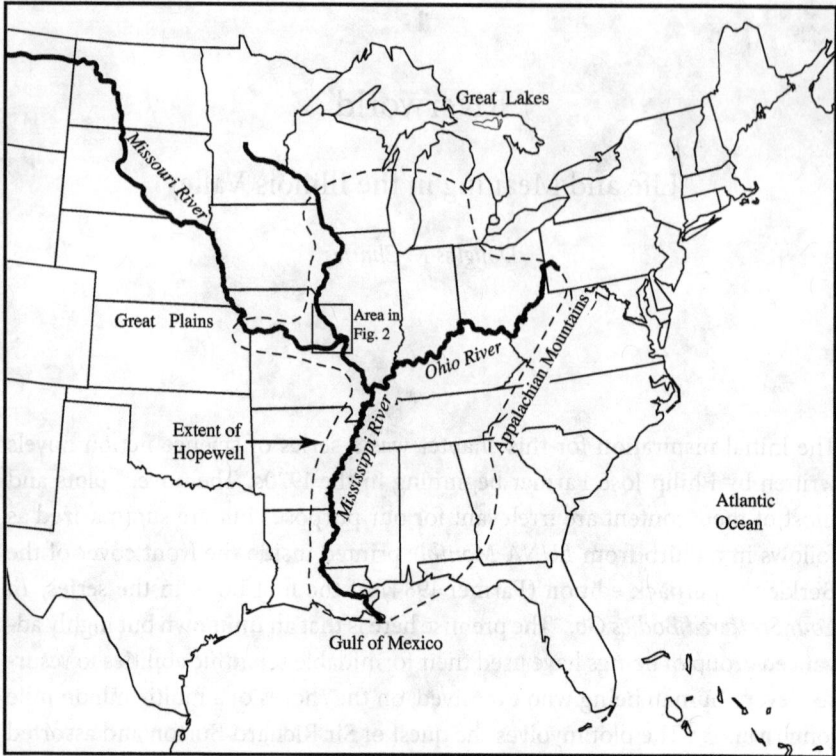

Figure 1.1. General extent of the Hopewell phenomenon in the Eastern Woodlands. Area around the confluence of the Illinois, Mississippi, and Missouri rivers is shown in Figure 1.2.

the Tennessee River valley (Walthall 1979). In this chapter I will explore the relationship between our understanding of the physical environment of the lower Illinois River valley and a putative landscape of the Middle Woodland Hopewellian people who lived there two thousand years ago.

The fact that this chapter was inspired by science fiction is perhaps more sensible than I appreciated when the first version was written for the symposium from which this volume originated. Fahlander (2001) has recently argued that archaeological interpretation would be more appropriately conceived of as science fiction rather than as ethnography of the past. He notes that archaeology's practice has been to take social theory generated under contemporary conditions and couple it with ethnographic analogies of extant "traditional societies," as if the latter were unaffected by contact and represent the complete range of such cultures in human history (Fahlander 2001: 35–36). Prehistoric societies thus become just additional examples of the contemporary Other. If we assume instead that current theory and ethnographically known cultures don't exhaust the full range of possible social, political, and economic conditions and ways of life, a situation increasingly likely as we go back in time, then we are engaged in "not simply a study of the Other, but rather a study of the *unknown*" (Oestigaard 2004: 86). Humans encountering the unknown is the essence of much science fiction. Thus, as ethnographers confronting the Other have come to acknowledge their writing as fiction rather than representation (e.g., Clifford and Marcus 1986), archaeologists confronting the unknown should recognize their work as science fiction (Fahlander 2001: 33). Archaeological "(re)constructions" should be evaluated in terms of "whether or not the interpretations of the past enhance our knowledge of the past" (Oestigaard 2004: 86; see also Fahlander 2001). Unless we confine ourselves to descriptions of basic data—densities of debris categories by excavation level or distributions of sites in a river valley, for example—meaningful, interesting (re)constructions of the past will be those that resonate with our own sensibilities, are developed through clearly marshaled logical arguments, and articulate with "reality" in believable ways. Given that these strictures also define good science fiction, Fahlander has a point. Before examining the connection between our views of the physical environment and the Hopewellian landscape, I will briefly explore the paradigms framing contemporary archaeological research and, more specifically, how these relate to the envisioning of prehistoric landscapes. This is necessary because the theoretical extremes that characterize archaeology at present—that archaeology is science *or* that it is fiction—would seem to make the term "science fiction" an oxymoron and Fahlander's argument nonsensical.

Sense and Sensibility

The preceding characterization of archaeology (and science fiction) is basically a request that we make sense. *Webster's New World Dictionary* defines sensibility, in the sense that I mean it, as "the capacity for being affected emotionally or intellectually, whether pleasantly or unpleasantly."[1] Archaeological interpretations should engage us. Logic, too, is about sense, in the formal sense, as in "the ability to think or reason soundly" (again from *Webster's*). Proposition C must follow from A and B, and cannot simply be sprung upon the reader. And, finally, archaeological constructions must engender a sense of reality, "the quality of being true to life" (*Webster's*). The relation between "reality" and our senses has been fundamental to much of Western philosophical discourse for the past several centuries, but we should at least accept that one's sense of reality will affect interpretation. My repetition of "sense" is not meant to be insensitive, sensational, or nonsensical but is meant, rather, to sensitize the reader to the many senses of sense embedded in the first sentence of this paragraph. My intent is simply to reiterate the often-made point that there is no one way to make sense of the past. Rather, we must strive to do it sensibly.

This is no easy task. Archaeological theory at the end of the twentieth century operated within one or the other of two mid-nineteenth-century paradigms (or what may also be termed metaphors or traditions) that were derived from the works of Darwin and Marx. The Darwinian paradigm originated in England and developed in the English-speaking world. Within archaeology, it is seemingly the more intact of the two after a century and a half, given the processual concern with adaptation in the 1960s and 1970s (e.g., Binford 1962, 1968) and the sort of "roots" movement of the more recent selectionist approach (e.g., Barton and Clark 1997; Dunnell 1980; O'Brien and Lyman 2000). The Marxian paradigm, also produced in large part in England, though written in German and derived from Continental thought, appears the more transformed, having shifted from its original emphasis on materialism, through the ideological focus of the Frankfort school of critical theory, to, in archaeology in particular, a concern with agency, meaning, context, and the notion of material culture as text (e.g., Hodder 1986; Shanks and Tilley 1987a). Although a Marxian approach occasionally impacted archaeology in the twentieth century, notably through the work of V. Gordon Childe in England and in a more muted fashion through the influence of Leslie White on Binford and others (Patterson 2003; Trigger 1989), the Marxian tradition remained largely a Continental phenomenon and only entered anglophone archaeology beginning about 1980 (e.g., Hodder 1982; Spriggs 1984).

In general, the Darwinian and Marxian paradigms[2] have underwritten the antithetical positions that define Western thought as expressed in the processual/postprocessual debates in archaeology in the closing decades of the twentieth century. The Darwinian paradigm has been associated with atomistic, ahistorical, abstract deductive, and prescriptive modes of Enlightenment thought, whereas the Marxian paradigm has tended to be anti-Enlightenment, with holistic, historical, particularistic, and descriptive concerns (Charles 1992a: 909–910; see also Bloor 1976: 54–57; Gibbon 1989: 129–134). The terms Giddens (1984: 1–2) uses to describe these two metaphors—"biology" versus "interpretative sociology"—are instructive if we think about the development of postprocessual thought in the last twenty years. "Interpretative" may still be a useful adjective, but it is not clear that "sociology" properly describes the phenomenology of Bender (1998), Tilley (1994), and others. This "slippage" over the last two decades suggests that the polarity of the metaphors is a function of the sociology of academia and is not inherent in the nature of the paradigms. In fact, the paradigmatic opposition developed in the twentieth century as others used the writings of Darwin and Marx. Materialism and evolutionary change were central to both Darwin's and Marx's thought, and they (particularly Marx) did not see their work as antithetical (Foster 2000).

Thomas (2004) has recently and cogently argued that archaeology, as a discipline, is very much a product and was made possible by the condition, or more aptly the process, of modernity. The modern era is characterized by "capitalism, the emergence of nation-states, industrialization, improvements in communications and transport, mercantilism, the control of violence by the state, surveillance, constant political struggle, an increasingly urban way of life, and an experience of agitation, turbulence and continuous change" (Thomas 2004: 2). There has also been a decline in the importance of tradition and religious conviction. The search for reasoned order under the emerging conditions of modernity is most clearly manifested in the Enlightenment, and thus the foundations of archaeology, for example, Thomsen's "three-age system," are readily situated in this context (Thomas 2004: 32–34). The question becomes, however: If we have entered a postmodern era, has archaeology as an academic discipline "outlived its usefulness" (Thomas 2004: 223)? Thomas (2004: 224) prefers to characterize the early twenty-first century as counter-modern rather than postmodern, thereby emphasizing continuity with the critiques of modernity present since its inception, for example, romanticism and, most recently, "phenomenology, hermeneutics, critical theory, post-structuralism, feminism, [and] queer theory." Thomas (2004) seeks to deem-phasize the need for certainty explicit in a scientific "modern" archaeology and argues instead for an ongoing dialogue with the past and among stakeholders, with the process itself, rather than certain knowledge, as the objective. Fur-thermore, he argues that a concern with ethics should become central to our practice. In the end, however, Thomas is essentially promoting the Marxian paradigm. This begs the question: Is Thomas's argument sensible?

The answer to this question must be a resounding "sort of." Euro-American archaeology has a less than stellar record regarding its ethical responsibilities toward indigenous communities (although vastly improved in recent years). As a strong program, the scientific method as generally conceived fails to ad-dress many of the crucial, or simply interesting, questions of archaeology. In particular, the meanings of things and places in the past elude, completely or partially, demands for empirical verification, statistical significance, or objec-tivity. At the same time, however, many of the countermeasures in postproces-sual archaeology are problematic in terms of issues surrounding the testing of knowledge claims, the extent to which reality exists or the past existed, and whether or not human behavior can be considered as something unique, completely apart from nature (e.g., Kuznar 2008). By contrast, as a weak program the scientific method is no more than a means of critical evaluation of claims of knowledge. To say that there can be multiple interpretations of the past is not to say that they are all equally valid, useful, or meaningful.

The empiricism underlying "science" is rooted in skepticism, and it is a manifest rejection of the cosmological centrality of humans. Thus to what extent is a rejection of the skepticism and empiricism of a scientific approach, and more important its decentering of human existence, a return to distortions of the past? Herein lies the challenge: to affirm human experience and our meaningful construction of the world in a way that makes sense to us while acknowledging sensibly our position in a "real" world with a "real" past. That we must find a middle ground is evident from the recent state of American politics. Consider the following:

> [President Bush's] aide said that guys like me were "in what we call the reality-based community," which he defined as people who "believe that solutions emerge from your judicious study of discernible reality." I nodded and murmured something about enlightenment principles and empiricism. He cut me off. "That's not the way the world really works anymore," he continued. "We're an empire now, and when we act, we create our own reality. And while you're studying that reality—judiciously, as you will—we'll act again, creating other new realities, which you can study too, and that's how things will sort out. We're history's actors . . . and you, all of you, will be left to just study what we do." (Suskind 2004)

The issue, rather graphically and frighteningly portrayed in the aide's remarks, is whether or not there are "real world" constraints on human action and knowledge. This is not a simple question of whether or not governmental policies can create reality. It is rather a question about the interplay between a constructed world believed by many and any resistance to that reality from outside that belief system. In questions concerning the past, the issue becomes, in the extreme, whether a situation at one point in time impinges on later times, or whether each point of time is created de novo. In biology, such questions relate to, for example, the role of chance in the history of life and to the validity of evolutionary developmental studies (e.g., Carroll 2005; Gould 1977, 1989). Likewise, in human history, does the past constrain the present and future?

I take the position that there is a real world out there, that it does in some fashion constrain our actions (Wylie 1992), and that, by extension, there was a real past that in part shaped the present. Thus, from this perspective, archaeological knowledge is conditional. To the extent that we can identify real-world constraints that would have structured people's actions and beliefs in the past, we can evaluate our (re)constructions and interpretations. As those constraints become less discernable, we increasingly imagine and project our understandings onto the past. All endeavors along this continuum are potentially equally sensible, provided we bear in mind the extent to which constraints come into play. An example of the conditional knowledge of archaeology lies in the growing interest in prehistoric landscapes. Also evident in landscape studies is the opposition of the Darwinian and Marxian paradigms.

Environments and Landscapes

The archaeology of landscapes is an arena particularly open to the judicious use of sensible (re)construction and interpretation. Landscape archaeology has ranged from the exploration of subsistence settlement systems (e.g., Willey 1953) to catchment analysis (e.g., Higgs and Vita-Finzi 1972) to, more recently, the investigation of ritual and sacred landscapes (e.g., Ashmore and Knapp 1999). Current practice spans the range of effects of evidentiary constraints from, in the simplest terms, probable to possible interpretations: from assessing diet and resource availability to experiencing a space to understanding the meaning of a sacred place.

The anthropology and archaeology of landscapes, or of space and place as it is sometimes framed, represents an important trend in cross- or interdisciplinary research in which spaces and places are seen as constructed, dwelt within, and imbued with meaning (e.g., Anschuetz, Wilshusen, and Scheick 2001; Ashmore and Knapp 1999; Bender 1993; Bowser 2004; Feld and Basso 1996; Hirsch and O'Hanlon 1995; Ingold 1993; Low and Lawrence-Zúñiga 2003; Tilley 1994; Ucko and Layton 1999). These approaches predominantly take landscape to mean either physical environment or cultural construction (the latter often given preferential designation as landscape) and "can be characterized in terms of the Weberian distinction between explanation and understanding" (Layton and Ucko 1999: 2). Viewed from modern versus postmodern perspectives, the distinction essentially becomes one between environment and landscape, as portrayed in Table 1.1. To attempt to make sense of the way in which the physical environment of the Illinois River valley (our modern ecological perspective) overlaps with the Middle Woodland landscape of nearly two thousand years ago (their meaningful construct) is to dive into the white space between the columns of Table 1.1, because we are confronting not only the environment/landscape dimension but also the dimension of archaeological (re)construction (see below).

Table 1.1. Environment and landscape: Modernist and postmodernist approaches

	Environment	Landscape
Interaction with	Explanation	Interpretation
	Cause or constraint	Representation
	"Bump into"	"Gaze upon"
Consequence	Adaptation	Meaningful action
Long-term	Process	History
Modernist representation	Etic (universal) theories	Emic (local) beliefs
	Us	Them
	Science	Arts
Postmodernist representation	Our interpretation	Their interpretation

Source: Modified from Layton and Ucko 1999: Table 1.1.

Landscapes can be more or less physically manifest in the sense of the degree to which elements of the environment are likely to impinge upon human consciousness. For example, a dense forest or broad desert, all trees or all sand, offer more subtle variability to the senses than a coastal setting where water, beach, and inland vegetation more starkly define spaces and places. The majority of recent archaeological and anthropological investigations of landscapes have concentrated on sacred places and how they may have been created and made meaningful (but see van Dommelen 1999). Layton and Ucko (1999: 8) cite Quine's (1960: 76) distinction between observation sentences and theoretical sentences in the context of the anthropological translation of theories of causality: "[Quine] argued that an anthropologist could easily learn statements in a foreign language such as 'there goes a rabbit,' since rabbits are objects of shared experience. Quine called this kind of statement an 'observation sentence.' A sentence such as 'neutrinos lack mass' can be understood only if one has learnt the theory of being that justifies it. 'Theoretical sentences' are less anchored to their references than are 'observation sentences.'" By analogy, elements of prehistoric landscapes that can be readily related to the physical environment ("Environment" in Table 1.1) correspond to observational sentences, while those elements meaningfully constructed without unambiguous references ("Landscape" in Table 1.1) are like theoretical sentences. I would argue, however, that rather than being a binary classification, environments and landscapes should be viewed as the ends of a continuum, that is to say, that elements of the environment/landscape can be more or less observational or theoretical. Put another way, any observational sentence has a "*degree of theoreticity*," as Quine (2000: 5) himself came to admit. From an archaeological perspective, our statements about elements of the environment/landscape range from observational statements with low levels of theoreticity to highly theoretical statements, that is, from statements having potentially shared (between archaeologists and subjects in the past) environmental references (experiences) to statements that are our (re)constructions of their meaningful constructions. Thus we not only confront the issues of translation with which Quine was concerned—how to understand another culture's (theoretical) landscape—but also attempt to construct that landscape based on presumably less theoretical (observational) statements about an experientially shared environment (or at least our reconstruction of the correspondence between the environment as we see it now and how it might have been then).

Braudel (1972: 20–21; see also Knapp 1992: 6) constructed a framework for interpreting history that offers a parallel to the observational/theoretical continuum. He envisioned history as moving in a series of planes: *la longue durée*, involving long periods of time, essentially environmental constraints on behavior; *conjoncture*, representing social and economic cycles of five to 50 years; and *l'histoire événementielle*, the events of traditional history. Archaeologically, we more readily observe environmental factors than we do social interactions or, at even further remove, individual actions. As an archaeological tool, *la longue durée* has been criticized as giving little insight into long-term change because for Braudel the environment was a static determinant of human behavior, given its very slow rhythm of change (Knapp 1992: 13; M. Smith 1992: 25). If, however, we are not interested in explaining change, but instead are focusing on observations we might share with prehistoric subjects, the relative immutability of certain aspects of the environment becomes a strength. We can thereby reconstruct aspects of past environments that we can sensibly assume would have been observed by, or would have affected, anyone living in the region at a given time. The following exploration of the Illinois River valley during the Middle Woodland period will move from contemporary observations about the prehistoric environment to statements about a theoretical Hopewellian landscape.

The Environment of the Lower Illinois River Valley

In Western scientific terms, the topography of a place like the lower Illinois River valley (Figure 1.2) is explained within a framework of deep time (e.g., Butzer 1977, 1978; Hajic 1990; Rubey 1952; Styles 1985; Van Nest 1997). The layers of bedrock underlying the region were formed eons ago during the Paleozoic. Glacial melt waters cut the river valley during the Pleistocene, leaving the windblown-loess-covered limestone bluffs towering 75 to 100 meters above the floodplain. The somewhat unusual character of the lower Illinois River,

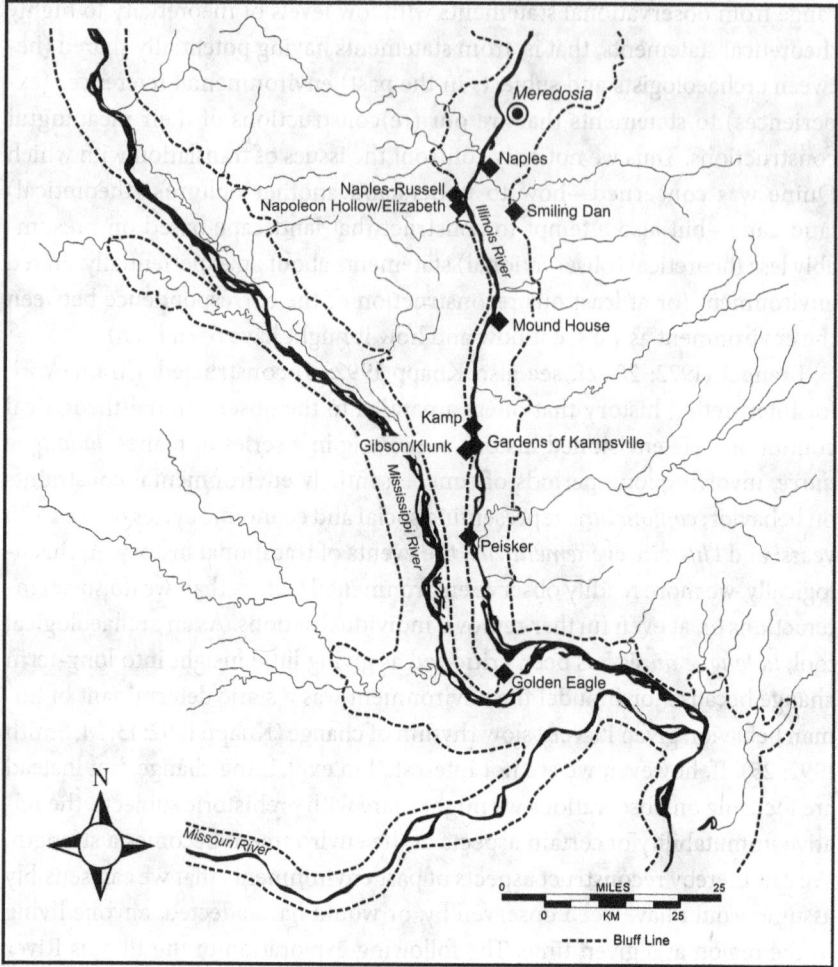

Figure 1.2. Middle Woodland/Hopewell sites in the lower Illinois River valley mentioned in the text. The location of the present town of Meridosia is indicated. Area depicted is delineated in Figure 1.1.

that of an underfit stream, results from the fact that the valley was originally the glacial melt water channel for what we now know as the Mississippi River. At some point during the Wisconsinan glaciation (c. 20,000 B.P.), the Mississippi carved a new channel several kilometers west of the old one. The width and depth of the lower Illinois Valley is thus out of proportion to the much smaller area drained by the river during the late Pleistocene and Holocene.

Glaciers never completely covered the lower Illinois Valley, the most southerly advance in part accounting for the transformation of the landscape in the vicinity of the town of Meredosia at the boundary between the central and lower valley. Above Meridosia the valley is wider and characterized by a more rolling topography. The lower valley floor did undergo significant reworking during the Holocene, and it has only been since the later centuries of the Early Woodland period (post-2500 B.P.) that the various relict river and tributary channels and interterrace zones have been largely infilled, creating the relatively flat topography of the present floodplain. This lack of relief, along with the low grade of the river, produces the conditions that promote the "gentle" spring flooding that have long been associated with the intensity of mudflat horticulture thought to characterize Middle Woodland subsistence in this area.

The ecology of the region is, generally speaking, that of a Holocene midcontinental temperate zone. The plant and animal communities mapped onto the highly structured topography of the area in a predictable manner (e.g., Asch, Ford, and Asch 1972; Hewitt 1983; Neusius 1982; Styles 1981; Zawacki and Hausfater 1969). Prehistorically, fish and mussels were distributed in the floodplain by species appropriate to the different conditions of the river, streams, and backwater lakes. Semiannually, enormous populations of migratory waterfowl would have streamed north or south along the valley, with the same bodies of water providing rest areas and food. Various species of seed- and tuber-producing plants would have been found across the floor of the valley. Deer and nuts would have been most densely distributed in the uplands, particularly along the transitional zones between upland forest and prairie, but would also have been present in the floodplain.

Three, and possibly four, types of sites characterize Middle Woodland settlement in the Illinois Valley (Ruby, Carr, and Charles 2005: 132–134). Small hamlets comprised the residential sites. The only such site that has been extensively excavated and reported, Smiling Dan, contained three houses, although there are indications that there may have been a fourth (Stafford and Sant 1985). One of the Smiling Dan houses was abandoned, and probably dismantled, before or during the occupation of the other two (Charles and Shortell 2002). The archaeological lore of the lower Illinois Valley assumes the existence of large residential "villages," such as the Gardens of Kampsville site (e.g., Struever and Houart 1972), but this assumption has yet to be adequately tested. Based on current survey and excavation records, we cannot at this time distinguish between large contemporaneous occupations and continuous or sequential small occupations shifting across sites over time. Bruce D. Smith (1992) therefore seems justified in his generalized model of hamlets as the primary form of residence during the Middle Woodland period across the Eastern Woodlands. There appears to have been a hierarchical "chain" of communities along the valley (Ruby, Carr, and Charles 2005: 138).

Individual hamlets constituted the daily, face-to-face residential communities. A group of hamlets, probably involving related lineages, comprised a second tier of communities focused around a second type of site—bluff-top burial mound groups such as Gibson/Klunk and the earlier mounds (1, 3, and 4) at the Elizabeth site (Charles, Leigh, and Buikstra 1988; Perino 1968, 2006). This pattern is consistent with the apparent size of the hamlets, the number of people buried in the mounds, and the genetic evidence gleaned from the cemeteries (Konigsberg 1990). Several of the mound-level communities came together to form a third tier of communities centered on the third type of site, represented by the six large floodplain mound complexes: Naples, Napoleon Hollow/Elizabeth/Naples-Russell, Mound House, Kamp, Peisker, and Golden Eagle (Buikstra, Charles, and Rakita 1998; Charles, Buikstra, and Konigsberg 1988; Struever and Houart 1972; Van Nest 2006; Wiant and McGimsey 1986). The hierarchical relationship among the three types of sites is geographically structured by the linear nature of the valley, and there was likely a fluidity to membership in the communities. In addition, there may be small special purpose sites that were mostly related to resource extraction, but these are not well known.

The Landscape of Riverworld

Integrating these characterizations of the geological, ecological, and human settlement environments, we can envision a pair of dimensions structuring the manner in which Middle Woodland people may have conceptualized the lower Illinois Valley: One axis is aligned with the river, while the second axis lies perpendicular to the first (Figure 1.3). The river flows southward along the first axis, and the bluffs parallel the course of the river. Huge numbers of migratory waterfowl would have flown in one direction along this axis in the spring (against the flow of the river) and in the opposite direction (with the current) in the fall. In general, resource zones run parallel to the river and the bluffs. The logic of resource collection strategies is such that catchments would have been oriented along the second axis, crosscutting and incorporating within only a few kilometers a complete array of resource zones. The territories would logically (from a behavioral ecology standpoint) extend from the river on one end, across the floodplain, and into the uplands on the other. Thus each side of the river would have been characterized by adjoining territories aligned consecutively along the river axis, with the different resource zones—river's edge; floodplain marsh, lake, prairie, and woodland; bluff base talus slope; small streams dissecting hollows; upland forest; and prairie—sequentially ordered along the perpendicular axis. The hamlets were

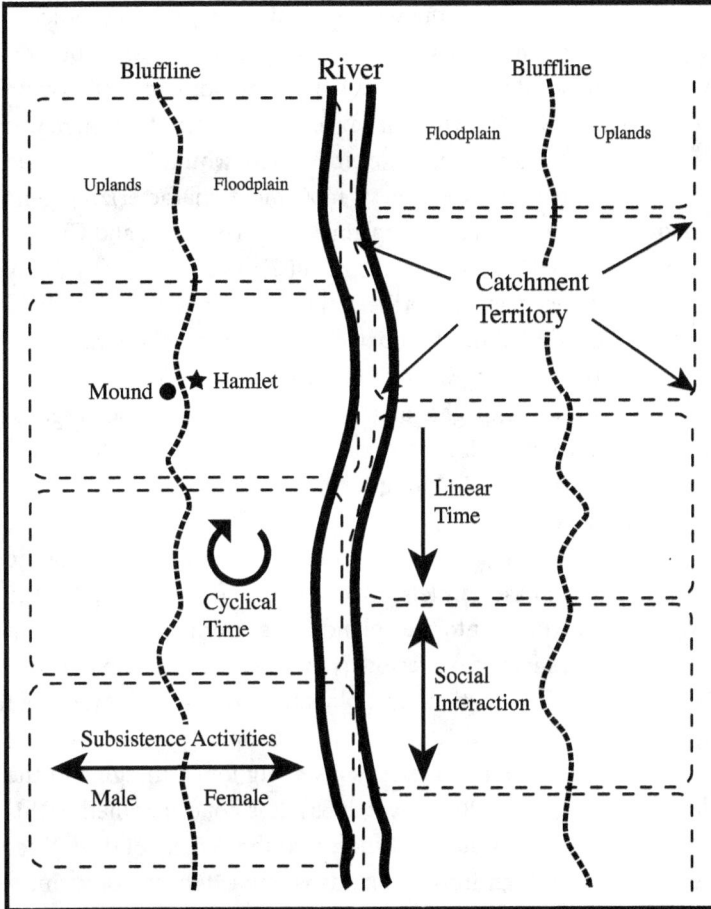

Figure 1.3. The landscape of "Riverworld" as discussed in the text.

situated in the main or tributary valley floors, generally in the vicinity of the bluffs separating the Illinois floodplain from the uplands. The burial mounds were constructed nearby but above the floodplain on the very edge of the bluffs. The large floodplain mound sites were spaced at intervals of roughly 20 kilometers.

How, then, would people have moved through the Illinois Valley and environs? The major transportation routes at the regional scale were apparently along the river axis, as suggested by the distribution patterns of Hopewell items and materials (Brose 1990; Seeman 1979; Struever and Houart 1972). At a smaller scale, gene flow, and presumably postmarital residence and extended kinship networks, also followed the river axis. This has been strikingly demonstrated in the lower Illinois Valley (Buikstra 1977), where the Mississippi River is between 10 and 50 kilometers to the west. Genetic distance data indicate, however, that gene flow was not crossing directly between the valleys but following the rivers. People would have converged on the floodplain centers from up and down the river, again following that axis. To the extent that there was visitation to more distant centers, that movement, too, would have followed the river axis. The similarity in direction of movement characterizing gene flow and the nature of interaction at floodplain centers (Buikstra and Charles 1999; Buikstra et al. 1998; Charles and Buikstra 2002) suggests the possibility that marriages were arranged as part of the activities routinely engaged in at these sites. In addition to the flow of Hopewell Interaction Sphere materials along the river axis, food or other resources may have been exchanged, and as an extension of these processes, rights of access to hunting or collecting territories may have been negotiated. Such rights, as well as direct exchanges of food, may have been a critical part of long-term strategies of subsistence risk management (e.g., Brose 1979).

The routine acquisition of resources would have been oriented along the second axis. From the bluff base hamlets, collectors would have moved either toward the river or away from it into the uplands. The river and its floodplain would have provided fish, shellfish, waterfowl, tubers, seeds, nuts, small game, and probably some deer. The horticultural plots have often been presumed to have been located in the floodplain, but in fact some species may have been cultivated in the well-drained loessic soils along forest margins in the uplands (Calentine 2005; Fritz 1990; Watson 1985). It is not clear whether this gardening activity would have reduced or increased the density of deer. Deer populations were probably high in the uplands where extensive forest margins were available. Of particular interest is the possible gendered nature of people's movement within the resource territories along the second axis. The types of resources generally associated with women's gathering would have been obtained from the floodplain by moving toward the river. The large game hunting often associated with men, of deer in this case, may have been accomplished via movement from the hamlet into the uplands away from the river. This is not to suggest that men never hunted deer or performed other subsistence tasks in the floodplain, or that women never gardened, collected nuts, or set fires in the uplands to increase deer and nut yields. I am suggesting, however, that those directions and spaces may have been gendered. In this light, it is also suggestive that the dead were placed in the liminal space at the midpoint between the resource directions/spaces. Hamlets were also located at this intersection, but the living were at the edge of the floodplain, while the dead were above, at the edge of the uplands. Within this scheme, the hamlets were located in the female space, the mounds in the male space (if these concepts were meaningful in the Hopewellian Illinois Valley).

Extending this line of argument, the river axis becomes a dimension of social interaction. The river flows in only one direction. The Illinois Valley had been almost totally abandoned by the end of the Early Woodland period (Charles, Buikstra, and Konigsberg 1986; Farnsworth and Asch 1986). The resettlement of the valley during the Middle Woodland period largely proceeded downstream from the central valley toward the river's junction with the Mississippi (Charles 1992b; King, Buikstra, and Charles n.d.; Kut and Buikstra 1998). Thus both in terms of the river and the settlement history of the valley time flowed in one direction. Relationships among the mound-based (second-tier) communities involved connections along the river. There may have been a temporal component to these relationships; for example, older communities would have been upriver. Interestingly, waterfowl migrate in both directions. Duck-billed, web-footed birds are one of only two recognizable animal images portrayed in Hopewellian ceramic designs in this region (Morgan 1988: 131). These waterfowl are possibly liminal in that they move among the domains of air, land, and water, but they might also be seen as liminal since they move both with the flow of time and the river and against it, toward the future and toward the past, in one direction in the spring and in the opposite direction in the fall.

Within this same framework, the orthogonal subsistence axis becomes a dimension of gender. Female is toward the river, male away from it. Oppositions can also be defined relating to female and male activities that have spatial relationships, for example, gather/hunt floodplain/uplands. The placement of the living sites in the valley floor and the cemeteries on the bluff tops, the former associated with the river, and the latter with the uplands, may have also been significant, adding the binaries of life versus death and up versus down. Time in this dimension is cyclical rather than linear. Life and death are often viewed as a cycle, as are the seasons. Spring and summer bring life, and they are also the seasons when gathered resources, particularly those derived from early seeding and fruiting plants after the long winter, would have been most important. The fall and winter are the seasons of death but are also the seasons when deer hunting and nut collecting would have been most important. Again, very interestingly, the other avian form portrayed on ceramics is the raptor (Morgan 1988: 131; although it has also been suggested that the images represent flamingos). Raptors include hawks, eagles, and vultures—birds that are hunters and carrion feeders. Raptors invoke their own liminality: They fly through the air, but many of them feed off terrestrial prey; and the vultures, in particular, draw their life by feeding off dead animals. Rather than the V shapes of migrating waterfowl traversing the skies from horizon to horizon, the raptor's signature flight pattern is circling in the updrafts in the vicinity of the bluffs.

Putting this all together, we can envision the complexities of Hopewellian life, encompassing the economic, political, and ritual aspects of existence, mapped onto the physical environment. Upriver and downriver related to linear time, to the past and the future. Interactions among lineage-based communities and among individuals within those communities, including those related to the Hopewell Interaction Sphere, were transacted along the river dimension. Morphological biodistance data suggest that women relocated along this dimension in terms of postmarital residence patterns (Buikstra 1976, 1977, 1980; Konigsberg 1988; Konigsberg and Buikstra 1995), although recent DNA evidence may indicate matrilocal postmarital residence patterns (Bolnick and Smith 2007). The subsistence activities of the local community, and notions of gender that gave meaning to those activities, were structured along the axis perpendicular to the river. Time as a cyclical phenomenon—life and death, the changing of the seasons—also played out in this dimension.

Conclusion

Naturally the question arises: Is the lower Illinois River valley our Rosetta Stone for interpreting Hopewellian landscapes? For now, I will leave that question to others. I will point out that the peculiarities of the lower Illinois Valley may make patterns and relationships more readily discernable—or imaginable. The demographic landscape of the valley is largely one dimensional: Communities and resource catchments are strung out along a very narrow riverine corridor. The Illinois River valley conveniently runs north and south and is located along a major migratory waterfowl flyway. As Ruby, Carr, and Charles (2005: 172–173) note, Hopewellian communities and intercommunity interactions were constructed very differently in the valley than seems to have been the case in either southern Ohio or southern Indiana, where the physical environments are very different from that of the Illinois River valley and from each other. Two other factors should also be kept in mind. The Middle Woodland history of the lower Illinois Valley was one of immigration into an uninhabited landscape, a movement of people into the valley largely from the north (Charles 1992b). Furthermore, despite the large-scale pattern of migration, at the local level mobility was very restricted. The productivity of the valley and surrounding uplands was conducive to permanently occupied hamlets and logistical subsistence practices. All of these factors contribute to the seeming clarity of the landscape dimensions outlined in this chapter.

But the question still remains: Does the "observational" quality of the physical environment of the Illinois River valley sensibly lead us to the "theoretical" landscape proffered, the landscape of the Middle Woodland people who inhabited it two thousand years ago? This is, ultimately, the point of this chapter. An environmental reconstruction of a region, in the modern ecological sense, is an insufficient method by which to perceive a prehistoric landscape because too much of a landscape is theoretical, in Quine's sense. Conversely, to categorically claim that our landscape is different from their landscape leaves us with no method by which to translate the Middle Woodland landscape into our terms, again because of the theoretical content. If, however, we accept a modicum of observational reality in the environment and in environmental reconstructions, we can, perhaps, begin to (re)construct and translate past landscapes.

At this juncture, we should recall the notion that was introduced earlier, to wit, that we are engaged in the writing of science fiction. As such, we cannot "prove" our (re)constructions in the sense of the experimental sciences. Rather, our endeavor is more akin to the historical sciences, where "proof" is attained by different inferential methods (Gould 1986). We are further burdened in that we attach importance to the meanings invoked by past people (which is not generally a problem for paleontologists and geologists). Essentially, we are writing fiction, that is, narratives, which should be internally consistent but which also relate to "science" and which should, therefore, be consistent with minimally theoretical observational statements (a.k.a., "reality"). The more our narratives incorporate archaeological "facts," the more confidence we can have in them.

The corroboration of the landscape (re)construction presented in this chapter entails establishing further congruence with additional aspects of the archaeological record. Areas of research to pursue include refinement of resource procurement locations, symbolism in mortuary ritual, movement of raw materials and finished goods at a microscale, and so forth. Perhaps more important will be attempts to invoke the above logic in other regions of Hopewell occupation, in particular Ohio. In the end, we are engaged in an endless endeavor, in that we will never complete a (re)construction of the past. Archaeological science fiction—as a synthesis of science and fiction—is a process, not a product.

Acknowledgments

I appreciate the very useful comments provided by Martin Byers, Juliana Shortell, and DeeAnne Wymer. The remaining overstatements are my responsibility.

Notes

1. Frege (1993) offers the classic distinction between sense and reference, specifically referring to names (or signs). In this formulation, a sign's *sense* is the meaning or cognitive content associated with it, and its *referent* is the object to which it applies. However, in more complex constructions, such as the sentence, the reference is no longer to an object but to its truth value: "Every declarative sentence concerned with the reference of its words is therefore to be regarded as a proper name, and its reference, if it has one, is either the True or the False" (Frege 1993: 28). For an archaeological (re) construction of the past, the truth value is an infinitely receding point, one that we can never attain. Ideally, we are at least trying to approach it. Nevertheless, archaeological explanation and interpretation, in practice, tend to be driven by methodological, theoretical, and/or political concerns. As such, a (re)construction that makes sense to us relates more to our emotional or intellectual satisfaction than to its truth value. Thus while Frege's logical definition of sense is applicable to archaeology, *Webster's* broader definition of sense more effectively encompasses actual practice.

2. I use the terms "Darwinian" and "Marxian," rather than "Darwinist" and "Marxist," to indicate the derived and transformed nature of much of the thought contained within these traditions. The "ist" terminology is restricted to those formulations that more closely adhere to the original writings of Darwin and Marx.

2

Why Move?

Ohio Hopewell Sedentism Revisited

Paul J. Pacheco

Were the builders of the famous earthworks and mounds of the Middle Ohio Valley, people we today call Ohio Hopewell, residentially mobile or sedentary populations? Both of these contrasting, and seemingly dichotomous, interpretations of the archaeological record have circulated in the recent literature concerning Ohio Hopewell settlement patterns. Before taking a detailed look at these contrasting interpretations, it is necessary to define a key term. Herein, the term "sedentary" is used to refer to populations who maintain stable, permanent residential bases (Rafferty 1985; Varien 1999), with the term "sedentism" representing the recognition of this general condition in the archaeological record. Permanence here does not imply that all members of a particular settlement are present at all times. It does imply, however, that members of a settlement who leave on trips do eventually return to the residential base.

My position, shared and developed with my colleagues William Dancey and Olaf Prufer (Dancey 1991, 2003; Dancey and Pacheco 1997; Pacheco 1989a, 1993, 1996, 1997; Pacheco and Dancey 2006; Prufer 1964, 1965, 1967, 1997a), posits that Ohio Hopewell populations lived in dispersed, sedentary households or hamlets, organized into communities affiliated with earthworks and/or mounds. At the local level, Ruby, Carr, and Charles (2005) and Carr (2008c) now refer to this scale of Hopewell social organization as "symbolic communities."

The most cogent and well-reasoned challenge to our interpretation of Ohio Hopewell settlement patterns has been presented by Frank Cowan at the Middle Woodland at the Millennium conference, held in Pere Marquette, Illinois, July 19–21, 2000. Cowan (2000) argues for the opposing view of residential mobility in his paper "A Mobile Hopewell? Questioning Assumptions of Ohio Hopewell Sedentism." A published version of his paper appears in the recently released volume *Recreating Hopewell* (Cowan 2006).

Cowan (2000, 2006) develops a complex, two-pronged argument in which he examines the meaning of permanent wooden architecture at earthwork centers and the meaning of lithic assemblage variability in proposed Ohio Hopewell domestic settlements. His conclusion is that housing facilities at earthwork centers imply the aggregation of residentially mobile populations and that domestic settlements lack the technological signature of sedentism. At the outset it is important to note that the phrase "Questioning Assumptions of Ohio Hopewell Sedentism" in Cowan's title is somewhat misleading. For Dancey and me, as well as Prufer, the idea of Ohio Hopewell sedentism originated first as an interpretation of our settlement data and only later became an important aspect of our settlement models.

Cowan sets the tone for his critique by accusing Dancey and me of shifting away from Prufer's (1964, 1965) view on sedentism as expressed in its original form:

> For nearly four decades, many Ohio archaeologists have held that Hopewell populations lived in small, dispersed, semisedentary hamlets near corporate ceremonial centers (Prufer 1964, 1965). Within the past decade, some researchers have dropped the qualifier "semi-," arguing that Ohio Hopewell populations were completely sedentary and that many of the hamlets surrounding earthwork complexes were occupied nearly continuously for long periods of time (Dancey 1991; Dancey and Pacheco 1997; Pacheco 1996, 1997). (Cowan 2006: 26)

First, it is important to note that Prufer referred to the hamlets as "semi-permanent," not "semi-sedentary" (Prufer 1964: 71, 1965: 137). Second, we have explained some of the confusion surrounding Prufer's terminology as a product of the era in which it was written (Dancey and Pacheco 1997: 6; Prufer 1997a: 124). Prufer used the term "semi-permanent" to refer to the Ohio Hopewell practice of periodically shifting their gardens as opposed to relying on permanent field agriculture. He still viewed hamlets as occupied year-round in this scenario, although he felt they moved periodically as the need arose to shift the locations of their gardens. Wymer (1987, 1993, 1996, 1997), Braun (1987), Crites (1987), O'Brien (1987), and Smith (1989, 1992, 2001) have documented specific aspects of this plant complex and the technological shifts associated with it in addition to the broader human-land relationships it creates. Taking these studies into account, we visualize a unique generalized (or diffuse) Ohio Hopewell niche focused on intensive use of diverse local resources in household-scale catchments (Pacheco and Dancey 2006: 13–16), which represent the culmination of a long-term process of human-land interaction based on seasonal scheduling of subsistence labor (Caldwell 1958; Rafferty 1985: 113).

The other issue confronted by Cowan in his opening statement refers to the length of time each domestic settlement is occupied. Dancey and I have discussed this issue as a reflection of the concept *duration of occupation* (Dancey and Pacheco 1997: 8–9; Pacheco 1997: 57–58; Pacheco and Dancey 2006: 13). At McGraw, Prufer (1965: 137) argued for an occupation of between 20 and 30 years, while we argued for a wider range of variation in duration and discussed how it affects the clarity of the signature of the household cluster in the archaeological record. The multiple, wide-ranging radiocarbon dates at proposed sedentary households such as McGraw and Murphy I may indeed reflect reoccupation of domestic loci over time (i.e., Prufer's shifting locations) as opposed to long-term occupations at single places or even interpretive deficiencies of the radiocarbon dating technique (Carr 2008c: 114; Carr and Haas 1996: 28–30; Clay 1998: 15; Dancey 1991: 66). But regardless of the actual duration of occupation at domestic sites, we maintain that the underlying pattern in these Ohio Hopewell communities is residential stability based on sedentism. Recently, Ruby, Carr, and Charles (2005: 153) make a plausible case that Ohio Hopewell residential settlements are unlikely to have been continuously occupied for more than 10 to 20 years at a time, which given current data seems like a reasonable estimate.

I argue that the generalized model of Ohio Hopewell community structure Dancey and I proposed (see Dancey and Pacheco 1997: 21, Figure 1.2) is still the best available general interpretive framework, despite Cowan's challenge. In our model, these sedentary communities used earthworks as corporate ceremonial centers to socially integrate dispersed populations.

The archaeological research supporting the interpretation of sedentary Ohio Hopewell households has come in a number of forms, including analyses of site distributions and assemblage variability (Burks 2004; Carskadden and Morton 1996, 1997; Dancey and Pacheco 1997; Keener and Biehl 1999; Lazazzera 2000; Pacheco and Dancey 2006; Pacheco 1989a, 1996; Prufer 1967; Seeman 1996), analyses of the maintenance and organization of space within settlements (Burks 2004; Dancey 1991, 2003; Kozarek 1997; Lazazzera 2004; Pacheco 1993, 1997; Prufer 1965), analyses of faunal remains (Blosser 1996; Parmalee 1965; Kozarek 1997), and analyses of gardening/subsistence strategies (Pacheco and Dancey 2006; Smith 1992; Wymer 1996, 1997).

At least some of the research listed above takes into account the seminal work of Rafferty (1985) and Kent (1990, 1992) on the topic of determining sedentism. Rafferty (1985) and Odell (1998) discuss how the sedentary versus residential mobility contrast is not an example of dichotomous variables but an expression of a continuum of mobility strategies representing many degrees and kinds of mobility; hence the existence of confusing terms such as "semisedentary." Similarly, Kelly (1992) argues for a wide range of variability in a group's mobility patterns, both within the group and from year to year. Such variation undoubtedly held true for Ohio Hopewell populations as well.

While we maintain that earthwork-building and moundbuilding populations of Ohio Hopewell people utilized dispersed, stable, permanent residential bases, we also recognize and document other mobility strategies as part of this settlement pattern (Pacheco and Dancey 2006). Like Cowan (2006), we see mobility expressed in visits to ceremonial centers by dispersed populations. But we maintain that these people utilized logistical mobility targeting spatially concentrated and seasonally available resources to supply their residential bases rather than residential mobility, where the whole group moves their residence to the resources (Pacheco 1989a, 1993; Pacheco and Dancey 2006; Seeman 1996). For many scholars, the issue of Ohio Hopewell sedentism will not be resolved in a satisfactory manner until a different approach to settlement research is developed and more extensive excavations are conducted in the core area (Smith 2006). To this end, a few strategies for future Ohio Hopewell settlement research are offered in the conclusion.

Structures at Hopewell Earthworks

To be sure, when excavations have occurred in the immediate vicinity of, or within, the walls of Ohio Hopewell earthworks, evidence of wooden structures has been found. This is not only true of the spectacular discoveries by Cowan, Sunderhaus, and Genheimer (1998, 1999, 2000) at Stubbs but also true at Fort Ancient (Connolly 1997; Cowan, Sunderhaus, and Genheimer 2004; Lazazzera 2000, 2004), Seip (Baby and Langlois 1979), and Mound City (Brown 1982). Similarly, wooden structures have been identified under numerous Hopewell mounds located within earthworks such as Seip (Greber 1979b, 1997a), Harness (Greber 1979b, 1983), Hopewell (Greber and Ruhl 1989; Greber 1991), and the Newark Fairgrounds Circle (Lepper 1989), to name just a few. Including the numerous post molds from presumably domestic structures at a few of our conjectured household/hamlet clusters (Burks 2004; Pacheco and Dancey 2006: 7; Pacheco, Burks, and Wymer 2006), it is clear that there is a rich diversity of Ohio Hopewell wooden architecture expressing a multitude of social purposes.

Cowan (2006: 36) misconstrues our designation of the specialized camp site type, extending it to cover all of his wooden structures at Stubbs and thereby thinking he has debunked a portion of our model because they do not appear to be all that specialized. Instead, he views the numerous wooden structures as temporary, episodically occupied camps, preferring the term "house-like" (Cowan 2006: 44). It was never our intention to claim that all sites near earthworks must by necessity fall into the catch-all category of specialized camps. However, based on the lack of a symbol for temporary earthwork camps in our model, it is easy to see how Cowan came to this conclusion (Dancey and Pacheco 1997: 21). Likewise, other logistical settlement types, representing activities such as gardening, flint quarrying, and upland hunting, have been documented and discussed, but in order to reduce clutter, symbols for them were not included on the schematic map of the settlement model either (Dancey and Pacheco 1997: 8–10; Pacheco 1989a, 1997; Pacheco and Dancey 2006; Seeman 1996). In actuality, the problem of recognizing temporary camps near earthworks as distinct settlement types has been discussed (Pacheco 1989a, 1993: 83–86), and they have been indirectly discussed as well (Greber 1997a; Pacheco 1996).

The concept of specialized camps was originally proposed by Prufer (1967: 289) to interpret the Russell Brown Upper Terrace and Middle Terrace #1 locations near Liberty Earthworks in Ross County. The surface assemblages of both clusters are dominated by the use and manufacturing of bladelets from prepared cores. Presumably, specialized camps represent the loci of craft activities associated with production of the artifact varieties discovered in Hopewellian mounds. Cowan (2006: 31) refers to these sites as "core patches" following Greber, Davis, and DuFresne (1981), who earlier had identified a number of other core and bladelet patches on the Harness Farm, both within and near Liberty, that also appear to match the specialized camp concept advanced by Prufer.

Analysis by Coughlin and Seeman (1997) and earlier large-scale surveys by Prufer (1967) show that in addition to the specialized camps, there are numerous other Hopewell artifact clusters in the vicinity of Liberty Earthworks. Presumably, some of these other settlements are temporary earthwork camps, while others may in fact be sedentary households, as both projects consider archaeological data which extend several kilometers out from the earthworks. Recent excavations at the Brown's Bottom #1 site on the Harness Farm (Blank 1965; Pacheco, Burks, and Wymer 2006) appear to confirm this impression. Work on Brown's Bottom in 2005–6 produced a well-preserved example of a Hopewell settlement with evidence of a permanently occupied, sedentary household cluster, including formal refuse deposits, abundant domestic ceramics, several large earth ovens, and a substantial 13.7-×-13.7 m^2 post structure containing a large center post, benches, internal hearths, thermal features, and a large, screened off, flat-bottomed storage pit.

At other major earthworks, wooden structures have been discovered which suggest a variety of functions. For example, some of the structures uncovered at Seip which contained bladelets and other nondomestic looking debris (Baby and Langlois 1979) have been interpreted as the loci of craft activities. Other structures, such as those inside the North Fort at Fort Ancient (Lazazzera 2000, 2004), may instead represent either temporary residences related to earthwork activities, like those Cowan (2006) proposes for Stubbs, or houses from a sedentary Late Hopewell/Early Late Woodland nucleated villages similar to Strait, Waterplant, and Zencor (Burks 2004). Lepper and Yerkes's (1997) report on Li. 79#1 (Hale's House), located near the Newark Earthworks, is a good example of the potential interpretive confusion surrounding sites located near earthworks. Structural remains of a small wooden windbreak, pit features, evidence of bladelet and core activity, and mica processing were discovered at this site. They argue for short-term use by a small domestic group for ceremonial purposes related to the earthwork (Lepper and Yerkes 1997: 197), yet use-wear patterns on bladelets at the site are generalized (see also Lepper 1989; Pacheco 1989a).

The critical issue for Cowan appears to be the rationality of constructing abundant, episodically used "house-like" structures at ceremonial centers, like the ones he and his colleagues have documented with their valiant salvage work at the Stubbs and Fort Ancient Earthworks:

> It is not clear why a sedentary community would need an abundance of well-built, special purpose housing facilities on the immediate fringes of a ceremonial gathering place if its year-round residences were located no more than an hour's walk away from the community center. The geographic scale of these communities is so limited that formal, highly visible community gathering places would not have been necessary to promote intracommunity communication and social solidarity. Everyday foraging and informal household visitation would have easily brought the members of such a community into daily, face-to-face contact without the necessity of constructing monumental architecture.
>
> The imposing grandeur of Ohio Hopewell ceremonial sites suggests that they were gathering places for much more widespread and probably much more mobile communities than is suggested by the Prufer-Dancey-Pacheco sedentary hamlet model. Monumental architecture implies a strong need for social integration, and the scale of the architecture implies the geographic scale of the attractive force. The abundance of "guest houses" further implies a highly dispersed population whose

members periodically traveled great distances to attend community gatherings. (Cowan 2006: 48)

Cowan (2006: 48) asserts that we have failed to specify the geographic scale of Ohio Hopewell communities in our model. His point is valid, but this is due to the fact that he is confusing our model with the description of a specific community. It is impossible to assign a discrete geographic scale to an abstract model of Ohio Hopewell settlement patterns because of the flexibility needed to cover "actual" Hopewell symbolic communities, which no doubt varied greatly in size.

Size variation is illustrated by our examples of proposed Ohio Hopewell symbolic communities (Pacheco 1996, 1997) and by those that have been documented by other researchers (Carskadden and Morton 1996, 1997; Church and Ericksen 1997; Connolly 1997; Coughlin and Seeman 1997; Genheimer 1997; Greber 1997a; Keener and Biehl 1999). These examples show that in small communities, such as Dresden, many households would have been located within short walking distance of the local earthwork (Carskadden and Morton 1997; Pacheco 1996: 29). In contrast, within regional-scale communities such as Newark (equivalent to Carr's (2008c) concept of a sustainable community), several documented households are located 20 kilometers or more from the regional center (see Figure 1.7, Pacheco and Dancey 2006: 20). While it is unlikely that Ohio Hopewell communities at the regional scale were more than 30 kilometers across (following Chisholm's Axiom), these dimensions will have to be established on the ground with settlement data.

Compounding the issue further is the possibility that some earthworks, in addition to having significance at the local and regional scales, acted at a higher scale as interregional centers that would have been frequented by the kinds of distant, far-traveling guests that Cowan envisions. These variations of scale create a nested set of social identities for Ohio Hopewell people of the kind which characterize segmentary social systems organized by sequential hierarchy. We have specifically argued that the Newark and Hopewell Earthworks represent interregional peer-polity centers (Pacheco and Dancey 2006: 21–23). Similarly, Ruby, Carr, and Charles (2005), Bernardini (2004), and Carr (2008c) have expanded on the many possible social meanings and spatial parameters of Ohio Hopewell communities which both reflect on and clarify the variation in scales of human organization apparent in the settlement data (Pacheco and Dancey 2006: 19–21).

Perhaps the most surprising of Cowan's arguments is his position that the very existence of these "house-like" structures near the earthworks rejects the type of sedentism we present in our settlement model. While intuitively appealing, perusal of his paper shows that this position is informed by neither archaeological nor ethnographic evidence. Instead, it appears to represent an application of common sense. What follows are several archaeological and ethnographic cases which provide examples contrary to the commonsense approach.

Monumental public architecture is typically associated with nucleated/urban societies throughout the world (Wenke 1999), but there are also somewhat rare archaeological and ethnographic examples of dispersed sedentary communities that used "vacant" corporate ceremonial centers defined by monumental public architecture to promote social integration—what Bernardini (2004: 331) refers to as the "village surrogate" concept. Prufer (1964, 1997a) specifically referred to examples of this settlement pattern among the Maya when he first formulated the model. Although the idea has been rejected for many of the prehistoric Mayan communities for which it was proposed (Becker 1979), it may still apply to a limited number of other ancient Mayan communities, such as those in the Belize Valley (Bullard 1962; Willey 1956), and especially to ethnographic Mayan communities in the highlands of Guatemala (Tax 1937) and the highlands of Chiapas (Vogt 1961, 1964, 1969). Similar settlement patterns are proposed for the Late Formative period in the Valdivia Valley of southwestern coastal Ecuador (Schwarz and Raymond 1996), the Early Intermediate period of the Nasca cultures of coastal Peru (Silverman 1988, 1994, 2002), the ethnographic Chachi of northwestern coastal Ecuador (DeBoer and Blitz 1991; DeBoer 1997), the ethnographic and protohistoric Mapuche of south-central Chile (Dillehay 1990, 1992), and some of the Megalithic cultures of Europe (Bogucki 1987; Chapman 1981, 1995; Sherratt 1990).

Importantly, these independent social systems express a wide range of variation, ranging from communities with "vacant ceremonial centers" supported by dispersed sedentary domestic settlements, to mostly vacant centers with limited specialist residential populations surrounded by dispersed sedentary domestic settlements, to rural dispersed sedentary domestic units evenly spaced along secondary river courses without ritual precincts, although they visit "vacant" pilgrimage centers at the regional level. This observation is especially important given that there must be variation within Ohio Hopewell too; in particular, this appears to be true for the southwestern Ohio earthwork sites at Turner (Prufer 1997a) and Fort Ancient (Connolly 1996, 1997; Connolly and Lepper 2004).

Yet as long as a specific community settlement pattern can be characterized as organized around dispersed sedentary households with associated ceremonial earthwork centers and/or mounds, the model should not be rejected because of the discovery of a range of variation in other Ohio Hopewell communities. This is especially true given that the spatial construct of the model has a dynamic component (i.e., variation might be due to change through time). Discussion should instead focus on the range of tolerance permitted by the model when it is extended to cover actual variation in time and space. Likewise, modification of the model should occur when the general model fails to serve as a useful heuristic device. Furthermore, the model should not be rejected on the basis of local symbolic communities identifying themselves with, or participating in, events at multiple rather than single ceremonial centers as long as the local landscape is still characterized by dispersed residentially stable households who built them (Bernardini 2004; Carr 2008c; Ruby, Carr, and Charles 2005: 159–172). In fact, the symbolic communities in Licking County at Granville and upper Jonathan Creek documented over a decade ago (Pacheco 1996) were presented as containing multiple centers. Such real variation clarifies the difference between actual settlement systems and the abstract models used to interpret their settlement pattern.

Several of the archaeological and ethnographic cultures which utilized the dispersed sedentary community–vacant ceremonial center settlement pattern built temporary structures at their centers to house community members and guests attending ceremonial events. Silverman (1988: 404) argues that the large Nasca center of Cahuachi "is a kind of vacant ceremonial center" based on years of extensive excavation and survey. The Nasca built a variety of structures at the site which were used as temporary quarters during pilgrimage events at the center. These structures ranged from clearly temporary housing made of cane and woven matting to wattle-and-daub huts to more permanent room blocks consisting of mud/adobe-plastered walls, some of which were whitewashed. Adobe rooms often had well-prepared hard packed floors which had been swept clean of cultural debris. Nonetheless, in the "125 hectares of open or unconstructed space at the site—corresponding to almost 85 per cent of Cahuachi's total area—no evidence of a large, residential, domestic occupation was found" (Silverman 1994: 6).

Less durable architecture for temporary housing is shown by Mapuche *trokinche* units (dispersed sedentary communities formed into peer-polities), who built numerous wooden structures at their vacant ceremonial centers:

All *trokinche* units share and maintain a permanent ceremonial field, usually a flat pampa adjacent to a creek or river, on communal land. A typical field is characterized by semipermanent *rukas* (dwellings) made of wooden posts, thatch, and tree branches. Fields range in size from approximately 60 m to 500 m in length depending upon the number and size of participating lineages and invited persons. (Dillehay 1992: 390)

The arrangement and placement of rukas around the ceremonial fields are a "microcosm of the actual community and household settlement patterns of lineages and families" (Dillehay 1992: 392). The Mapuche example provides a counter to Cowan's commonsense logic about building wooden structures at otherwise vacant ceremonial centers despite living in the same region. The use of these structures by invited guests, in addition to the local household members of the trokinche, is a notable aspect of their function.

The ethnographic Chachi are another well-documented example of a society organized around dispersed, single-household, sedentary communities integrated through vacant ceremonial centers (DeBoer and Blitz 1991; DeBoer 1997; Greber 1997a). An eloquent description of the Chachi is presented and discussed by DeBoer and commentators in his 1997 *Cambridge Archaeological Journal* article. A few observations about the contents of this article will suffice to add to this discussion. First, Chachi ceremonial centers also contain guest houses, "either regularly sized houses microcosmically arranged, as at Punta Venado, or 'big houses,' as at other centers. This observation provides a springboard for the more general suggestion that the ceremonial centre, symbolically conceived is a 'big house'" (DeBoer 1997: 227). Second, DeBoer links the concept of the ceremonial center as "big house" to ethnographic examples in the Eastern Woodlands. He then extends this analogy to explore aspects of the Ohio Hopewell settlement pattern. And third, DeBoer shows that Chachi communities display considerable variability in geographic scale. Finally, Fagan makes an important observation about DeBoer's research in the comments section of the article, connecting the Ohio Hopewell dispersed sedentary community settlement pattern to issues concerning regional sociocultural change:

The important point is that DeBoer also tries to demonstrate that there has been change from the past, and that he is not merely extending the ethnographic present into the past. This change is measured by the intrusion of new earthwork shapes, which DeBoer considers indicative of growing internal social contradictions. He perceives the trajectory of Ohio Hopewell "nervously poised" between egalitarianism and tyranny. If DeBoer is right, then the Hopewell reflects Native American groups in a long period of transition, where monuments symbolically map a changing social order, in which marriage and women's labor played a dominant role, before giving way to the aggregated settlements of the Late Woodland period after A.D. 400. (Fagan 1997: 247)

In summary, there is clear archaeological and ethnographic evidence of dispersed sedentary communities building episodically used structures in the vicinity of their otherwise vacant corporate ceremonial centers. While these examples do not, in and of themselves, demonstrate that Ohio Hopewell people used such a practice, they do show that the mere idea of creating temporary housing at vacant centers by dispersed sedentary communities is not irrational. These examples are superior to Cowan's commonsense logic, even if on face value it is intuitively more appealing to question why sedentary Ohio Hopewell communities located near enough to their vacant corporate ceremonial centers to be able to walk "home" would build wooden guest houses at their centers.

Lithic Assemblage Variability Issues

Cowan's arguments concerning lithic assemblage variability at our proposed households/hamlets (like the Murphy Tract clusters, Jennison Guard, and McGraw), and how it reflects on the question of sedentism in Ohio Hopewell communities, are complex and well reasoned. Two intertwining comparative themes underlie his analysis: whether or not Ohio Hopewell assemblages are characterized as curated or expedient and whether or not the Ohio Hopewell mobility pattern represents logistical mobility or residential mobility. Both of these comparative themes can be traced back to the ground-breaking work of Binford (1979, 1980, 1982) among the Nunamiut and the expedient core research of Parry and Kelly (1987). Cowan (1999), to be sure, has made a significant contribution to this literature by showing a strong relationship between mobility and the organization of lithic technology in a sample of Late Archaic through Late Woodland lithic scatters in western New York.

Yet the relationships between lithic technology and these two strategic continuums of *expediency versus curation* and *logistical mobility versus residential mobility* are far from conclusive. Most certainly, the relationships are not well enough understood to represent behaviors governed by laws of human behavior. At best, what is understood today represents empirical generalizations. And these generalizations offer few consistent means by which to understand lithic assemblage variability in the archaeological record.

Parry and Kelly (1987), for instance, argue that sedentary populations often shift to expedient lithic technologies, while Binford (1980: 16–18; 1982: 26) suggests sedentism implies complete adoption of a logistical mobility strategy, as by necessity, all resources except those immediately available within local catchments must be moved to the stable residential bases. Yet Binford (1979, 1980) also links foragers to preferring curated lithic technology when they use logistical mobility embedded within a cycle of seasonal residential moves. This, in fact, is the crux of Binford's argument for the Nunamiut. Thus logistical mobility has been linked to both curated and expedient technology depending on whether or not the settlement system is sedentary.

Other researchers have argued against a straightforward relationship between mobility and either curated or expedient organization of lithic technology. Bamforth (1986) argues that raw material availability, rather than mobility, is the key variable which governs the systemic organization of lithic technology in a settlement system. Bleed (1986) concludes that the design alternatives of hunting weapons, measured in terms of maintainability in comparison to reliability (both alternatives are affected by the mobility of and spatial density of prey species), also affect the curation/expediency issue. Finally, Keeley (1982) illustrates how the decision to haft a particular tool type is an additional mitigating factor in choosing either strategy for organizing lithic technology.

Cowan (2006: 27) argues: "Throughout the Americas, bifacially flaked stone tool production strategies predominate among mobile populations." Here Cowan relies on research which suggests that bifacial technology is the sine qua non of a curation strategy, which then declines in popularity as sedentism increases (Parry and Kelly 1987; Odell 1998). Cowan (2006: 48) suggests that the lithic assemblages of documented Ohio Hopewell households are best characterized as a veneer of bladelet tools "with a biface-dominated assemblage suggestive of high mobility, not sedentism," and that they represent a highly mobile people who utilized a long-distance logistical strategy to provision resources for their seasonally shifting residential bases. The underlying reason for promoting residential mobility is Cowan's stance that Ohio Hopewell people are fundamentally foragers, a view recently favored by Yerkes as well (2002, 2005, 2006). Because of their residential mobility, these groups organized their lithic technology with a curation strategy emphasizing bifaces. This type of mobility strategy is therefore similar to the one outlined by Binford (1979, 1980, 1982) for Nunamiut foragers. Another similar strategy emphasizing long-distance logistical mobility has been suggested for Great Lakes foragers of the Mid-Holocene (Lovis, Donahue, and Holman 2005).

A potential source of confusion exits in Cowan's argument surrounding expediency versus curation. This is found in his Table 2.2 (2006: 29), in which he lays out the expectations for lithic assemblages in sedentary base camps. Under the category functional expediency, Cowan lists opportunistic use of local raw materials, extensive retouch, resharpening, reuse, recycling, and considerable use wear on discarded tools. Bamforth's (1986) research, however, suggests that the widespread availability of a raw material sidesteps dependence on opportunism and moves a given lithic technology toward expediency. Furthermore, the notion of extensive retouch, reuse, recycling, and considerable use wear applies more appropriately to a strategy emphasizing curation. These principles represent the anathema of expedient technology as explained by one of Cowan's key sources:

> Second, no explicit distinction is made between "tools" and "waste." Every piece is regarded as a *potential* tool. In practice, tools are selected by trying them out empirically, and the pieces best suited for the specific task at hand are chosen for use. . . . Third, tools are seldom modified. If a piece has an unsuitable shape, or its edge is dulled from use, it is usually discarded and a new piece is selected rather than being retouched to reshape or sharpen it. Most tools are used only once, although a flake that is unsuited for one task may later be reused in another. . . . The tools are made with little expenditure of time or effort, to be used in a specific task. Once the task is completed, the tools are discarded just as quickly as they were made. (Parry and Kelly 1987: 287–288)

While sedentary Hopewell groups may have recycled and reused (especially by resharpening) formal bifaces used for local and logistical hunting activities, they rarely recycled flake tools. By arguing that retouch is rare and use-wear polishes are poorly developed (based on Yerkes 1990, 1994), Cowan attempts to strengthen the case for his interpretation that the sites represent curated, biface-dominated assemblages, characteristic of highly mobile logistical parties (Cowan 2006: 35). Instead, what his analysis actually does is underscore the predominantly expedient nature of the lithic assemblages at documented Ohio Hopewell residential sites. As will be shown next, this is especially true for sites from the Murphy Tract in the Licking Valley.

Lithic Assemblage Variability in Household Clusters

Has Cowan correctly characterized the lithic assemblage variability of documented Ohio Hopewell household clusters as biface-dominated? To be sure, he recognizes the abundant evidence for bladelets, but he views them as a tool which can be filtered out of the underlying biface-dominated assemblages. Cowan's only comment concerning possible candidates for expedient tool types is to assert that "[unretouched] flakes, for the most part, are limited to the by-products of bladelet core shaping and maintenance and to the by-products of bifacial tool retouch" (2000: 8). However, I contend that Cowan incorrectly characterizes the lithic assemblage variability from my dissertation research and that his decision to "filter-out" the bladelets is not valid because bladelets in these domestic contexts are tools too (Genheimer 1996). One could easily turn the argument around and view the assemblages as dominated by flake tools (including both bladelets and unretouched and retouched flakes), which are expediently organized and to which are attached a household level pattern of biface production and use (Pacheco 1993: 60–64).

There are two good explanations for the continued emphasis on a biface industry within the Ohio Hopewell lithic technology. First, as part of their dispersed sedentary niche, individual households are primarily responsible for hunting activities to procure meat protein. Without reliable domesticated animals, exploitation of white-tailed deer remained at a premium throughout Ohio prehistory. Deer hunting occurred at seasonally occupied upland logistical camps, but also occurred at the scale of the local household catchments. Furthermore, Middle Woodland land-use patterns created a synergism which increased the density of locally available deer (Pacheco and Dancey 2006). Hunting locally available deer would have promoted biface use within the household catchments and maintenance of bifacial projectile points within the households. Second, there is an equally important emphasis on biface production for inclusion within the ceremonial context and possibly for interregional trade and exchange, exactly as Cowan argues is the case for bladelets. Numerous biface caches exist within mounds. Perusal of the famous photograph of the biface assemblage from Mound 2 at the Hopewell Earthworks (Greber 1996: 152) makes this impressively clear. Simply put, some aspects of biface production in Ohio Hopewell households may be equally "ritually charged" (Cowan 2006: 32).

Like Cowan, I will focus the remaining discussion in this section on the lithic assemblages from my surface survey of the Murphy Tract, but I also maintain that the lithic assemblages from Jennison Guard (Blosser 1996; Kozarek 1997) and McGraw (Sunyer 1965), despite representing distinctly different recovery contexts, also represent sedentary households. In fact, the McGraw midden, because of its diverse ceramics, bone, and shell tools, closely matches Cowan's expectations for a functionally complete toolkit exhibiting a sedentary coresidential group.

The data Cowan (2006: 35) uses in his analysis are from my surface survey of the Murphy Tract (refer to Tables 2.3 and 2.4, Pacheco 1997: 74–75 for this discussion), for which he claims "most of the Hopewell artifact concentrations are interpreted as residential hamlets." This claim is not quite true. Only five of 11 identified clusters, Murphy I, III, IV, V, and VI, were interpreted as the locations of sedentary households (Pacheco 1993, 1997). Furthermore, Murphy IV represents a complex palimpsest with three distinct components. Two of these components are spatially distinct, although both are distinguished by use of local Van Port (Flint Ridge) chert. One of these components represents a Hopewell household while the other represents a Late Archaic occupation based on the recovery of three Matanzas side-notched points (Justice 1987: 119–121). These two components are partially overlapped by a third, later component, which is interpreted as a specialized camp that extended across a larger, four-hectare space called the South Block. The specialized camp is distinguished by a high frequency of exotic Wyandotte chert from Harrison County, Indiana (Munson and Munson 1990). I have argued that the procurement and use of the Wyandotte chert occurred during the occupation of this specialized camp. Analysis suggests this event occurred sometime around A.D. 190 ± 60 in uncorrected radiocarbon years (Pacheco 1997: 49–58).

In Cowan's (2006: 35–36) Figure 2.7 and Figure 2.8, the mixing of all assemblages, but especially the two Murphy IV Hopewell components, distorts the bladelet/biface ratios used to make his argument. Cowan calculates a 14:1 bladelet to biface ratio for the Murphy IV cluster. But the ratios are very different if the Wyandotte chert and the Van Port chert in this assemblage are separated. For Wyandotte, the ratio of bladelets (n = 124) to bifaces (n = 6) is really much higher at 20.7:1. For Vanport chert the ratio of bladelets (n = 64) to bifaces (n = 23) is less dramatically weighted toward bladelets, with a ratio of 2.8:1.

Cowan ignores the overall pattern of coarse-grained redundancy (Binford 1980: 18) exhibited by the proposed households and the intersite variability exhibited by the smaller clusters and intercluster space, which were crucial to my argument for sedentism. The smaller clusters and intercluster space exhibit a wide range of variation including some very low bladelet/biface ratios. Cluster 4, for example, has a 1:1 ratio of bladelets to bifaces (n = 5 and n = 5), and Cluster 5/8 has a ratio of 1:2.5 (n = 2 and n = 5). The ratio in intercluster space is even more skewed toward bifaces, especially when the Wyandotte chert is separated out as a product of the specialized camp event. The ratio of probable Middle Woodland Van Port chert bladelets to bifaces in intercluster space is 1:2.7 (n = 3 and n = 8). But as the three bladelets are all classic examples with trapezoidal cross-sections, they may relate to the South Block specialized camp, making the ratio even more skewed at 0:8.

More important than the high ratio of bifaces in intercluster space are the kinds of bifaces found there and in the other small clusters located between households. Eight of the nine specimens recovered are thinned and broken, including one of the four recognizable Middle Woodland projectile points recovered during the survey (Pacheco 1993: 123). In fact, 13 of the 59 (22%) thinned broken bifaces are from either small clusters or intercluster space, comprising just over 2 percent of all artifacts in these assemblages, while only 10 failed biface rejects were recovered in these contexts (a ratio of 1.3:1). This pattern is very different from the proposed Hopewell household clusters where there are 46 thinned broken bifaces, comprising less than 0.002 percent of the household assemblages (Pacheco 1997: 74–75), to 112 failed biface rejects (a ratio of 1:2.4). Thus bifaces are primarily produced in the proposed households but are extensively used/broken in the small clusters and intercluster space in between the households. Dancey (1991: 55) reports the same biface pattern in the excavated sample from Murphy I. Given the spatial parameters of the project area, and the arguments for density/distributional patterns within clusters, this is the kind of pattern of inter-assemblage lithic assemblage variability expected within a sedentary community (Binford 1982). The documented assemblages from upland Middle Woodland rock shelters (Seeman 1996), which Cowan acknowledges, are characterized by assemblages similarly skewed toward biface use (especially projectile points), supporting their use as logistical hunting camps.

Cowan likewise ignores the abundant evidence and supporting arguments for a predominantly expedient approach to lithic technology present in the Hopewell households of the Murphy Tract. One aspect of this expedient technology is the use of the residual aspects of bladelet production. Cowan recognized the short use lives of bladelets (2006: 30) but missed the significance of their presence in these assemblages. Dancey (1991, n.d.) addressed this issue when he argued that bladelets are being produced in the proposed Murphy Tract households, with classic examples being exported, exchanged, or taken elsewhere. He based his argument on the presence of bladelet cores and the ratio of triangular to trapezoidal cross-sections in these assemblages. In other words, several of the proposed Murphy households, especially Murphy I, III, and VI, may have engaged in the production of bladelets as a craft or lapidary cottage industry (Flannery and Winter 1976: 36). Based on the distributional pattern of bifaces discussed previously, this cottage industry may have included biface production too. The regional proximity of the Vanport quarries at Flint Ridge likely facilitated the development of this lapidary cottage industry by Licking Valley Hopewell households.

The bladelet cross-section evidence is straightforward. Triangular cross-section bladelets come off a core earlier in the bladelet core flaking process (Greber, Davis, and DuFresne 1981) and are not as uniform in shape and size as trapezoidal shaped cross-section bladelets which come from the interior of the core. Sheets and Muto (1972) have shown experimentally that the expected ratio of triangular to trapezoidal cross-sectioned bladelets produced from prepared bladelet cores is about 1:2. The Murphy Tract household clusters have bladelet assemblages which are opposite of these expected ratios. Combining the Murphy I, III, V, and VI assemblages produces a ratio of 1.6:1 (triangular n = 315 versus trapezoidal n = 195) in favor of triangular bladelets, suggesting a large proportion of missing trapezoidal bladelets but leaving the triangular cross-section bladelets behind to form a large pool of relatively straight, sharp-edged flakes available for expedient, generalized domestic use.

On the other hand, the ratio of triangular to trapezoidal cross-sections for Wyandotte chert bladelets associated with the proposed specialized camp event in the South Block (Murphy IV, Cluster 1, Cluster 2, and Intercluster space) has a combined ratio of 1:2.15, which is very close to Sheets and Muto's expectation (triangular n = 53 versus trapezoidal n = 114). This ratio supports interpretation that the Wyandotte bladelet assemblage represents on-site bladelet manufacturing and use, distinct from the blade-core activities proposed for the households. The Murphy IV Wyandotte assemblage also includes seven bladelet cores or core fragments and abundant evidence of on-site core preparation using spherical cobbles possessing distinctive chalky tan cortex. The bladelet assemblage has a widely scattered spatial pattern of deposition representative of casual refuse disposal that further supports this interpretation (Pacheco 1997: 69).

Yerkes's (1990, 1994) microwear analysis of a substantial sample of flakes, bladelets, cores, and bifaces from the Murphy I assemblage found evidence of a variety of domestic tasks. Use-wear polishes were poorly developed, especially on the flakes and bladelets, suggesting that their use was expediently organized. Both flakes and bladelets had use-wear polishes on 18 percent of the specimens examined. First, this suggests that the residual products of the bladelet industry (i.e., early stage triangular cross-section bladelets) are treated just like other debitage (i.e., they may be ritually charged in other contexts, but they are not in a domestic refuse dump). Second, while 18 percent may not sound like a substantial proportion, multiplied over the entire assemblage, the number of expedient tools in the assemblage is immense, since a conservative estimate of the flake debitage at Murphy I is about three-quarters of a million specimens (Pacheco 1993: 64). The Murphy III assemblage is equally large. Extrapolating out Yerkes's use-wear frequency of 18 percent indicates that there may be 135,000 expedient tools in the assemblage (with hundreds of thousands of potential tools lying along side them). This vast reserve of available cutting edges explains why use-wear polish is not well developed in the

Murphy I assemblage, and it is the hallmark of a sedentary residence utilizing an expediently organized lithic technology rather than a residentially mobile residence dominated by curated bifaces.

Similarly, Cowan ignores the columns listing macroscopically identified flake tools from the Murphy survey, those that have visibly utilized edges or some retouch. In the proposed household clusters, identifiable flake tools versus bifaces occur at ratios ranging from between 14:1 and 7:1. Bamforth's (1986) argument about raw material availability, given the presence of abundant Van Port chert in the region, provides another reason to suspect that the proposed Murphy Tract household clusters would prefer an expedient, as opposed to a curated, approach to organizing their lithic technology.

The final issue is the lack of flake cores in the Hopewell household assemblages to match the occurrence of these items in the sedentary assemblages which Cowan (1999) is familiar with in western New York. First, it should be noted that the surface survey did recover 24 flake cores, but these are not sufficient to match the criteria based on the research of Parry and Kelly (1987) which Cowan is applying to the assemblages. However, the reason for the lack of flake cores is rather easily explained. Widespread availability of quality raw material, combined with the production of bladelets and bifaces (for perhaps both domestic use and export), provides an immense stock of usable flakes for expedient use. Ohio Hopewell households in the Licking Valley did not need flake cores to make their expedient approach to lithic technology feasible.

Conclusion

Even though the case for sedentism in these proposed dispersed Ohio Hopewell households appears solid, there is still a great deal of reluctance to accept this view, as demonstrated by Cowan's paper and other recent papers as well (Clay 1998; Lepper and Yerkes 1997; Yerkes 1994, 2002, 2005, 2006). Unfortunately, Ohio Hopewell scholars lack a set of well-reported comparative data for interpreting settlement patterns (Smith 2006). While these deficiencies could be remedied with robust, redundant, interregional data, several alternative strategies to acquiring settlement data could be employed in the interim. A few of the more feasible approaches at this time include:

1. Utilizing noninvasive geophysical surveys, like magnetometry, at potential domestic settlements to establish settlement structure with a relatively cheap remote sensing methodology. Jarrod Burks, DeeAnne Wymer, and I employed this strategy on our Brown's Bottom project; the results were more than gratifying and are still in the initial stages of

publication (see Burton 2006; Dalan 2008; Pacheco, Burks, and Wymer 2006).

2. Focusing limited resources on complete excavations of Ohio Hopewell domestic settlements to reveal evidence of structures and facilities such as storage pits and refuse deposits (Smith 2006: 495–496). At this point, Murphy I (Dancey 1991) is the only completely excavated, and published, Ohio Hopewell household, and there are only a couple other robust data sets from excavated sites such as McGraw (Prufer 1965) and Jennison Guard (Blosser 1996; Kozarek 1997).

3. Concentrating limited excavation resources on domestic settlements which contain well preserved faunal remains. The last item on this list may be most crucial of all potential approaches to resolve the sedentism issue, since, unlike with floral remains, it is theoretically possible to demonstrate year-round occupancy of a site with faunal remains. To date the only well-published and -interpreted Ohio Hopewell faunal collection is reported by Kozarek (1997) and Blosser (1996) from Jennison Guard.

Cowan concludes his paper with the sentence "Somewhere out there, there must be an Ohio Middle Woodland that doesn't look particularly 'Hopewell'" (2006: 49). Application of Occam's Razor suggests otherwise. A complete Ohio Hopewell settlement pattern has already been documented. Ceremonial precincts containing earthworks and/or mounds, specialized camps, temporary housing in the vicinity of ceremonial precincts, dispersed residential bases (i.e., household clusters), upland hunting camps, rock shelters, chert quarries, lithic reduction camps, isolated projectile points, and interhousehold clusters probably representing garden areas have all been identified with Middle Woodland Hopewell components. Given these visible localities, Ohio Hopewell mobility is unlikely to represent residential mobility and instead is best viewed as the product of logistical work parties moving between fixed residential bases and spatially incongruous resources, in addition to wide-ranging mobility associated with visits to various local, regional, and far distant ceremonial centers. Invoking Griffin's (1996) admonishment about an Ohio Hopewell housing shortage is slowly becoming less and less necessary.

3

The Land between the Mounds

The Role of "Empty" Spaces in the Hopewellian Built Environment

Lauren Sieg and Jarrod Burks

When Squier and Davis (1998 [1848]) surveyed the "Ancient Monuments of the Mississippi Valley," they were captivated by the immense earthen architecture of the Middle Ohio Valley. Like other nineteenth-century explorers (e.g., Atwater 1820; Whittlesey 1852), they focused on the most pronounced archaeological features of southern Ohio—the earthworks and mounds. Excavations within and in the immediate vicinity of these earthworks were a focus for archaeologists in many subsequent explorations (e.g., Fowke 1902; Mills 1902, 1907, 1909, 1916, 1917, 1922; Moorehead 1890, 1897–1898; Putnam 1885, 1886; Shetrone 1926; Shetrone and Greenman 1931). A much larger portion of the Hopewell landscape, the area between the earthwork sites, was not systematically explored until the 1960s. The inter-earthwork space began to receive substantial archaeological attention only in the last decades of the twentieth century, especially as a result of mitigation work prompted by the passage of the Archaeological Resources Protection Act (ARPA). This mitigation work has led to the accumulation of additional data on the space between earthwork complexes. As a result, we can now begin to integrate these two lines of field research: one oriented toward the earthworks and the other on the space around and between these earthworks (e.g., Byers 2006a). In this chapter, we use an integrated data set—earthworks, habitation sites, and iconography—to examine the use of space at Hopewell horizon[1] sites from a structuralist perspective. With a structuralist perspective, we can focus on the formal patterning of space rather than the meaning of such patterns.

Hopewell has been described as "minimally . . . an ideological system . . . [that] is really the conjunction of two types of cultural systems—one, social structural and the other, symbolic" (Seeman 1995: 122–123). Here we focus on one structural element in Hopewell artwork, the interrelation of negative and positive space, and attempt to show that a similar use of space occurred across the landscape and probably at multiple scales. We propose that the interplay of negative and positive space in Hopewell artwork, which produced complementary pairs and a means of ordering the images, is useful for interpreting the Hopewellian built environment and use of the landscape. As explained by Levi-Strauss (1963: 21), "If . . . the unconscious activity of the mind consists in imposing forms upon content . . . it is necessary and sufficient to grasp the unconscious structure underlying each institution and each custom, in order to obtain a principle of interpretation valid for other institutions and other customs." Sackett (1990: 41) termed these structures "deep style." Following this principle, the structural relation of negative and positive space in artwork is used as a heuristic device to understand the delineation of space into positive (earthwork) and negative[2] (nonearthwork) zones. The construction of monumental architecture was paired with the construction of hamlets, gardens, workshops, resource procurement zones, trails, and other smaller-scale components of the built environment in a complementary arrangement of positive (earthwork) and negative (nonearthwork) space. In short, the structural principles found in art from the Hopewell horizon of the Scioto region (Greber and Ruhl 2000 [1989]: 223) are writ large on the landscape.

Negative Space in the Hopewell Art of the Chillicothe Area

In art, "negative" space is the portion of a drawing or painting that serves as a framing or background for the subject matter. Negative space is frequently represented by white or black in Western art. In Hopewell art, negative space consists of "open" areas in copper cutouts, cross-hatched areas in pottery and engraved bone, darkened areas on painted textiles, and blank spaces on incised stone (Figure 3.1). The negative and positive spaces are rendered in a manner to produce two intertwined images, similar to a yin-yang symbol or an Escher drawing. For example, a piece of engraved antler from the Hopewell site contains bear imagery in the positive space and bird imagery in the negative space (Figure 3.2a). A similar but more subtle pairing of bird and bear motifs is present on an engraved human femur from the same site (Figure 3.2b). Bird and bear motifs are also seen on a Hopewell site copper cutout that utilizes both positive imagery and positive/negative space imagery (Figure 3.3) (Greber and Ruhl 2000 [1989]). This pairing of bird and bear motifs through the use of positive and negative space is repeated in the textiles that accompanied the copper plates. Some plates were wrapped in layers of textiles made from bird feathers or bear fur and at least one plate had the bird and bear textiles placed on opposing sides of the plate (Wymer 2004: 66). The

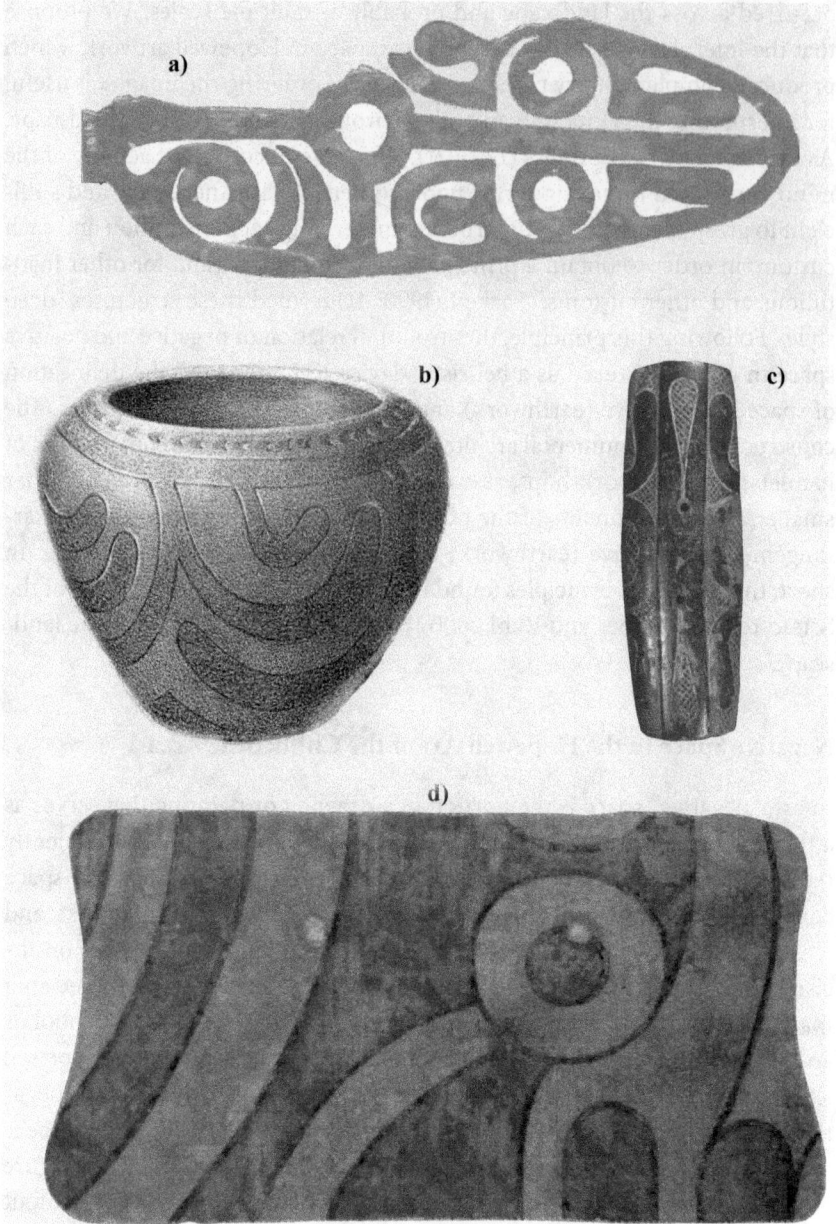

Figure 3.1. Examples of negative space in Hopewell art. Key: a = copper cutout object from Hopewell Mound Group; b = zoned vessel from Mound City (from Squier and Davis 1848: Figure XLVI); c = zoned-incised bone bead from the Hopewell Mound Group; d = copper breastplate and textile from Seip Mound Group. Objects not to scale.

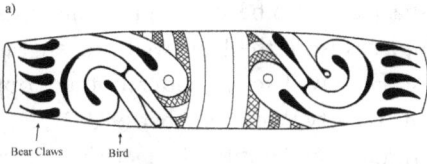

Figure 3.2. Hopewell carved
(a) antler and (b) human
femur revealing use of
positive and negative imagery.
Objects not to scale (adapted
from Greber and Ruhl 1989:
Figures 6.59, 6.63).

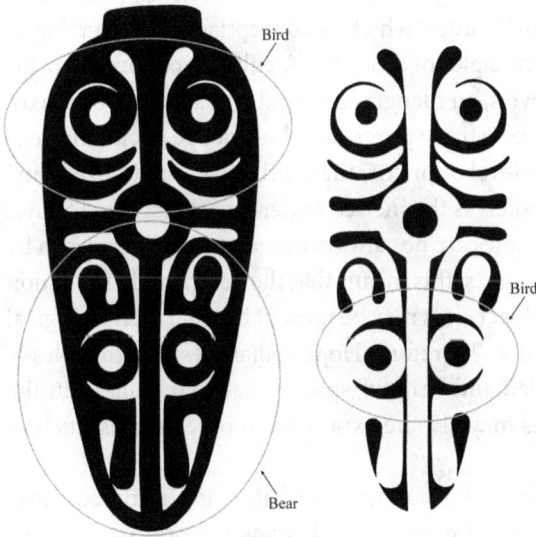

Figure 3.3. Bird and bear
imagery on copper cutout.
Objects not to scale.

interplay of positive and negative space can also be seen on the hundreds of fragments of other engraved bone pieces from the Hopewell site, engraved bone at the Turner Earthworks site, Hopewell series pottery, other copper cutouts, and a pipe fragment from the Liberty Works (Greber 1983: 32, Figure 3.5). The variety of media on which negative and positive imagery is expressed and its presence at multiple sites in southern Ohio suggest that the use of such imagery was an essential component to the design of some Hopewell art.

The negative spaces in Hopewell artwork from the Scioto Valley region play an important function in the creation of imagery and meaning. They generate a second set of images portrayed in the artwork. They also project a sense of interrelatedness and complementarity. This sense of complementarity is emphasized by the lines that are shared between two different images and by the continuous nature of the lines. In the examples discussed above, the bird and bear are depicted as complementary pairs. Greber and Ruhl (2000 [1989]: 217–220) have noted the presence of contrasting or complementary duality in animal symbolism at Hopewell sites. Greber has also found evidence for complementary basin features at the Hopewell site and has suggested that a similar principle of duality and complementarity may be present in the distribution of copper and mica objects at the site (Greber 1996: 162–163, 168–169).

The integration of designs in Hopewell art suggests that a design principle of interrelated imagery was present. As suggested by Firth, symbols reveal more than a "meaning"; they also have an underlying structural content (Firth 1975: 20). Symbols express the world order, which is conceptualized according to the specific organizational principles of a culture. A culture's organizing principles exist on at least two levels, an ideographic level and at a level of praxis. At an ideographic level, they constitute procedural knowledge, including general design principles. At the level of praxis, these principles are utilized during the creation of an object such as the incised antler object discussed above. Design and production principles are not always domain specific; they can be broadly applied. For archaeologists, this means that the design and production principles identified in one object class may be present in other archaeological remains from the same culture. Therefore, Hopewellian design principles—such as a combination of filled and "empty" space—that were utilized in the creation of decorated objects may also be expressed in other arenas, such as the built environment.

Here, we suggest that the earthworks and the habitation/resource zones were complementary, interrelated parts of the Hopewell world in the same way that positive and negative spaces were complementary, interrelated parts of Hopewellian art. If both spaces were integral to the Hopewell built environment, an artificial polarization of the two (such that some research focuses only on earthworks and other research only on settlements) would limit our understanding of the Scioto region Hopewell world. To better understand this world, we need a wide variety of data from both contexts of the Hopewell built environment. Yet despite more than 150 years of scholarly research on earthworks and the societies that constructed them in the Middle Ohio Valley, there are still few archaeologists who publish information on Hopewell activities beyond the walls of the earthworks (for exceptions, see below). Multiscalar, integrated efforts to understand the organization and use of the Hopewell landscape, including material objects, settlements, earthworks, and natural features, are rare (cf. Seeman and Branch 2006). Below, we utilize data on earthwork and nonearthwork space in the Chillicothe, Ohio, area to construct a more complete picture of the Hopewellian built environment and illustrate how the negative and positive spaces are integrated in economic and symbolic ways. We begin by discussing the history of landscape studies in the region. We present data on the distribution of earthwork and nonearthwork sites, and then use this distribution to illustrate how the negative and positive spaces are integrated in economic and symbolic ways.

Negative Space and the Hopewell Landscape in the Chillicothe, Ohio, Area

In the mid-twentieth century, Ohio archaeologists began to examine the possibility that Hopewell people may have lived in places other than within their ceremonial centers (e.g., Morgan 1952). In the absence of data on habitation from contexts outside the earthworks, researchers still had to rely on data from the earthwork sites—focusing on the nonmound debris—to reconstruct Ohio Hopewell domestic life (e.g., Griffin 1952). For example, the extensive deposits of debris at Fort Ancient inside the North Fort and south of the parallel walls were thought to be solid evidence supporting the presence of villages within and next to earthworks (Morgan 1946).

In the early 1960s, Olaf Prufer initiated a new line of Hopewell research in the Scioto Valley with his Scioto Valley Survey. Prufer and his crew identified approximately 20 concentrations of Hopewell debris outside and away from the earthworks and burial mounds (Blank 1965; Prufer 1965, 1967). The first well-documented Hopewell habitation site, the McGraw site, was excavated as a result of this survey. Prufer concluded that the Hopewell must have occupied small settlements in the hinterlands of their "vacant" earthworks, similar to the scattered settlements observed outside vacant (as understood in the 1960s) ceremonial centers in Mesoamerica (Prufer 1965, 1967, 1997a). Prufer considered this "Vacant Ceremonial Center-Dispersed Agricultural Hamlet" pattern a hypothesis, not a model (Prufer 1997a). It has been variously referred to as the Hamlet Hypothesis (Pacheco 1989a), the Prufer model (Dancey 1991), and the Vacant Center model (Pacheco 1993). Dancey and Pacheco (1997: 8) have most recently reinvigorated the idea of the Hopewell settlement pattern as one of dispersed households and residentially (permanent residences) vacant ceremonial centers—a model they call the Dispersed Sedentary Community model (discussed below). Although Prufer never tested his hypothesis with additional large-scale survey, he introduced an important paradigm shift in Ohio Hopewell archaeology. Prufer demonstrated that archaeologists should not look for Hopewell habitation sites in the form of villages at earthwork complexes. Instead, they should look for small, scattered settlements in the vast expanses of land outside the earthworks. While the Vacant Center model is no longer considered valid by Mesoamerican or Hopewell archaeologists, Dancey and Pacheco's Dispersed Sedentary Community model has proven useful.

Despite Prufer's success at finding Hopewell settlements and his call to conduct surveys in other regions, it was not until the mid- to late 1980s that archaeologists began to intensively search for the remains of Hopewell settlements (e.g., Dancey 1991; Genheimer 1984; Kozarek 1987; Pacheco 1989a, 1993). By 1997, Dancey and Pacheco were able to amass data from more than 90 documented Hopewell settlements to formulate their Dispersed Sedentary Community model of Hopewell community organization (Dancey and Pacheco 1997). This model, a generalized roadmap or schematic of Hopewell land use that is based upon the Hamlet Hypothesis, proposes that the Hopewell lived in small, sedentary settlements on the terraces of main stream valleys and at the convergence of intermittent streams in the uplands surrounding the earthwork sites. These settlements, though occupied year-round, varied greatly in the number of consecutive years they were inhabited. Wymer (1997) has hypothesized that the need to shift garden locations to ensure adequate yields was a major determinant in the duration of settlement occupation. Differences in settlement duration were also affected by varying household longevity (Dancey and Pacheco 1997). Earthworks were the focal point of each community's social-ceremonial life (Dancey and Pacheco 1997; Greber 1997a). Yet despite the centrality of earthworks to social and ceremonial functions, early, nucleated communities may have formed first in areas peripheral to the main Hopewell centers during the Middle Woodland period (Burks 2004; Dancey 1992).

Although there has been an increasing amount of research on the topic of Middle-Late Woodland period settlement (e.g., Burks 2004; Church and Ericksen 1997; Coughlin and Seeman 1997; Cowan, Sunderhaus, and Genheimer 2004; Dancey 1992; Keener and Biehl 1999; Kozarek 1997; Lazazzera 2004; Pacheco 1996; Pacheco and Dancey 2006; Pacheco, Burks, and Wymer 2006; Yerkes 2006), projects at Hopewell ceremonial sites still far outnumber investigations of domestic settlements. Furthermore, regional surveys focused on documenting an entire settlement system have yet to take place. In fact, few surveys of Middle Woodland period sites equaling the scale of Prufer's work in the 1960s (Prufer 1967) have occurred since, though some important surveys have been conducted (e.g., Blank 1972; Genheimer 1984, 1997). For example, Pacheco's (1996) presentation of a potential community in the Jonathan Creek area of Perry County, Ohio, shows what might emerge from an intensive survey of an entire drainage. Due to the lack of published information on Hopewell settlement practices (except in the recent literature, see above), someone new to the study of Hopewell land use would get the sense that much of the Hopewell landscape was empty or unused. This is simply not the case.

Analysis of the distribution of monumental architecture in the Chillicothe region suggests that earthworks appear in very specific areas—the relatively broad, flat floodplains of major streams. Earthwork size is, however, not related to the width of the floodplain. The Hopewell site, the largest complex in the Ross County area, is located in one of the smallest floodplain areas. Moreover, there is more to this equation than broad, flat floodplains. Some earthworks are located close to important natural features. For example, Rock Mill (Squier and Davis 1998 [1848]: Plate XXXVI, no. 3) and Trefoil (Squier and Davis 1998 [1848]: Plate XXXII, no. 5) were built adjacent to waterfalls.

High hills also play an important role in the Hopewell landscape. The distribution of earthworks is highly correlated to the location of the glacial margin. In the Ross County area they occur within the hills just beyond the Wisconsinan end moraine (except for Frankfort), not out into the glaciated plateau (Figure 3.4). Except for the earthworks that once existed at Circleville, Ohio, nearly all major earthwork complexes in southern Ohio (not including hilltop forts) follow this pattern and are located near the glacial margin, where dramatic hills are commonly found. Not all areas that offer a relatively broad floodplain at the glacial margin, however, have earthworks. For example, Deer Creek in northern Ross County has wide, flat terraces in the floodplain and it flanks a region with low hills, but it has no known Hopewell horizon earthworks. The same is true for the upper reaches of Paint Creek before it dives into the hills. Though they lack major earthworks, these areas do have mounds, many of unknown (but possibly Hopewell) origin.

The places on the landscape where no earthworks or other known sacred spaces occur are not barren of Hopewell remains. They contain numerous

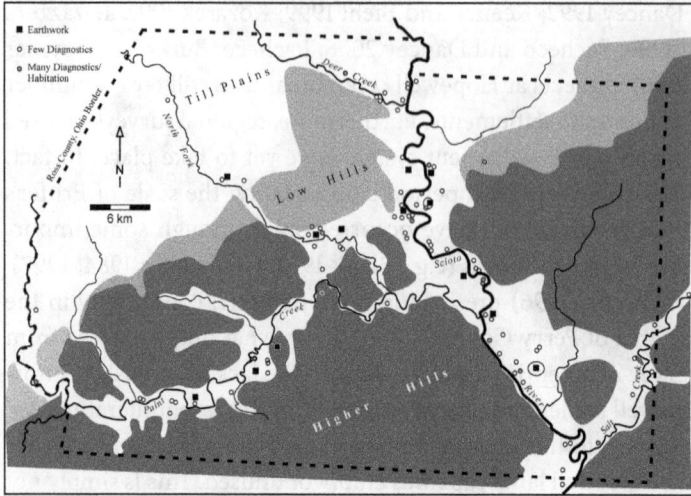

Figure 3.4. Distribution of Hopewell Earthworks and habitation debris in
Ross County, Ohio.

clusters, in varying densities and sizes, of Hopewell occupation debris. For
example, a plot of sites in Ross County containing bladelets and Lowe Cluster
projectile points shows the location of a number of possible Hopewell habitation sites (Figure 3.4). The habitation sites shown represent a growing list
of sites documented by professional and amateur archaeologists,[3] but they
represent a small percentage of the habitation sites that likely exist in Ross
County. Based on this growing body of settlement data, it is clear that the
space between Hopewell earthwork complexes (especially on the floodplains
of the Scioto River) is far from empty. Rather than containing large earthwork
complexes, negative space on the landscape contained houses, activity areas,
temporary campsites, gardens, cleared forest areas, hunting territories, raw
material deposits, trails, waterways, small mounds, and perhaps other features. "Negative" space is evident in places as large as entire drainages, such as
the Deer Creek valley, where suitable space (large, flat floodplains) for earthworks is plentiful but no monumental earthen architecture is found. Because
of the multitude of other features in "negative" space—the space between the
earthworks—such spaces must have been an important part of the Hopewell
landscape.

   The creation of negative space can be seen on multiple scales. As discussed
above, it is apparent on a macro scale, at the level of the entire drainages. It is
also apparent at particular earthwork sites. While some earthworks enclose
space that contained mounds, structures, and other architectural elements,
many other earthworks are seemingly devoid of aboveground earthen archi-

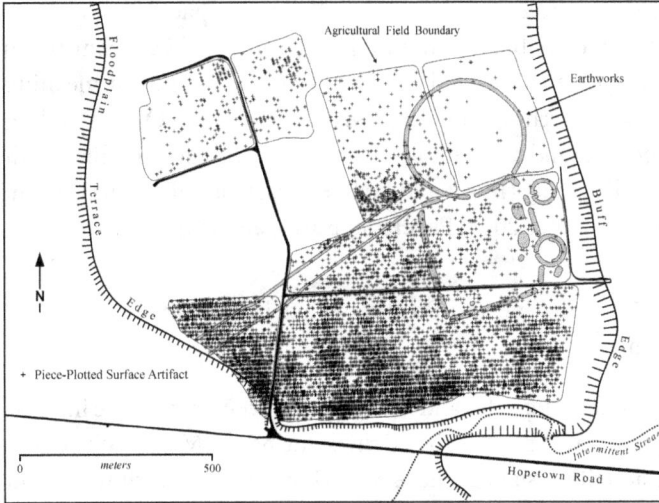

Figure 3.5. Distribution of surface debris across 172 acres surrounding the Hopeton Earthworks. The objects from this 10 percent sample of the surface were piece plotted using a Trimble ProXR global positioning system (GPS). The earthwork drawing is an amalgamation of the Squier and Davis (1848) and Thomas (1889) maps as anchored by GPS data. All prehistoric objects found during the survey, including those from the Middle Woodland period and other periods, are shown.

tecture within their walls. The intentional setting aside of space in earthworks is not only evident in the lack of visible facilities within earthwork enclosures. It can also be detected in the distribution of debris (i.e., artifacts) at some earthwork complexes. For example, at the Hopeton Works in Ross County, Ohio, a plot of systematically collected surface material within and around the earthwork walls found very few objects within the enclosure but many just outside (Figure 3.5) (Burks, Pederson, and Walter 2002; Burks and Walter 2003). This lack of debris within the earthworks suggests the existence of rules governing the use of space and the deposition of waste (Byers 2004). Discarding noticeable amounts of waste on the surface within the earthworks was apparently prohibited. This does not appear to be the case outside the earthworks, where Hopewell debris is very common—though low in density—in most of the area immediately surrounding the embankments.

In sum, earthwork patterning at a variety of scales indicates that negative spaces were a deliberate part of landscape design. Many earthen enclosures and mounds occur in dense clusters, or earthwork complexes. These complexes were present in a limited number of locales, and few ancillary earthworks existed between these complexes. The "negative space" between the earthworks constituted the bulk of the built environment. Far from being empty, however, negative spaces in Hopewell society were full of meaning and utility. Ongoing research at many Hopewell earthworks in Ohio is finding that the spaces between and adjacent to earthwork complexes are filled with evidence of Hopewell activity (Burks and Walter 2003; Connolly 1997; Cowan, Sunderhaus, and Genheimer 2004; Pederson, Burks, and Dancey 2001).

The Interrelation of Negative and Positive Space in the Hopewellian Built Environment

Taken together, the habitation sites and the earthwork centers give the impression of a landscape that was filled with activities during the Middle Woodland period, but some activities, such as those requiring the use of facilities found only at large earthwork centers, were very restricted in their positioning on the landscape. Thomas Crump wrote that "in any geographic context there is an ideal arrangement of the topographic features. Any man-made alteration to the landscape . . . had to satisfy the requirements of order, as defined in local culture" (Crump 1990: 140). We suggest that the earthworks and settlements of the Chillicothe area followed the same design principles as the artwork in their use of "negative" space. Both earthwork and nonearthwork spaces were required in order to constitute a culturally meaningful landscape. Because the positive and negative spaces are interrelated, they must be studied in conjunction with one another to understand the Hopewell built environment in toto.

The widespread use of the landscape by the Hopewell, as exemplified by the growing number of known Hopewell habitation sites, emphasizes the choice of locales for constructing earthwork complexes. Clearly the Hopewell used the entire landscape, economically and symbolically, but chose very particular places for their earthwork complexes. The earthworks were central points at which social, ceremonial, political, and economic activities occurred and provided the symbols that charged the landscape with social and symbolic meaning (e.g., Byers 2004; DeBoer 1997; Greber 1997a). The earthworks contained monumental architecture and large deposits of unique finished goods and raw materials. They were the loci for many types of ceremonies and for the congregation of groups as small as two or three people or as large as corporate units (Greber 1996).

Earthworks were constructed in, around, and possibly on top of those areas in which people went about their everyday lives. Around earthworks were large swaths of land that were available for settlement, resource procurement, subsistence, and other quotidian uses. Although habitation debris and features are present at earthwork sites, they were not the locus for extended habitation (e.g., Burks and Pederson 2006; Burks, Pederson, and Walter 2002; Coughlin and Seeman 1997; Dancey and Pacheco 1997; Pederson, Burks, and Dancey 2001). On the other hand, the hamlets and resource procurement zones contain evidence of a dispersed, semisedentary settlement pattern of small family groups (Dancey and Pacheco 1997). They were not places for large rituals or the deposition of extensive deposits of well-crafted, symbolically charged objects or exotic (i.e., nonlocal) raw materials, though they likely contained some of these objects in middens or pits (e.g., Gehlbach 1985 [Strait site]; Pacheco, Burks, and Wymer 2006 [Brown's Bottom #1 site]; Prufer 1965 [McGraw site]). The settlements and resource zones, where no monumental architecture was present, provided a backdrop against which the earthwork space could be recognized as functionally and ritually different. The earthworks, by their significance and high visibility, served as a social and ceremonial backdrop to the nonearthwork areas. Thus earthwork and nonearthwork space were integrated into the totality of the Hopewell cultural landscape. Neither could be fully recognized or understood without the other.

As described above, there are marked differences between earthwork and nonearthwork spaces in terms of the architecture, scale of construction, types of deposits, and other features present at the respective locales. The differences between these spaces are accentuated by the architecture that separates the earthwork and nonearthwork spaces. The borders between earthwork and nonearthwork spaces were delineated by massive earthen walls, wooden structures, and water features. As explained by Douglas (1984: 4), "It is only by exaggerating the difference between within and without . . . that a semblance of order is created." The walls, wooden structures and water features of Scioto region Hopewell earthworks were rendered on a massive scale to establish proper order. They may have served not only to separate spaces, but also to provide a means for safely navigating between them. Entrants may have been ritually prepared to enter the earthworks by passing between walls or across waterways, while potentially dangerous spiritual powers were removed by exiting in the same manner.

Although the differences between earthwork and nonearthwork space have been readily apparent to archaeologists for over one hundred years, they should not be used to artificially dichotomize the Hopewell world into sacred and profane spaces. For example, raw materials such as mica and copper and ceremonial objects such as pipes are found at habitation sites. It is likely that certain features outside the earthworks, such as springs, were ritually significant. Rather, the earthwork and nonearthwork spaces were complementary parts of the same whole, imbuing one another with meaning and significance.

The interrelated nature of meanings has long been recognized by linguists, who have noted that objects can be interpreted only in relation to other objects (e.g., de Saussure 1966; Peirce 1931).

The concept of complementary "pairs" has been discussed by Greber (1996, 1997), Greber and Ruhl (2000 [1989]), and DeBoer (1997). Pairs of features, raw materials, artifacts, earthwork forms, and earthwork sites have been delineated and assigned symbolic meaning. The repeated appearance of complementary "pairs," such as red and white, male and female, circle and square, and negative and positive, suggest that such pairings were a fundamental concept and structure through which the Hopewell ordered their world. If it was such a fundamental principle, it may be expected that earthwork and nonearthwork spaces were also paired.

Pairings of earthwork sites have already been identified (DeBoer 1997; Greber 1997a). A well-developed interpretation of paired earthworks has been discussed by Greber (1997a) for Seip and Baum, for example. Greber suggests that "a single social group" who lived in the Paint Creek valley "claimed the two geometric enclosures in the Paint Creek as its corporate cultural expression" (Greber 1997a: 219). This pair of earthworks and the surrounding habitation sites may be termed a "precinct." The distribution of the earthworks suggests that a "precinct" concept may be useful for analysis of the Hopewell landscape. There are many potentially suitable places that the earthworks could have been built but were not. Their clustering in the Ross County area, versus other parts of central Ohio, suggests that their locations are strategic, but probably unrelated to the nearby presence of fertile soils or abundant ecotones, which abound in many areas of southern Ohio. This controlled placement of earthworks gives the impression of the intentional creation of negative space between the earthworks in Ross County and between the Ross County group and other earthwork centers such as Circleville, Portsmouth, or Newark. The use of a "precinct" as an analytical unit may allow us to identify central social-ceremonial points on the landscape and the surrounding areas to which they were linked. This perspective is not intraregional or interregional, per se, but is guided by the identification of socially significant space.

Conclusion

The positive and negative imagery in both Hopewell earthworks and artwork in the Chillicothe region reflects underlying cultural beliefs about the ordering of the world. This world was perceived in terms of complementary, interconnected parts, as seen in many engraved bone and copper cutout objects. The repeated appearance of complementary, interrelated pairs at earthwork sites suggests that this concept was not restricted to symbols in artwork. Rather, it was utilized in a variety of media, from inorganic objects to textiles to large earthworks. The presence of complementary pairs in multiple media suggests that it was more than a unique concept for expressing beliefs about birds, deer, bears, and quartered circles. Instead, these pairs were part of a wider domain of design principles that structured the creation of objects, earthworks, and the cultural landscape. If the objects and earthworks from Chillicothe region sites do reveal a fundamental underlying design principle, then this principle may be applied to other aspects of the Hopewell archaeological record. For instance, the presence of burial subgroups within a common structure (Greber 1976) implies a relation between the subgroups. This relation might be interpreted as a complementary relation between clans or moieties (e.g., Greber 1996). Trade may also show elements of complementarity. For example, Seeman found an overall relation between the Scioto Valley and the Santa Rosa regions (Seeman 1979). Copper objects were sent south from Ohio, while conch shell appears to have been the primary export heading north from the Gulf Coast. This complementary relationship may have an extensive history that dated back to the Archaic period and lasted until European contact (Seeman 1979).

In addition to utilizing an interpretive approach that blends settlement and symbolic studies, we support another potential concept for approaching the study of Hopewell earthworks and settlements: the "precinct." The precinct may be an appropriate and underutilized concept for analysis of the Hopewell landscape at an intersite level. The concept of the precinct implies that zones around the earthworks, the "empty" or "negative" spaces, were tied to the earthworks. However, the correspondence may not have been 1:1. Earthworks may be related to zones, and people, outside their immediate area, and vice versa (Byers 2004). Many Hopewell habitation sites have been found well away from regions with earthwork centers. If the earthwork center was an important part of the lives of all Hopewell peoples, then those groups living outside the main precincts (e.g., the earthwork complexes in Ross County, Newark, and Portsmouth) must have had to travel great distances on a regular basis to participate in earthwork-related activities (e.g., Bernardini 2004; Byers 2004; Greber 1997a: 220).

Although this study has explored the question of whether or not the "empty" spaces between the mounds were really empty, it has not addressed the question of why the earthwork and settlement spaces existed where they did. This is due in part to the limitations of a structural analysis. Such analyses provide models for patterns but do not explain why these patterns existed. However, the question of "why" is also somewhat rhetorical. The people who lived in the Chillicothe area during the Middle Woodland period required shelter, food, and other resources for survival. The activities related to basic necessities occurred in areas where people gathered and lived near and between earthworks. The earthworks may have been constructed on space that was recognized as sacred, though the basis for such recognition may not be fathomable today. Perhaps some locations were already marked as ritually significant by the time of the Middle Woodland period. For example, Hopewell Mound Group has ample evidence of Early Woodland period use of the site for nondomestic (ceremonial?) activities (i.e., small circular earthworks and isolated heating/cooking facilities of unusual proportions that have been radiocarbon dated to the Early Woodland period [Pederson, Burks, and Dancey 2001]). Many other Hopewell earthwork sites have elements with design principles that predate the Middle Woodland period: Hopeton, Seip, High Bank, and Newark, for example. It is also possible that the earthworks were not the only venue for rituals. Smaller-scale rituals may have occurred outside the earthworks at campsites and hamlets and isolated mound sites. Only through additional landscape-scale surveys will we be able to address the "why" question and more fully explore the nature of the land between the mounds.

Notes

1. Archaeologists have used the term "Hopewell" in varying senses, ranging from a cultural tradition to an exchange system (e.g., Caldwell 1964; Struever and Houart 1972). Because of its multiple definitions, the meaning of the word "Hopewell" can be ambiguous. For the sake of clarity, we use the term "Hopewell horizon" to make it clear that we are dealing with a unit that is an archaeological construction, not a culture or social group. The term "horizon" is used here to denote "a primarily spatial continuity represented by cultural traits and assemblages whose nature and mode of occurrence permit the assumption of a broad and rapid spread" (Willey and Phillips 1958: 33). Hopewell horizon sites are broadly distributed across the Midwest and beyond. The horizon spread throughout the area during the Middle Woodland period. Horizons are defined by horizon styles and markers. For example, Hopewell horizon styles include cross-hatch filled zones on stone, bone, and pottery, while rectangular copper plates are horizon markers (Sieg and Hollinger 2005).

2. Labeling these spaces as "negative" is a heuristic device; it is doubtful that the prehistoric occupants of the region would have described the spaces as "negative" in the sense that they were devoid of cultural significance. As in art, the term "negative" does not equate to an absence of feature.

3. The locations of Hopewell occupation sites depicted in Figure 3.4 are derived from two sources. Some of the site locations were recorded by Burks during interviews (from 2000 to 2004) with three amateur archaeologists who live and surface

collect in the Ross County area. These three individuals visited some of these sites on multiple occasions over a period of 10–20 years. The Figure 3.4 map also shows all nonmound/earthwork sites with Hopewell/Middle Woodland period debris that have been recorded for Ross County in the Ohio Archaeological Inventory (as of January 2005). The sites in Figure 3.4 in no way represent all Hopewell/occupation sites in Ross County.

COMMENTARY

Commentary on Douglas K. Charles's "Riverworld: Life and Meaning in the Illinois Valley"

Commentary by Paul J. Pacheco

After reading Doug Charles's chapter, I became cognizant that my contribution to this book is quite possibly not what the editors were looking for when they invited me to be part of their 2004 Society for American Archaeology symposium on Hopewellian settlement patterns and sacred landscapes. In retrospect, my efforts clearly represent one side of an interpretive spectrum in Hopewell archaeology (apparently I'm an old-fashioned materialist) rather than a successful bridge of the materialist-idealist dichotomy broached by A. Martin Byers and DeeAnne Wymer in the book's introduction. On the other hand, I think Charles's chapter has successfully bridged this dichotomy, and has done so in a creative and interesting manner.

As I ponder what to say about this chapter that is both constructive and insightful, my initial focus is on the idea that archaeology represents an enterprise akin to the writing of science fiction. My initial reaction is to argue against this view and how it denies or denigrates the empirical and pragmatic foundations of the materialist archaeology I hold dear. On closer reading, I came to realize that Charles is on to something important. But I will argue that this something is not really that new; instead, it is a new wrapping for an approach to prehistory that many archaeologists, me included, already practice.

My starting point for this realization came a few weeks ago when a student from a previous semester of an archaeological theory course brought up the article "The Golden Marshalltown" by Kent Flannery (1982) during a discussion we were having. Flannery's tongue-in-cheek parable is an archaeological science fiction with a message that I can sink my teeth into, allowing me to comprehend and bridge the materialist-idealist dichotomy, if only for a moment. To quote a section of the text which I believe to be particularly relevant:

> Son, all of prehistory is hidden in a vast darkness, and my generation was taught that it was better to light one tiny candle than curse the darkness. Never did I dream we'd have people whose career was based on cursing our *candles*.
>
> In the old days we mainly had one kind of archaeologist: a guy who scratched around for a grant, went to the field, surveyed or excavated to the best of his ability, and published the results. Some guys labored patiently, in obscurity, for years. And one day, their colleagues would look up and say, "You know, old Harry's doing good solid work. Nothing spectacular, mind you, but you know—I'd trust him to dig on my site." (Flannery 1982: 277)

Flannery puts his finger on the heart of the issue. Archaeology explores a past that is impossible to reconstruct in any complete sense. We will never know exactly what happened in the past or what the participants in past events thought about their lives. Yet we still seek answers because we are fascinated by the mystery of it. But our work does more than just make stuff up—it shines a tiny light on what once was. Still, it has become the vogue since the 1980s for there to be archaeologists who sit on the sidelines and point out that the interpretations of the materialist "diggers" are less than perfect, and sometimes even naïve. They are probably right to a certain degree, but without old Harry continuing to dig up the past, eventually the sideline commentators will have nothing to critique. For me, this is one of the great conundrums of bridging the materialist-idealist dichotomy.

Turning back to Charles's chapter. What follows is an abstracted summary of the flow of his argument from my perspective: Archaeology is like science fiction because we study the unknown. Our reconstructions of the past need to be sensible and based on clearly marshaled logical arguments. We should seek to understand the meanings of things in the past through sensible reconstruction but shouldn't be fooled into thinking our reconstruction is the only possible interpretation. Archaeological knowledge is conditional but seeks to understand a real past that constrained and helped to shape the present. The archaeology of landscapes provides an opportunity for sensible reconstruction and interpretation, especially through reference to past physical environments that would have affected the people of a region. The lower Illinois River valley provides a unique north-to-south trending structure to the environment of the Middle Woodland people who lived there which is further defined by a zonation of east-west floodplain to upland resources. The Middle Woodland people organized themselves in three primary settlement types, the smallest divisible unit being residential households/hamlets. These were grouped into communities that focused around bluff top burial mounds. Several of these adjacent communities came together to interact at large floodplain mound complexes. And finally, the river and its axes created a Riverworld landscape for these people which structured and gendered their use of space. This reconstruction is a sensible interpretation but is written more like a historical narrative than a scientific proof.

The reason Charles's approach represents a new wrapping for a practice that already exists is relatively straightforward and stems from the realization that archaeology is best characterized as a historical-materialist science rather than an essentialist science (Dunnell 1982; Lyman, O'Brien, and Dunnell 1997: 3–6). Charles basically says this himself at the end of the article. The best any historical-materialist scientist can do is to write a narrative account reconstructing the real past. Such narratives are not tested in the sense of an experiment, but they are subjected to sensible evaluation of their ability to account for the facts (Charles references Gould 1986 here, but see also Braun 1991). When new "facts" come to light, the narratives may need to be rewritten and we should not be surprised that we often get it wrong. After all, this is, as Charles notes, "a process, not a product." Importantly, Darwinian theory, and hence evolutionary biology, is the quintessential example of historical-materialist science, although it is also true of paleontology, geology, astronomy, and archaeology as well. Darwin's approach is first and foremost a form of historicism (Lewis 2001).

That Charles did not recognize this is perhaps my only real quibble with what is otherwise an excellent work. Charles contrasts the Darwinian paradigm with the Marxian paradigm as part of his discussion concerning the processual/postprocessual debate (an aspect of Byers and Wymer's materialist-idealist dichotomy). In my opinion this contrast contributes little to the paper except confusion and is even partially erroneous. He characterizes the Darwinian paradigm as "associated with atomistic, ahistorical, abstract deductive, and prescriptive modes of Enlightenment thought, whereas the Marxian paradigm has tended to be anti-Enlightenment, with holistic, historical, particularistic, and descriptive concerns." While there is no quibble with the

Enlightenment part, Marx was foremost a progressive evolutionist, which is a theoretical perspective based on classic essentialism, even if modern Marxists tend to focus more on analyzing ideology in particular cases. Darwinian theory, on the other hand, is clearly the more historical of the two; in fact, Darwin is probably the most important historical scientist to have ever lived. Likewise, Darwinian analysis tends toward the particularistic, although this is not a necessary corollary of the approach. That Charles concludes his paper by advocating historical narrative in my mind throws him in with the Darwinists, which is the approach to archaeology that I find most attractive. After getting past the confusion created by this unnecessary contrast, I think that Charles's paper is in the end an excellent and sensible story.

Commentary by Lauren Sieg and Jarrod Burks

Charles's chapter is a terrific example of the interpretive potential of Hopewell horizon data. The extent to which he can document habitation, seasonal resource exploitation, and interactions, and then use this information to interpolate symbolism, is something that Ohio Hopewell researchers would envy. As noted by Charles, he is in a unique position to make such interpretations by virtue of the archaeological record that is present in Illinois. The Ohio archaeological record, or at least that which has been documented to date, lacks the linearity in space, time, and resources that is apparent in the lower Illinois Valley. Although the Illinois and Ohio data sets do not parallel one another, Charles's work is inspiring and contains concepts that we may be able to apply to Ohio. For example, the ecozones surrounding the river valleys are roughly similar and similar resource extraction zones may have been present. Although it may take longer to reach interpretations that are as multilayered as those of Charles, his work should inspire those of us working in Ohio to persevere.

Charles also addresses problems of archaeological theory in his chapter, using his work in the lower Illinois Valley to explore the basis of archaeological interpretation as well as questions of validity. As Charles points out, not all interpretations are created equal. We contend that "the meanings emerging from the data have to be *tested* for their plausibility, their sturdiness, their 'confirmability'—that is, their *validity*. Otherwise we are left with interesting stories about what happened, of unknown truth and utility" (Miles and Huberman 1994: 11). Interpretations based on qualitative data should be evaluated using the same principles that are important in quantitative data analyses, such as robust sample sizes, control of variables, use of appropriate methodologies, adequate attention to theory, and evaluation of competing interpretations. Interpretations should be logical, parsimonious, and internally consistent, and it should be possible to derive testable hypotheses that further support or refute a particular conclusion from them. Peer review should be rigorous. Principles of qualitative data analysis are fully discussed in social science literature (e.g., Corbin and Strauss 2008; Creswell 2007; Miles and Huberman 1994; Patton 2002).

Many of the practices described above are evident in Charles's work. He situates his research within the larger body of landscape studies and hermeneutics. He makes his theoretical orientation explicit. His sample size is large and he uses multiple methods to reconstruct the landscape. He controls for variables such as space and time by limiting his study to a specific valley during a specific period. From his interpretations, it would be possible to generate a set of hypotheses that could be tested. For instance, gendered roles in subsistence practices could be tested through statistical tests of the relationship between the sex of individuals and the presence/absence of stress markers that are indicative of hunting or plant food processing. Evidence for gendered subsistence roles could then be used to support the hypotheses that there were gendered work spaces. Finally, Charles's work is being submitted to peer review in this volume.

Last, a word of caution must be sounded to archaeologists who call their work "fiction" for postprocessual or "countermodern" reasons. In his chapter, Charles notes that there are parallels between historical sciences and archaeology and advocates a bridging of science and interpretation. We maintain that there are many reasons that archaeological interpretation should not be equated to fiction. Fiction is a literary genre, the archaeological record is not. Fiction does not have measures of validity or reliability like those discussed above. Calling archaeological interpretation "fiction" can quickly render professional archaeology irrelevant. Doing so jeopardizes the preservation and study of archaeological resources. Why should the United States have cultural resource protection laws or spend taxpayer money on fieldwork if the end result is a work of fiction? Why should archaeologists be given any authority—legally, scholarly, professionally—if their interpretations are fictitious? Granted, some literary license might make Phase I survey reports more interesting to read, but it would not be useful for determining the impact of development on cultural resources. Calling interpretation "fiction" because it can never be proven true perpetuates a misunderstanding of science and the role of falsifiability. Similarly, archaeologists must be careful in their use of the word "theory." In science, a theory is an idea or set of ideas so supported by the data that it becomes an operational assumption. A theory is not the same as an inference, a hypothesis, or an interpretation.

Charles is to be commended for providing such a data-rich, "thick description" of the landscape in the lower Illinois Valley during the Middle Woodland period. The environmental reconstructions literally and figuratively ground his interpretations. The parts of his interpretation that deal with gender, the cycle of life and death, and the flow of time add a human dimension to the landscape. The combination of hard and soft science techniques produces results that are far more robust than just one set of techniques would. Miles and Huberman state that "numbers and words are *both* needed if we are to understand the world" (Miles and Huberman 1994: 40). Charles's Riverworld uses both, and in so doing it provides a valuable insight into the Hopewellian world.

Rejoinder by Douglas K. Charles to Comments by Pacheco and Sieg and Burks

I very much appreciate the overall positive responses to my chapter expressed by Pacheco and Sieg and Burks. The editors have asked that we keep our responses brief, so I will concentrate on the "literary motifs" fittingly isolated in the comments: fiction and narrative. I say "fittingly" because the commentators' focus on those terms illustrates some of the points I was attempting to make. Sieg and Burks, like Pacheco, see themselves as scientists, and Pacheco states that "archaeology is best characterized as a historical-materialist science rather than an essentialist science." Many postprocessual approaches to archaeology (and post- or countermodernism in general) take specific issue with the notion of archaeology as science, and even with the Enlightenment concept of science itself as a means of knowing. I give credence to elements of this critique while still harboring a respect for the scientific method. My chapter is part of an attempt to resolve this tension (no doubt kept palpable by teaching osteology, human evolution, and archaeology lab courses while inhabiting a department otherwise filled with increasing post-postmodern cultural anthropologists).

Fiction, as a descriptive term, was adopted to convey the constructivist nature of ethnographies that was apparent to many by at least the mid-1980s (e.g., Clifford and Marcus 1986), and archaeologists writing about those aspects of the past that are not physically, chemically, or statistically quantifiable venture into the same constructivist realm. Thomas (2004) and others would not even excuse the scientists. I presume by the term "archaeological record" that Sieg and Burks mean the physical elements we recover, associations among objects, and so on, and thus strictly speaking the archaeological record does not constitute a literary genre (although Hodder [e.g., 1990] and others have advocated reading material culture as text). Archaeological reporting is, however, a writing genre (literary would seem too flattering an adjective for most publications and reports in our discipline), and the analytical categories, attributions of significance, and so on in the reporting—and in the preceding data collection and analysis—should be critically and reflexively examined in terms of our categories and values. An ethnography (or its archaeological equivalent) is fiction, not because it can not be proven but because it potentially informs us more about the author and her or his culture than it does about the culture of which it purports to be a study. The significance of this point relates specifically to removing the ethnographer or archaeologist from a position of privileged authority over interpretation and opening up the possibility of multiple points of view, particularly to those people being studied (or their descendants). Indeed, issues around historic preservation should be articulated by a number of stakeholders. Preservation should not be co-opted as a rationale for the employment of archaeologists.

Different meanings of the term narrative are employed by Pacheco and me. A narrative can serve as a method of verification in historical sciences, for example, as a means to explicate an evolutionary sequence. Pacheco makes this point and I wholeheartedly agree. However, narrative in the sense in which I used it means to simply tell a story. The narrative conveys a hypothesis. It is not a test of, or evidence in support of, the hypothesis. In the one case, a (diachronic) hypothesis based on a presumed series of contingent events is supported by a story that connects those events; in the other case, a number of "facts" are connected in order to render comprehensible a (synchronic) situation. I would argue that my (re)construction of Riverworld conforms to the latter meaning of narrative and in that sense is not at all Darwinian.

This raises a second point. In the perhaps too-obscure means of an endnote, I tried to distinguish between Darwinist and Darwinian approaches. The former refers to the writings of Darwin (and later works securely in the tradition narrowly defined), while the latter refers to the various permutations of Darwinism that have come down to us. Darwin was very aware of the role of history: homologies and atavisms constituted some of the most powerful evidence for his theory of evolution by natural selection. A phrase he used was "descent with modification." History is embedded in the descent component as connections with past states. An overemphasis on the modification component, as in current selectionist models in archaeology, has created the contemporary situation in which Darwinian models are effectively ahistorical because explanation resides in natural selection in the moment and there is a focus on analogies (e.g., Braun 1991), not on the retention of homologies—the evidence of descent and history. History as an explanatory dimension currently resides in the Marxian (not necessarily Marxist—using the suffixes in parallel fashion) approaches.

So I still contend (Charles 1992a) that we are largely stuck with choosing between Darwinian (scientific, explanatory, Enlightenment) and Marxian (constructivist, interpretive, Romantic) approaches. Not that some sort of resolution/synthesis is not desirable (Charles 2006).

Commentary on Paul J. Pacheco's "Why Move? Ohio Hopewell Sedentism Revisited"

Commentary by Douglas K. Charles

At the heart of the disagreement between Pacheco (along with Dancey) and Cowan (as well as Yerkes) are dimensions of continuous variability forced into contrasting variables. While postulating dichotomies can be analytically useful (e.g., Charles, this volume; Sieg and Burks, this volume), dichotomization can be misleading, seductive, and simplistic if we are accentuating the ends of a continuum—or if people simply behave less rigorously than their conceptual frameworks might suggest.

Pacheco acknowledges the dimensional, rather than dichotomous, nature of residential mobility, citing Rafferty (1985) and Odell (1998), and he accepts Kelly's (1992) argument for seasonal and annual variation in mobility. Indeed, a continuity of mobility patterns, not contrasting modes, was the frequently overlooked essence of Binford's (1980) original formulation. Nevertheless, the disagreement predominantly focuses on whether Hopewell populations in Ohio were sedentary or mobile. Pacheco and Dancey (e.g., 2006), following Prufer (1964, 1965), argue for "dispersed, sedentary households or hamlets, organized into communities affiliated with earthworks and/or mounds" (Pacheco, this volume). Cowan (e.g., 2006) counters that Hopewell people were highly mobile, and that they periodically gathered at earthwork complexes.

Either of these models is likely to be a gross oversimplification that fails to capture the complexity of Hopewellian economic and social life. Bernardini (2004) and Ruby, Carr and Charles (2005) suggest that individuals participated in several different communities operating on different spatial and temporal scales. A given individual might thus have occupied/utilized numerous hamlets, special purpose camps and loci, mound sites, and earthworks seasonally, annually, and over the course of their life. Each of these site "types" would have encompassed a range of sizes, configurations, and depositional patterns. No single individual would have necessarily operated within the same field as any other, depending upon their age, gender, clan, status, and so on. In other words, membership in communities would have been very fluid, and direct correlations between sites and people would not have been clearly structured. Different people would have attended different sites, different sites would have been attended by different people, and the patterns of site use and the distributions of people would have differed seasonally and annually throughout the Middle Woodland period.

Similarly, arguments focusing on expedient *versus* curated tool technologies as alternatives may likewise mask continuums of seasonal and annual variation. Depending upon the location of chert sources, and their quality, access to raw material can vary relative to a group's location in the seasonal round (assuming some residential mobility or variation in logistic mobility over the course of a year), whether affecting longer distance exchange or transport, and presumably other factors. Furthermore, there may well be social dimensions to consider. The use, function and/or meaning of the prismatic bladelets that serve as a diagnostic for Hopewell are, ironically, poorly understood. Pacheco and Cowan disagree over the role of blades in expedient or curated technologies as these factors relate to mobility. In Illinois, Morrow (1987, 1988) and Odell (1994) could only conclude that bladelets were socially, rather than functionally, significant. Byers (2004: 236–239) develops this line of argument further, suggesting that bladelets, routinely manufactured from contrasting cherts—Wyandotte and Vanport in Ohio, Cobden-Dongola and Burlington-Crescent Quarry in Illinois—were used within a dualistic ritual context. As an example, he cites the meat versus milk food preparation practices in Orthodox and Conservative Jewish households. Alternatively, Buikstra (1976) and Morrow (1988, 1998) noted the association of bladelets with women in Middle Woodland cemeteries in Illinois, and Charles (2005) has suggested that the bladelets served as specifically women's tools, something like the Inuit *ulu*.

Commentary by Lauren Sieg and Jarrod Burks

Pacheco's chapter underscores the importance of carefully evaluating each half of Prufer's Vacant Ceremonial Center-Dispersed Agricultural Hamlet Hypothesis. Although the "Dispersed Agricultural Hamlet" is the second half of the model, it is the primary source of contention today. Most would agree that the Ohio Hopewell occupied small settlements, often referred to as hamlets in the literature, in the hinterlands surrounding the earthworks. What is at question is how long these hamlets were occupied. While some (e.g., Dancey 1991, 1992; Dancey and Pacheco 1997; Kozarek 1997; Pacheco 1996, 1997; Pacheco and Dancey 2006; Prufer 1964, 1965; Wymer 1993, 1996, 1997) have found evidence for sedentary, hamlet-based residential patterns, others (Cowan 2006; Yerkes 2002, 2006) have concluded that habitation was highly mobile, with hamlets intermittently and perhaps repeatedly occupied during particular seasons. We agree with Pacheco that Cowan's evidence from a site immediately adjacent to an earthwork in Warren County, while a very significant contribution to our understanding of Ohio Hopewell, is not sufficient to refute the hypothesis that the Hopewell lived in permanent (i.e., year-round) settlements away from the earthworks in other regions.

The data to address the sedentism question lie in the settlements themselves. While Dancey and Pacheco (1997) list nearly 100 documented Ohio Hopewell settlements, very few of these have been studied enough to address issues of settlement permanence, seasonality, or even settlement layout. We lack a large set of thoroughly and systematically examined habitation sites and we do not have control over interregional and temporal variability. Thus we would argue that much of the debate surrounding Ohio Hopewell settlement might be a bit premature given the current state of our knowledge.

Ohio Hopewell settlements are difficult to find, especially in today's no-till agricultural fields. They are fairly small sites whose archaeological traces have been further diminished by a century of plowing, 1,500 years of flooding and other kinds of erosion, and at least 50 to 100 years of artifact collecting. A good example of the extent to which formation processes can affect settlement sites is the Strait site in central Ohio (Burks 2004). Strait is a large, permanent settlement consisting of multiple, contemporaneous households dating to about A.D. 250. Much of the site has been under cultivation for at least 150 years, and it has been heavily surface-collected by artifact collectors and archaeologists. As a result, stone tools and even lithic debitage are now rare on the plowed surface. Pottery, if present, has been broken into tiny fragments because of weathering and plowing. The story is quite different in an unplowed section of the site, where there are thick (40–60 cm) secondary refuse deposits with hand-sized pieces of pottery and dozens of projectile points and other large tools. The spatial distribution of these objects is so good that discrete activity areas and refuse deposition zones are evident in the unplowed section. The contrast between the plowed and unplowed contexts is striking. Given that most Ohio Hopewell settlements are thoroughly plowed and regularly surface collected, it is no surprise that their surface signature may today include just a few diagnostic objects, some lithic debitage, and a cluster of fire-cracked rock—an assemblage that likely would not warrant special attention during a typical survey. Nevertheless, these meager surface remains can be underlain by very large numbers of intact features, as was found recently at the Brown's Bottom #1 site in Ross County, Ohio (Pacheco, Burks, and Wymer 2006).

The second half of Prufer's hypotheses, the "Vacant Ceremonial Center," is also a source for some debate. The term itself is a basis of some of the confusion, as it combines two site functions, habitation (or lack thereof) and civic-ceremonial activities. If the two types of sites are differentiated on the basis of their primary function, their terminology should reflect this distinction, that is, simply a ceremonial center or a hamlet. This is not to suggest that the characteristics of habitation at earthwork sites are not important to research. Rather, it is to suggest that we should free ourselves to explore the nature and extent of habitation at the earthworks by not presupposing an absence of habitation in the site terminology.

Finding evidence for habitation at civic-ceremonial sites is even more difficult than finding evidence for outlying hamlets, just as finding evidence for rituals at habitation sites is much more difficult than finding evidence for them at civic-ceremonial sites. In addition to the disturbances described above for all Hopewell horizon habitation sites, the visibility of habitation at earthworks has been further impacted by prehistoric activity. The civic-ceremonial functions of the earthwork sites comprise the bulk of the material record at earthwork sites. Artifacts and features that relate to habitation can be intermixed or obscured by artifacts and features that relate to the civic-ceremonial functions. For example, soil that contained habitation material could have been used to construct embankments or mounds. Refuse disposal patterns that utilized natural swales or bluff edges as dump zones at the earthworks may result in artifact concentrations that do not correlate to habitation features. Reoccupation of earthwork areas after the Middle Woodland period disturbed Hopewell horizon features.

In addition to the formation processes that obscure habitation visibility, there are questions of spatial and temporal relations between earthworks and habitations. First, there is difficulty in delineating the spatial boundaries of civic-ceremonial sites. At what point would a domestic structure be too far from a civic-ceremonial site to not be considered habitation at that site? Second, it is difficult to assign dates or duration of occupation to possible habitation structures at earthwork sites. Chronometric dating techniques are not refined enough to precisely date the sequence and length of occupation, even if residential structures were uncovered.

The types of habitation sites, the change in such sites through time, and the nature of habitation at the civic-ceremonial sites are much better understood today than they were 20 years ago. There is, however, much more to learn. It would be useful to create hypotheses about the archaeological signatures of short- or long-term residences at earthwork sites. Based on the variability in earthwork form, earthwork size, mound form, mound size, workshops, features, and assemblages, we can expect a great deal of variation across space and time in the habitation at earthworks. As described by Pacheco in his chapter, expectations for habitation could range from short-term, temporary

structures used by a single family to substantial structures that were periodically inhabited by one or more groups. The former would leave little to no archaeological trace (e.g., Burks and Pederson 2006). The latter would include
a combination of feature patterns that are identified as "habitation" alongside
evidence that shows a range of duration of occupation. These expectations
have parallels in the sizes of groups involved in rituals at civic-ceremonial
sites, as outlined by Greber (2006).

It is also important that we explore in greater detail the habitation sites
from areas other than Ross and Licking County, and then compare these data
to Pacheco's model of how the components of a hypothetical Hopewell community articulate. Hopewell horizon settlements and camps have been found
all over southern and central Ohio, from the floodplains of major streams
to upland settings along drainage divides. In areas without major earthwork
centers, what is the glue that binds communities together? With so many
Hopewell horizon sites spread all across southern and central Ohio, why are
the major earthwork centers so clustered in just a few areas? With an expanding database, continuing debate, and refinement of our models, the advances
in our understanding of the Hopewell settlement pattern during the next 20
years should keep pace with the last two decades.

Rejoinder by Paul J. Pacheco to Comments by Charles and Sieg and Burks

First of all, I wish to thank my colleagues for the opportunity to participate
in this process with them. In general, I agree with most of their critiques and
have gained insight from their comments. What follows are a few comments
which I hope clarify certain aspects of these critiques.

In his comment, Charles argues that both my model and Frank Cowan's
model are "likely to be a gross oversimplification that fails to capture the
complexity of Hopewellian economic and social life." I think he has hit the
proverbial nail on the head. Archaeological models are by nature gross over-
simplifications. The purpose of these models is to organize existing data about
a cultural phenomenon which has been obscured by formation processes and
the vastness of time. In other words, the ultimate purpose of archaeological
models is heuristic. When Dancey and I first proposed our update of Prufer's
model, we were not trying to squash variation into dichotomous and unvarying
essentialist settlement types. Rather, our purpose was to provide a base from
which to proceed to design ongoing research that facilitates interpretation
of Ohio Hopewell sociopolitical organization. We fully expected intra- and
interregional settlement variation in both space and time. Our discussion of
the Licking region documents such intraregional variation and also provides
an interregional contrast for the central Scioto region (Pacheco and Dancey

2006). Similarly, recent efforts by Bernardini (2004), Ruby, Carr, and Charles (2005), and Carr (2008) refine the multiscalar concept of Ohio Hopewell communities while proposing cultural historical hypotheses about the meaning of the earthwork variation within the central Scioto. Like any model, ours should be either replaced or revised when it no longer does a good job of organizing Ohio Hopewell settlement variability.

It is ironic how closely our model mirrors the currently accepted model of Illinois Hopewell community organization, a model Charles relies on as a basic assumption in his chapter and from which he proceeds to his interpretive reading of the Riverworld landscape. This is not a coincidence; dispersed households likely form the basic building block of Middle Woodland/Hopewellian societies throughout the Woodlands (Smith 1992, 2006). As Charles indicates, those in Illinois were very stable with a structured and engendered use of local and regional space (see Charles, this volume, Figures 1.2 and 1.3). The polarized debate about residential mobility in Ohio Hopewell goes deeper than just dichotomizing contrasting variables. As Charles points out, "Pacheco acknowledges the dimensional, rather than dichotomous, nature of residential mobility, citing Rafferty (1985) and Odell (1998), and he accepts Kelly's (1992) argument for seasonal and annual variation in mobility." I would also point out my discussion of the important role of logistical mobility in Hopewellian settlement systems, in addition to obvious participation of dispersed households in corporate activities. What Cowan and Yerkes propose is more than a continuum of mobility. They are arguing that the earthworks and mounds of Ohio Hopewell are built by residentially mobile hunter-gatherer populations, who ranged widely across the landscape (i.e., they are not characterized by residential stability). Charles fails to see that his Riverworld reconstruction would not be applicable to the itinerant travelers of the Cowan and Yerkes model; they did not hold still long enough to structure and engender the use of local space. Likewise, other social reconstructions, like those in Bernardini (2004) and Ruby, Carr, and Charles (2005), are probably not applicable to the Cowan and Yerkes reading of Ohio Hopewell settlement variation, either. For me, the core of this debate is the basic understanding of what the Ohio Hopewell landscape looked like. Was it a landscape composed of residentially stable but dispersed households engaging in a combination of low-level food production and primary forest efficiency? Or was it composed of ever-shifting Archaic-like hunters and gatherers? Charles assumes residential stability on the Illinois Hopewell landscape, but he sees the unsettled nature of the debate in Ohio as polarizing. Just say no to the hobo Hopewell.

Charles's comment about expediency and bladelets is very insightful and has helped me to refocus one of my research projects. Sieg and Burks's point about the premature status of the sedentism debate in Ohio is also well taken, as is their point that settlement variation within Ohio Hopewell includes the diverse signature of occupations within earthwork precincts. In future modifications of the model, I propose to drop the terms "sedentary" and "vacant"; both appear to have outgrown their usefulness.

Commentary on Lauren Sieg and Jarrod Burks's "The Land between the Mounds: The Role of 'Empty' Spaces in the Hopewellian Built Environment"

Commentary by Douglas K. Charles

At the risk of being a large cooking vessel hurling rocks within my siliceous abode, I must admit to being less than persuaded by the binary interpretation of the Ohio Hopewell landscape offered by Sieg and Burks. The question I will address is the following: Is the conception of the Hopewellian landscape composed of a complementary pairing of earthwork and nonearthwork space a meaningful (re)construction of their world or an imposition of our archaeological categories? Identifications and interpretations of the symbolism represented in Hopewellian art—bears; birds; deer; animals that cross the boundaries between sky, land, and water—is widely accepted, even if there might be disagreement over specific cases. Similarly, complementarity and pairing seem to be important elements in Hopewellian art. The point at issue is whether or not these structures were integral to the built landscape as conceived, consciously or not, *by the Hopewellians.*

One way to approach the question is to examine one of the examples Sieg and Burks offer. Their Figure 3.5 is meant to illustrate that at the Hopeton Works site the distribution of debris is structured by the earthwork/nonearthwork opposition. The relative paucity of debris inside the walls of the earthwork is taken as evidence of the differential use of the "positive space" of the earthwork and the "negative space" of the inter-earthwork occupation/resource zones. An alternate interpretation of the debris distribution seems equally plausible. The densest debris concentrations are along the southwest corner of the terrace edge. Density drops off to the east and the north. There is a sharply lower debris density inside the boundary of the earthwork walls—but this is only apparent along the southern and western walls. To the east and north a similar break is not perceptible. In fact, an interruption in the debris distribution is barely discernable, if at all, at the walls of the circle. Only at the southwest corner of the rectilinear component is this aspect of the debris patterning marked. Furthermore, the west-southwest to east-northeast gradient also describes the distribution of debris *inside* the walls of the earthwork. In other words, a fall-off pattern of activity emanating from the southwest corner of the terrace edge, interrupted at some point by the construction of the earthwork, which altered the deposition patterns from then onward, is a scenario that at least as readily explains the ultimate debris distribution. The lack of debris-producing activity at any time to the north and east of the earthwork would seem, in fact, to undermine Sieg and Burks's argument.

Another approach to the question of whether Hopewellian or modern archaeological practice defined an earthwork/nonearthwork landscape is to look outside Ohio. Ironically, the archaeological literature from Illinois over the past several decades is dominated by a concern with the habitation component of the Hopewellian landscape, not the mounded ceremonial component. Again, however, the content of archaeological publications does not address the question of whose duality is being represented. I would argue that this difference between Ohio and Illinois archaeological practice supports the notion that the earthwork/nonearthwork opposition is an imposition on the data in line with Western conceptions of, for example, sacred/profane, ritual/ domestic, and religious/secular. The multilayered community structure posited by Ruby, Carr, and Charles (2005; see also Bernardini 2004) for southern Ohio, southern Indiana, and west-central Illinois does not readily lend itself to a straightforward binary interpretive scheme, suggesting that the landscape for Hopewellian populations was more complex. Sieg and Burks are right to argue that we need to integrate the earthwork/inter-earthwork components to achieve a fuller representation of Hopewellian landscapes, and life in general, but the dichotomy reflects our archaeological practice, not Hopewellian practice.

Commentary by Paul J. Pacheco

The chapter by Sieg and Burks is well written and well conceived, although in the end it may not say much that we do not already know. In my opinion, the most important contributions of this chapter are somewhat marginalized by the authors. Viewed from my materialist perch, I think the most important contributions are the plot of Hopewell sites in Ross County and the impressive map of the systematic surface collection in and around the Hopeton Earthworks. I see them as marginalized because they are only used in support of the thesis of the argument rather than forming a centerpiece of the analysis representative of time-consuming field and lab research.

Like Charles, Sieg and Burks utilize a landscape approach, although in distinctly different ways. I agree with them that this approach is underutilized in Hopewell archaeology and that it has great potential for future application. I want to point out a minor oversight that applies to both of the chapters, however. Neither of them makes reference to the work of Helaine Silverman (1988, 1994, 2002). Silverman's research on settlement archaeology for the Early Intermediate period of the Nasca cultures of coastal Peru has contributed significantly to the growth of a landscape approach in archaeology. Silverman specifically proposes what she calls a "full landscape" approach (2002) for investigating the dispersed settlement patterns of people who aggregated at spatially isolated ceremonial precincts. This approach provides her a unique insight into the social meaning and spatial placement of the Nasca ceremonial center at Cahuachi, paralleling to some extent what Charles and Sieg and Burks have independently accomplished in their chapters.

Sieg and Burks propose a structuralist approach to focus on the formal patterning of space rather than trying to understand the meaning of the spatial patterning. They then demonstrate that Hopewell artwork is stylistically composed of the complementary use of positive and negative space. Relating this artistic rendering to a yin-yang symbol or an Escher drawing is an important and visually stimulating insight. But then Sieg and Burks go on to propose that the artwork can serve as a heuristic device to understand the delineation of space in the Ohio Hopewell settlement pattern, with positive space representative of earthworks and negative space representative of nonearthwork zones. This is the primary aspect of their paper that in the end, in my opinion, does not say much beyond what we already know, especially since the heuristic device of using the artwork interplay of positive and negative space is a stretch to apply to the settlement pattern. Sieg and Burks argue that the negative space in artwork consists of open areas or blank spaces which are paired with the positive spaces of the image. For the settlement pattern, the supposed blank spaces are the spaces between the earthworks where "hamlets, gardens, workshops, resource procurement zones, trails, and other smaller-scale components of the built environment." In other words, these nonearthwork areas are not really open and not really blank! In fact, they represent what the authors just called them, "smaller-scale components of the built environment." Their own map of the habitation sites in Ross County shows quite well that the nonearthwork areas are not really blank. Instead, they are full of the imprints of all kinds of nonearthwork activities created by the Hopewell during the course of their occupation of the Scioto Valley. Since the authors do not add any new elements to the Hopewell settlement pattern of this region, I would contend that all they are doing is describing and discussing what we already know, but from a unique perspective.

So why did the authors choose this particular heuristic device, which only works if we grant them that nonearthwork space can count as complementary negative blank spaces to the positive spaces of the earthworks? I would argue that the contrast of positive = earthwork, negative = nonearthwork originates in the work of Squier and Davis, who only show positive spaces in the form of earthworks and mounds on their maps, such as "Twelve Miles of the Scioto Valley." The visual effect of the Squier and Davis map leaves the impression that the spaces between the earthworks are blanks. This idea was carried to its logical conclusion by Prufer in his presentation of the Vacant Ceremonial Center-Dispersed Agricultural Hamlet Hypothesis. If the Hopewell did not live in their earthworks, they must have been dispersed around them. They are right about the paradigm shift which focused attention outside the earthworks if one is concerned with Hopewell residential space.

Sieg and Burks later point out that the creation of negative space by the Hopewell "can be seen on multiple scales," especially at the macro-scale level of entire drainages. Examination of a map of the distribution of earthworks and proposed Ohio Hopewell polities shows that Ohio Hopewell groups were quite restricted within Ohio, especially concentrating along the glacial margin (Pacheco and Dancey 2006: 17, Figure 1.6). I would contend that the space between polities is a more legitimate example of the use of negative space in the Ohio Hopewell settlement pattern. The authors assert that "many Hopewell habitation sites have been found well away from regions with earthwork centers." I argue that this assertion is not empirically valid (Dancey and Pacheco 1997) and contend instead that Hopewell habitation sites are rarely found outside the areas of the proposed polities shown on the map referred to previously. In other words, the space between the polities is a better approximation of the "actual" negative spaces on the Ohio Hopewell landscape. The authors point out that another scale at which the positive-negative complement occurs is the space within the earthworks themselves. Here their evidence is interesting and important but somewhat marginal to the main argument. This is where the authors include the data from the surface survey of the Hopeton Earthworks.

Toward the end of the chapter the authors discuss the idea of complementary pairs of earthworks. Here they propose the concept of precincts as a useful analytical device. I think this is an innovative idea and support its adoption. The precinct concept may allow us to sidestep the multiple meanings of the community concept (see Ruby, Carr, and Charles 2005). As I read their argument, the author's precinct concept is close to the meaning of Ruby, Carr, and Charles's symbolic community concept. However, it may be a superior concept in that it is "guided by the identification of socially significant space," which I see as a landscape device as opposed to a sociopolitical hypothesis, which is how I understand the symbolic community concept.

In conclusion, I think this chapter contains many interesting ideas, some of which are innovative and significant, and some of which are simply new ways to say what we already know. I would have liked to have seen the new data which they present in the chapter as more central to their main argument, but it is a fine contribution to the literature nonetheless.

Rejoinder by Lauren Sieg and Jarrod Burks to Comments by Charles and Pacheco

The reviewers raise several important questions about our analysis of the Hopewellian landscape. One can be addressed by introducing a revised figure (Figure 3.6). When only the definite (bladelets and projectile points) and probable (Vanport and Harrison County chert objects) Hopewell horizon markers from the 2001 Hopeton survey results are plotted, the surface artifact distribution has a couple of clear patterns. First, Hopewell tools such as bladelets and projectile points are fairly evenly spread across the area between the earthworks and the western terrace edge. They occur even in areas lacking fire-cracked rock and other chert debris. The scattered, low-density distribution of bladelets suggests that intermittent occupations occurred across the terrace outside the earthworks. However, there are almost no Hopewell

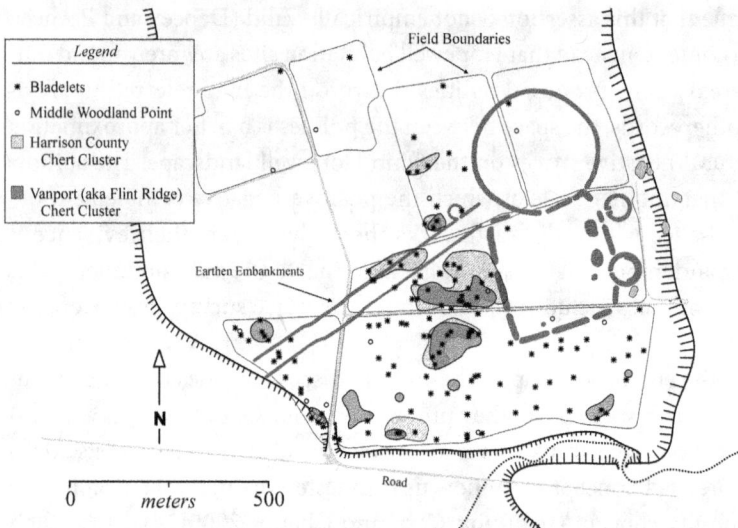

Figure 3.6. Map of the Hopeton Works, Ross County, Ohio, showing the locations of Middle Woodland period objects and clusters of lithic debitage made from raw materials typically used during the Middle Woodland period. Note the general absence of objects within the earthwork enclosures. Based on Burks, Pederson, and Walter (2002); Burks and Walter (2003).

diagnostics inside the earthwork, although some of the highest densities of Vanport and Harrison County chert lie along the outside, western edge of the earthwork. The lack of bladelets and chert debris inside the earthworks suggests that (1) the earthworks were present when the lithics were deposited and (2) there was some kind of proscription against the disposal and perhaps the use of certain types of objects inside the earthworks (see Byers 2004, 2006). In this case the absence of materials on the surface, that is, the negative space inside the earthworks, is a good indication of the differential use of space.

Charles and Pacheco question the validity of the dichotomy between earthwork and nonearthwork space that we have presented, although for different reasons. Charles suggests that the dichotomy may restrict interpretations of social, political, economic, and ritual organizations of the people who lived in this space. We have tried to make the argument that the differences in landscape use do not create opposites. They create complementary parts of the built environment and do not preclude multilayered systems, tripartite social structures, sodalities, clans, and other social, ceremonial, or economic constructs. Charles also questions if the distinction that we have drawn in this chapter is a correct reflection of how the Scioto area people viewed their world. We do not presume that the people who used the earthworks would have described their landscape in the same manner as we have in this chapter (i.e., earthwork/nonearthwork, positive/negative), but we can only describe them today using archaeological terms in ways that have empirical validity. For example, the differences in artifact distribution reflect differences in the use of earthwork and nonearthwork spaces. At a different scale, the dense clustering of earthworks around Chillicothe and the lack of major earthwork clusters in other regions is clear. It is our belief that empirically valid concepts enable us to more closely approximate the structuring of space 2,000 years ago.

Pacheco does not dispute the validity of etic-derived archaeological interpretations, but questions the utility of negative/positive space for settlement studies. He is correct that the first visual representation of this dichotomy can be seen in the Squier and Davis maps and that the dichotomy has remained in the archaeological literature for more than 150 years. Here, we have attempted to use it in a way that may be more appropriate for discussion of Hopewell remains—not as a dichotomized presence/absence distribution but as complementary parts of the same whole. The nonearthwork space and/or areas with low artifact density are important to include in our analysis of the built environment. The data may not be new, but we hope that our use of concepts documented in other Hopewell artifacts as a framework for understanding the built environment at multiple scales will intrigue our colleagues. Design principles (complementary parts, pairings) can be a parsimonious basis for arguments about a variety of Hopewellian behaviors. For example, Greber (2006) has used the design element of open and filled spaces for discussion of earthwork designs at Junction, Works East, and Liberty. Pacheco also disputes our assertion that Hopewell settlements are found far from the earthwork sites. Although space is too limited for presentation of additional data here, a review of state site file records (i.e., Ohio Archaeological Inventory forms) shows "Hopewellian" artifacts, such as bladelets, are present in the spaces between polities. Whether or not these objects are associated with substantial (i.e., year-round) Hopewell settlements is certainly debatable.

Both Charles and Pacheco suggest that we should utilize analyses of landscape patterns from other regions to understand Scioto Hopewell. We agree that there are many landscape studies, among them the work of Silverman (e.g., Silverman 1994, 2002), which present concepts useful for analysis of the Hopewell landscape. However, we have chosen to remain as Hopewell-focused as possible, using data from Hopewell sites and concepts (e.g., pairings and precincts) that have already received considerable attention from other scholars of Hopewell archaeology (e.g., Byers 2004; DeBoer 1997; Greber 1996, 1997a, 2006). As already demonstrated by Ruby, Carr, and Charles (2005), the Scioto region is different in both the natural and built environment from other regions in the Midwest. It is certainly different from the environment of Peru. While transregional concepts and comparisons can be helpful, the differences between regions leave such comparisons fraught with interpretive hazards. It is our contention that the Hopewell literature already contains useful building blocks for understanding the Hopewellian built environment. Although they may be found in literature that is either settlement focused or earthwork focused, they can be combined to forge a more complete understanding of the Hopewell world.

SECTION 2

The Earthworks and
Their Geospatial Relations

The authors of the three chapters of this section worked independently of one another (although they are very aware of one another's past work) and yet that their themes in each case converge in a profoundly interesting manner. Bradley T. Lepper's paper has situated the Newark Earthworks, probably the most complex of known Ohio Hopewellian works, within the larger framework of the Raccoon Valley and has shown that understanding the former requires appreciation of the complexity of the overall history of earthwork construction. Ray Hively and Robert Horn have extended the implications of their pioneer work on the astronomical alignments of the geometrical earthworks of Newark and Chillicothe by also taking a more global approach, not only situating the Newark Earthworks within the wider natural landscape of the Raccoon Valley but also directing their attention to the Chillicothe region, undertaking a very ambitious analysis of how the multiple, large-scale earthworks of this region may be deliberately aligned both with one another and with local natural-astronomical points of relevance. Hence both Lepper and Hively and Horn address how the earthworks of a given region (Newark and Chillicothe) may have been historically related. Warren DeBoer goes one step further and explores the possibility that the geometrical earthworks of Chillicothe might have been related by direct alignment and that this alignment may have been extended down the Scioto River to more distant earthworks. This alignment, thus, may mark a deliberate invoking of the historical connections between social groups.

Lepper's contribution to this volume has accomplished a truly gargantuan task that will serve to advance Hopewellian monumental studies. He has undertaken to research the large archival literature having its roots into the early nineteenth century to winkle out a truly impressive list of references to Hopewellian and even earlier Adena earthwork construction in the Raccoon Creek area. This alone will be of tremendous value to future researchers in this area. Thus in this chapter he has synthesized his own considerable fieldwork in the region along with that of Hopewellian colleagues in Ohio as well as many of his archaeological colleagues expert in other New World prehistoric and historic monumental works. In addition, Lepper has undertaken to integrate these empirical data under a wholistic cognitive-normative model of Native American cultural traditions that postulates these and similar earthworks served ongoing needs of pilgrims in the pursuit of experiencing *communitas* with the spiritual beings that were immanent in the cosmos. This ambitious work challenges his colleagues to extend themselves in pursuit of a common task of clarifying the possible purposes and meanings of these ancient works and certainly raises important issues about the type of social and symbolic structural organization that must have existed in the Eastern Woodlands of the Middle Woodland period that would make such collective efforts possible.

Hively and Horn raise the extremely important issue concerning the planning depth and scope of the earthwork construction strategies of the populations responsible for these earthworks. They also introduce a new approach to azimuth alignment analysis by using and applying the notion of zero-altitude azimuth alignments. Overall, they argue and present relevant evidence to the effect that the earthwork constructions represent a major period of time and that this would have entailed a series of building episodes, each prior episode being the context and the constraining and enabling conditions for the next episode. They postulate that this was the case in both the Newark and the Chillicothe regions and, indeed, suggest that the populations responsible for these two regional construction programs sustained long-distance interactive relations mediated through their common interests in earthwork construction. They persuasively argue that individual earthworks were themselves tied into astronomical azimuth events and go on to argue that in each of the two regions, there were in place certain guidelines that afforded increased accuracy of alignments as well as a generalized developmental program so that as one or more earthworks were "abandoned," the new ones that were built were situated according to certain central coordinating points.

They are cautious in presenting their evidence and point out the statistical difficulties in establishing the plausibility of their postulates. Their main concern is establishing the effective statistical method to support their argument. Without denying that this is a proper cautionary approach, in fairness to them, it should be noted that they are dealing with distinctly different types of "alignment intentions" and demonstrating these types should not be subject to the same statistical rigor. The demonstration of astronomical alignments can be subjected to rigorous statistical techniques, as they point out; however, the demonstration of a generalized planning by which the placement of the individual earthworks with regard to what existed and what may exist in the future really requires a carefully elucidated theory about the plausible nature of the earthworks as these were perceived in the collective understanding of the Hopewell. This would establish the generalized nature of the interests that earthwork construction was serving and such generalized interests are not served by means of strict rules of conduct but by general guidelines that manifest a collective sensibility of how best to proceed. Thus "ball park" linear associations will serve adequately since these would express an etiquette rather than a strict set of constitutive rules. Their analysis may be best read in these dual terms: rather narrow statistical accuracy for specific earthworks and their claimed astronomical alignments, on the one hand, and more generalized considerations of appropriateness of positioning such that respect for the past and the future will be honored, on the other. Their work will serve as another major contribution that they have made to the growing understanding that archaeology is developing in this area.

The earthwork interaction theme embedded in spatially long distant and historically developmental inter-earthwork alignment notion is also developed by Warren DeBoer. While Hively and Horn synthesize both Newark and the Chillicothe regions, DeBoer focuses on the Chillicothe region and even extends his analysis of the possible spatio-alignment relations among the earthworks down the Scioto River to incorporate the Seal site, thereby delineating what he terms the "Scioto Ceremonial Zone" (SCZ). Using a statistical methodology different from that of Hively and Horn, he tentatively concludes that the region-wide patterning of the placement of SCZ earthworks manifests a historical strategy in which ancestral earthworks are the targeted anchors in the placement of their lineal "descendants" and concludes by linking this vast and intricate patterning to the outcome of possibly a combination of ancestral and world renewal rituals.

A careful reading of these three contributions clearly indicates both convergences and interesting differences, generating the conditions of an ongoing and highly illuminating debate. The ideas developed by these three chapters are an excellent start to delineating the most plausible dynamics underwriting these patterns, and with ongoing debate and the pursuit of additional empirical data, we may well approach a contingently true account of this fascinating archaeological record of Native American monumental architecture.

4

The Ceremonial Landscape of the
Newark Earthworks and the Raccoon Creek Valley

Bradley T. Lepper

So old the moon can only know
How old, since ancient forests grow
On mighty wall and pyramid.
(Madison Cawein, *Dead Cities*, 1911)

Ever since the first scientific presentations of the earthworks of eastern North America (e.g., Atwater 1820; Squier and Davis 1848), our perception of them has been constrained by the margins of the maps that portrayed the various sites (see also Cowan, Sunderhaus, and Genheimer 2004). Indeed, the earliest cataloguers of these monumental structures seem to have appreciated this limitation. They presented a few maps that showed portions of river valleys with more or less schematic views of the more prominent earthworks and their relationships to one another (Figure 4.1). Atwater, for example, presented a portion of the Paint Creek valley showing the Seip, Baum, and Spruce Hill Earthworks (1820: Plate VII, facing p. 145) and much the same view was presented by Squier and Davis (1848: Plate III, no. 1, facing p. 4), although their map included many additional mounds and enclosures.

Although these small-scale maps lacked accuracy and could not match the detail in the larger-scale representations of individual sites, they reflected the crucial, if nascent, insight that the earthworks could not be understood in isolation from their geographic and cultural contexts. Greber (2003: 88) made this point clear with her observation that "people transformed the natural environment of the Hopewell valleys into a unique planned landscape." This landscape included the natural features of hills and streams as well as the cultural features superimposed upon and articulated with those natural features—the earthworks, habitation sites, and networks of interconnecting paths. This integrated whole is what Sauer (1925) referred to as the "cultural landscape."

Consequential cultural modifications of the American landscape began as soon as humans entered this hemisphere. Hunters selectively sought particular game animals and gatherers favored certain varieties of plants over others.

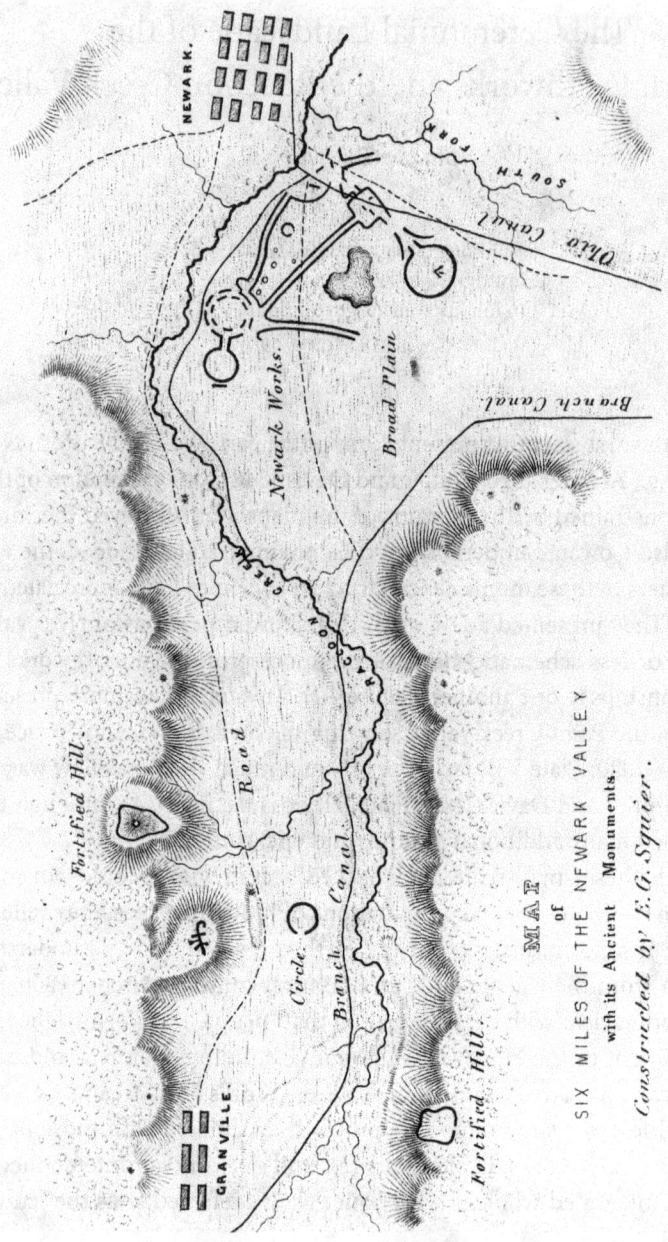

Figure 4.1. Squier and Davis's (1848) map of "Six miles of the Newark Valley with its Ancient Monuments."

Fires were set as a means of driving game as well as to encourage habitats favorable to preferred prey species. These practices changed the character of the regional flora and fauna, reducing or even eliminating some species while introducing or favoring others. Some of this pruning and grafting of the biosphere was intentional, but much of it doubtless was incidental.

A significant change in the relationship between humans and the cultural landscape is marked by the creation of monuments often, but not invariably, linked to mortuary ritual. Although the hunting and gathering peoples of the Paleoindian and Early Archaic periods certainly invested some natural landscape features with ritual significance, they did not mark these places with substantial or lasting architecture. The earliest well-documented examples of monument building in eastern North America are the Middle Archaic period mound group at Watson Brake and the Late Archaic earthworks at Poverty Point in Louisiana (Gibson 1996; Saunders et al. 1997). In Ohio, no such earthen structures are known until the Early Woodland period (c. 500 B.C. to A.D. 100). The acme of monumental earthwork construction in the Ohio Valley occurred during the Middle Woodland period (c. 100 B.C. to A.D. 400). The Hopewell culture built a variety of circular, square, and other geometrically shaped enclosures across southern Ohio, principally in the valleys of the Great and Little Miami, the Scioto, and the Muskingum rivers (Squier and Davis 1848). The largest concentration was centered on modern Chillicothe, whereas the largest individual centers were at Newark and Portsmouth. In addition, these people built many more or less irregularly shaped earthworks that enclosed prominent hilltops (Riordan 1996). Fort Ancient and Fort Hill are the most spectacular examples. The succeeding Late Woodland (A.D. 400 to 1000) and Late Prehistoric (A.D. 1000 to 1500) cultures built small burial mounds of stone and earth, an occasional earthwork or ditch surrounding a village, and the animal effigy mounds long considered to have been the work of either the Adena or Hopewell cultures (Lepper and Frolking 2003).

The following chapter is an attempt to consider the Newark Earthworks within the context of a broader cultural landscape. From the standpoint of archaeological visibility, this is predominantly a ceremonial landscape; but the evidence also indicates that habitation sites were present throughout this area, often in close proximity to the earthworks (e.g., Bernhardt 1976; Dancey 1991; Lepper and Yerkes 1997; Pacheco 1997; Yerkes 1990).

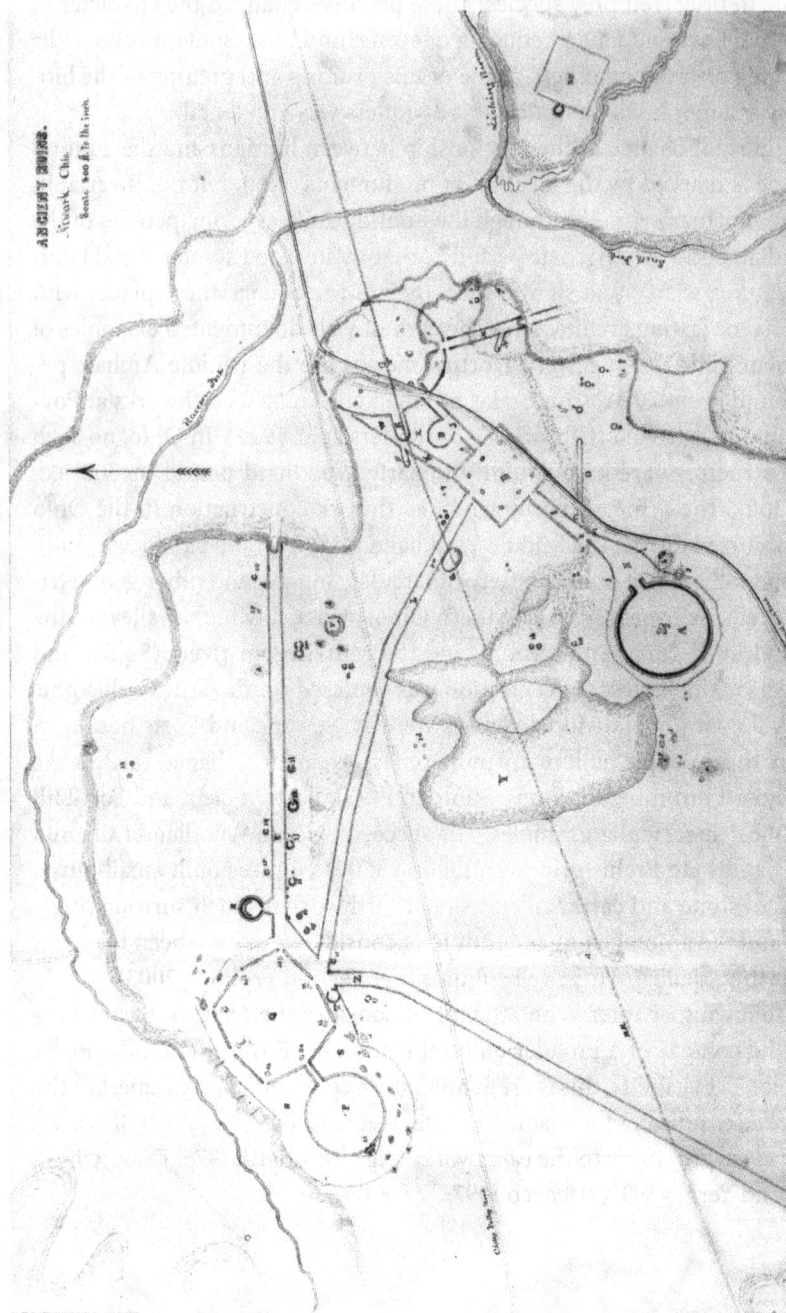

Figure 4.2. Map of the Newark Earthworks as surveyed by James and Charles Salisbury, c. 1862. Courtesy of the American Antiquarian Society.

The Archaeology of the Newark Earthworks and the Raccoon Creek Valley

> The Raccoon Valley and contiguous territory constitute, probably, the most interesting territory in the State, or even in the United States for the antiquarian. Mounds of different sizes and heights, earthworks of every kind known to the historian exist here in great numbers. Numbers yet to be seen and traced may almost be counted in the hundreds. (Hill 1881: 426)

The Newark Earthworks

The Newark Earthworks originally consisted of a series of monumental geometric enclosures connected by a network of parallel-walled roads (Figure 4.2). The primary enclosures included a circle (the so-called Observatory Circle) connected to an octagon, a circle with an interior ditch (the Great Circle), a square, and an oval surrounding a number of large and small, conical and loaf-shaped mounds (Cherry Valley enclosure and mounds). I have reviewed the archaeology of the Newark Earthworks in some detail elsewhere, so readers who desire more than a cursory review may consult those references (Lepper 1989, 1996, 1998, 2002, 2004a).

The Observatory Circle is a nearly perfect circular earthwork with a diameter of 321 m (1,054 ft). It is connected by a neck of parallel walls to the Octagon, which encloses an area of 20 ha (50 acres). There is a small platform mound located at every opening into the Octagon. A gravel-filled pit located adjacent to one of these mounds yielded radiocarbon dates[1] of 1650 ± 80 years B.P. (Beta-76908) and 1770 ± 80 years B.P. (Beta-76909). The circle is named for the "Observatory," or Observatory Mound, a large, loaf-shaped platform mound located on the outside of the circle opposite the gateway leading into the Octagon (Squier and Davis 1848: 70).

The Great Circle, located a bit less than 2 km southeast of the Octagon, is 358 m (1,176 ft) in diameter with walls that are between 1.5 and 4 m (3–13 ft) high. It has an interior ditch 2–4 m (7–13 ft) deep. In 1992, excavations through the enclosure wall revealed a three-stage construction sequence that utilized different colors and textures of soil (Lepper 1996: 233). A buried paleosol at the base of the embankment yielded a radiocarbon date of 2110 ± 80 years B.P. (Beta-58449). Pollen and phytoliths from the A horizon indicated the environment at the time the earthworks were constructed was dominated, at least locally, by a prairie. At the center of the Great Circle is a three-lobed mound named Eagle Mound for its supposed, if dubious, resemblance to a bird. Eagle

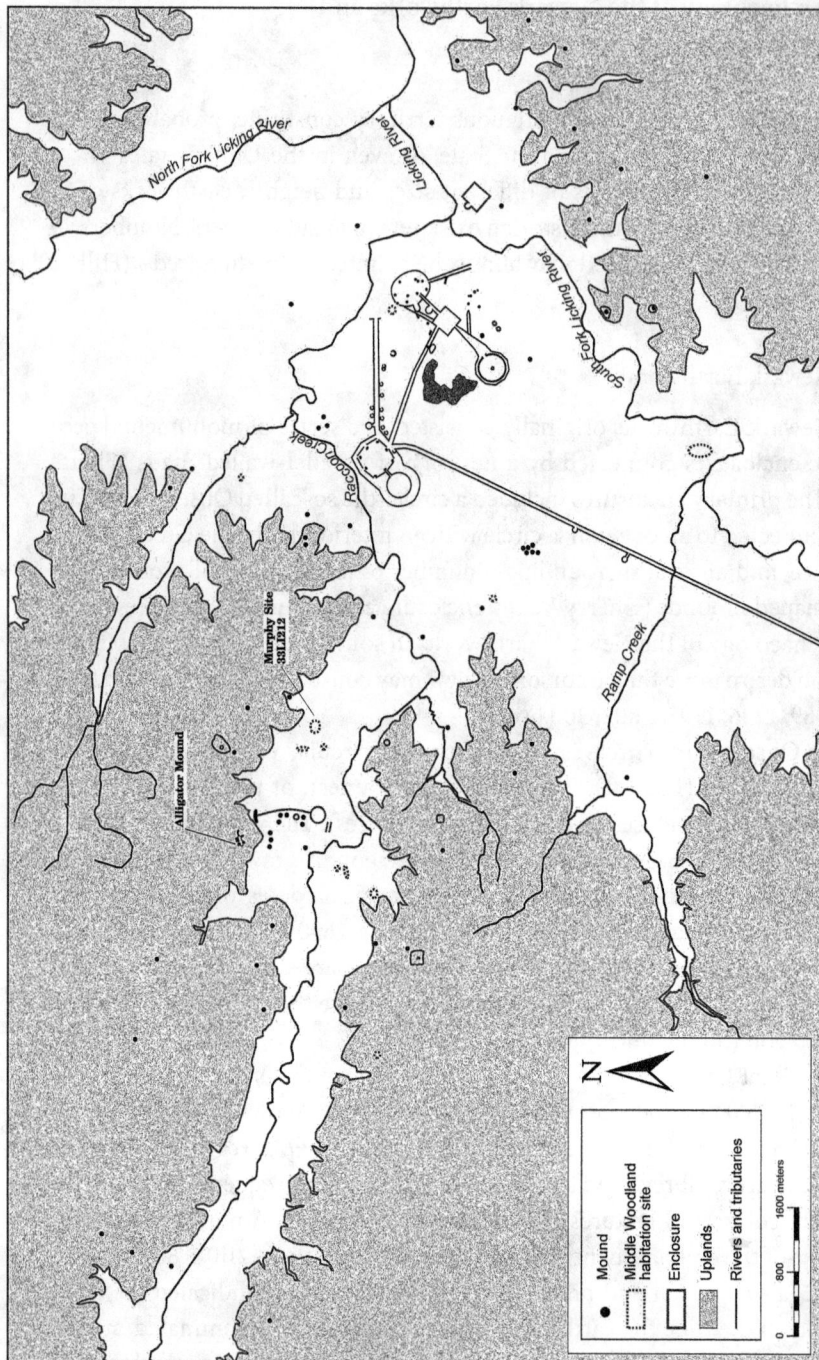

Figure 4.3. Map of lower Raccoon Creek valley showing the distribution of mounds, enclosures, and Middle Woodland habitation sites. The data were derived from a number of sources, including the Ohio Archaeological Inventory, Bushnell (1889), Hooge (1993), Mills (1914), Salisbury and Salisbury (1862), Squier and Davis (1848), and Unzicker (1860).

Mound was excavated in 1928 and found to cover the remains of a Hopewellian Big House (Greber 1996: 166).

The Newark Square was a nearly perfectly square enclosure with walls between 286 and 290 m (939–951 ft) long. Little of the square has survived, but a remnant is preserved as the Wright Earthworks. The Cherry Valley enclosure was an elliptical earthwork approximately 550 m (1,800 ft) long by 450 m (1,500 ft) wide. Within this enclosure were at least 11 mounds of varying sizes and shapes, most of which included interments of human remains, a small circular enclosure, and a small platform mound (Salisbury and Salisbury 1862; Squier and Davis 1848: Plate XXV; Wyrick 1866). In addition to the main components of the Newark Earthworks, there were numerous small circles mainly concentrated along the network of parallel-walled avenues (Figure 4.2; see also Reeves 1936; Wyrick 1866). Kennedy (1994: 55) has compared these to the Stations of the Cross on the Via Dolorosa. Hall (1997: 126), on the other hand, suggested such features were similar in form and function to Lakota sweat lodges. There were, in addition, several small conical mounds associated with the Newark Earthworks (see Figures 4.2 and 4.3). The Wells Mound Group (33LI13) was a cluster of three Middle Woodland mounds located west of the Great Circle along the southern margin of a large pond. Mound No. 1 of the group, the remnants of which were excavated in 1928, produced a Lowe Expanding Base point, an anchor pendant, and a large lamellar flake (Lepper 1989: 125), indicating a late Middle to early Late Woodland affiliation (e.g., Justice 1987: 208). According to James and Charles Salisbury (1862: 18), "some 8 or 10 small mounds" were situated on the large kame located southwest of the Octagon, typically on the "highest points" of this irregular feature (Figure 4.2). The affiliation of these mounds is unknown, but given the context, they are possibly Early Woodland or even Late Archaic in age.[2]

There are only four Middle Woodland habitation sites documented in close proximity to the Newark Earthworks. Considering that very few surveys for such sites have been undertaken in this area, it is unlikely that this number provides a reasonable approximation of the frequency of domestic sites that existed here.[3] Hale's House site (33Li252) is located just outside the Cherry Valley mounds oval enclosure (Lepper and Yerkes 1997). It consisted of several post molds that defined a roughly rectangular structure with a prepared floor. Several features were spatially associated with this structure, including a hearth, an earth oven, a refuse pit, and an hourglass-shaped basin lined with pebbles and covered with small sheets of mica. Radiocarbon dates obtained on charcoal from these features indicated there were at least two components present. The earth oven dated to 2670 ± 70 B.P. (Beta-27446), placing it in the Early Woodland period. Charcoal from a shallow basin returned a date of

1845 ± 60 B.P. (Beta-28062/ETH-4593), and the hourglass-shaped pit yielded a date of 1640 ± 90 B.P. (Beta-58450), placing them solidly within the Middle Woodland occupation.

Bernhardt (1976: 49) described the DiGiondomenico site (33LI56) as a "rich site" located at the confluence of the South Fork of the Licking River and Ramp Creek. The artifacts recovered from the surface included Hopewell projectile points, cores, bladelets, and a small fragment of obsidian. Bernhardt suggested that the site's location "would have commanded access to and from the ceremonial complex" and that it "may have enjoyed a central role in the Hopewell religious (and political?) system" (1976: 49). The Southgate Development site (33LI57) was discovered during a 1977 Ohio Department of Transportation survey (Addington 1977). Surface investigations yielded a McGraw Plain body sherd, a small, corner-notched point made from white Flint Ridge flint, and a large quantity of Flint Ridge flint debitage. Finally, Carskadden and Donaldson (2008) described a small amateur collection of Hopewell projectile points, preforms, bladelet cores, and bladelets along with a single sherd of McGraw Cordmarked pottery and a slate gorget fragment from a garden a short distance to the southwest of the Great Circle. They interpreted the Indianhead Drive site as a domestic location.

These four sites establish that Hopewellian habitations are present in close proximity to the Newark Earthworks. None of these documented sites appear to represent long-term or substantial occupations; therefore, without further investigation, it is not possible to establish whether they are ordinary domestic sites, the temporary encampments of visitors to the earthworks, or some sort of specialized activity areas. Lepper and Yerkes (1997: 188) argued that Hale's House site, at least, was functionally equivalent to "typical" Hopewell domestic sites.

Beyond the Newark Earthworks

The Raccoon Valley has been recognized for its spectacular archaeology since Squier and Davis published their map of six miles of the Newark Valley in 1848 (1848: Plate XXXVI, no. 4; see Figure 4.1). Hooge (1993) undertook the most recent thorough review of the archaeology of this area, and those wishing a more comprehensive description of particular sites should consult his unpublished dissertation (see also Lepper 2004b). Though dominated by the Newark Earthworks, there is an impressive number and diversity of lesser known earthworks in the surrounding region.

The Salisbury Square was a rectangular earthwork with a small circular enclosure that projected from one wall (Salisbury and Salisbury 1862; Lepper 1998). The dimensions of the rectangular enclosure were 226 m by 232 m (740 ft by 760 ft). The circular enclosure was 43 m (140 ft) in diameter. The earthwork was located east of the Great Circle on the opposite side of the South Fork of the Licking River (see Figure 4.2). It almost certainly is a Hopewellian construction and appears to have been closely related to the Newark Earthworks. It is situated on a remnant of the same glacial terrace on which the more narrowly defined Newark Earthworks were built, separated from the main complex only by the South Fork of the Licking River (Forsyth 1966). Also, the form of the enclosure is similar to the Anderson Earthwork in Ross County, which yielded a radiocarbon date of 2010 ± 60 B.P. (Beta 68758/ CAMS 10484) (Pickard and Pahdopony 1995).

The Salisbury brothers (1862: 19) reported that a deposit of 194 leaf-shaped Flint Ridge flint bifaces had been found buried 0.6 m (2 ft) below the surface of the embankment at the southeastern corner of the Salisbury Square: "They were placed points upward in a conical pile like stacked arms, resting upon a large flat stone" (Salisbury and Salisbury 1862: 19). In 1970, a deposit of diagnostic Hopewell artifacts (33LI36), including more than 150 bladelet cores and core fragments and as many bladelets, was discovered in the general vicinity of this enclosure; but the exact nature of the association is unclear because the precise location of the Salisbury Square has not been identified (Lepper 1998: 128–129).[4]

An ovate hilltop enclosure with an exterior ditch (33LI7) is situated on a prominent bluff south of the Great Circle and on the opposite side of the South Fork of the Licking River (Whittlesey 1852: Plate V, no. 2). The enclosure, which the Salisbury brothers refer to as "Hill Fort No. 1," is about 150 m (500 ft) in diameter along the north-south axis and 230 m (760 ft) in diameter along the east-west axis.[5] A low mound, reported to have been just over 1 m (4 ft) tall in 1862, is located near the center of the enclosure (Salisbury and Salisbury 1862). There are no documented accounts of any excavations that may have been undertaken here, so its cultural affiliation is unknown. Its proximity to the Newark Earthworks, however, and the dramatic view the location affords of what Squier and Davis (1848: 69) described as the "remarkable plain" below suggests it was built by the Hopewell culture. Whittlesey (1852: 14) concluded that it was, "no doubt, part of the great system of works constructed about Newark and Granville."

Approximately 0.5 km south of 33LI7, on a neighboring hilltop, there was a circular enclosure of an unusual character. It was surveyed by the Salisbury brothers in the early 1860s and they identified it simply as "Hill Fort No. 2" (Figure 4.4). The earthwork also appears on Unzicker's map of the Newark Earthworks (Unzicker 1860). It consisted of an outer semicircular or C-shaped

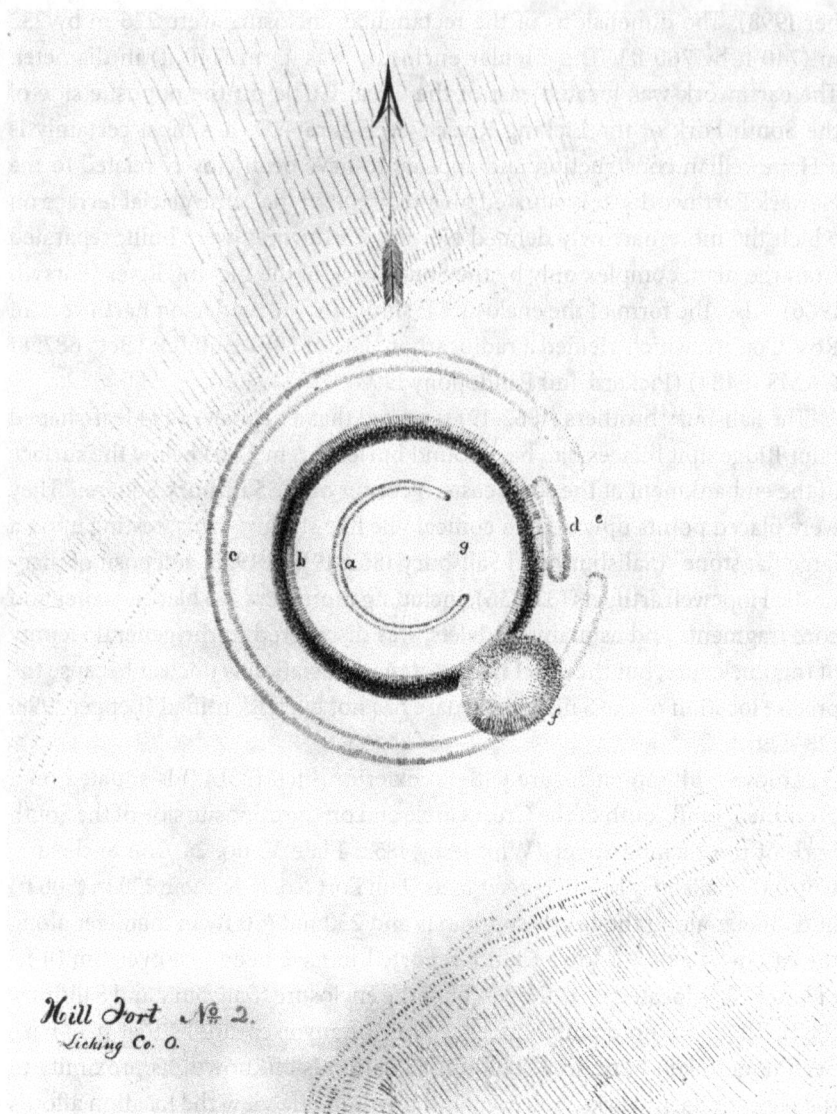

Hill Fort № 2.
Licking Co. O.

Figure 4.4. Map of "Hill Fort No. 2" as surveyed by James and Charles Salisbury, c. 1862. The enclosures and mound are situated on a prominent hilltop south of the Newark Earthworks. Key: a = semicircular enclosure about 33 m in diameter; b = interior ditch; c = the outer wall, which was about 88 m in diameter; d = wall 23 m in length that blocks the entrance to the outer circle; e = the gateway into the outer semicircular enclosure; f = conical mound about 4 m in height; g = the gateway into the inner semicircular enclosure. Courtesy of the American Antiquarian Society.

wall 88 m (287 ft) in diameter and barely 1 m (3 ft) high, surrounding a smaller semicircular wall about 33 m (107 ft) in diameter and less than 0.5 m (1–2 ft) high. Between these walls ran a ditch 6 m (20 ft) wide and about 1 m (3 ft) deep. A relatively large mound, 21–24 m (70 by 80 ft) in diameter and about 4 m (12 ft) in height, had been erected on top of the outer wall and was extended into the ditch. The Salisbury brothers reported that excavations into the center of this mound "disclosed several human skeletons together with burnt stone, charcoal and ashes" (1862: 24). Although the enclosures and ditch have been almost entirely obliterated, the mound has been preserved. This site appears to represent a set of Adena circular earthworks upon which a subsequent group built a conical mound, perhaps as a way of appropriating the site.

The most prominent earthwork of the Raccoon Creek valley is the Granville Circle (Bushnell Fort 2), with its associated arcuate wall, known as the Hill Earthwork (Bushnell 1889: 11–12; Hill 1881: 426–427; Hooge 1993: 84–87). The Granville Circle is shown on Squier and Davis's map of the Newark Valley (Figure 4.1), but their accompanying description says only that it is "a large and beautiful circular work" (1848: 99). Bushnell (1889) identifies it as his Fort 2 and states it was 60 rods (302 m) in diameter.

The Hill Earthwork was an earthen wall that extended 986 m (2,250 ft) from the Granville Circle across the Raccoon Creek floodplain to a large crescent-shaped mound located at the base of the northern bluffs that frame the valley (Hooge 1993: 85). The Crescent Mound was a large earthwork 50 m (165 ft) in length and 30 m (99 ft) wide "composed largely of gravel" (Hill 1881 46). Although it had been "plowed over for fifty or more years," it was about 2 m (6 or 7 ft) high when studied by Hill. Bushnell stated that a "large quadrangular stone two or three feet across and sinking deep into the earth" projected from the north side of this embankment (1889: 12).

Bushnell reported that a set of parallel walls was located southwest of the Granville Circle. Hooge rediscovered these features on a 1940 aerial photograph (1993: 93–94). They were 38 m (125 ft) apart and extended from the base of the circle to the northwest "toward a meander of Raccoon Creek for approximately 250 feet [76 m]" (Hooge 1993: 94). Parallel walls are almost exclusively associated with Middle Woodland architecture, suggesting the complex consisting of the Granville Circle, the Crescent Mound, the Hill Earthwork, and the Parallel Wall was built by the Hopewell culture. The Bushnell Circle (Bushnell's Fort 3) was 151 m (495 ft) in diameter and enclosed 3 ha (8 acres) (Bushnell 1889: 11, 13; Hooge 1993: 94). It appears to have been a typical Adena culture circular earthwork.

The Granville Fort Hill (33LI6), or Bushnell's Fort 1, was situated on a prominent south-facing hilltop overlooking Raccoon Creek. Although Bushnell

(1889) depicted this hilltop enclosure as a circular earthwork, it was mapped more accurately by Squier and Davis as heart-shaped (1848: Plate IX, no. 1). According to Bushnell it was 59 rods (297 m) in diameter. Its walls varied in height from 2 m up to a maximum of 3 m (8–10 ft), as measured from the bottom of its outer ditch (Squier and Davis 1848: 24). Within the enclosure, on the highest ground in the interior, was a small, circular earthwork 31 m (100 ft) in diameter with a gateway facing to the east. There were two mounds within the small circle and a third "truncated mound" to the north (Squier and Davis 1848: 24). Moorehead (1886: 297) claimed that the two mounds were conjoined and constituted "an effigy mound in the shape of a butterfly, or double bladed mace," 12 m (40 ft) long by 5.5 m (18 ft) wide. Squier and Davis reported that excavations within the mounds disclosed "altars" that were "covered with ashes, intermixed with small fragments of pottery" (1848: 24). The Ohio Archaeological Inventory identifies this enclosure as a Middle Woodland site, probably because of the presence of the so-called altars, but the small circular enclosure with an eastward facing opening also would be consistent with Adena culture architecture. E. F. Appy (1887) conducted excavations into one of the mounds within this enclosure and claimed to have "exhumed the entire skeleton of a bison . . . in a good state of preservation" (Appy 1887: 1; see also Moorehead 1892: 19). Bison burials are recorded in Late Woodland or Late Prehistoric mounds in Minnesota (Wilford 1970: vi–vii, 2; Wilford, Johnson, and Vicinus 1969: 42), but no other such occurrence has been reported in Ohio. Since the bones recovered by Appy were neither preserved nor illustrated, their identification as bison is open to question. Bushnell (1889: 11, 13) documented a circular enclosure (Fort 4) with a diameter of 60 m (198 ft) on a hilltop almost directly across the valley from the Granville Fort Hill enclosure. Hooge (1993: 99) identified traces of a circle at this location in a 1940 aerial photograph and designated it the Munson Enclosure. It is likely either an Adena or a Hopewell earthwork.

In 1829, Chidlaw produced a map of a subrectangular enclosure with a small, circular earthwork in the center indicating only that it was located "near Granville Ohio" (Chidlaw 1829). Squier and Davis (1848) show a similarly shaped enclosure as a "Fortified Hill" immediately south of Granville (Figure 4.1). Bushnell's (1889: 11) map plots a roughly circular enclosure (Fort 5) in this location and indicates it was 60 m (198 ft) in diameter. Hooge (1993: 81) identified the site in a 1930 series aerial photograph and visited the location. He determined that Chidlaw's description was substantially correct (Hooge 1993: 81). The small circular enclosure with its eastward facing opening is suggestive of an Adena cultural affiliation.

The enigmatic "Salt Wall" (33LI1043) is a 150-m remnant of an arcuate earthwork south of Raccoon Creek along the west bank of Salt Run. Mickelson (2000) suggested it was Woodland in age, but its affiliation and purpose remain uncertain. According to Squier and Davis there were "numerous mounds upon the hilltops and in the valley" of Raccoon Creek (Squier and Davis 1848: 99; see also Unzicker 1860). Their map of six miles of the Newark Valley (Figure 4.1), however, shows only "a small proportion of the mounds occurring with this range" (Squier and Davis 1848: 101; see also Moorehead 1892: 16, 19). Only a few of these mounds have survived. Most were dug into by treasure seekers or plowed over by farmers and generally little information was recorded on what they may have contained. Many of them probably were Early Woodland burial mounds, but a particular mound might have been Early, Middle, or Late Woodland, or even Late Prehistoric in age.

Bushnell claimed that "a dozen or more [mounds] used to lie in the vicinity of the crescent and its connected works" (1889: 14), but his map shows only six. This constellation of earthworks suggests something similar to the cluster of Early Woodland earthworks at The Plains in Athens County (Squier and Davis 1848: Plate XXII; Skinner 1985). Clay (1998) persuasively has suggested that such prominent clusters of mortuary and ritual structures represent "the archaeological expressions of negotiations between groups" (1998: 16).

In 1836, the Calliopean Society of the Granville Literary and Theological Institution excavated half of the conical mound located along Raccoon Creek northwest of the Octagon earthworks (Figure 4.3). This Adena burial mound was 4 m (14 ft) high and the excavated portion yielded five or six burials, "each in distinct layers of earth" and "disposed in conical form, one above the other" (Lepper 1991: 6). Among the artifacts found with the burials was a tubular pipe, a characteristic Adena artifact.

Appy excavated several mounds in the Raccoon Creek valley during the late nineteenth century (Moorehead 1892: 18–19), but the results of only one of these investigations were published. The Sherman mound (33LI1045) is located about 1.6 km (1 mile) southwest of Granville on "a ridge commanding a beautiful view of the Raccoon valley and the surrounding country" (Appy 1887: 1; see Bushnell's map [1889: 11]). It was about 19 m (62 ft) in diameter and approximately 3 m (10 ft) in height. Appy excavated a portion of the mound and uncovered a central burial chamber made from clay containing the remains of an individual "lying on his back, with arms extended. The head toward the west . . . and his hands pointing north and south" (1887: 1). Artifacts found with this person included a necklace of "fresh water pearl shells," two flint spear points, a triangular slate pendant, a bone awl, a "thin plate of iron" (probably copper, but possibly meteoric iron), and several bear bones (Appy 1887: 1).[6] Appy uncovered 12 additional sets of human remains, including six skeletons reportedly buried "in a sitting posture" near the northern margin of the mound (1887: 1). These facts, if accurately reported, suggest a Middle Woodland mortuary facility with possibly Late Woodland burials added at a later time.

Deeds Mound is located on a high point overlooking the Raccoon Creek valley just west of the Munson enclosure (Beers 1866: 26; Mills 1914: 45; Hooge 1993: 100–102). Excavations in the 1930s produced a bowl made from a human skull, considered by Webb and Baby (1957: 23–24) to be a diagnostic Adena artifact. An obsidian bladelet core was recovered from a bundle burial deposited into the top of the mound (Hooge 1993: 101). Therefore, this would seem to be an Adena mound that continued to be used as a mortuary facility into the Middle Woodland period.[7]

The Licking County Archaeology and Landmarks Society discovered a small mound at the Munson Springs site east of Granville (Frolking and Lepper 2001; Lepper and Gill 1991; Reustle 1993). Charcoal from the base of the mound yielded two virtually identical radiocarbon dates of 2445 ± 60 years B.P. (Beta-34437/ETH-6064) and 2445 ± 65 years B.P. (AA-5061), indicating the initial construction episode was during the early Early Woodland period. A complex succession of layers subsequently was added culminating in a layer of fire cracked rock deposited on the eastern flank of the mound, evidently during the Middle Woodland period as some diagnostic Hopewell artifacts were recovered from this stratum.

Alligator Mound is an animal effigy mound situated on a low but prominent bluff that projects into the valley east of Granville (Figure 4.5). Traditionally, it has been considered to be a Middle Woodland mound based solely on its proximity to the Newark Earthworks, but radiocarbon dates along with other data indicate it was built during the Late Prehistoric era (Lepper and Frolking 2003). The builders of Alligator Mound therefore appear deliberately to have situated this remarkable effigy in a landscape already saturated with ancient ritual architecture.

Moorehead (1892) described several large "village sites" in the Raccoon Creek valley. Although the ages of these apparent habitation sites are not known, Moorehead observed that the material recovered from the surface at two of the locations was "largely similar in character" to the "contents of the mounds" in the vicinity (1892: 19).

The Licking County Archaeology and Landmarks Society and the Ohio State University investigated the Murphy site (33LI212) in the 1980s (Dancey 1991). It is primarily a Middle Woodland residential site and one of the most comprehensively studied in Ohio (Dancey 1991: 68). It is located north of Raccoon Creek on an outwash terrace near the base of the bedrock bluffs to the

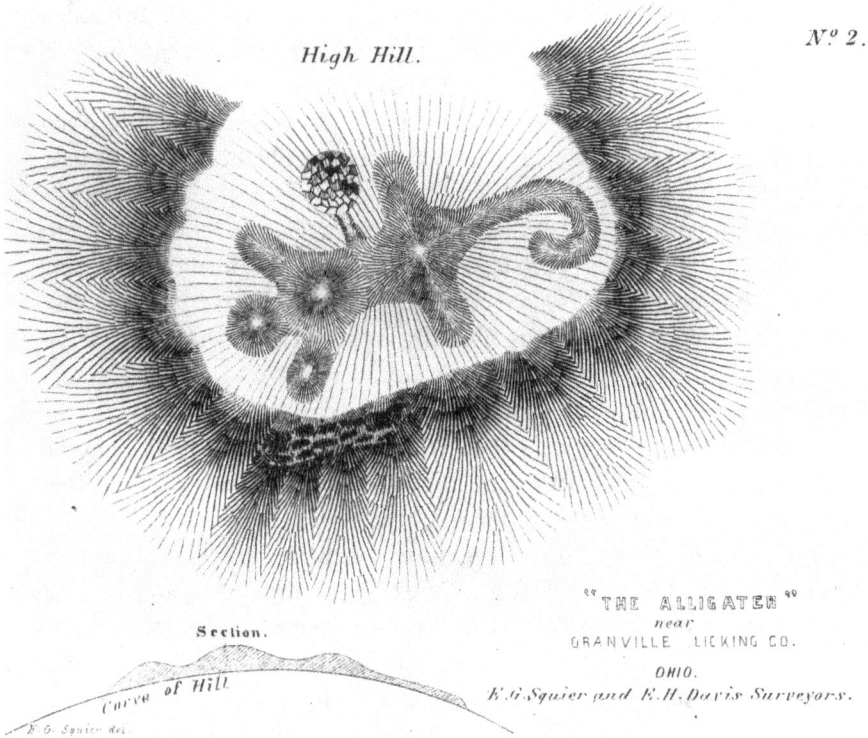

Figure 4.5. Map of the "Alligator" earthwork, Licking County, Ohio (from Squier and Davis 1848: 99).

north. The site is 3.1 km (2 miles) east of the Octagon earthworks (Figure 4.3). The Murphy site covered an area of about 1 ha and included 43 cultural features including post molds, hearths, earth ovens, and a variety of pits and basins distributed more or less in discrete food processing, structure, open yard, and refuse zones. Four radiocarbon dates were obtained on wood charcoal: 2040 ± 110 B.P. (Beta-15267), 1890 ± 110 B.P. (Beta-16619), 1760 ± 60 B.P. (Beta-16620), and 1740 ± 60 B.P. (Beta-16621) (Dancey 1991: 49). A fifth date of 1820 ± 80 years B.P. was obtained on carbon residue from pottery sherds. More than 18,000 lithic items were collected, including bladelet cores, bladelets, and other tools. The ceramic assemblage from Murphy includes only 858 sherds, which Carr and Hass (1996: 29) suggest might derive from only 10 to 20 broken pots. Dancey (1991: 67) interprets the Murphy site as a permanent habitation that was occupied for nearly 100 years. However, Carr and Haas (1996: 29) and Yerkes (1990) propose that the site represents a number of overlapping short-term occupations.

Pacheco (1997) intensively surveyed a 50 ha (124 acres) tract of land that included the Murphy site. He identified four dense clusters of artifacts and five low-density artifact clusters. The former he interpreted as small Hopewell hamlets like the Murphy site (Murphy I). These included Murphy III, Murphy IV, Murphy V, and Murphy VI. He suggested the low-density clusters of material were special purpose sites or activity areas possibly related to the more permanent occupations.

The J. J. Substanley site (33LI233) corresponds to Pacheco's Murphy IV site. It is a multicomponent site with a substantial Middle Woodland component, including fragments of a tetrapod ceramic vessel, quartz crystal, and numerous bladelets, many of which are made from Wyandotte chert. This site represented something of an anomaly in Pacheco's survey. It was the largest cluster, yet it yielded "the lowest estimated artifact density of any of the clusters" (Pacheco 1997: 48). I have suggested elsewhere that this site might represent a temporary encampment of a group of pilgrims from the Wyandotte chert source area that was visiting the Newark Earthworks (Lepper 2006: 128).

The Field Site 1 (33LI851) is a single component, Middle Woodland habitation site located south of Raccoon Creek across from the Granville Circle (Weller Von Molsdorff 1998). A Phase I archaeological survey recovered numerous bladelets, three bladelet cores, one leaf-shaped biface, four ceramic sherds, a pitted stone, and abundant fire-cracked rock.

The Newark Earthworks as a Ritual Machine

> Much Indian knowledge involved the technique of reproducing the cosmos in miniature and invoking spiritual change, which would be followed by physical change. Hardly a tribe exists that did not construct its dwellings after some particular model of the universe. The principle involved was that whatever is above must be reflected below. This principle enabled the people to correlate their actions with the larger movements of the universe. Wherever possible the larger cosmos was represented and reproduced to provide a context in which ceremonies could occur. Thus, people did not feel alone; they participated in cosmic rhythms. (Deloria 2001: 25–26)

It is obvious that the Newark Earthworks were built in the shapes of various geometrical figures. The sophistication of the underlying geometry is, however, not so obvious (Hively and Horn 1982 and this volume, Marshall 1996, Romain 2000, and Volker 2004). For example, the distance from the center of the Great Circle to the center of the Observatory Circle is precisely six times the diameter of the Observatory Circle (Hively and Horn [1982: S8] refer to this fundamental unit as the "OCD" measure, i.e., the Observatory Circle Diameter); the distance from the center of the Octagon to the center of the square also is six times the OCD; and the distance from the center of Observatory Mound to the center of the Octagon is two times the OCD (Hively and Horn 1982: S8–9). These examples relate simply to linear measurement. There are other, more esoteric geometric principles encoded into this architecture. The circumference of the Great Circle is equal to the perimeter of the square (Romain 2000: 40). In classical geometry, such a correspondence is an example of rectifying the circumference (Volker 2004). It is not exceedingly difficult to execute, but it reflects the establishment of an intentional geometric relationship between the two figures. According to Romain (2000: 41), this is "the only Hopewell example of its kind." And other geometric correspondences tie the Newark enclosures together even more closely. The area of the square is equal to the area of the Observatory Circle and a hypothetical square with sides equal to the diameter of the Observatory Circle, which would in fact circumscribe it, would have an area equal to the area of the Great Circle (Hively and Horn 1982: S8). Such a square may not be so hypothetical because it corresponds to the square formed by connecting four alternate corners of the Octagon. It may have been the underlying geometrical figure from which the Octagon was derived (Hively and Horn 1982: S8). As John Volker (2004:32) has expressed it, the "Octagon circumscribes the square which in turn circumscribes the Observatory Circle." These area correspondences exemplify the geometrical conundrum referred to as "squaring the circle," which is much more difficult to accomplish than simply rectifying the circumference (Volker 2004; see also Romain 2000: 197). In a similar vein, the Octagon is precisely double the area of the Observatory Circle and the parallel-walled avenue that connects them (Hively and Horn 1982: S20). Civil engineer James Marshall surveyed a large number of Hopewellian earthworks and believed he identified "cryptographic" geometric forms that underlie this architecture. He argued that a line drawn from the center of the Great Circle to the center of the Octagon formed the hypotenuse of a 3-4-5 right-angled triangle the other sides of which are defined by the cardinal directions (Marshall 1996: 12). Once again, these correspondences establish a definite, if somewhat more esoteric, relationship between the various enclosures.

These many interrelationships demonstrate that the principal elements of the Newark Earthworks are systematically integrated and are not simply independent structures tacked onto one another more or less haphazardly. The geometry of the site bespeaks a coherent and intentional design, but more than geometry ties the site plan together. The architecture of the Newark Earthworks also incorporates alignments that define the 18.6-year-long cycle of moonrises and moonsets (Hively and Horn 1982, 2006a). Hively and Horn (1982) determined that the main symmetry axis of the Newark Octagon is aligned to the northernmost rising of the moon. Other earthwork alignments mark the southernmost moonrise, the northern minimum moonrise, the southern minimum moonrise, and the four corresponding moonsets. Hively and Horn (1982) also claim that the walls framing the gateway of the Great Circle are oriented to the minimum northern moonrise. Moreover, Hively and Horn (1982: S9, S15) showed that the axis of the Great Circle's gateway is parallel displaced from the corresponding axis of the Observatory Circle along a mean azimuth that corresponds to the maximum southern moonrise. The displacement of the square with respect to the Octagon is similarly aligned to the minimum southern moonrise. Finally, Hively and Horn (1982: S17) assert that the alignment extending from the western corner of the square to the eastern corner marks the rising of the moon at the midpoint in the lunar cycle, and the parallel walls that connect the square enclosure with the Octagon were aligned, where they entered the square, to the minimum northern moonset. While they found "no convincing evidence" for any solar alignments at Newark and did not consider possible stellar alignments (1982: S11), Romain (2004a: 117), on the other hand, claimed the east-west axis of the square was aligned to the equinox sunrise and that it shares this alignment with the Liberty Square in Ross County. He also asserted the symmetry axis of the Great Circle is aligned to the heliacal rise of the Pleiades star cluster but acknowledged that "the intentionality of that alignment is less than certain."

The many astronomical alignments encoded in the structure of the Newark Earthworks, and their predominantly lunar emphasis, corroborate the idea that the several enclosures were designed and built as a distinct and unified architectural composition. The integration of geometry and astronomy in this architecture, combined with the functional differentiation of the various components and their distribution across the broad expanse of the glacial terrace, suggest to me that the Newark Earthworks were built according to a design conceived by an individual or a small group of people. Given what we know about the social structure of the Hopewell peoples in this region (see, for example, Seeman 2004: 58–61), it seems unlikely that this person or group, however influential they may have been while they lived, had any way of ensuring that such an ambitious project could be sustained much beyond their deaths. If this inference is correct, the construction must have been completed within the lifetimes of at least some of the individuals who originally conceived the design. In the absence of an hereditary leadership with authority over subsidiary social classes, I am not aware of any sociocultural mechanisms for effectively sustaining a multigenerational effort of such magnitude (cf. Gibson 2004).

Greber (1997a) asserts that the many and various components of the large monumental earthworks, such as Newark's, were not coeval: "In determining the true human scale probably represented by such sites, we must consider pace" (1997: 209). It is, indeed, prudent to consider the possibility that such sites are products of a series of contingent historical events and that what we see in the maps of Squier and Davis (and others) is the end result of a prolonged process of accretionary development. Intensive archaeological efforts by Essenpreis, Connolly, and others at Fort Ancient (see Connolly and Lepper 2004) and by Riordan (1995) at the Pollock Works have demonstrated that these sites, at least, changed significantly through time as new architectural components were added. Nevertheless, I suggest it would be a mistake to assume that all large sites must have been built in this way.

Byers (1987, 2004) and others have proposed that the Great Circle, with its interior ditch, was an Adena enclosure and that it was the first of the major elements to be built at Newark. The Great Circle does conform to the architectural canons of Byers's Mt. Horeb tradition (2004: 28), but the antiquity of the structure has not been determined.[8] In spite of the Great Circle's apparent Adena affinities, its architectural relationships to the other elements of the Newark Earthworks suggest that it is likely to have been built by the Hopewell culture. Similarly, Byers (2004: 98) also has claimed the many small circular enclosures at Newark are Adena "sacred circles" that predate the grander Hopewellian constructions. Most of these circular works, however, are closely associated with the network of parallel walls that certainly are Hopewell features and which, regardless, must postdate the principal enclosures they link together (Figure 4.2). Such seemingly anachronistic architectural elements may reflect a conscious retention of conservative architectural canons, or they may represent a deliberate revival of archaic earthwork forms. As Kubler (1962: 4) has written, "Style describes a specific figure in space better than a type of existence in time."

The scale and the degree of geometric and astronomical integration of the Newark Earthworks are unprecedented in the Hopewell world. The evidence for an integrated design suggests to me that the Newark Earthworks constituted some sort of device with a specific purpose. Given the astronomical and/ or cosmological implications of the earthworks and their clear association with mortuary activities, that purpose must have been related primarily to ritual (Anschuetz, Wilshusen, and Scheick 2001: 179). I argue that the functionally differentiated earthworks, such as the Cherry Valley burial mounds, the Great

Circle with its central Big House, and the astronomically aligned Octagon, all interconnected by a network of ritual conduits, represent the integrated components of a monumental ritual machine.[9] This was not just some kind of three-dimensional representation of the cosmos; it was an engine of ritual, built to do something, to achieve some momentous end possibly, but not exclusively, related to world renewal (Byers 2004: 78–79; Carr 2008a: 632–634; Romain 2004a). Determining more specifically the intended function of the Newark Earthworks may be difficult, since so many of its component parts have been damaged or destroyed, but important clues surely lie in the physical remnants of the remaining earthworks and, perhaps, in surviving oral traditions that may be remnants of the intangible ideology behind the labyrinthine geometry.

The Newark Earthworks were the dominant feature of the Raccoon Creek valley. They occupied a broad, roughly triangular section of outwash terrace at the confluence of Raccoon Creek with the South Fork of the Licking River (Figure 4.3). The main components of the site were framed by streams and the earthworks, in turn, surrounded a large pond (Lepper 2004a). Raccoon Creek defined the northern boundary of the complex, the South Fork of the Licking River determined the eastern perimeter, and Ramp Creek ran along the southern and southwestern edges of this "remarkable plain" (Figure 4.3). An examination of the Salisbury map (Figure 4.2), the most comprehensive map of the Newark Earthworks so far documented, shows that the principal ways of gaining access to the enclosures were along the three parallel-walled passages leading from each of these surrounding waterways. This simply may be an indication that streams and rivers provided a primary route of travel to the site. Ramp Creek, however, is a short, local tributary of the South Fork with its headwaters in the hills to the west. Such a small stream could not have been a major transportation artery, so it may be that the three sets of parallel walls were more than simple access roads for visitors arriving via canoe.

In the cosmology of many Eastern Woodlands Indian tribes, the universe is composed of three layers: the celestial "Above World," the "Middle World" in which we normally live, and a "Beneath World" or Underwater World upon which the disk of the Middle World floats (Lankford 2004: 208; Reilly 2004: 126–128; see also Hudson 1976; Lankford 1987; Vecsey 1983). Streams, springs, and ponds provided links to the powerful energies of the Beneath World. Thus if this or a related cosmology were in operation 2,000 years ago, and there is compelling archaeological evidence to suggest that it was (e.g., Brown 1997; DeBoer 1997; Hall 1997; Penney 1985), the Newark Earthworks would have been linked to the Beneath World by the three ritual conduits that connected the earthworks to each of the surrounding water sources (Lepper 2004a).

Possible connections between Newark's earthworks and the Above World are more subtle but equally integral to the architecture. The alignments framing the 18.6-year lunar cycle were built into the Observatory Circle and Octagon as well as other earthwork elements. The Newark Earthworks, therefore, may be viewed as a geomantically forged link between the three layers of the Eastern Woodland Indian cosmos. Perhaps its machinery was intended to facilitate shamanic travel or communication between those worlds.

Seeman (2004: 68) stated that the earthworks of the Ohio Hopewell culture represented "'cosmic centers' for ritual performance." The "cosmic" significance of Newark's earthworks is evident from the astronomical alignments woven into the warp and woof of the structure, and the giant enclosures do appear to be monumental stages for grand ritual theater. Certainly they were not built for small groups of people in which to perform intimate ceremonies (although groups of varying size could have used the facilities once they had been built [Carr 2008a: 255–264]). Bernardini (2004: 350) argued that Hopewellian earthworks "enclose spaces so large as to be socially unusable." He estimated that sites such as Newark's Great Circle "could have held more than 280,000 people" (2004: 350) and concluded that such improbably vast congregations never actually assembled at these places. Instead, he suggested that the most important event in the "life history" of the largest enclosures, "and the most important experience of a participant, was the act of construction" (2004: 350).

Although the enclosures indeed are built to a seemingly cyclopean scale, Benardini's estimate of congregation size is not realistic. He came up with such a large number by using cross-cultural data suggesting that each 1 m^2 of interior space would have contained one person (2004: 350). There are two things wrong with applying such an equation to the Hopewellian enclosures. First, it assumes the enclosures were devoid of structures such as wooden frame buildings. This certainly was not the case for sites such as Seip (Baby and Langlois 1979). Second, it assumes that "participants" were relatively passive and stationary occupants of their assigned square meter of space, much like a worshipper in a church pew or a fan at a sports stadium. It is much more likely that people actively moved through these spaces in ceremonial processions and dances. For example, these expansive ritual stages may have been used for large dance formations of men who, in a manner similar to the Tsembaga studied by Rappaport (1968, 1971), displayed their vigor and wealth to potential mates. Their health and vigor would be evident in their performance in the dance, whereas their wealth would be "signaled by the richness of a man's shell and feather finery" (Rappaport 1971: 62). Such massed dancing also would communicate information about the relative sizes of participating groups to potential rivals and allies (Rappaport 1971). Thus while Bernardini probably is correct in concluding that Hopewellian enclosures were not amphitheaters or churches with a single, centrally located stage or pulpit, I suggest he is wrong to conclude that they must then have been kinds of performance art that once built were more or less immediately abandoned.

Bernardini analyzed the time and labor necessary to construct the Hopewellian earthworks and concluded they "could not have been built exclusively by the people living in close proximity to them" (2004: 348). "Thus, the gathering of people to construct an earthwork was not *experienced* by participants as the aggregation of a dispersed community, but instead as the assembly of a much wider social network" (2004: 349). I suggest this wider social network did not just participate in the construction of an earthwork but also viewed it as a ritual nexus to which adherents would return periodically at significant times in the life of the extended community. The Newark Earthworks, simply by virtue of their monumental size, would have become a powerful spiritual magnet for people who shared aspects of the ideology represented by its architecture. According to Preston (1992: 33), "Spiritual magnetism derives from human concepts and values, via historical, geographical, social and other forces that coalesce in a sacred center."

The Newark Earthworks as a Pilgrimage Center

The Creek oral history repeatedly mentions that the Creeks traditionally went north to special mounds for pilgrimages in spring and autumn.

(Chaudhuri and Chaudhuri 2001: 9)

The spiritual magnetism exerted by the Newark Earthworks, the preeminent architectural monument of its age, would have drawn pilgrims from the ends of the Hopewell world. Elsewhere I have argued that the parallel walls that extended to the southwest from the Octagon constituted a "Great Hopewell Road" connecting the Newark Earthworks with the center of Hopewell culture near modern Chillicothe (Lepper 1998: 2006). Similar long, straight roads are associated with other North and South American cultures (Trombold 1991). The best documented are the Anasazi roads of Chaco Canyon and the *sacbeob* of the Maya. In the case of the Maya, there is reliable native testimony as to the purpose of these roads. In 1688, Diego Lopez Cogolludo reported that "there are remains of paved highways which traverse all this kingdom and they say they ended in the east on the seashore . . . so that they might arrive at Cozumel for the fulfillment of their vows, to offer their sacrifice, to ask for help in their needs, and for the mistaken adoration of their false gods" (Tozzer 1941: 109). A similar function for the Chacoan roads is supported by "the use of constructed roads as sacred pilgrimage avenues by historic and modern Puebloan peoples" (Marshall 1997: 71).

The linkages between the Hopewell culture and the groups historically associated with the Ohio Valley are not as strong as they are for the Anasazi and the modern Puebloan tribes, and few documented oral traditions can be shown to relate unambiguously to the ancient earthworks and mounds. There are, however, ethnohistorically documented traditions from some Eastern Woodlands tribes that appear to echo salient elements of the Mayan statements regarding the sacred nature of the straight roads and the pilgrimage centers with which they are associated.[10] The Creek Indians have oral traditions of traveling northward on "spiritual journeys," or seasonal pilgrimages, to "special mounds" in Ohio (Chaudhuri and Chaudhuri 2001: 9, 135). Moreover, the Creeks affirm that mounds were important for "observation and ritual interactions with the cosmos" (Chaudhuri and Chaudhuri 2001: 6) and that "Creek stargazers, astronomers, or *miccos*" paid particular attention to the moon and its cycles (Chaudhuri and Chaudhuri 2001: 10):[11] "In Creek beliefs when the 'wedding' of the moon and the sun takes place every eighteen years, a new set of spirits is created which invigorates the earth under the blessings of the seven *miccos* of the Pleiades. It is in these eighteen-year adjustments that the creative 'miracles' of new spirits and energies are infused in nature and in human societies and cycles" (Chaudhuri and Chaudhuri 2001: 11).[12]

The Rev. Albert Seqaqknind Anthony, a Delaware Indian, told anthropologist Daniel Brinton that "in the good old times," before any European had landed on their shores, the Lenape had "a string of white wampum beads . . . which stretched from the Atlantic to the Pacific, and on this *white road* their envoys traveled from one great ocean to the other, safe from attack" (Brinton 1890: 188; emphasis added). It is interesting to note that the Mayan word for their sacred roads is *sacbe*, which means "white road." The Maya use the same word to indicate the Milky Way, which the Delaware and other Eastern Woodland tribes similarly refer to as the "White Path" (Speck 1915, 1931). It is, therefore, plausible to infer that the Lenape "white road" might refer to the same sort of long, straight "white roads" used by the Maya for making pilgrimages to their holy places and that such roads were the principal avenues by which far-faring pilgrims would approach Ohio's sacred centers.

Although plausible, it may be impossible to know whether these fragments of oral traditions provide any meaningful insight into the historic American Indian understanding of the function of the ancient earthworks, to say nothing of the meaning these sites held for their builders. Nevertheless, my appeal to them is at least an attempt to take the evidence of oral traditions seriously

(Echo-Hawk 2000; cf. Mason 2000). Turner has written that "pilgrimages are liminal phenomena" (1974: 166) and the pilgrimage center "represents a threshold, a place and moment 'in and out of time'" (1974: 197). Pilgrims traveling on the Great Hopewell Road and gathering at Newark, perhaps to celebrate some rite of passage, fulfill a vow, offer a sacrifice, or participate in the construction of a mound, would experience, according to Turner, a sense of communitas or sublime unity with those with whom the mystery was shared. This may have been one of the most important social functions of sites such as Newark, although Byers (2004: 7) believes it was an unintended consequence of "the exercise of the collective intentions, duties, and beliefs that brought about the construction of these monuments." Sallnow (1981) argued that communitas may not be an inevitable consequence of gatherings at pilgrimage centers. He concluded, based on a study of Andean pilgrimage, that pilgrimage centers do not create communitas, but simply provide "a setting in which social interactions can take place ex novo" (1981: 180). For the people that Sallnow studied, group pilgrimage "is a complex mosaic of egalitarianism, nepotism and factionalism, of brotherhood, competition and conflict" (1981: 176).

Regardless of whether any sort of spiritual *communitas* was achieved or even desired, "the symbiotic linking of pilgrimage, periodic festivals, and entrepreneurial activity provides a means for the integration of an extended population" (Malville and Malville 2001: 339). This social integration must have been linked to the construction of the earthworks as Bernardini suggests, but it didn't end with their construction. The continuing periodic performance of rituals at this site would have reinforced "the cognitive and emotional substrates of individual commitment to group ideals and values . . . [and] the willingness to perform costly religious behaviors," such as the building of the earthworks and the transport of magnificent offerings to this ritual center, would be reliable signals of "beliefs and commitment to the group" (Sosis and Alcorta 2003: 267). More fundamentally, the long-term (18.6-year) ritual cycle inferred for the periodic use of the Newark Earthworks and other Hopewellian earthworks (e.g., Hively and Horn 1980, 1984, this volume) may have served to articulate local and regional cultural systems with each other and with their environment. Rappaport (1968: 224; see also 1971: 60) argued that such a ritual cycle among the Tsembaga of New Guinea helped to "maintain an undegraded biotic environment," limited warfare to frequencies that did not endanger the survival of the regional population, and facilitated trade.

Finally, such pilgrimages may have played a role in the rise of sociopolitical complexity in the region that would culminate in the chiefdoms of the Late Prehistoric period. According to Helms (1979: 161), early Spanish records relating to the indigenous societies of Colombia note that they exchanged a variety of goods at periodic festivals or markets. Helms infers that these gatherings were held at "political-religious centers or perhaps recognized places of pilgrimage." The people who traveled great distances to participate in these events did so, at least in part, to obtain esoteric knowledge along with the exotic items, which would signal the elevated status of those pilgrims who had completed the great "Hadj." The spiritual power individuals accrued in this way, thus could translate into a measure of sociopolitical power.

Conclusion

> While stands the Coliseum, Rome shall stand.
> (Lord Byron, *Childe Harold's Pilgrimage*, 1812–18)

Greber (2003: 88) has observed that over centuries "people transformed the natural environment of the Hopewell valleys into a unique planned landscape." The Raccoon Creek valley is one example of such a region transformed into a landscape of ceremony. The Newark Earthworks complex is, in Byers's terms, "a monumental iconic warrant constructed in order to embody the totality of the cosmos" as conceived by the American Indians of the Eastern Woodlands (2004: 101).[13] The occurrence of Middle Woodland habitation sites throughout the valley indicates this landscape was not restricted solely to ceremonial pursuits. The monumental earthen architecture dominates the archaeological record, however, and would have dominated the experience of native peoples moving through this valley from the Middle Woodland period through the historic era. If we view the Newark Earthworks and similar sites simply as sets of large enclosures and the spaces enclosed by them, the lack of evidence for extensive habitations therein might allow us to conclude that these places were "vacant" ceremonial centers. When such sites are placed within the context of the cultural landscapes they helped to create, however, the notion that they were, in any important sense, "vacant" becomes untenable. The documented habitation sites, such as the Murphy cluster and Hale's House site, are embedded in the ceremonial landscape. The Newark Earthworks complex was not an urban center, but neither was it a sacred no-man's land devoid of habitations. I agree with Buikstra and others who have called for the development of "a perspective that de-emphasizes partitions between economic, ritual, and other behaviors" (Buikstra, Charles, and Rakita 1998: 4; see also Greber 1997a: 211). Byers's (2004) Proscriptive/Prescriptive Ecological Strategy model for the Ohio Hopewell represents an important step forward in this regard.

American Indian cultural landscapes were not confined to the manageable limits of European American mapping conventions and standard archaeological surveys (see Cowan, Sunderhaus, and Genheimer 2004). The Hopewell culture, in particular, created a ceremonial landscape of unprecedented scope. The map I present of the Newark Earthworks and its environs (Figure 4.3) is an improvement on some more restrictive views of Hopewell cultural geography, but the rectangular boundaries of this map are every bit as arbitrary as the maps of Atwater (1820) and Squier and Davis (1848). Hively and Horn (this volume) suggest the ceremonial landscape fashioned by the architects of the Newark Earthworks was even vaster than what I have suggested here, an assertion that is corroborated by the observation that, whatever their ultimate length proves to be, the walls of the Great Hopewell Road extended well beyond even this map's margins.[14] Nevertheless, I offer the map as an attempt to present a more contextualized view of the Hopewellian cultural landscape in this region than has been presented heretofore.

The ceremonial landscape of the Raccoon Creek valley assuredly is not exclusively a Middle Woodland landscape; but the Hopewellian Newark Earthworks dominate the region. Early Woodland precursors were perched on more or less isolated hilltops or were clustered together in the more intimate confines of the valley. On the other hand, the integration of features, such as the small circular enclosures, typical of Adena architecture, with the quintessentially Hopewellian Newark Earthworks suggest a continuity of canons and traditions that make determinations of cultural affiliation on the basis of single traits problematic.[15] Sites such as the Salisbury brother's "Hill Fort No. 2," with its mound built apparently astride an Adena circular earthwork; the Deeds Mound, a possible Adena burial mound with a Hopewell burial added at a later time; and the Munson Springs mound, an Early Woodland structure partially covered by a mantle of Hopewell midden, suggest the Middle Woodland inhabitants of the valley made an effort to appropriate the existing monuments and to make them a functioning part of their contemporary ceremonial landscape. The Hill Earthwork may have been a Hopewellian attempt to incorporate the (possibly) Adena mound group into their active ceremonial landscape, or alternatively, it may have served to insulate the newly shaped sacred landscape from the remains of an earlier and somehow incompatible sacredness. Likewise, Alligator Mound may have been a Late Prehistoric attempt to neutralize, capitalize upon, or pay homage to the earthworks of the preceding eras. Kohler (1997: 19) observed that "forms of appropriation, or co-optation, are fundamental to the historical trajectories" of eastern North American indigenous groups and that it could be expected that such strategies "extend even further back in time." Newark's Great Circle may be another example of this strategy. It either was designed following architectural canons that harkened to an earlier age, or it was, as Byers suggested, the earliest large structure at the site. If the latter scenario is correct, then the Great Circle became the pivot around which Hopewellian architects laid out the other earthworks at Newark so as to fully incorporate this archaic element into a grand unified design. In either case, the Great Circle served to link the other components of the site to a living past.

Dillehay (1990) asserted that, for the South American Mapuche, ceremonial landscapes are not temporary or ephemeral configurations of built monuments and natural features, such as sacred streams and hills. Instead,

> Mapuche monuments are permanent ceremonial fields and earthen mounds where public activities are spatially located and anchored, and where kinship and other lineage relations are historically and continuously formed. As viable social places, these monuments do not just emerge temporarily out of a local group, go out of use, collapse, and, after their abandonment, become part of past lineage history. They contribute to local history in a specific spatial and temporal context through the perpetual and intergenerational creation and utility of particular geographical and ceremonial locations. Participation in group activities at these locations leads to the reinforcement of pan-Mapuche social, economic, and religious institutions (e.g., alliances, public ceremony, ancestral worship). (Dillehay 1990: 226)

Surely, this is more or less how the ceremonial landscape of the Raccoon Creek valley functioned and evolved from the earliest monuments of the Early Woodland to the occasional visits of historic American Indians, such as those the eighteenth-century frontiersman Simon Kenton reportedly witnessed at Fort Ancient (Moorehead 1908: 31).

The interpretations I have offered here are speculative, but they represent an attempt to view the several and varied earthworks of the Raccoon Creek valley as components of a ceremonial landscape with a history. Only further research at Newark and the few existing remnants of satellite works will resolve basic questions of chronology, which will provide a sound basis for moving forward with confidence to more interesting questions about these sites and the landscape they transformed. My idea that the Newark Earthworks were constructed within a single generation should be regarded as an "outrageous hypothesis" in the provocative sense in which this term was used by Davis (1926).[16] DeBoer (1997; this volume) and Hively and Horn (this volume) demonstrate a remarkable level of integration between the Hopewellian earthworks of the Scioto River and Paint Creek valleys. It is difficult to argue that it would have been humanly possible, even for these extraordinary societies, to construct all of this architecture within a single generation. So we must turn as well to the further exploration of social mechanisms whereby egalitarian peoples would find it useful or felicitous to link the monuments of preceding generations to their own, such that their final form and distribution produced a unitary cosmographic composition (see, for example, Clark 2004: 211–212 and Lekson 1999). "Beneficent obligation," as discussed by Gibson (2004), is a potentially powerful mechanism that I think will figure in the solution of this riddle, as will the strategies of appropriation and co-optation (see, for example, Kohler 1997). Certainly, these processes were at work in the larger context of the Middle Woodland Raccoon Creek valley, but the disparate elements of the Newark Earthworks proper seem to be so functionally specialized and so extraordinarily well integrated with one another and with their cultural landscape that I think a master plan must have guided its construction from the outset. The Newark Earthworks were a North American Kaaba, Sistine Chapel, and *Principia* all rolled into one. The spiritual magnetism generated here drew pilgrims from distant regions to share in the wonder of the place. The *communitas* they likely experienced, here and at the other great earthwork complexes, made them a part of something larger than themselves, something that archaeologists have recognized, if only through a glass darkly, and subsumed under the term "Hopewell."

There is a paradox at the heart of this chapter. On the one hand, I have attempted to show that the Newark Earthworks must be understood as part of a larger ceremonial landscape. On the other hand, I argue that the earthworks, as traditionally defined, do appear to constitute a discrete machine-like set of components. The resolution of the paradox lies in the recognition that places have a history and cultural landscapes are continuously evolving. The Newark Earthworks emerged from a unique cultural context, and once created, its presence had profound repercussions for all subsequent residents of and visitors to this valley. As Knapp and Ashmore (1999: 8–19) note, "We forget that a seemingly abandoned monument is still part of an active landscape. Ancient sites, monuments and even entire landscapes may be transformed and re-used as people encounter and interact with particular places, as they re-create the past (Bender, Hamilton, and Tilley 1997: 149)."

Acknowledgments

I extend my sincere appreciation to Martin Byers and DeeAnne Wymer for inviting me to participate in the original SAA symposium on which this volume is based, for graciously understanding why I could not, and for inviting me to submit this contribution to the published proceedings in spite of my absence from the symposium. I also thank them for their constructive criticisms of a previous draft of this paper.

I thank Tina Hartman Davis, ASC Group, Inc., for her assistance with drafting Figure 3 and to Shaun Skinner, ASC Group, Inc., for allowing Tina to work on this underfunded research project. Thanks also to Brent Eberhard, OHPO, for the OAI data, to John Volker for his invaluable insights on the Hopewellian geometry of Newark and for copies of, so far, unpublished manuscripts, and to Ray Hively and Robert Horn for the same privilege. Warren DeBoer drew my attention to several relevant ethnohistoric sources and has contributed much to my understanding of Hopewelliana. I extend special thanks to Jerry McDonald for the information about bison burials in Minnesota mounds. I also thank William Romain for presenting me with a copy of his unpublished dissertation and for providing comments on an early draft of this paper. Finally, I extend my thanks to Paul Hooge for his efforts to preserve and help us to understand the archaeology of the Raccoon Creek valley.

I dedicate this chapter to Mary Borgia, Linda Woolard, their fourth grade students at Newark's Miller Elementary School, and William Hughes, a retired teacher at Miller, for their passionate appreciation of the Newark Earthworks and for their efforts to translate that passion into action by initiating a bill in the Ohio legislature to have the Newark Earthworks recognized as the state's official prehistoric monument.

Notes

1. All radiocarbon dates reported in this paper are uncorrected and uncalibrated.

2. Romain (2005a) regards these mounds as likely Hopewell burial mounds and makes an interesting argument that the kame (Geller Hill) is integrated into the structure of the Newark Earthworks. I would argue, instead, that the burials associated with the kame relate to Late Archaic/Early Woodland burial practices and that this prominent topographic feature was regarded as part of the cultural landscape from an early period. The Hopewellian designers of the Newark Earthworks then may have anchored their architecture on this already sacred feature as a way of appropriating its power for new purposes (Kohler 1997).

3. Fowke (1902: 163) referred to numerous "lodge-sites" in association with Newark's "geometric figures," and local avocational archaeologist Jim Hahn (personal communication 1994) reported finding more or less extensive remains of Hopewell habitation material at various locations along the western banks of the South Fork of the Licking River southwest of the Great Circle.

4. The Sunkle cache, named for its discoverer Marie Sunkle, was on loan to the Ohio Historical Society and exhibited at the small museum in Newark until 2004, when Marie Sunkle rescinded the loan and sold the collection on eBay.

5. The dimensions of 33LI7 are based on Whittlesey's (1852: Plate V, no. 4) map. The Salisbury brothers' map (1862: Plate IX) differs significantly from Whittlesey's rendering. In the Salisbury map, the enclosure is nearly circular with its longest diameter, 644 ft (196 m), along the north-to-south axis. Whittlesey more correctly shows an ovate enclosure with its long axis oriented from east to west. On the other hand, the Salisbury map more accurately represents some features, such as a narrow ridge that gradually descends from a northeastern gateway in the enclosure to the river. The site currently is owned by the City of Heath.

6. Andrew Mickelson (personal communication 2006) has suggested that the extant mound, which is somewhat smaller than Appy's description, may not be the mound Appy excavated. Appy also discovered a stone engraved with the profile of an Indian with a feathered headdress in apparent association with the central burial at the Sherman Mound (Appy 1887: 1). This enigmatic artifact was a hoax planted in Appy's excavation by two boys, one of whom later confessed to the act (Jones 1935). His confession came long after Appy's death.

7. Discoveries of obsidian are not unknown for Early Woodland sites in eastern North America (see Stoltman and Hughes 2004), but flintknappers of the Adena culture are not known to have produced bladelet cores.

8. The radiocarbon date of 2110 ± 80 years B.P. (Beta-58449) does not provide an accurate measure of the age of the enclosure. The sample did not consist of charcoal from a cultural burning event, such as the clearing of the original forest. It was, instead, natural humates from the buried soil horizon on which the earthwork was built. Therefore, the date only establishes a *terminus post quem*. The actual construction may have begun a century or more later, and the original land-clearing activities may have begun millennia earlier.

9. I am aware that some regard the "machine" metaphor as inapt or at least infelicitous, evoking visions of Blake's "dark, Satanic mills." By using this metaphor, I intend only to convey a sense of disparate elements purposefully integrated to achieve some desired end. In a previous essay, I appear to have written that "the Newark Earthworks can be viewed not merely as arcane symbols built upon the landscape, but as a gigantic machine *or factory* in which energies from the three levels of the Eastern Woodland Indian's cosmos . . . were drawn together and circulated through conduits of ritual to accomplish some sacred purpose" (Lepper 2004a: 80; emphasis added). The extension of my metaphor from machine to "factory" was not mine. That phrase appears to have been added, without my knowledge or consent, by an editor of the volume. I disavow the use of the term "factory" in the context of my intended metaphor.

10. My references to the oral traditions of particular Eastern Woodland Indian tribes should in no way be read as a claim that these particular peoples are the sole modern heirs to the legacy of the Hopewell. It may not be possible to single out any particular modern group as the certain descendants of the Hopewell. Indeed, a recent study of mitochondrial DNA from the teeth of several individuals from the Hopewell Mound Group found genetic links between one or more of the individuals from the Hopewell site and tribes as culturally diverse and geographically widespread as the

Apache, Chippewa/Ojibwa, Iowa, Kickapoo, Micmac, Pawnee, Pima, Seri, Southwest Sioux, and Yakima (Mills 2003). These results are perfectly consistent with our understanding of gene flow (e.g., Rohde, Olson, and Chang 2004) and, moreover, might reflect the extent to which distant peoples came to Newark and related sites on pilgrimage, remaining at least long enough to exchange genes. Regardless, they demonstrate that no particular contemporary Native American tribe reasonably can claim any exclusivity with regard to biological and/or cultural links to the archaeologically defined Hopewell culture, while many disparate groups might be expected to retain some traditions relating to the societies we have lumped together under the "Hopewell" rubric (e.g., Hall 1997; cf. Mason 2000).

11. *Miccos* refer to headmen or leaders. Some Creek towns could have more than one *micco*.

12. This reference to the importance of the Pleiades for Creek astronomers casts Romain's assertion that Newark's Great Circle is aligned to the heliacal rising of this star cluster in a more favorable light. The 18-year cycle referred to here is the Saros eclipse cycle, not the 18.6-year Metonic cycle. Nevertheless, it documents a traditional interest in making observations of the moon over extended periods.

13. Byers (1987, 2004) presumably would disagree with the presumption that all aspects of the Hopewell world view are inaccessible to modern analysts. He has argued that the earthwork data can "serve as an expressive signature of the collective beliefs, duties, and intentions of the builders, and therefore, as a verifiable cultural entry into their social world" (2004: 7).

14. An argument could be made that many of the monumental Hopewellian earthworks of central and southern Ohio formed a continuous network of linked pilgrimage centers. DeBoer (1997), Hively and Horn (1984, personal communication 2004), Kennedy (1994), and Romain (2000, 2004a) have proposed various formal connections between widely dispersed Hopewellian earthworks. Byers (2004: 488, 624) inferred the existence of a Turner-Hopewell ideological axis that was the "complementary equivalent" of the "Chillicothe-Newark axis" embodied in the Great Hopewell Road (See Byers, this volume). Finally, there are suggestions that other Hopewell roads might have linked these and other earthwork centers (Lepper 2006): "Sing the benediction: More research is necessary" (Lekson 1999: 187).

15. Abrams and Freter (2005) assign the circular earthworks of the Plains, which appear to be typical "Adena" structures, to the Middle Woodland period.

16. Even more "outrageously," Clark (2004: 209) argues that the much older Archaic period earthwork sites, such as Watson Brake and Poverty Point, "were planned as totalities before they were built and that whole complexes were laid out and built according to master plans."

5

Hopewell Cosmography at Newark and Chillicothe, Ohio

Ray Hively and Robert Horn

The construction of large geometric earthworks is generally attributed to the Hopewell culture in Ohio during the period A.D. 1–400. The objective of our research for the past 25 years has been to test the hypothesis that astronomical knowledge played a significant role in the location and design of the large, geometrically sophisticated earthworks for which Ohio Hopewell is best known. Our work has established that some of these earthworks are aligned to significant rise or set points of both the sun and moon. However, the intentionality of such alignments remains a difficult and unresolved problem. In the absence of written sources, reliable oral tradition, or small art clearly related to the design of the earthworks, it is hard to justify compellingly either belief or doubt when features of these structures are interpreted as deliberate alignments to solar or lunar events visible on the horizon.

The maps of the earthworks published by Squier and Davis in 1848 afford a first approach to their design and scale, but well-known inaccuracies render them unreliable as a basis for a precise quantitative study of the geometry and orientation of the sites and, without corroboration, useless for astronomical analysis. Fortunately, beginning with the Smithsonian Bureau of Ethnology's surveys in the 1880s, major geometric earthworks have been mapped with greater accuracy (Thomas 1894). Since the 1930s these surveys have been tested and supplemented by aerial photography, remote geophysical sensing, and scientific excavation.

In this chapter, we summarize our work during the past decade at Newark and Granville and in the Ohio Hopewell core near Chillicothe. In the early 1980s, we published papers on the geometry and astronomy of the earthworks at Newark, Ohio, and High Bank, near Chillicothe, Ohio. That work depended on the accuracy of James Middleton's surveys of the sites for the Bureau of Ethnology. More recently we have been able to utilize the newly rediscovered 1862 Salisbury survey of the entire Newark site (Salisbury 1862) as well as to draw on the results of aerial photography, pollen analysis, remote geophysical sensing, and excavation at Newark and other Ohio Hopewell sites.

The qualitative interpretations we outline here are analyzed in quantitative detail in a statistical study of five key lunar alignments along features of the Circle-Octagon earthworks at Newark (Hively and Horn 2006a) and in forthcoming papers. In these papers we will detail the possible role of astronomical observations made from high hilltops in the planning and construction of Newark-Granville and major sites in the Chillicothe region and more closely examine the role played by regional and celestial "topography" in the location and layout of the Newark-Granville and Chillicothe sites. The general theme of these studies is Hopewell cosmography and its landscape. We have found that the Hopewell builders were concerned not only with the geometry and astronomical alignment of some of their works but also with the place and location of those works in the local terrain. That place and those places appear to have been chosen not only for broadly economic suitability but also for their significance in the builders' view of their world (Buikstra and Charles 1999: 216; Sahlqvist 2001: 79–102).

Statistical Analysis

We have recently completed a Monte Carlo statistical analysis of the most accurate and compelling lunar alignments associated with the Newark Octagon (Hively and Horn 2006a). In our original papers, we found at the Newark site 17 possible alignments to local horizon rise and set extremes of the moon over its 18.6-year cycle.[1] Rise extremes are shown in Figure 5.1. The plausibility of these alignments being deliberate depends upon the likelihood that the five well-defined alignments on the avenue axis and walls of the Observatory Circle-Octagon, shown in Figure 5.2, are accidental. The structure is a unique combination of geometrical and empirical symmetries—the geometrical symmetry of the octagon and the astronomical symmetry of the long lunar cycle. Five of the eight lunar extremes are aligned with the octagon (the maximum possible on the walls and avenue axis of the nearly perfect Circle-Octagon). The remaining three lunar extremes are aligned with other features of the Circle-Octagon but are not aligned on the walls. The shape of the octagon conforms to a precise geometrical plan, and its size is related to the associated circle as shown in Figure 5.3.

In most cases, statistical analysis cannot establish the probability that the builders intended chosen properties of a single site. At Newark, the scale, geometrical precision, and complexity of the Circle-Octagon make it possible to use Monte Carlo techniques to assess the statistical distribution of random

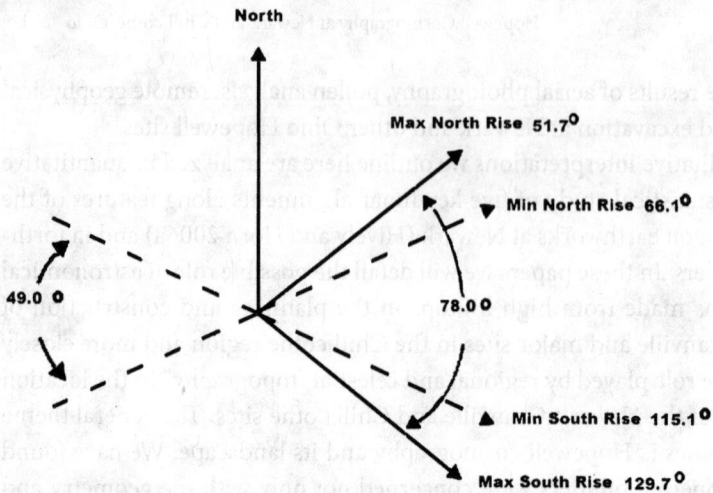

Figure 5.1. Range of movement of moonrise along the eastern horizon from the Newark Circle-Octagon.

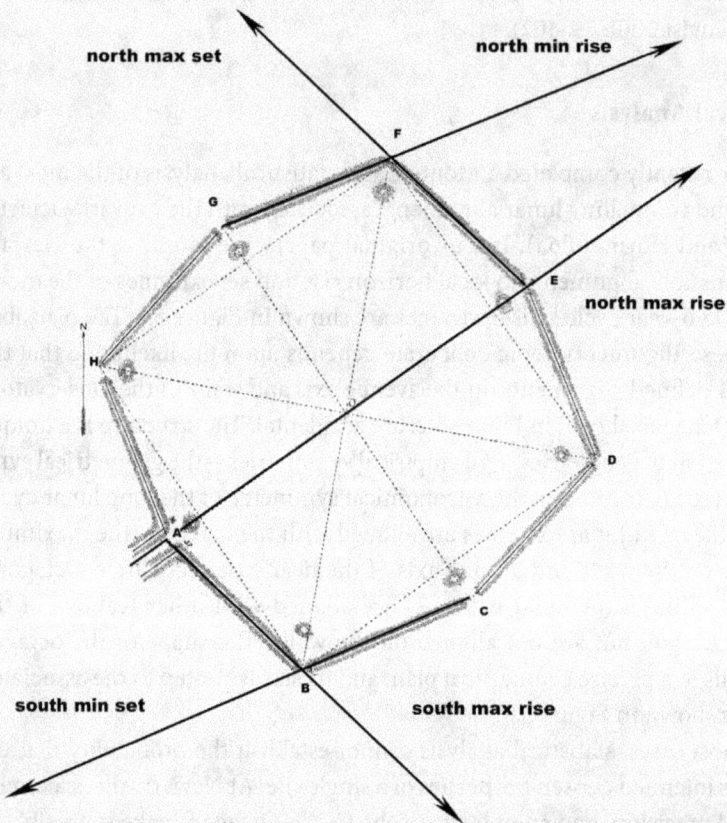

Figure 5.2. The five lunar alignments embedded in the Newark Octagon.

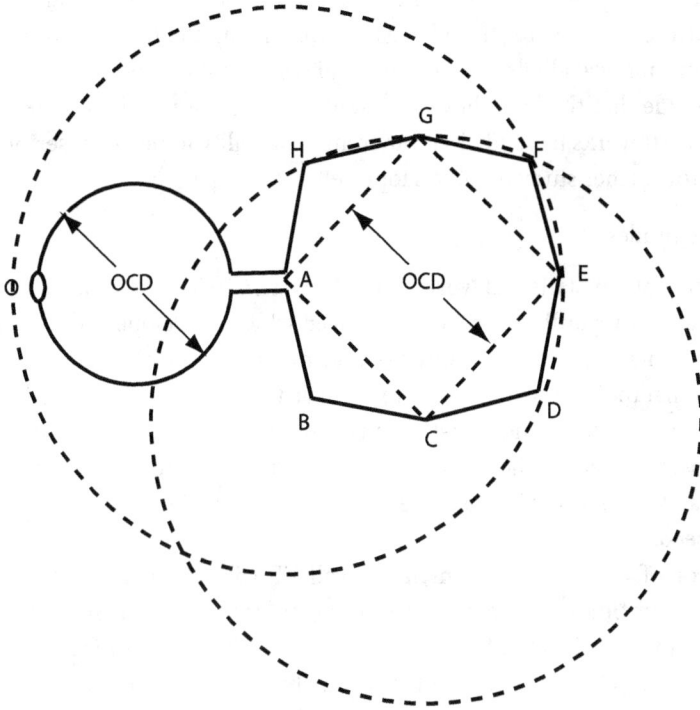

Figure 5.3. The OCD Geometry of the Newark Circle-Octagon.

astronomical alignments in such structures by building and analyzing billions of comparable sites by computer. With well-defined computer-generated data sets we can compute the probability that astronomical alignments comparable to those found at Newark are random accidents. We tested 72 models that made a range of assumptions, which we believe are persuasively indicated by data at the site, about intended geometrical plans, wall errors, alignment tolerances, exclusive lunar alignments, and deliberate geometrical distortion. Our analysis showed that for the most plausible models, the probability that the octagon design achieves five lunar alignments (comparable to those actually found) on its symmetry axis and four walls by chance varies between 4.1 .6 $\times 10^{0-8}$ and 2.8 .2 $\times 10^{0-7}$.

The dependence of the probability of comparable chance alignments on the assumptions underlying the models is discussed in detail in the aforementioned work (Hively and Horn 2006a). Although the precise probability of comparable chance alignments varied with the modeling assumptions, the conclusion that the probability was less than .001 was quite robust and was true of all reasonable models. The Monte Carlo analysis does not by itself prove that the Hopewell builders of the octagon intended these lunar alignments, but it does militate strongly against dismissing the hypothesis of deliberate astronomical alignment on statistical considerations alone. This leads us to conclude that the hypothesis of intentional astronomical alignment in Hopewell earthworks has sufficient inherent plausibility to be taken seriously as a basis for further study of Ohio Hopewell.

Horizon Altitudes

In the course of our statistical work on the Newark Circle-Octagon, we tested two hypotheses regarding the horizons over which the Hopewell builders viewed the lunar extremes at moonrise and moonset. In our original paper we judged that the lunar extremes were observed and presumably recorded at first gleam on moonrise and at last gleam on moonset as seen over local horizons by observers within the Circle-Octagon earthworks. This gave the best fit to the data. A statistically implausible error in one of the five core alignments led us to reconsider.

An error of 1°.7 in the alignment of wall EF with the north maximum moonset is four times the average error of the other four alignments. The 1°.7 error results from a local hill on the azimuth of wall EF 1.9 km from vertex E of the Newark Octagon. If the intent of the builders had been to mark the northern maximum moonset with high accuracy as observed from vertex E, it would seem strange to choose a location where the distant horizons were obscured by local obstructions. Moreover, the local hill forming the visible horizon does not appear to distinguish itself in any way as being particularly useful as an astronomical foresight. If a primary priority of the designers had been to conduct precise observations of the lunar maximum north set point along wall EF, it would appear to have been better to move the octagon farther south, away from obstructing hills north of Raccoon Creek. The alignment error of wall EF relative to the moonset as it would appear on a zero-altitude horizon for lower limb tangency is negligible (0°.2). These considerations led us to formulate a zero-altitude hypothesis which we now believe gives a better explanation of the astronomical alignments at the site.

The zero-altitude hypothesis asserts that the key lunar alignments found in the Circle-Octagon earthworks were designed to fall along lunar lines which had been determined by observations conducted from high points with distant horizons and not by observations made from the valley floor where the earthworks are located. If the intent of the builders was to accurately record the "true rise and set points" as they would be seen unobscured by local topography, then it is plausible that these astronomically significant lines would be determined from observations made from high hilltops in the region rather than from positions within the octagon structure itself.

The question of how the lunar extremes might have been discovered and marked with an accuracy of about 0°.5 is also addressed by the zero-altitude hypothesis. Such a feat would have required determined observation over several generations. Consistent and precise observations would have been difficult to make from valley floors, where the directions to rise and set points appear to vary significantly due to obscuration by local topography and seasonal vegetation. The most logical place to make and record repeatable observations of lunar rise/set points would indeed be from high places with unobstructed views of distant horizons. Such high places could be dedicated to long-term observations, as they would not have been prime areas for other activities.

The zero-altitude hypothesis would predict that suitable elevations should be found in positions where they could function as long-distance backsight for the lunar alignments found in the Circle-Octagon structure. Skeptics will rightly observe, however, that the fulfillment of such a prediction is likely to be vacuously true by chance alone given the large number hills which surround the valley. Consequently, evidence for this hypothesis will only be compelling if high points can be found which have additional characteristics (beyond their functioning as a backsight for a single alignment) suggesting that they were deliberately chosen and used to make the observations which the hypothesis requires.

As we reflected on empirical problems involved in the initial planning and layout of the Circle-Octagon, we studied the local topography to locate vantage points that command a view of the earthwork location on the flood plain of Raccoon Creek. The terrain of the nearby Appalachian foothills affords many such points. We have used three criteria in looking for sites which may have played a role in the planning and layout of the earthworks: (1) the site can serve as a backsight which allows a zero-altitude horizon view of a lunar (or solar) extreme over the length of an octagon wall or along the symmetry axis of one or more geometrically regular constructions, such as the Circle-Octagon, the Great (or Fairground) Circle, the Wright Square, the Salisbury Square; (2) the site is prominent among the many eligible hill sites, affording an optimum view of the earthworks; and (3) the site may show evidence of Hopewell or Early Woodland activity.

One site, the most prominent hill (H1) southwest of the earthworks, fits these criteria in an impressive fashion. From the highest elevation on H1 the azimuth to the north maximum moonrise passes through the long axis of the Observatory Circle-Octagon, and the azimuth to the north minimum moon-

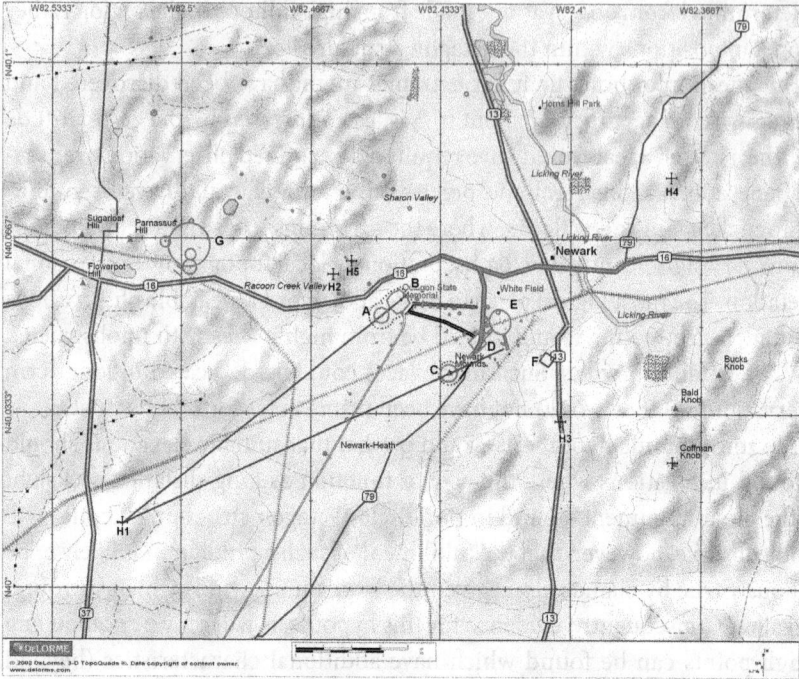

Figure 5.4. H1 alignments of the Newark Earthworks. Courtesy © 2002 DeLorme (www.delorme.com) 3-D TopoQuads Æ and with the authors' additions.

rise passes through the centroid of the Great Circle, as shown in Figure 5.4. Samuel Park, in fact, noted that in 1870 a "circumvalation" (enclosure) and mounds near the H1 location site afforded a clear view of Cherry Valley and the Newark Earthworks (Park, 1890).

Here, and throughout this paper, unless specified otherwise, the azimuths for rise/set events will be defined in terms that we believe offer the best fit to the data for the Circle-Octagon. The horizon over which the rise and set points are observed is assumed to be zero, consistent with the evidence that the astronomical observations that discovered and marked the positions were made from high elevations. We further assume the rise/set events were determined by lower limb tangency to the horizon. We also have assumed a date of A.D. 250 in computing lunar rise/set azimuths, although the maximum deviation of azimuth for any date in the interval A.D. 1–400 will be less than 0.05 degrees, that is, negligible. Finally, all the astronomical alignments proposed in this study have an accuracy of 1 degree or better. Given the observational difficulties associated with weather, daylight, and lunar phase, this is consistent with the best accuracy that could reasonably be expected for marking the lunar extremes.

A second site may suggest one reason the Hopewell chose to build so extensively at Newark. Coffman's Knob, southeast of the Newark Works (the highest hill overlooking the area), commands a view of the confluence of Raccoon Creek and the South and North Fork of the Licking River. The view from Coffman's Knob also suggests a fourth criterion for sites which may have played a role in the layout of earthworks: a site from which lunar extremes appear aligned with both earthwork architecture and prominent features of the local terrain. Viewed from Coffman's Knob, the moon at its north maximum extreme sets in Sharon Valley. Seen at its north minimum extreme, the moon sets in the valley of Raccoon Creek. Over the 9.3-year period between maximum and minimum standstills, the observer would see the extreme north set point of the moon cross slowly from one valley to the other, certainly a striking visual phenomenon (Figure 5.5).

Major features of the earthworks at Newark and Granville appear to conform to these views of moonset from Coffman's Knob. The azimuth through Sharon Valley to the north maximum moonset passes through the center of the Salisbury Square parallel to the walls of the square (within 2 degrees) and passes through the approximate center of the elliptical enclosure to the north.[2]

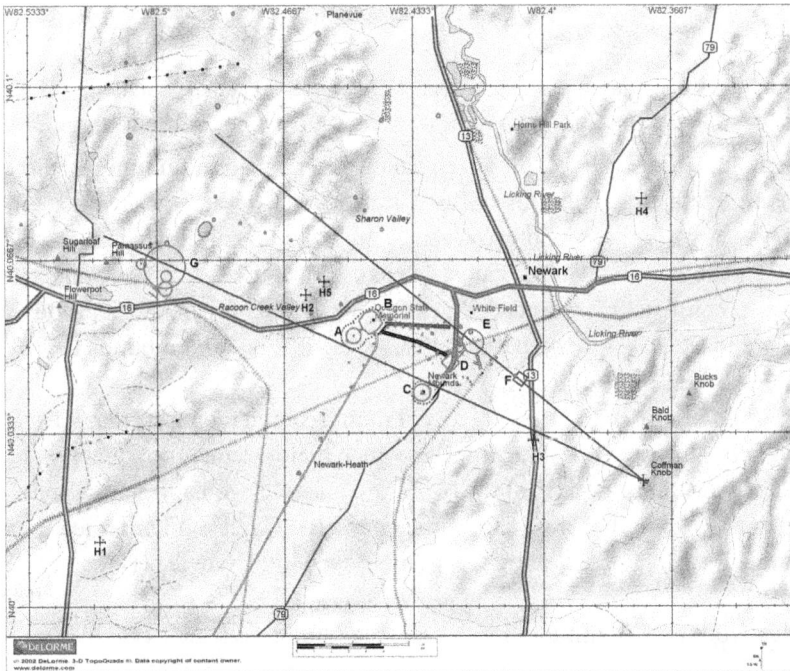

Figure 5.5. Coffman's Knob alignments of the Newark Earthworks. Courtesy © 2002 DeLorme (www.delorme.com) 3-D TopoQuads℗ and with the authors' additions.

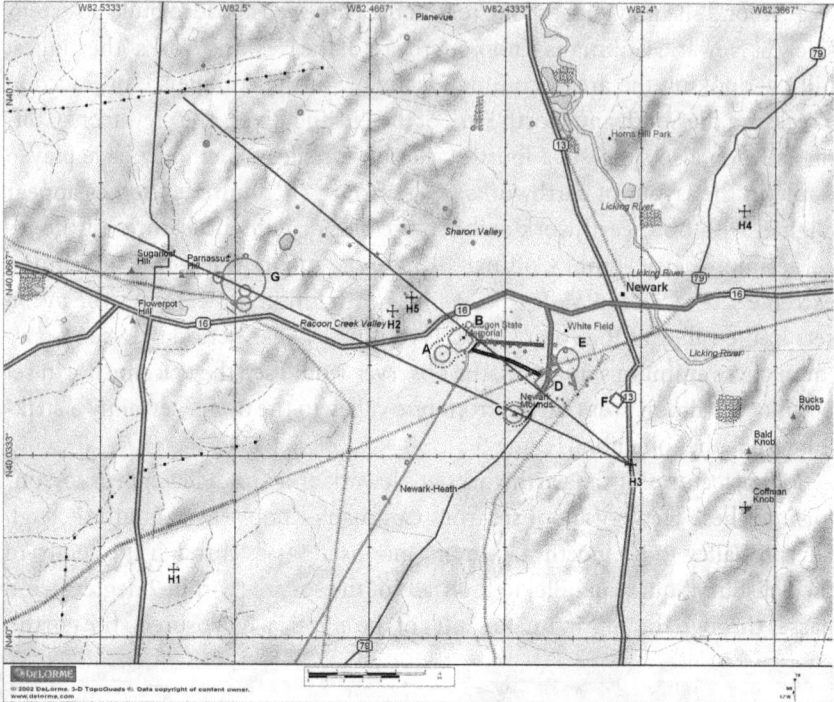

Figure 5.6. Newark Earthworks showing Prominence H3 alignments. Courtesy © 2002 DeLorme (www.delorme.com) 3-D TopoQuads℞ and with the authors' additions.

The azimuth through Raccoon Creek valley to the north minimum moonset passes near the entrance to the Great Circle of the Newark Earthworks and through a large, perhaps incomplete, circular embankment situated in the valley below the well-known "Alligator" (or panther) effigy east of Granville. No Hopewell construction is recorded near the peak of Coffman's Knob, though there are Middle Woodland habitation sites, enclosures, and mounds nearby (Pacheco 1997: 51, Figure 2.1).

Zero-altitude horizon views of tangent moonrise and moonset from H1 and from Coffman's Knob are along lines on which major elements of the Newark design reside—the long axes of the Newark Circle-Octagon and the Salisbury Square and Ellipse; the Great Circle; the Granville "Circle" and other features along the Raccoon Creek valley between Newark and Granville (Hooge 1993: 156–198).

Seen from a zero-altitude horizon vantage point, wall EF of the Newark Octagon is aligned accurately with the north maximum moonset. This suggests that this wall may have been carefully constructed to fall on that line as observed from high hilltops. When moonset is viewed over the local horizon from vertex E of the octagon, wall EF misses the north maximum (similarly defined by lower limb tangency) by nearly four lunar diameters. Consistent with the roles we have suggested for H1 and Coffman's Knob in the layout of Newark, it is pertinent to look for a hill on the bearing of wall EF which could serve as a backsight for wall EF and allow a zero-altitude horizon for moonset observation. Across the valley to the southeast, a small prominence (H3) in the first range of hills 4,300 meters distant from vertex E allows a zero-altitude view of the north maximum moonset on the line of octagon wall EF (Figure 5.6). The local topography affords comparable locations for long-distance backsights associated with the three remaining lunar oriented walls of the octagon. We examine the plausibility of these as vantage points, given the minor differences between the horizons seen along these walls from high points or from within the octagon, in a forthcoming paper.[3]

Comparison between Hopewell site planning at Newark and in the Chillicothe region is appropriate for many reasons. There are obvious similarities between the Newark Circle-Octagon and the High Bank Circle-Octagon, south of Chillicothe. It will also be necessary to test at Chillicothe the two hypotheses we have proposed in our recent work at Newark and Granville: (1) relatively high, zero-altitude horizon vantage points overlooking suitable second-terrace locations for earthworks were used in the planning and layout of ceremonial centers, and (2) some earthwork alignments to lunar extremes also incorporate alignments to major features of local topography, such as linear valleys and high prominent peaks.

Newark and High Bank

Design similarities between the circle-octagon components at Newark and High Bank are salient here, as is the fact that these are the only such constructions known in Hopewell or in American antiquity. The Newark Observatory Circle diameter (OCD unit) is accurately repeated at High Bank. At both Newark and High Bank, the dimensions of the octagons are derived from the circle diameters. Both octagons encode alignments to lunar extremes. The axis of the High Bank Circle-Octagon, however, does not replicate the Newark Circle-Octagon axis. As shown in Figure 5.7, from a point on the perimeter of the High Bank Circle-Octagon (13) opposite the avenue, the observer does not see the moon rise at its north maximum extreme. Instead, one looks down the broad valley of the ancient, preglacial Teays River through which the present Scioto River flows.

In contrast to the Newark Octagon, only one of the eight alignments on lunar extremes that are achieved at the High Bank Circle-Octagon follows an octagon wall. Only one of the four solar alignments on the Circle-Octagon fol-

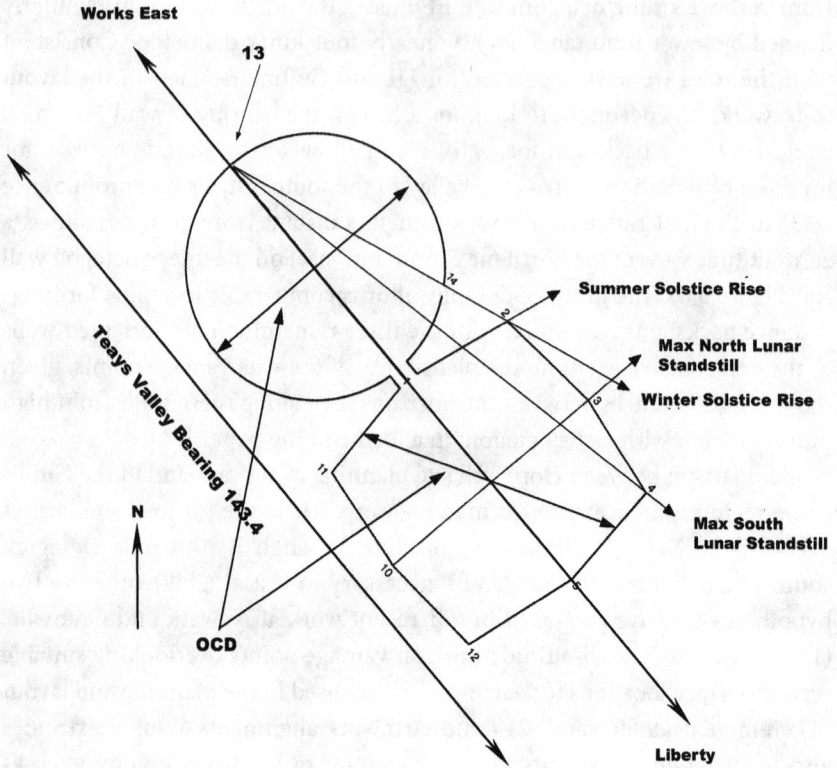

Figure 5.7. Teays River valley alignment from point 13 on the perimeter of the High Bank Circle.

lows an octagon wall. At the High Bank Circle-Octagon the best fit with all of these alignments is to local rather than zero-altitude horizons. The High Bank alignments, with the lower limb of the moon or sun tangent to the horizon at rise and set, do, however, correspond with the zero-altitude interpretation of Newark.

In our Monte Carlo statistical analysis of randomly built equilateral octagons (with fourfold rotational symmetry) we discovered that there were only two precise octagon shapes which achieved the greatest number of alignments to lunar/solar extreme rise/set points along octagon walls or along an avenue axis (a maximum of five alignments is possible). These shapes were defined by the choice of a single vertex angle. Equilateral, symmetric octagons could have been built with a large variety of different shapes. Our analysis shows that at the latitude of Newark, the shape that aligns most accurately with the lunar extrema is defined by a maximum vertex angle (at the adjoining avenue) of 153°.6. The actual Newark Octagon has an average large vertex angle of 154°.8.

Similarly, the octagon shape (at the latitude of High Bank) which aligns with the most lunar/solar extrema is defined by a large vertex angle at the adjoining avenue of 165°.7, whereas the actual High Bank Octagon has an average large vertex angle of 165°.5. Thus the hypothesis of deliberate experimentation to determine the shapes which aligned with the most lunar/solar extrema "explains" the design of both octagons known to have been constructed by the Hopewell. In these cases, in the absence of other more compelling reasons for the choice of shape we believe this is a very notable fact.

The design of the High Bank Octagon is the optimum shape for aligning with a combination of solar and lunar extreme rise/set points at its latitude; yet compared with the Circle-Octagon at Newark, it fails to encode that astronomical design on the most prominent feature, its long axis. As the High Bank Circle-Octagon avenue is not aligned with a solar extreme, only two sides of the octagon rather than a possible four are aligned with lunar or solar extremes. The 0°.75 difference in latitude between the Newark Earthworks and the High Bank Earthworks makes it impossible to replicate the accurate match to lunar extremes achieved on the Newark Circle-Octagon merely by repeating the Newark design in Figure 5.3 at Chillicothe. Some change in design is required.

High Bank in Context

In considering the differences between the two circle-octagon designs above, do we perhaps take up the problem from the wrong end by beginning with Newark, then finding High Bank anomalous? This finding reflects our initial approach. Because we could better document the Newark site, we began our study of the archives, surveying, and analysis there. When we reached the conclusion that there could be deliberate astronomical design at Newark, we tested that hypothesis against the available evidence at High Bank.

Let us reconsider, beginning with High Bank in the context of the Chillicothe Hopewell. What is the focus of the long axis of the High Bank design? From point 13 (Figure 5.7) on the circle opposite the avenue, features of the Circle-Octagon (symmetry axes, vertices, the single opening in the circle embankment other than the avenue) are aligned with (1) the southern maximum moonrise, (2) the winter solstice sunrise, and (3) the broad valley of the preglacial Teays River (Figure 5.8).[4]

The latter orientation deserves attention for four reasons: (1) south of High Bank, the Scioto abandons its meandering course to hug the west wall of the Teays Valley on a straight bearing of 143°.4 for more than 10 km; (2) the 143°.4 bearing from point 13 on the High Bank Circle bisects the large circle of the Liberty Works 6.3 km to the south (Figure 5.8); (3) the opposite 323°.4 bearing

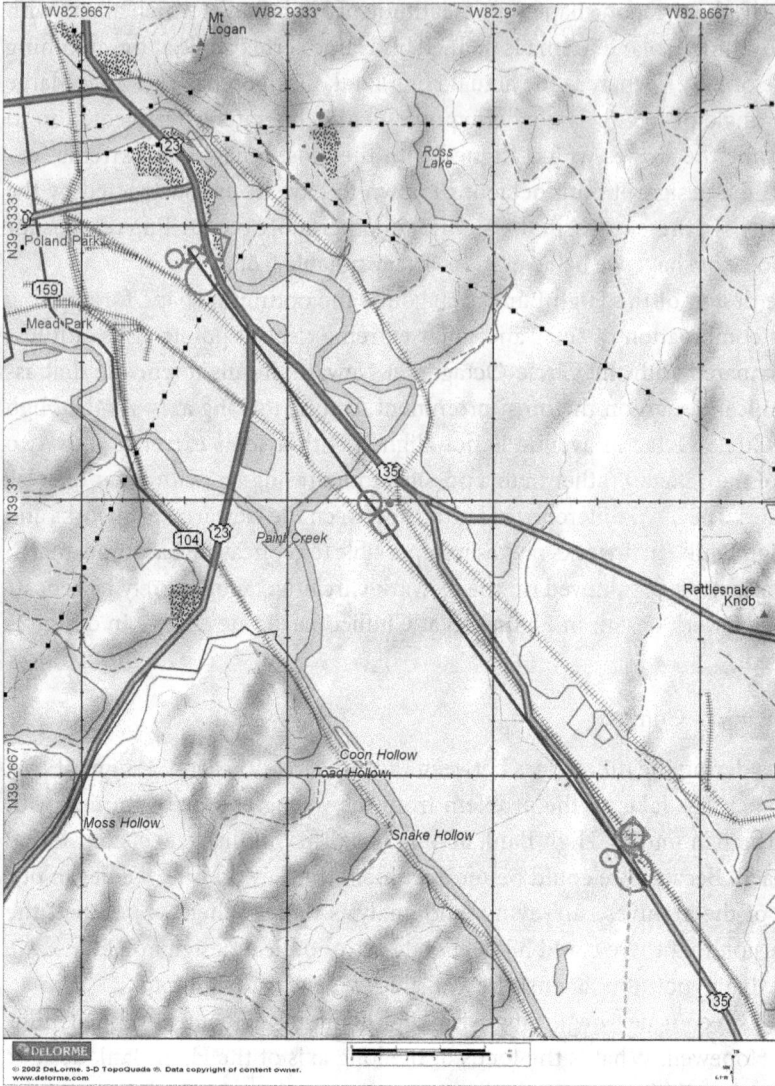

Figure 5.8. Teays River valley with Liberty–High Bank–Works East alignment. Courtesy © 2002 DeLorme (www.delorme.com) 3-D TopoQuadsÆ and with the authors' additions.

from point 13 on the High Bank Circle bisects the large circle of Works East 3.5 km to the north;[5] and (4) the north lunar maximum rise (53°.4, tangent to the local horizon) occurs at a 90-degree angle to the major axis of the Circle-Octagon.

As is evident in Figure 5.8 the siting of High Bank, relative to the Teays Valley and to both Liberty and Works East, suggests that these works belong to a common plan. The design incorporates the empirical symmetries of the lunar and solar extremes, and the geometrical symmetry of the octagon, with the nearly unique linear topography of a long segment of the ancient river valley. Though High Bank appears anomalous to the viewer who approaches it with Newark as the norm, it not only fits its local context, but offers clues to a better understanding of that context, and perhaps many features of Newark as well.

We have seen the manner in which the design of Hopewell earthworks from Newark to Granville may have incorporated local topography with the geometrical symmetry of the octagon and the empirical symmetry of the long lunar cycle. At Chillicothe we find additional evidence of such design, supporting one hypothesis framed at Newark—some earthwork alignments that function to mark lunar extremes also incorporate alignments to major features of local topography. No geometric-astronomical feature of the Newark Earthworks is as demonstrably integrated with its topographic setting as is High Bank with this linear segment of the Teays-Scioto valley. Yet this coincidence of geometric, astronomical, and topographic features at High Bank is consistent with our findings at Newark.

The second hypothesis framed at Newark, that relatively high, zero-altitude vantage points overlooking suitable second-terrace locations for earthworks were used in the planning and layout of ceremonial centers, is not confirmed at High Bank.[6] It remains to be seen whether it is supported by other earthen enclosures in the Hopewell core region near Chillicothe.

Paint Creek Valley

We have seen the alignment of Liberty, High Bank, and Works East along the bearing of the Teays Valley south of Chillicothe. Strong as this evidence of alignment is in the context of High Bank, it is important to ask if other regional sites are aligned both with local topography and with each other. The valley of the ancient Paint Creek is an obvious place to begin, as shown in the bedrock geology map of Ross County (Figure 5.9).

The course of the preglacial valley of Paint Creek bearing northeast is evident in Figure 5.9, beginning at lower left. Although the valley walls are not as straight as the west wall of the Teays Valley below Chillicothe, the valley itself is prominent, as anyone approaching Chillicothe along U.S. Route 50 from the west can see. On the north side of the valley, three earthwork enclosures, Bourneville, Anderson, and Dunlap, are aligned with the approximate center of the large circular enclosure at Seip. On the south side of the valley, three enclosures, Spruce Hill, Mound City, and Cedar Bank, are aligned with the geometric center of the Baum Earthworks. The location and dimensions of these eight enclosures confine each of these "alignments" to a narrow range

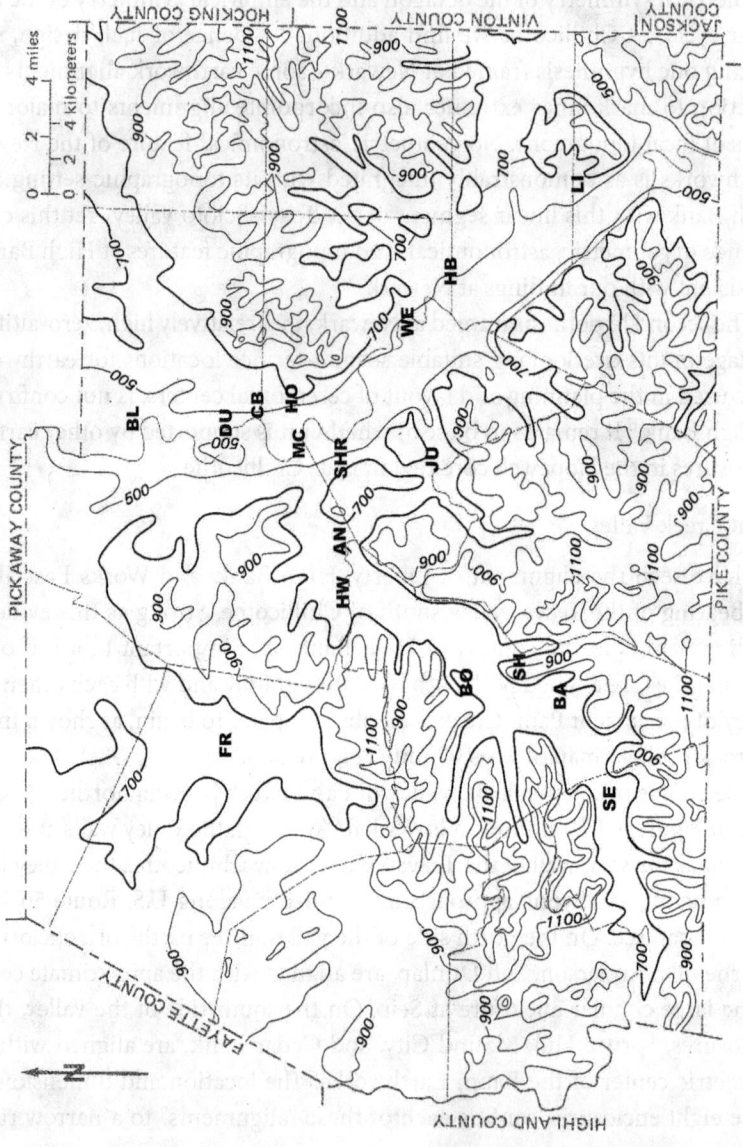

Figure 5.9. Bedrock geology and distribution of major sites in the Chillicothe region. Contour interval 200 ft (Quinn and Goldthwait 1985: Figure 3, p. 5, and with the authors' additions). Courtesy of Ohio Geological Survey. Key: AN = Anderson; BA = Baum; BL = Blackwater; BO = Bourneville; CB = Cedar Bank; DU = Dunlap; FR = Frankfort; HB = High Bank; HO = Hopeton; HW = Hopewell; JU = Junction; LI = Liberty; MC = Mound City; SE = Seip; SH = Spruce Hill; SHR = Shriver; WE = Works East.

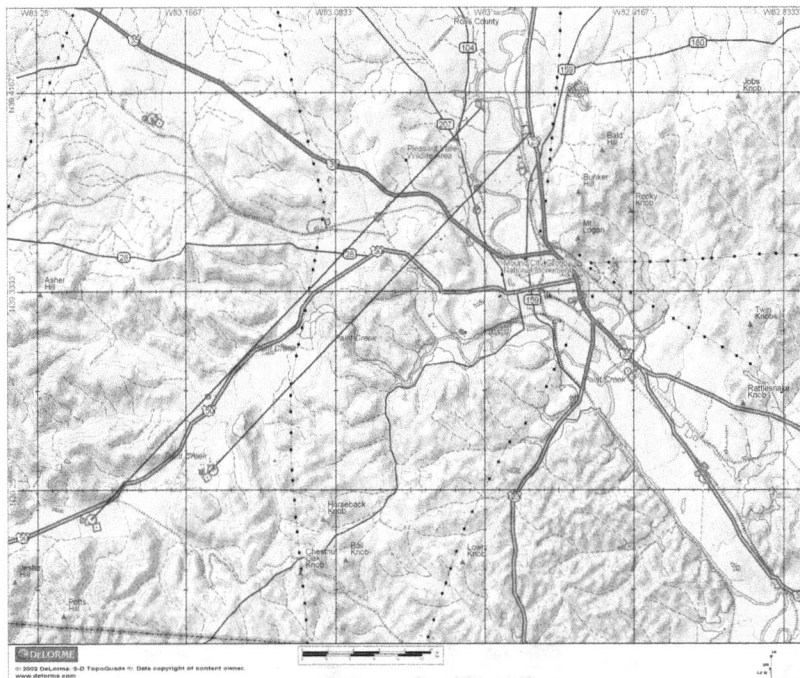

Figure 5.10. Parallel alignments on Old Paint Creek valley and Teays River valley. Courtesy © 2002 DeLorme (www.delorme.com) 3-D TopoQuadsÆ and with the authors' additions.

within ± 0°.3 of 44°.3. The northern of the parallel 44°.3 alignments passes through the center of the enclosure at Anderson. The southern passes through Mound City at Mound 3 and through the eastern "gate" of the Mound City enclosure near the Scioto River. As with the Teays Valley alignments, suitable soils determine in part the location of large second terrace enclosures, but this does not explain the extension of the "alignments" beyond the preglacial Paint Creek valley to intersections with the Teays Valley near Dunlap and Cedar Bank (Figure 5.10). The 44°.3 bearing of the old valley aligns with no lunar or solar extreme.[7]

Two bearings from the Seip-Pricer Mound (near the center of the large circular embankment at the Seip enclosure) through other ceremonial centers do align with lunar extremes. As shown in Figure 5.11, a 52°.2 bearing from the Seip-Pricer Mound on the north maximum moonrise passes close to the centroid of the Shriver enclosure (south of Mound City) and through the center of the southern small circle at the east wall of the Hopeton Polygon. A 66°.4 bearing from the same position on the Seip-Pricer Mound across the

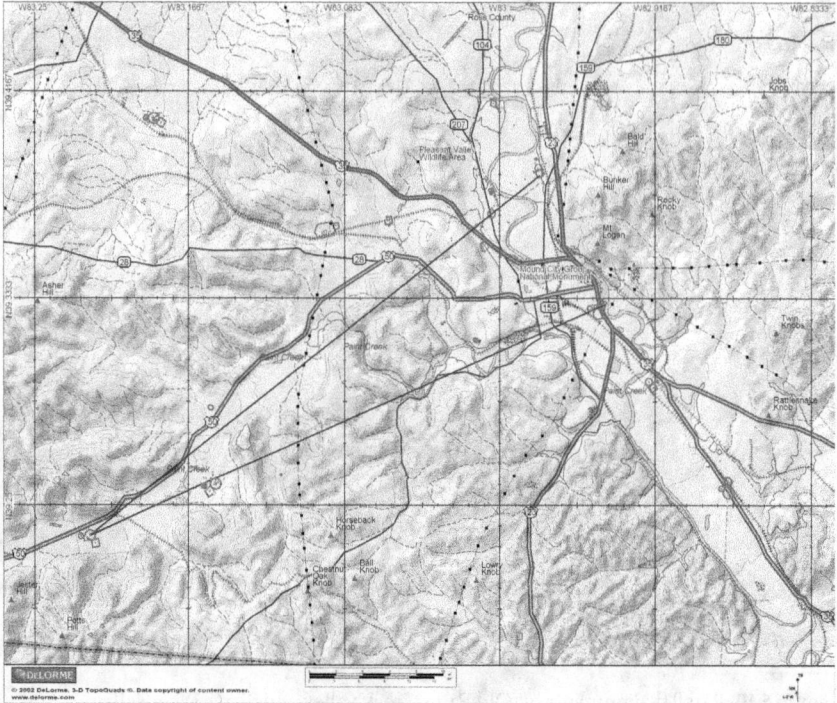

Figure 5.11. Seip-Pricer Mound alignments. Courtesy © 2002 DeLorme (www.delorme.com) 3-D TopoQuads/Æ and with the authors' additions.

northern boundary of the Baum enclosure and through the estimated center of the Works East Square aligns with the north minimum moonrise. The situation here recalls H1 at Newark, where zero-altitude, lower limb tangent bearings taken from the same position pass along the symmetry axes of the Circle-Octagon and the Great Circle to the northern maximum and minimum moonrise. Yet the Seip enclosure is located in a valley, not on a prominence like H1.[8] The corporate center at Seip appears to play a focal role among the Paint Creek sites, as it anchors alignments to lunar extremes and to other Hopewell enclosures, in some cases to both.

Some of these possible alignments may be accidental. Patterns consistent with astronomical alignment may result from choices based on properties of water and soil, sun, wind, and other factors that have not entered our reckoning. The question we must consider is whether the evidence we cite supports the conclusion that it is reasonable to believe the builders of these works were drawing patterns on a scale larger than the already extensive earthworks themselves. Were the Hopewell builders, and perhaps their Early Woodland predecessors, thinking in terms that drew patterns in earth and sky on a common map?

Mound City and Shriver

The impression of singular local topography is strong where the northeast-bearing valley of ancient Paint Creek intersects the Teays Valley near Mound City. From this point the Appalachian range (the Logan Range) east of the Scioto River appears in sharp relief, from Sugarloaf Mountain on the north to Mount Logan on the south. This range is the most prominent signature of Chillicothe topography, visible from high points in the region to the west for as much as 35 kilometers (Figures 5.12 and 5.13). This profile may have played a role in the siting of both Mound City and the Shriver "Circle" 728 meters south of Mound City.

Viewed from Mound 7, which forms the most prominent peak within the walls of Mound City, the Appalachian profile from the peak of Sugarloaf to the peak of Mount Logan defines the 48°.5 range of the monthly north-south movement of the moon during the season of minimum extremes which recurs every 18.6 years. During that "season," which lasts about 18 months on either side of the extreme, the rising moon will repeatedly approach the limits of 66°.3 at the north and 114°.8 at the south, but it will appear to the observer as if bound within those limits. During the 9.3 years after the minimum extreme, the rising moon moves gradually toward the season of maximum extremes, where it travels monthly from 52°.1 at the north to 129°.3 at the south (see Figure 5.1; the range of lunar extremes shown at Newark is slightly wider than at Chillicothe).

At the maximum extreme the rising moon travels 77°.2 from north to south each month, a visible increase of 28°.7, or 57 lunar diameters, over the minimum season. The profile of the Appalachian range to the east, viewed from Mound City, makes this difference, more than 28 lunar diameters at each boundary of the range, hard to miss. Skeptics have wondered why the minimum lunar extremes would be noticed (Aveni 2004). At Mound City the answer is in the mountains.[9]

The view of the Appalachian range from Mound 7 is salient for a second reason. From the same position where the minimum moonrise extremes occur over the peaks of Sugarloaf and Mount Logan, the observer will see the summer solstice sun rise at the northern base of Sugarloaf, and the winter solstice sun rise over the southern base of Mount Logan (Figures 5.13 and 5.14). Today trees obscure this view of the eastern horizon from Mound City. It would have been necessary to clear trees as far away as the location of Hope-

Figure 5.12. Eastern profile of the Appalachian range from Chillicothe. This photograph, taken from the intersection of Clinton Road and Pleasant Valley Road 9 km east of the Logan Range, shows the entire range from north to south. Today trees and construction obscure the view of the range from Mound City. Photo by the authors.

Figure 5.13. The Logan Range profile from Mound City. Photo by the authors. Key: ss = summer solstice sunrise; nm = north minimum moonrise; sm = south minimum moonrise; ws = winter solstice sunrise.

Figure 5.14. Profile of Sugarloaf from Mounds 3 and 7, Mound City. Photo by the authors.

ton, 2.5 kilometers across the Scioto River, for the views described here to have been possible. Kendra McLaughlin's recent findings at Fort Ancient are consistent with such land clearing, as are Brad Lepper's and DeeAnne Wymer's earlier findings at Newark (McLauchlan 2003: 557–566; Lepper 1996; Wymer 1997: 153–171).

Although this view of the solstices and of the minimum standstills of the moon over the Appalachian range from Sugarloaf to Mount Logan is possible anywhere within the embankment walls at Mound City, it is most accurate when viewed from Mound 7. When Squier and Davis excavated Mound 7, they found a large deposit of round, 10- to 12-in mica sheets which they interpreted as a segment of a mica crescent 20 ft long. They assumed the rest of the figure was still hidden in their unfinished excavation (Squier and Davis 1848: 154). In 1920 Mills's exploration of the Mound City group reduced the 20-ft crescent to an 8-by-4-ft mica deposit "made to conform to the rounded contour covering of the base of the small mound covering burial number 9" (Mills 1922: 493). It appears from this later excavation that Squier and Davis were wrong about the crescent. But Mound 7 does appear to have a lunar context, both in terms of its location and aspects of its design.[10]

The monthly swing of the moon from Sugarloaf to Mount Logan during the season of minimum extremes would have called attention to the 57 lunar diameter difference between the minimum and maximum moonrise extremes. In this context, some features of the Shriver "Circle" a short distance south of Mound City deserve attention.

One astronomical feature of the Shriver "Circle" may indicate a common element in the designs of Shriver and Mound City. As documented in the Squier and Davis survey of Shriver, they described a large, irregular circle wall, bounded by an exterior ditch, with a mounded area near the "center" of the circle. Unlike many Early Woodland circles, but comparable to Hopewell cir-

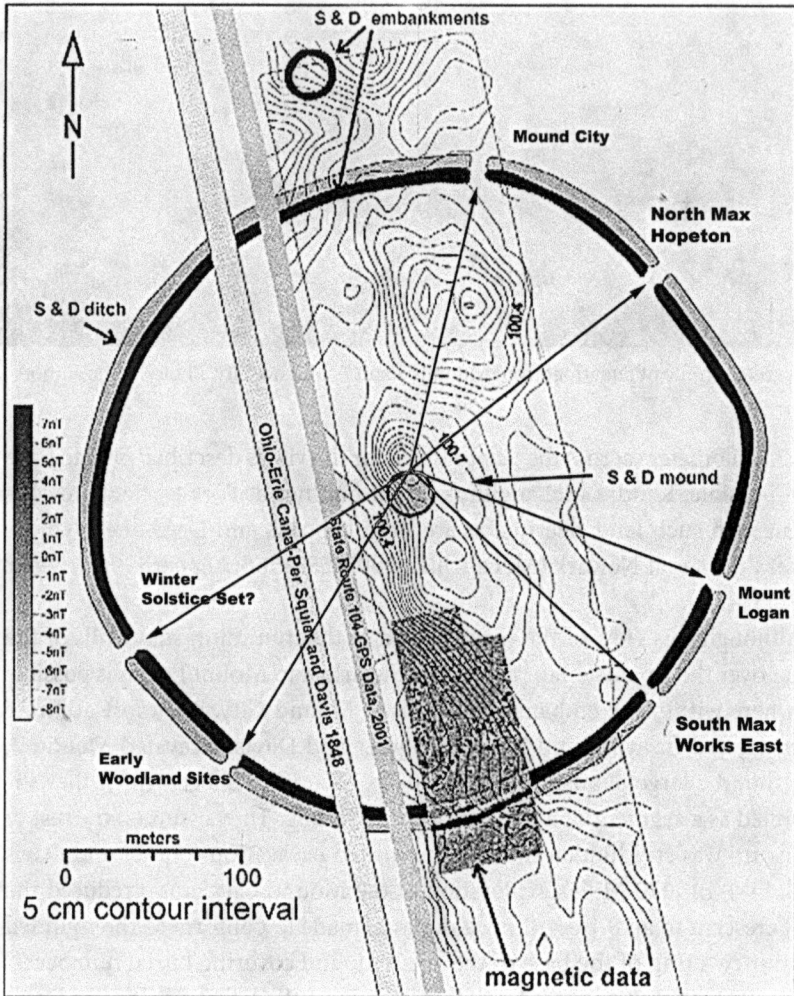

Figure 5.15. The Shriver "Circle." From Pederson and Burks 2002: 15, Figure 1.
Courtesy of the Midwestern Archaeological Center and with the authors' additions.

cles at Liberty, Seip, and Baum, Shriver has many openings, or "gates." Like the
large circle at Seip, there is a mound near its center. When one looks east from
the central mound at Shriver, two of the gates frame the maximum moonrise
extremes (zero-altitude, tangent) as seen over other Hopewell sites, Hopeton
at the northeast, Works East at the southeast (Figure 5.15).[11]

Since Squier and Davis surveyed six openings in the Shriver wall, with an
average width of about 10 m, this coincidence of two such openings with lunar
extremes may well be accidental. Yet the orientation of the remaining four
openings is also consistent with an intent to indicate other Hopewell or Early

Woodland sites and prominent features of the local terrain. One additional opening may have an astronomical orientation.

Reading clockwise from the north (Figure 5.15), the breaks in the Shriver embankment, viewed from the central mound, open a 2-degree window on (1) the Scioto River opposite the eastern opening or "gate" in the Mound City wall, (2) the north maximum moonrise extreme (52°.1) and the southwest corner of the Hopeton "Square," (3) the highest point on Mount Logan, recorded by Squier and Davis (1848: 92, and Plate II) as the site of a mound which "afforded the most extended view that can be obtained in the entire region," and (4) the south maximum moonrise extreme (129°.3) and the southwest quarter of the Works East Square. Neither gate 5 nor gate 6 is aligned with a recorded Hopewell site. Numerous Early Woodland mounds, including the eponymous Adena Mound, were located near Lake Ellensmere at the northeastern base of Mount Prospect (see next section). Gate 6 is aligned with the zero-altitude horizon bearing of the winter solstice sunset (239°.0), but the observer would see the sun set south of gate 6 because the local horizon is not zero but 2°.5.

Each of these bearings considered individually is inexact, based at present on the Squier and Davis survey alone. Aerial photography and recent geophysical survey have confirmed the Squier and Davis location of the southern segment of the Shriver wall and ditch (Pederson and Burks 2002). With geophysical sensing and excavation it may still be possible to ascertain the location of the two western gates at Shriver. These findings should be compared, where possible, with the locations of enclosure openings in the large "circles" at Baum, Seip, and Liberty (see Appendix 2 below).

Shriver and Mount Prospect

We have sought evidence to test the zero-altitude hypothesis (originally formulated at Newark) in the Chillicothe region by asking two questions. First, is there an elevation in the region that seems to be best suited for observing the rise/set of the sun and moon at zero-altitude? Second, does the distribution of Hopewellian earthworks in the region seem to have any astronomical relation to this point? We have found an affirmative answer to both questions. As always one has to confront the issue of whether the evidence for intentionality is more than one would expect by chance alone. Nevertheless, given the astronomical context already established we believe the evidence bears further examination.

Shriver is on the second terrace of the Scioto, in a position where fire beacons lit up and down the Teays Valley from Liberty in the south, to Dunlap, perhaps Blackwater, in the north would have been visible. Horizons to the east average 0°.5. But 1 km to the southwest, local horizon altitudes are higher. A

275-meter-high plateau 1.5 km southwest of Shriver, for which we will revive an old Chillicothe name, Mount Prospect, blocks any view of sites on Paint Creek. Anderson and Hopewell are near but hidden. Shriver is not a promising site for zero-altitude views of moonrise or moonset.

In this context Mount Prospect is promising. It is not the tallest peak in the region. But it is the highest land close to the broad terraces of the Scioto River where Mound City, Shriver, and Hopeton were built early in the Middle Woodland period. It is also the best known today. Thomas Worthington, one of the Chillicothe founders and the sixth governor of Ohio, built his home there. He first named his estate Mount Prospect Hall for the view of the valley and the Appalachian range to the east that it offered. Later he changed its name to Adena, whence it lent that name to the Adena culture.[12] The view of sunrise over Mount Logan across the Scioto was placed on the Great Seal of Ohio in 1803.

Worthington's Mount Prospect commands a view of the Teays Valley north and south, and Shriver, Mound City, Hopeton, and Cedar Bank are easily seen from Mount Prospect. Beacons at Dunlap and Blackwater to the north would have been visible, as also at Works East, High Bank, and Liberty toward the south. Mount Prospect also overlooks the North Fork of Paint Creek, bringing Anderson and Hopewell into the range of visible sites, assuming the use of beacons and some extensive clearing. Only the sites on Paint Creek, and Frankfort, distant on the North Fork, would have been beyond direct view.

Mount Prospect and the Zero-Altitude Hypothesis

Sketches in Squier and Davis indicate mounds on Mount Prospect, but no Hopewell enclosure is known there (Squier and Davis 1848: Plate II). Nevertheless, the view from Mount Prospect may have played a role in the site planning for Shriver, perhaps also for Hopeton and other corporate centers. If one stands on Mount Prospect above Shriver and looks toward the northeast, the moon at its north maximum will rise near a line that passes through the "center" of the Shriver "Circle" and passes through Hopeton. There is no place closer than Mount Prospect from which this zero-altitude view of the north maximum moonrise over Shriver and Hopeton is possible.

As shown in Figure 5.16, eight major Hopewell earthworks fall on bearings to lunar extremes when viewed from a single position on Mount Prospect: (1) the north maximum moonrise (52°.1) aligns with the center of Shriver and the southwest corner of Hopeton,[13] (2) the south minimum moonrise bearing (114°.8) passes near the estimated center of the large circular enclosure at Works East, (3) the south maximum moonrise bearing (129°.3) passes through the southern extension of High Bank and touches the northeast corner of

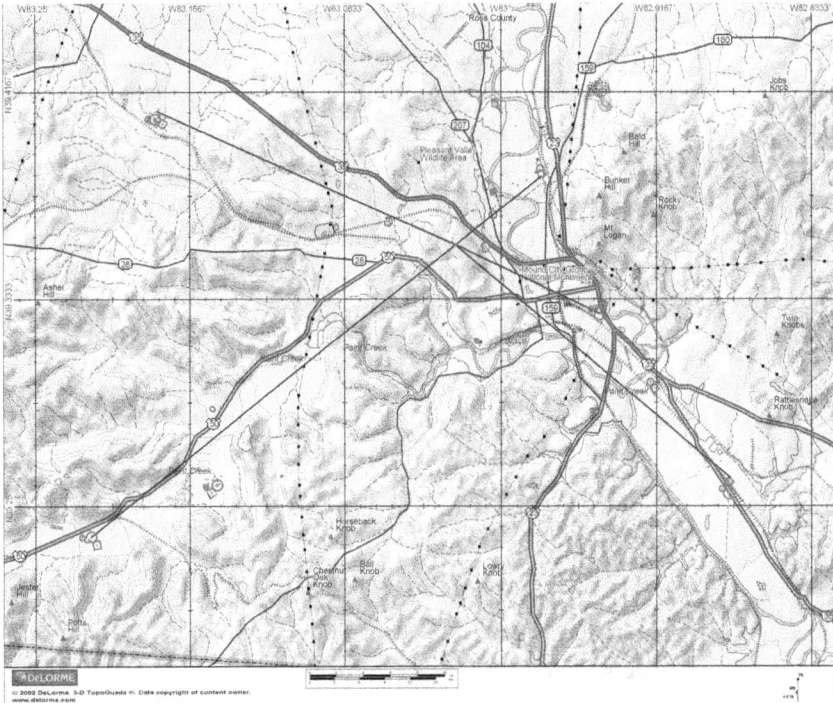

Figure 5.16. Mount Prospect Plateau alignments. Courtesy © 2002 DeLorme (www. delorme.com) 3-D TopoQuadsÆ and with the authors' additions. Key: Shriver-Hopeton: north maximum rise, 52°.1; Works East: south minimum rise, 114°.8; High Bank–Liberty: south maximum rise, 129°.3; Seip: south maximum set, 230°.8; Anderson-Frankfort: north minimum set, 293°.6.

the Liberty Square, (4) the south maximum moonset bearing (230°.7) passes through the southeast corner of the Seip Square, and (5) the north minimum moonset bearing (293°.7) passes within 10 m of the northeast corner of the Anderson "Square" and misses the northeast corner of the Frankfort Square by perhaps 100 m, an "error" of less than .05°.[14] Zero-altitude horizons and a tangent moon at rise and set define all of these bearings.

It is difficult to estimate the probability that these alignments are accidental. The earthwork "targets" are large, ranging from 7 degrees at Works East, the site closest to Mount Prospect, to 1 degree at Frankfort, the most distant site. Defining the earthwork target is also problematic. One could choose among circle centers large and small, corners and centers of squares, and geometric centers of entire enclosures. Here we have considered alignment as a bearing passing through or within 1 degree of an enclosure. Some insight about the probability of accidental alignment could be gained from a Monte Carlo study of the likelihood that randomly positioned high points would have alignment relations to the Hopewell sites comparable to those actually found at Mount Prospect.

If this position on Mount Prospect, which we will call Prospect Point, served as the common backsight for lunar extremes seen over Shriver and Hopeton, Works East, High Bank and Liberty, Seip, and Anderson and Frankfort, its role in the large design of the Chillicothe core resembles the roles of Coffman's Knob and H1 in our earlier interpretation of the smaller design of works at Newark and Granville. In that respect the zero-altitude hypothesis framed at Newark gains support.

Yet there are significant differences. At Newark, bearings on lunar extremes from both Coffman's Knob and H1 bisect major earthworks and the Observatory Circle-Octagon and the Great Circle, and pass through centers at the Salisbury Square and the elliptical enclosure north of the Salisbury Square. At Chillicothe there is no consistently accurate pattern. At Newark the aligned sites are visible from H1 and Coffman's Knob. At Chillicothe there is no direct line of sight from Prospect Point to Seip or Frankfort, or even to Anderson and Hopewell, unless the observer leaves Prospect Point and moves toward the western edge of the plateau.

Prospect Point could have served as a position from which to lay out or coordinate roughly the locations of as many as seven Hopewell enclosures: Shriver, Hopeton, Liberty, Works East, Seip, Anderson, and Frankfort. Observations of zero-altitude lunar rise/set points may have played a role in the placement of these enclosures.

A Regional Plan?

The suggestion of a larger regional plan calls our attention back to earlier discussion of the array of sites along the Teays Valley north and south of High Bank—Works East, High Bank, and Liberty aligned along the 143°.4 bearing of the old valley. If Mount Prospect played the role in the layout of the Shriver–Mound City–Hopeton complex that we have begun to suspect, there is reason to believe it may have played a further role in the layout of the Teays Valley array. The long axis of the High Bank Circle-Octagon and the bearing of the valley determine the line on which Liberty and Works East fall. As viewed from Mount Prospect, the intersections of the azimuths of the Seip south minimum and maximum moonrise extremes with the Teays Valley–High Bank axis could have determined the places where Liberty and Works East would be built (Figures 5.11 and 5.16). It remains for experimental archaeology to determine the feasibility of laying out such a design on such a scale.[15]

On the preglacial Paint Creek valley we have established another array of sites along both sides of the northeast-bearing valley. We have seen already that bearings on the north maximum moonrise and the north minimum moonrise connect Seip with Shriver-Hopeton, and with Works East. Now we discover that the 52°.2 north maximum moonrise bearing from Seip through Shriver and Hopeton passes over Prospect Point, drawing the Seip enclosure into a possible regional plan centered on Mount Prospect. Seip, as we noticed earlier, is the focus of lunar bearings on Shriver-Hopeton and Works East. It is also the origin, with Baum, of the double array of sites ranged in parallel along the bearing of the old Paint Creek valley (see Figures 5.10 and 5.11).

If we look at Mount Prospect as the possible center for the development of a larger regional plan, we can utilize the astronomical evidence we have gathered to frame testable hypotheses about stages in the discovery and implementation of such a plan. We must remind ourselves that even where the alignments we have described are solid evidence, the question remains whether the alignments add up to evidence of intent. On the assumption that the alignments are intentional, the following scenario offers a rough guide for such a plan:[16]

1. Lay out the Shriver–Mound City–Hopeton complex, with moonrise and sunrise events seen over the Appalachian range to the east as the focus of many aspects of earthwork location and orientation.
2. Build the High Bank Circle-Octagon, emulating the style of Hopeton. The symmetry axis of the Circle-Octagon determines the bearing on which the future sites of Liberty and Works East will fall (Figures 5.8, 5.16, and 5.17).
3. Build Liberty at the intersection of the Teays Valley–High Bank axis with the south maximum moonrise extreme as seen from Mount Prospect.
4. Build Works East at the intersection of the Teays Valley–High Bank axis with the south minimum moonrise extreme as seen from Mount Prospect.

Given the attention of the Hopewell builders to the long, linear Appalachian range east of the Scioto, and to the long linear valley of the Teays south of Mount Prospect, it is reasonable to believe they saw something special too about the long, linear valley of the preglacial Paint Creek. Perhaps its major attraction was that it led back to the origin of the regional array at Mount Prospect, Shriver, Mound City, Hopeton, and Cedar Bank (see Figure 5.10).

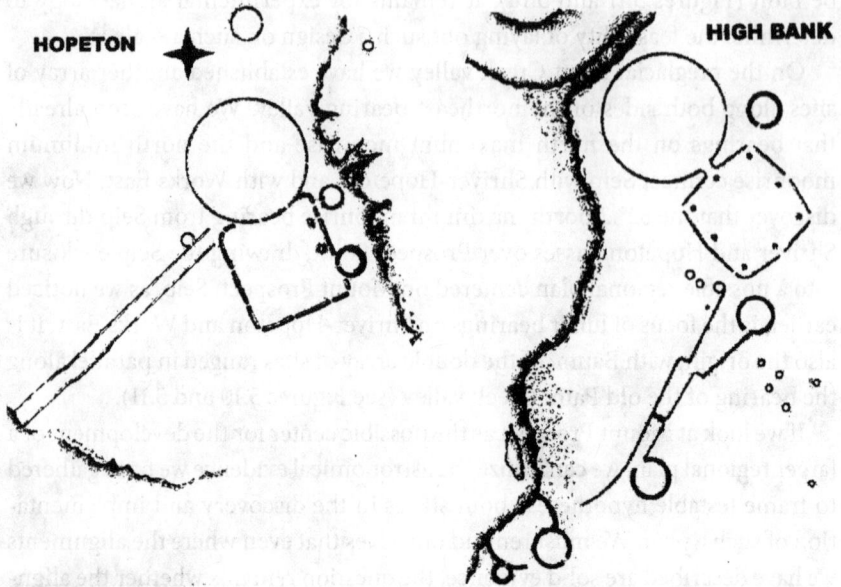

HOPETON

HIGH BANK

Figure 5.17. The Hopeton and High Bank Circle-Polygons (Hopeton: Squier and Davis 1848, Plate XVII, corrected to true north; High Bank: Squier and Davis 1848: Plate XVI).

The sites along the ancient course of Paint Creek could be drawn into the larger plan in the following manner:

5. Build Seip on the intersection of the south maximum moonset bearing from Mount Prospect and the south minimum moonset from Works East. This would be a challenging task, a "sightline" of nearly 26 km from Works East to Seip, crossing three intervening ridges with an average elevation gain of 115 m (see Figure 5.18).

If Anderson, Cedar Bank, and components of Hopeton were already in place, as some archaeological evidence suggests (for Cedar Bank and Hopeton see Byers, 2004: 538–539; for Anderson see Pickard and Pahdopony 1995), the next stage in the implementation of the plan may have been:

6. Build Baum to the east of Seip on the intersection of a north minimum moonrise bearing from Seip to Works East, and the 44°.3 bearing of the old Paint Creek valley. That bearing following the south side of the valley passes through Mound City and Cedar Bank. It will also pass through the present or future site of Spruce Hill (Figure 5.10). This is another challenging task, 27 km over four intervening ridges.

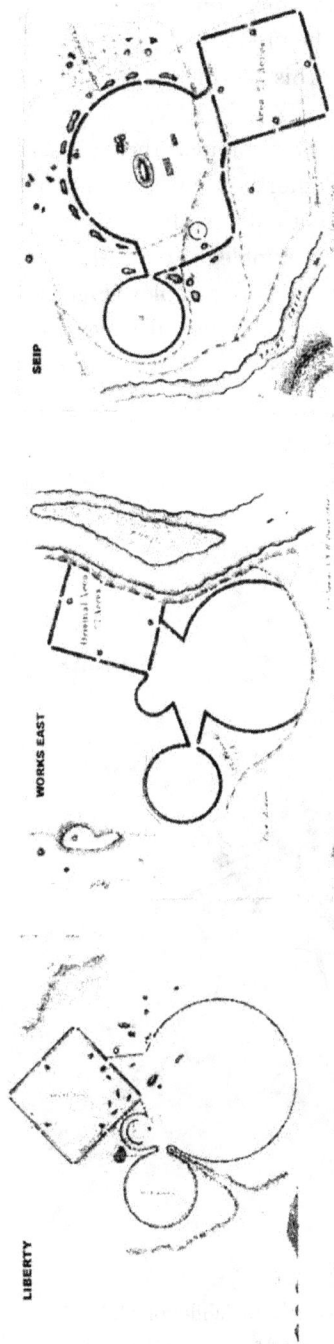

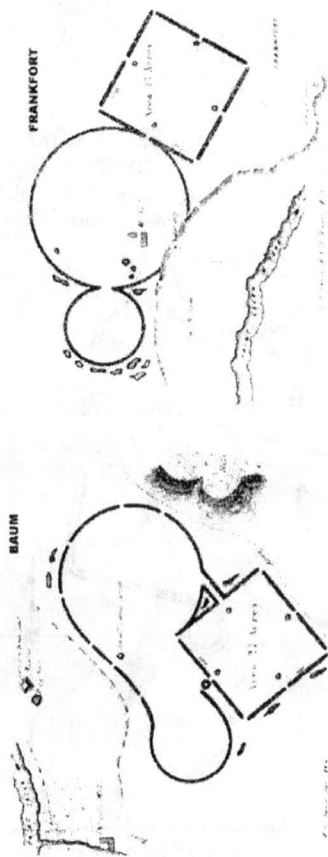

Figure 5.18. Plan maps of Liberty, Works East, Seip, Baum, and Frankfort. All at same scale (Liberty: Squier and Davis 1848: Plate XX, corrected to true north; Works East, Seip, Baum, and Frankfort: Squier and Davis 1848: Plate XX, nos. 3, 2, 1 and 4)

7. Draw attention to the parallel bearing of sites on the north side of the valley by building a new enclosure at Dunlap which completes an array of sites that begins at Seip, passes through the present or future site of Bourneville, and passes through Anderson. This 27-km "sightline" will cross four intervening ridges.

8. Design Dunlap so that it is clear that it is meant to complete the regional plan. Include an Anderson-like circle on the north side of the Dunlap polygon (Figure 5.19). Add long parallels that both recall the parallel alignment beginning at Seip and Baum, and resemble the parallel walls that connect Hopeton with the Shriver–Mound City complex (Figures 5.10 and 5.16). Align the parallels with the bearing of the old Teays Valley, recalling the Liberty–High Bank–Works East axis, and the second stage in the development of the regional plan (Figure 5.8).

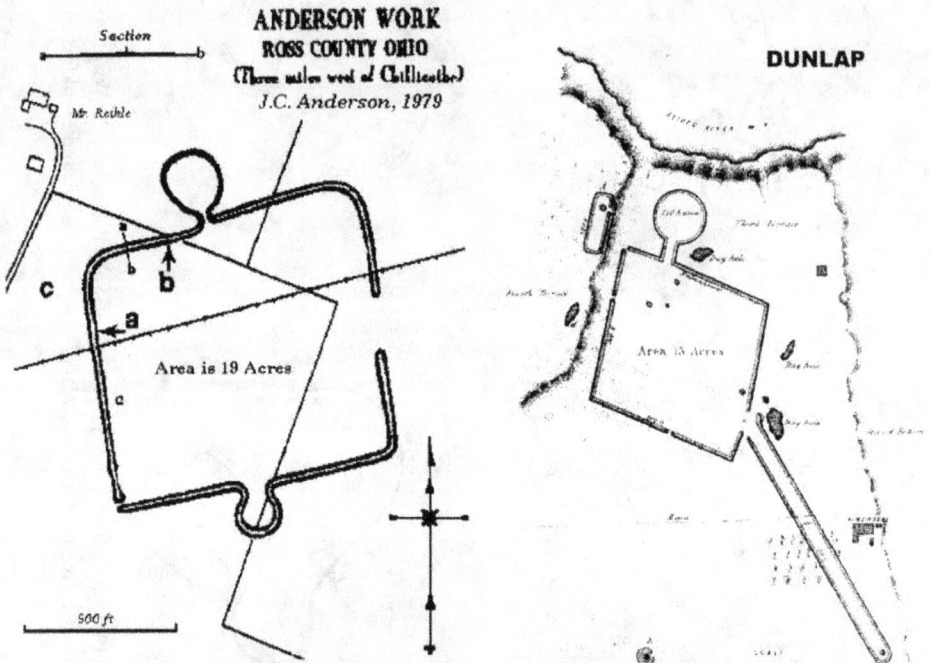

Figure 5.19. Anderson site and Dunlap site (Anderson: Pickard and Pahdopony 1995: 4, Figure 1, mapped by J. C. Anderson, 1979, courtesy of Midwest Archaeological Center; Dunlap: Squier and Davis 1848: Plate XXIII. no. 2).

If we return now to Mount Prospect and the radial array of sites aligned from Prospect Point to lunar extremes, only one further step is required to complete the plan:

9. Build Frankfort, extending the alignment on the north minimum moonset from Anderson. The addition of Frankfort completes the regional plan by incorporating sites on the North Fork of Paint Creek beyond Anderson, most important in this respect, Hopewell (Figure 5.16).[17]

If anything like what is suggested here is true of Mount Prospect, and of Prospect Point, the situation is quite different from what we have found at Newark. As already noted, alignments made from Prospect Point most often do not indicate symmetry axes or other geometrically determined features of enclosures. Yet Mount Prospect, with its zero-altitude vantage point over perhaps 260 degrees of the horizon, could have played a major, perhaps determining, role in the location of ceremonial architecture in Chillicothe Hopewell.

Arguments for planning on this scale, with the demands on the economy, social organization, information storage and retrieval, and investment of time and labor required, place the burden of proof on those who accept the alignments as deliberate rather than accidental. The choice of Mount Prospect as the focus of an array of alignments on lunar extremes marked by sites 26 km distant is problematic, especially since there is no known Hopewell site at Prospect Point. Yet individual components of the argument are more secure:

1. Alignments to two lunar and two solar extremes seen from Mound City over prominent points on the Logan Range.
2. Alignments to four solar and eight lunar extremes on the Circle-Octagon at High Bank.
3. Three sites (Works East–Liberty–High Bank) aligned on the 143°.4 bearing of the Teays Valley, orthogonal to the minor axis of the High Bank Octagon and to the 53°.4 azimuth of the north maximum moonrise.
4. Alignments from a single point at Seip to Shriver and Hopeton on the north maximum moonrise, and to Baum and Works East on the north minimum moonrise.
5. Eight Paint Creek valley sites (Baum–Spruce Hill–Mound City–Cedar Bank, Seip-Bourneville-Anderson-Dunlap) aligned along opposite sides of the valley on 44°.3.

None of these alignments involves Mount Prospect. Yet if we assume that the Hopewell builders did utilize Mount Prospect as a regional focus, further elements fall into place:

1. Eight of the sites which fall on the above more secure alignments also fall on five lunar extremes as viewed from Prospect Point (Shriver-Hopeton, Works East, High Bank–Liberty, Seip, Anderson-Frankfort).
2. Liberty and Works East are located at the intersection of lunar rise extremes, as viewed from Prospect Point, with the Teays Valley 143°.4 axis.
3. Seip is located at the intersection of two lunar set extremes, as viewed from Prospect Point and from Works East, and the 44°.3 line which passes through Bourneville, Anderson, and Dunlap.
4. Baum is located on the intersection of a lunar rise extreme as viewed from Seip and the 44°.3 line which passes through Spruce Hill, Mound City, and Cedar Bank.

If we assume that Mount Prospect played a central role in Hopewell planning at Chillicothe, the suggested scenario accounts for these phenomena:

1. The location of the Shriver–Mound City–Hopeton complex, in terms of its broadly economic suitability and in terms of its situation relative to the Logan range and the visible extremes of the rising sun and moon.
2. The locations of Liberty and Works East along the Teays Valley, by their relation to the long axis of High Bank and their position on lunar extremes as viewed from Prospect Point.
3. The location of Seip relative to lunar extremes from Works East and Prospect Point.
4. The location of Baum relative to lunar extremes and the old Paint Creek valley topography (44°.3 parallels).
5. The locations of Anderson and Frankfort on a lunar extreme as seen from Mount Prospect.

Certainly alternative scenarios can be constructed, but any scenario that assumes that all or most of the recorded alignments are not accidental must explain how so many archaeologically related sites could have been placed on these lunar extremes in another order of construction and without adopting Mount Prospect as a focal location. We believe the logic of the argument requires serious consideration.

Conclusion

On the basis of our recent work at Newark and Chillicothe, these hypotheses are plausible and deserve continued testing:

1. The five lunar alignments defined by walls of the Newark Octagon and the connecting avenue are an intended part of the Newark design.
2. The location and design of major features of many earthworks at Newark and Granville are coordinated with lunar extremes and local topography as viewed from vantage points which afford a zero-altitude view of the distant horizon.
3. The location and design of major features of earthworks in the Hopewell core at Chillicothe are coordinated with local topography and with lunar (and solar) extremes as viewed from vantage points that afford a zero-altitude horizon.[18]

It remains for further research to discover whether these alignments, which cannot be tested with the rigor possible on the perhaps uniquely precise and complex Newark Circle-Octagon, are more plausibly regarded as accidental or deliberate. Field testing of the plausibility of astronomically oriented construction on the scale suggested here is required. As we have seen, the third hypothesis appears to be disconfirmed at High Bank. There is no evidence on the Circle-Octagon that the alignments to lunar and solar extremes are made from high zero-altitude horizon locations. All of the alignments are along local horizons.[19] There is no unambiguous evidence for alignments on zero-altitude horizons in the layout of individual Hopewell enclosures in the Chillicothe region.

At Newark and Granville the evidence for zero-altitude observations from high elevations is much stronger. The large design of the Great Circle, the Observatory Circle-Octagon, and the Salisbury Square and Ellipse conforms to lunar extreme azimuths viewed from H1 and Coffman's Knob. In some cases the local horizons at individual enclosures are too low to make it possible to decide whether the builders aimed at the zero-altitude moonrise or moonset or built so that the local observer would see the rise and sets defined by the geometry over nearby, local, non-zero-altitude horizons.

To this point we have found no site in the Chillicothe region that displays the accuracy achieved on the Newark Circle-Octagon. Consequently, we have no other site where the distinction between local and zero-altitude horizon alignments can be as readily decided. One is tempted to believe that the builders at High Bank decided to go to Newark and "do it right," to build a circle-octagon which displayed the symmetry of the octagon and the 18.6-year cycle of the moon unambiguously on its walls and long axis.

We do not yet have a comprehensive view of Hopewell at Newark or at Chillicothe. We understand too little about the economy, social structure, and social-cultural education among these Middle Woodland peoples to test a priori the plausibility of planning on the scale suspected here. At present we know too little about the relative chronology of works at Newark-Granville and in the Hopewell core at Chillicothe to do more than guess at the scale and scope of design or the pace and pattern of building.[20]

Our current hypothesis is that Hopewell planners understood not only the yearly cycle of the sun but also the longer 18.6-year cycle of the moon, and that they sought to express this understanding in the siting and design of corporate ceremonial architecture. Where the natural environment itself suggested links, for example, between the paths of rivers, valleys, mountain ranges, and the long journey of the moon, they sought to build on that suggestion. They linked their corporate centers to salient features of the land, to one another, and in some cases to the heavens. Something like this cosmographic vision seems to us to be required in order to account for the ingenuity, the meticulous craft, and the labor invested in this remarkable architecture.

Appendix 1: Motivations

We generally believe that there is considerable virtue in not speculating about the motives of a prehistoric culture for which there is no unambiguous evidence. Nevertheless, one must also recognize that some skepticism about the inherent plausibility of Hopewell astronomy arises because possible motives are not widely understood. As a result, we will include here a brief description of possible motivations.

First, it should be remembered that observing and understanding the moon almost certainly was a high priority for any society advanced enough to be interested in geometrical symmetry and regularity as well as the practical necessity of understanding seasonal and repetitive natural phenomena relevant to survival. Observing and understanding the moon would have been of high cultural priority for at least four broad reasons: (1) the moon would have appeared to be mysterious and powerful and to embody the fundamental rhythms of the natural environment through its predictable changes in position, shape, and brightness; (2) the cyclical change in the extreme rise/set points of the moon would be easily noticed in a context where the local horizons provided many reference points (valleys and hills) which made the changes obvious, (3) at the latitude of Newark the amount of moonlight at north lunar maximum (15.25 hours) was much greater than that at south lunar maximum (8.75 hours), a striking phenomenon calling even more attention to the monthly north-south swing of the moon; and (4) the cycles of the moon (the month and 18.6 years) provide convenient calendrical time scales for organizing human activity. The 18.6-year cycle roughly equals one human generation.

The impressive scale of the earthworks (especially the Newark Circle-Octagon earthworks, which enclose more than 60 acres) is difficult to understand as being required for any obvious utilitarian purpose. Indeed, the shape and precision cannot be clearly seen by any human observer on the ground. It can only be seen and appreciated from a vantage point high in the sky overlooking the earthworks, precisely the vantage point of the powerful and ever mysterious moon. The large scale of the earthworks also gives the encoded alignments an accuracy and permanence that has survived almost 2,000 years.

The geometrical earthworks themselves constitute undeniable evidence of a cultural passion and fascination for geometrical experimentation and construction on a large scale. The recognition that symmetrical geometrical structures could also encode an understanding of the moon's motions would have been a marvelous and powerful but not implausible discovery. Even today when one stands inside the Newark Circle-Octagon earthworks (especially under the light of a low altitude full moon when the octagon walls cast dark bold shadows across the softly illuminated interior) one cannot help but be stirred by the stunning expenditure of physical, cultural, and intellectual energy involved in their construction. They stand today as impressive testimony to what a culture can achieve when motivated by ideas with sufficient power to inspire its collective imagination, intellect, and courage.

Appendix 2: The Baum Circle Segment

Perhaps, with the aid of aerial photography, geophysical sensing, and excavation, the plausibility of purported alignments at Shriver can be tested at the Baum, Seip, and Liberty circles. Here, tentative results are cited for the large circular component of the Baum Circle, based on Squier and Davis as well as Middleton's resurvey of the site (Thomas 1894: 483).[21] Although the Baum Circle has no central mound, the geometrical center of the Baum site is at the northeast corner of the square. The wall of the large circular segment, extended southwest toward the smaller circle (Figure 5.20), is broken by seven openings that average 10 m in width. Reading clockwise from north, a bearing from the geometrical center of Baum through these openings aligns to the following locations within 1 degree: (1) the entrance to the Bourneville oval, 1°.1; (2) the southwest corner of the Hopewell Square, 26°.2; (3) the southern slope of Spruce Hill, Shriver, and the northwest quarter of the Hopeton Polygon, 46°.8; (4) the point (13) on the High Bank Circle-Octagon wall opposite the avenue, 76°.3; (5) the southern quarter of the large circular component at

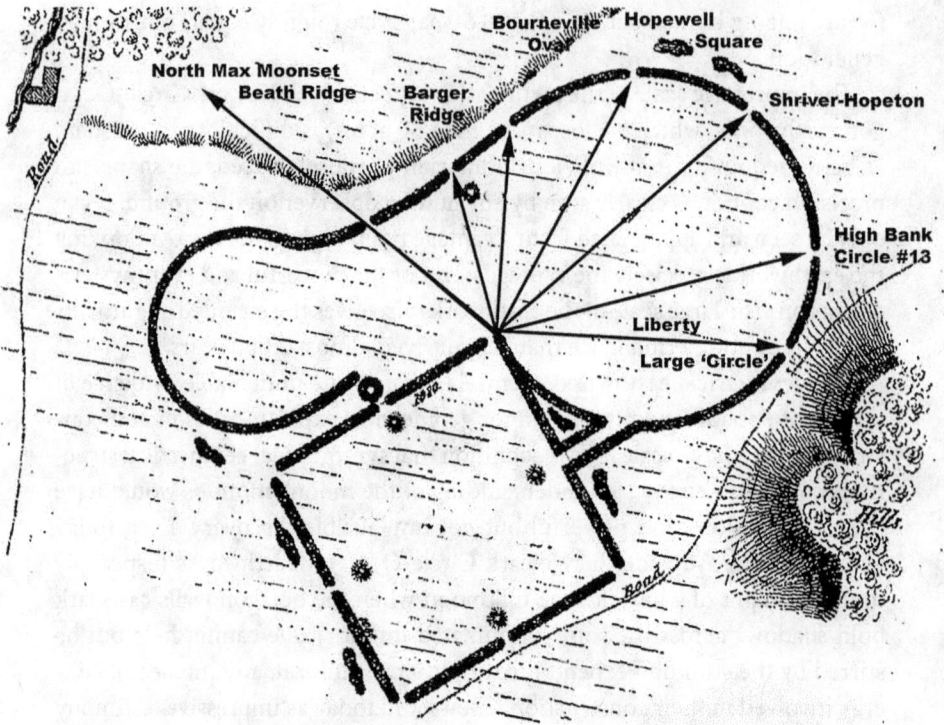

Figure 5.20. Baum: Rotation of enclosure altered to match Middleton's resurvey (Squier and Davis 1848: Plate XXI, no. 2).

Liberty, 91°.0; (6) the western slope of Beath Ridge 6.5 km northwest of Baum, 307°.8, and (7) a narrow and prominent peak on Barger Ridge 6 km northwest of Baum, 329°.8. The 307°.8 bearing through enclosure "gate" 6 also coincides with the tangent zero-altitude azimuth of the north maximum moonset.

Seen from the geometrical center of the Baum enclosure, five of the seven openings in the circle walls at Baum align with other Hopewell or Adenan sites. Two align with nearby features of the Appalachian ridge that flanks the northern side of the old Paint Creek valley. In contrast to Shriver, only one of these bearings through gaps in the circle walls at Baum is aligned with a lunar or solar extreme.[22] Beath Ridge and Barger Ridge stand out in the local terrain less than many other peaks and valleys.

Notes

1. Unlike the sun, which travels *each year* between the same rise and set extremes defined by the summer and winter solstices (standstills), the rising moon makes the journey from its northeastern extreme to its southeastern extreme *each month*. The

lunar extremes themselves change slowly. For 9.3 years they move gradually from a narrow range on the horizon (minimum extremes) to a broad range (maximum extremes). The entire cycle, from maximum to maximum or minimum to minimum, repeats every 18.6 years. The local range of these extremes, like those of the sun, is determined by latitude. Between Newark and Chillicothe the range of difference is about 1°.

2. James and Charles Salisbury first mapped this square, to the north of the confluence of Raccoon Creek and the south fork of the Licking River, in 1862. Neither the Salisbury Square nor the ellipse to the north of the confluence has survived (Salisbury and Salisbury 1862). According to the Salisbury survey, the walls of the "square" are not parallel. The northeast and southwest sides of the square differ by 4°; the northern and southern sides by 2°. The average of the azimuths of the northeast and southwest sides of the figure is 307°, within 1.3° of the north maximum moonset extreme as seen from Coffman's Knob.

3. Since the acceptance of this chapter for publication, we have found that the pattern described here for H1 and H3 is repeated at two comparable hill positions (H2 and H4) from which the north and south maximum and minimum moonsets are seen along octagon walls EF and BC, through the Great Circle or the Wright Square. Further, we were surprised to find that (1) the bearing between H1 and H4 aligns with the summer solstice sunrise and winter solstice sunset and (2) the bearing between H2 and H3 aligns with the winter solstice sunrise and the summer solstice sunset. It now seems plausible that the monumental, complex earthworks were planned using this solstitial "template" and built on the valley floor below the surrounding observation points to incorporate lines to the extreme rise and set points of the moon in their geometrical structure (Hively and Horn 2008).

4. Greber's recent excavation at the High Bank Circle indicates that the circle wall near Middleton's survey station 13 (which corresponds to the location of the "Observatory Mound" at Newark) was a focus of activity at High Bank. Plausible evidence of more than 200 posts was found in a 2 m × 18 m excavated trench (Greber 2002: 2).

5. This is the best current estimate of the location of the Works East enclosure (N'omi B. Greber personal communication, August 2004.

6. Our work at High Bank since this paper was accepted for publication lends some support to the conjecture that high zero-altitude vantage points did play a role in the layout of the High Bank Works, and other Chillicothe sites. This will be discussed in forthcoming papers.

7. See Waldron and Abrams (1999: 97–111) for a discussion of the intervisibility of Adena hamlets and mounds in the Hocking River valley. Few of the enclosures along the old Paint Creek valley would have been intervisible. A plausible test of the intentionality of these alignments would be to look for evidence of Early and Middle Woodland activity on the ridges along the both sides of the valley which these 44.3° lines cross.

8. Jester Hill (390 m) lies on the same bearing as Seip and Hopeton 4.6 km southwest of the Seip enclosure, affording a view of the valley locations of Seip and Baum.

9. It should be noted that the peaks of Sugarloaf and Logan necessarily would have been marked with fires, as the profile of the range would seldom have been visible at moonrise.

10. We had completed this research before we read Byers's account of possible lunar symbolism at Mound 7. His interpretation of Mills's account of the content of Mound 7 converges with our own findings regarding its lunar (and solar) context (Byers 2004: 354–358, and chap. 15). Romain's discussion (Romain 2000: 152–157) of the orientation of the floor plans of some Mound City charnel houses is germane, as is his study of the diagonal solstice orientations of Mound City and other "squares" among Chillicothe region Hopewell enclosures (Romain 2004a, 2004b, 2004c).

11. The Shriver enclosure may be deliberately oriented to the Logan Range, as the figure is oriented toward the peak of Bunker Hill, the most distinct prominence on the Appalachian profile visible from the Shriver location.

12. National Historic Landmark Nomination, Adena (Thomas Worthington House), United States Department of Interior, National Park Service, 2003.

13. The line on the same bearing can be extended backward to its beginning at the Seip enclosure, a distance of 26 km.

14. The exact location and orientation of the Frankfort Square is uncertain.

15. Lekson (1999: 117–118) contributes to early stages of a discussion of these problems.

16. The scenario draws on both Greber's essay on enclosures (Greber 2006) and Byers's *Hopewell Episode* (Byers 2004). Neither is to be blamed for the obviously precipitate suggestions we make here. Many, perhaps most, of the Chillicothe sites are accretional. Any serious effort to work out a chronological sequence for specific features of individual sites will have to deal with this problem in detail. See Greber 2006.

17. Ascertaining the place of Hopewell among the Chillicothe sites is a more complex issue than we can discuss here.

18. As indicated in note 3 above, our recent work finds that the geometric earthworks in Newark's Cherry Valley may have been planned and laid out from four sites in the surrounding hills that together form a pattern aligned to the summer and winter solstices. If so, both Newark and High Bank are lunar and solar sites.

19. See note 6 above.

20. Current evidence is reported and reviewed in Byers 2004.

21. Thomas says that the resurvey of the circular portion of Baum agreed essentially with the Squier and Davis figure given in *Ancient Monuments*, Plate XXI, no. 1. Yet he continues, "The circular portions of the work are considerably worn and two sections of considerable length are so nearly obliterated that the line cannot be retraced with any certainty."

22. In 1990 Greber and Linsay, utilizing Middleton's survey data and their own examination of the topography at Baum, found local horizon altitude alignments with the north maximum moonrise and moonset among the openings or gates in the square. They found no solar azimuths aligned on "gates" (N'omi B. Greber personal communication, 1991). Allowing for the local horizon altitude and lower limb tangency, two sides of the Baum Square are aligned with the winter solstice sunset.

6

Strange Sightings on the Scioto

Warren DeBoer

Space that has been seized upon by the imagination cannot remain indifferent
space subject to the measures and estimates of the surveyor.
(Bachelard 1964: xxxii)

Once placed in motion, imagination leaves palpable and measurable traces.
In which case, the problem for archaeology is not so much the ineffability of
the imaginary as the crafting of "measures and estimates" that permit some
degree of engagement between images *from* the past and images *of* the past.
This meeting should be more than a time-travel seance that, however enchant-
ing, unnerves our scientific sensibilities. Yet in deference to our anthropological dispositions, it cannot be handed over to any lofty science that claims to
levitate above, rather than walk upon, cultural terrain. A middle ground is
needed.

The Scioto Valley of Ohio, dubbed by some the "Hopewell core," affords
such a meeting place. During the first few centuries A.D., the Scioto landscape
was memorialized by the construction of numerous earthen monuments.
In their geometric plans projected at colossal scales, these monuments intimate many stories. Nearly two centuries ago, Caleb Atwater, the postmaster
of Circleville, argued that the earthworks were fortifications, in spite of interior ditches having dubious defensive use. Atwater chided "gentlemen of the
Atlantick [*sic*] cities, who have never crossed the Alleghanies [*sic*]" and yet
were convinced that the monuments had a "religious purpose" (Atwater 1997
[1820]: 145). Later, Squier and Davis (1998 [1847]) acknowledged the presence
of "works of defense" but added "sacred enclosures" that were often accompanied by "mounds of sepulture." These burial mounds yielded the distinctively
crafted items that later came to carry the label "Hopewell." In a huff of Yankee
practicality, Lewis Henry Morgan dismissed Squier and Davis's sacred enclosures as "going for nothing" (1965 [1881]: 230) and instead advanced his own
theory-driven notion that the Scioto embankments were topped by Iroquois-
like longhouses arranged around enormous plazas of the kind found at Chaco

Canyon in what was then the Territory of New Mexico. In an unanticipated sense, this early Chaco allusion was perhaps perspicacious, as we shall see.

The monuments continue to spawn debate. Although more complete surveys might change the picture, available information suggests that the Scioto "heartland" during the Middle Woodland period was studded with monuments and short on residential sites. Bender's 1985 contrast between large, enduring ritual centers and small, fugitive settlements remains an apt verdict. Local labor catchments seem inadequate to the task of exhuming and transporting the more than one million metric tons of earth congealed in the major monuments stretching from Circleville in the north to Seal in the south (Bernardini 2004). This mismatch between labor and its product strains the view that each monument acted as a "surrogate village" for a nearby swirl of hamlet-based foragers. Nor have the social or ideological mechanisms that might account for these extraordinary construction projects been spelled out, although there have been ingenious, if somewhat unconvincing, attempts to make sense of their seemingly "wasteful" character (Dunnell and Greelee 1999). At least one scholar, however, is apparently unimpressed by massive dirt piling and argues that Scioto Hopewell, when stripped of its earthen monuments, was just a routine tribal society, whatever that might be (Yerkes 2002). Of course, when differences are eliminated from consideration, similarities are likely to remain.

Rather than dismissing the monuments or claiming that their sheer salience deflects attention from a more tractable, if humdrum, backdrop of deer hunters and desultory gardeners, other research continues to address the specificities of earthwork design and layout. Evidence for alignments with solstices or even longer-term lunar periodicities is indeed tantalizing (Hively and Horn 1982, 1984; Romain 2000). According to Marshall (1995a, 1996), however, careful remapping of earthworks casts doubt on some of the claimed astronomical orientations, while other geometric regularities intimate that a sophisticated school of architects was at work in ancient Ohio. In either case, however, the roles played and served by these feats, whether geomantic or astronomical, remain obscure. After this quick and somewhat irreverent survey, one might settle for the default conclusion accepted by Squier, Davis, and those anonymous gentlemen from the Atlantick, namely, that many of these monuments were "sacred enclosures" made for "religious purposes."

Groundworks

The will to a system is a lack of integrity.
(Friedrich Nietzsche, *Twilight of the Idols*, 1889)

The present attempt at system building began as a rhetorical ploy in a re-view article dealing with archaeoastronomical matters (DeBoer 2003). There I noted that several of the Scioto earthworks, in addition to any celestial bear-ings that they may display, also tended to align with each other, forming a ground-based system of mutually referencing sites. At the time, this obser-vation was offered with skepticism. I was not aware that Romain (1992) had already anticipated such patterning but later came to disavow its likelihood. Here I wish to resurrect Romain's insight and to atone for my own skepticism, even while sacrificing claims to integrity.

Figure 6.1, divided into two sections, plots major earthworks on maps com-posed from the relevant USGS quadrangles. Amending some obvious typo-graphical errors, I have taken site coordinates from Romain (2000, Table 6.2). Salient peaks that border the Scioto drainage are also indicated as, at some point, they may be relevant either as horizon markers by which, or vantages from which, site orientations were laid out (see Hively and Horn, this vol-ume). Table 6.1 gives intersite angles, or azimuths, in degrees measured clock-wise from north, while Table 6.2 gives intersite distances in kilometers and the angles subtended by sites, treated as targets, at these distances. Angles and distances were determined through protractor and sharp pencil technology, and the results were checked against the Distance and Azimuth Program of the Federal Communications Commission. Plus or minus 1 degree is treated as a minimal cutoff for distant sites. For nearby sites that present themselves as larger targets, the angular center point is listed. In both tables, the bold-outlined cells mark sites that are targeted by alignments where alignments are the projected extension of linear embankments, either the sides of square en-closures or the parallel walls of so-called avenues. Elsewhere, I have expressed misgivings about privileging the diagonals of squares in assessing astronomi-cal alignments (DeBoer 2003). Why use diagonals as sightlines rather than the embankments created in the actual earth-moving experience?

One can emphasize the diversity or the modularity of earthwork plans. In Figure 6.2, I chose the latter course in order to develop a terminology that streamlines the description of individual monuments. Circles and squares of the three size modes defined in Table 6.3 constitute the major units. One such unit is called a "monad," two conjoined units a "dyad," and three units a "triad." Octagons are treated as derivatives of inscribed squares. Alternative

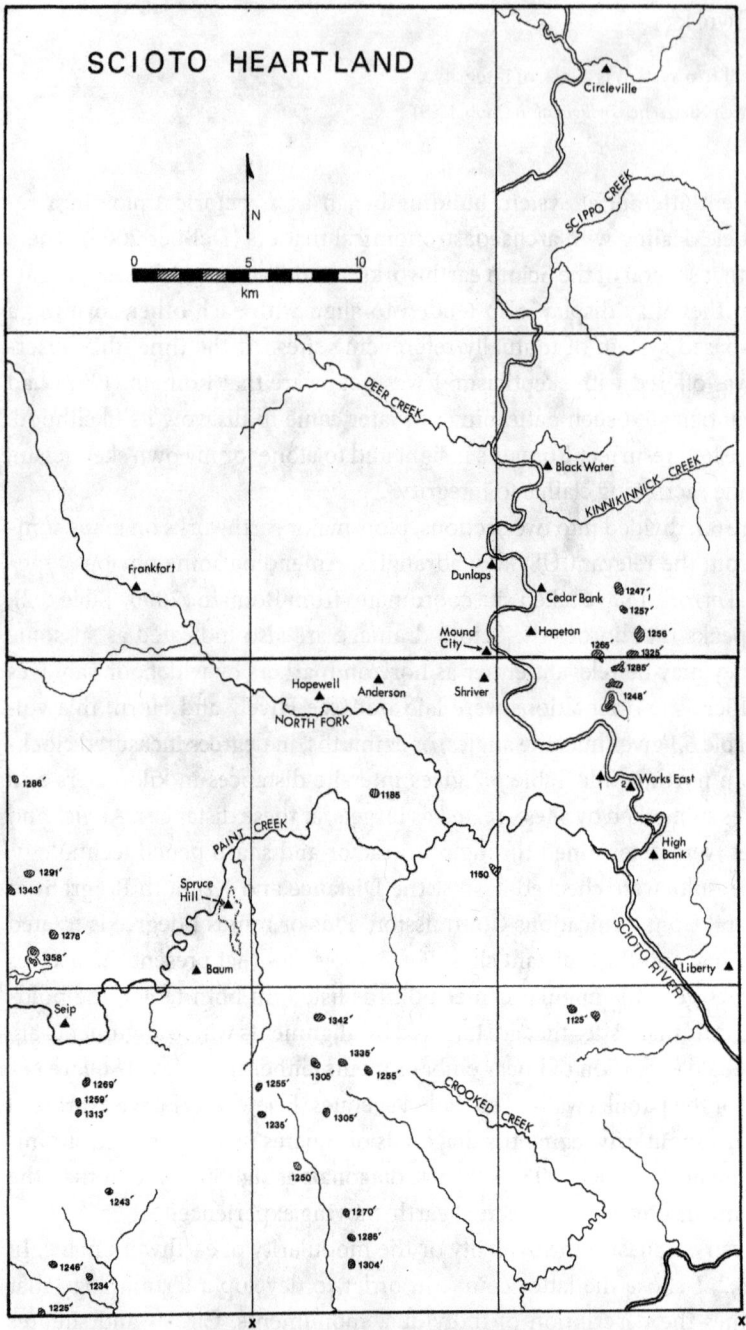

Figure 6.1. Major archaeological Scioto monuments and topographical features plotted on composite maps based on USGS quadrangles 7.5-minute series. The two x's at the bottom mark coincident points on the two maps.

Table 6.1. Declinations between monuments of the Ross County earthworks (in degrees clockwise from north)

	Cv	BW	Du	CB	Ht	MC	An	Hw	Fr	WE	HB	Li	Ba	Sp	Pk	Se
Cv		189	194	188	188	192	201	205	223	181	176	172	205	211	186	186
BW	9		210	184	187	199	219	226	255	170	165	160	216	222	184	186
Du	14	30		121	150	183	224	233	267	152	150	148	217	224	182	182
CB	8	4	301		185	223	240	244	270	164	157	153	223	228	186	186
Ht	8	7	331	5		253	254	255	276	155	150	148	226	232	185	185
MC	12	19	3	43	73		254	257	280	138	140	141	223	230	181	182
An	21	39	44	60	75	74		262	290	113	121	127	212	223	173	176
Hw	25	46	55	64	74	77	82		300	105	115	123	205	219	167	173
Fr	43	75	87	90	96	100	110	120		112	117	122	170	190	159	163
WE	1	350	332	344	335	318	293	285	292		143	144	245	246	191	190
HB	356	344	330	337	330	320	301	295	297	323		143	255	254	197	194
Li	352	340	329	333	328	321	307	303	302	324	323		270	266	208	204
Ba	25	36	37	43	46	43	32	25	350	65	75	90		250	150	159
Sp	31	42	44	48	52	50	43	39	10	66	74	86	70		137	148
Pk	6	4	2	5	5	1	353	347	339	11	17	28	330	317		185
Se	7	6	2	5	5	2	356	353	343	10	14	24	339	328	5	

Note: Cv = Circleville, BW = Blackwater, Du = Dunlaps, CB = Cedar Bank, Ht = Hopeton, MC = Mound City, An = Anderson, Hw = Hopewell, Fr = Frankfort, WE = Works East, HB = High Bank, Li = Liberty, Ba = Baum, Sp = Seip, Pk = Piketon, and Se = Seal. In rows, bold-outlined cells indicate sites hit by alignments emanating from sites listed in the left-hand column, while underlined cells mark sites that share the same declination or bearing orthogonal to that declination.

Table 6.2. Intersite distance matrix of selected central Ohio earthworks

	Cv	Du	D^A	C^A	Ht	MC	An	Hw	H^D	Fr	WE	HB	Li	Ba	Sp	Pk	Se	Σ
Cv		21 1°	21 1°	22 1°	24 1°	26 1°	28 1°	30 1°	30 1°	30 1°	31 1°	33 1°	32 1°	42 1°	47 1°	59 1°	68 1°	544 .13
Du	21 1°			2.2 8°	4 4°	4 4°	7 2°	10 1°	10 1°	16 1°	10 1°	14 1°	20 1°	24 1°	27 1°	38 1°	46 1°	253 .26
D^A	21 1°			2.2 8°	4 4°	4 4°	7 2°	10 1°	10 1°	16 1°	10 1°	14 1°	20 1°	24 1°	27 1°	38 1°	46 1°	253 .16
C^A	22 1°	2.2 8°	2.2 8°		2.0 9°	4 4°	8 1°	11 1°	11 1°	18 1°	8 1°	12 1°	18 1°	22 1°	28 1°	38 1°	46 1°	253 .16
Ht	24 1°	4 4°	4 4°	2.0 8°		2.2 8°	7 2°	10 1°	10 1°	17 1°	7 2°	11 1°	17 1°	21 1°	26 1°	35 1°	43 1°	240 .31
MC	26 1°	4 4°	4 4°	4 4°	2.2 8°		5 3°	8 1°	8 1°	16 1°	7 2°	11 1°	17 1°	19 1°	24 1°	35 1°	42 1°	232 .28
An	28 1°	7 2°	7 2°	8 1°	7 2°	5 3°		2.6 6°	2.6 6°	11 1°	11 1°	14 1°	20 1°	15 1°	20 1°	33 1°	41 1°	232 .23
Hw	30 1°	10 1°	10 1°	11 1°	10 1°	8 1°	2.6 6°			9 1°	13 1°	16 1°	21 1°	13 1°	18 1°	33 1°	41 1°	246 .19
H^D	30 1°	10 2°	10 2°	11 1°	10 2°	8 2°	2.6 6°			9 2°	13 1°	16 1°	21 1°	13 1°	18 1°	33 1°	41 1°	246 .11
Fr	30 1°	16 1°	16 1°	18 1°	17 1°	16 1°	11 1°	9 1°	9 1°		22 1°	25 1°	31 1°	16 1°	19 1°	40 1°	47 1°	342 .16
WE	31 1°	10 1°	10 1°	8 1°	7 2°	7 2°	11 1°	13 1°	13 1°	22 1°		4 4°	10 1°	19 1°	26 1°	30 1°	38 1°	259 .18
HB	33 1°	14 1°	14 1°	12 1°	11 1°	11 1°	14 1°	16 1°	16 1°	25 1°	4 4°		6 3°	21 1°	27 1°	27 1°	35 1°	286 .19
Li	32 1°	20 1°	20 1°	18 1°	17 1°	17 1°	20 1°	21 1°	21 1°	31 1°	10 1°	6 3°		23 1°	29 1°	24 1°	32 1°	338 .18
Ba	42 1°	24 1°	24 1°	22 1°	21 1°	19 1°	15 1°	13 1°	13 1°	16 1°	19 1°	21 1°	23 1°		6 3°	24 1°	31 1°	333 .16
Sp	47 1°	27 1°	27 1°	28 1°	26 1°	24 1°	20 1°	18 1°	18 1°	19 1°	26 1°	27 1°	29 1°	6 3°		26 1°	32 1°	400 16°
Pk	59 1°	38 1°	38 1°	38 1°	35 1°	35 1°	33 1°	33 1°	33 1°	40 1°	30 1°	27 1°	24 1°	24 1°	26 1°		8 1°	521 .07
Se	68 1°	46 1°	46 1°	46 1°	43 1°	42 1°	41 1°	41 1°	41 1°	47 1°	38 1°	35 1°	32 1°	31 1°	32 1°	8 1°		637 .12

Note: Each cell: upper number gives straight line distance in kilometers; lower number gives degrees subtended by target site at that distance. DA = Dunlaps avenue; CA = Cedar Bank; HD = the central D-shaped enclosure at the Hopewell site. Cells with bold outlines are as defined in the note to Table 6.1. Row totals at right exclude underlined or "overshot" entries, for reasons discussed in text.

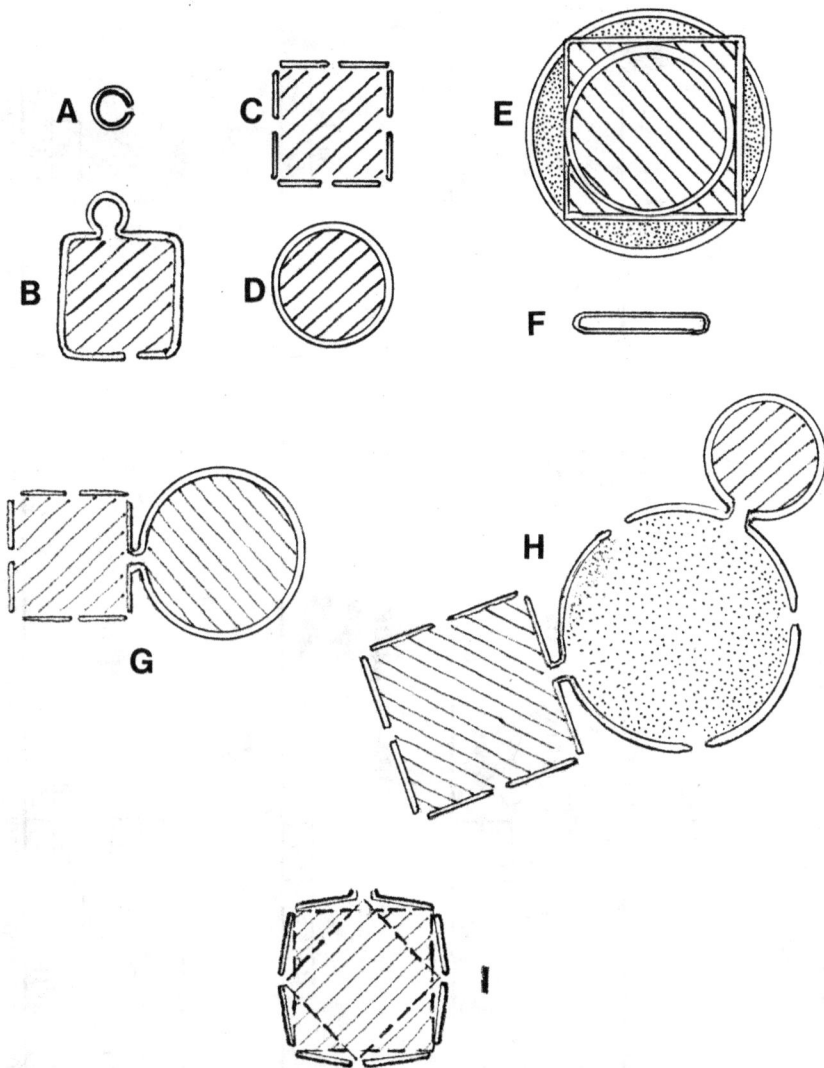

Figure 6.2. Schematic geometry of Scioto monuments. Key: A = "polyp" circle with interior ditch; B = polyp circle incorporated into small-sized square with acentric gateways; C = small square with centered gateways; D = small circle; E = inscribed relations among medium-sized circle and square (hatched) and large circle (stippled); F = avenue; G = dyad formed by small square and medium circle; H = triad formed by medium square, large circle with multiple openings, and small circle; I = octagon, the corner points of which are generated from two superposed, small squares.

Table 6.3. Sizes of major units forming Scioto Valley monuments

SIDE OF SQUARE

DIAMETER OF MINOR CIRCLE

DIAMETER OF MAJOR CIRCLE

TOTAL

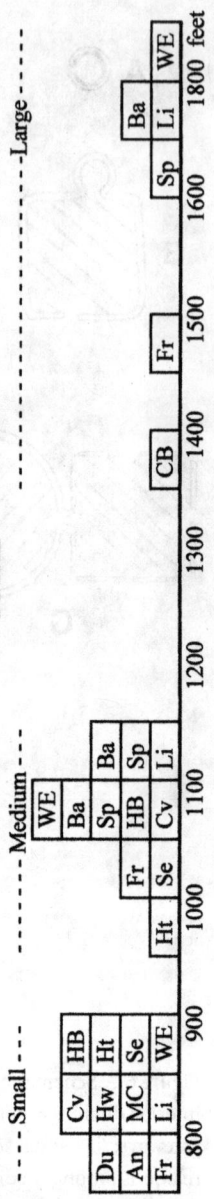

terminologies are also in use, most notably the elaborated one devised by Byers (2004). The terms crafted by Byers, however, are so tightly bound to his interpretive framework that their use requires that the reader be familiar with, and committed to, that framework. The simpler scheme used here is sufficient for the following survey.

A Tour of the Monuments

As treated here, the Scioto Ceremonial Zone extends from Circleville in the north to Seal in the south and from Frankfort and Seip on the west to Liberty on the east. Connected by lines, these delimiting sites enclose an irregular polygon of some 1,500 km^2. Our tour, keyed to Figure 6.1, begins at the northernmost site of Circleville.

Circleville

At first glance, Circleville appears to be an archetypal dyad composed of a medium-sized circle affixed to a small-sized square (Figure 6.3A). As Byers (2004: 50–51) points out, however, the monument displays some novel features. For example, the circle incorporates two concentric embankments separated by a ditch. According to Atwater's 1820 description, the outer embankment was built up from earth taken from the adjacent ditch, while the inner circle, and the square as well, were composed of soils scraped or otherwise borrowed from a low-lying swale located immediately to the north of the site (Atwater 1997: 141–142). Atwater's plan (his Plate 7) suggests that the square was constructed after the outer circle had been completed. Although this circle-square construction sequence will be encountered at other monuments, the Circleville arrangement in which the square is upstream from the circle (in this case, the stream being Hargus Creek, a tributary of the Scioto) is atypical.

In Marshall's updated map of Circleville, the minor axis of the square bears 201 degrees to the southwest (Marshall 1995a: Figure 8). This azimuth intersects the edge of the Anderson site a full 28 km away. This alignment could be fortuitous for the distance is great and there is no obvious rationale for connecting these two particular sites. Pickard and Pahdopony (1995), however, note that the Anderson square with its attached polyps resembles the Salisbury Square found at the eastern edge of the Newark site. Similarly, the Wright Square at Newark and the Circleville Square share eight mound-studded gateways. Thus a set of features tenuously links these three sites, although such linkage alone does not necessarily strengthen the case for the Circleville-Anderson alignment.

Dunlaps

It would be nice if the "twisted" aspect of the Dunlaps "Square" could be explained in terms of some orienting imperative. Indeed, the western wall almost fulfills this wish by pointing northward toward the Circleville vicinity. This would-be pointer, however, misses the actual earthwork by several degrees. The avenue extending southeastward is more promising (Figure 6.3B). Its proximal walls are open and flare to meet the enclosure, suggesting that the latter was already present when the avenue was constructed. With an azimuth of 150 degrees, the Dunlaps avenue points directly toward the avenue of Hopeton and, in overshoot fashion, goes on to skirt the edge of High Bank.

Anderson

The northern and southern walls of the somewhat rhomboidal square hit Mound City and the Hopewell site respectively (Figure 6.3C). The Anderson-Hopewell segment is particularly evident in 1938 aerial photographs (McGraw Aerials of Ross County, photo 3-51). These alignments could be coincidental given that both Mound City and Hopewell are only a few kilometers distant from Anderson and consequently comprise rather large targets. An uncalibrated radiocarbon date of 60 B.C. ± 60 on charcoal from a hickory post of 30-cm girth pertains to a pre-embankment context (Pickard and Pahdopony 1995: 6). As such a hickory could be a century or more in age at the time of cutting, this date must be regarded as a rather wide-ranging *terminus post quem*.

The Blackwater Group

Neither the small, open circular embankments nor the nearby avenues were necessarily working parts of the Scioto Ceremonial Zone (Figure 6.3D). In overall plan, Blackwater resembles the Junction Group (see Figure 6.6), and both likely pertain to earlier "Adena" times. Thus it is unsurprising that Blackwater remains untouched by alignments emanating from other Scioto sites, nor do its avenues point to such sites.

Cedar Bank

Cedar Bank has problematic status. Its flat-topped pyramidal mound might suggest Mississippian affiliation, but such attribution is unfounded as similar mounds of uncontested Hopewell authorship are present at Marietta (Pickard 1996). Byers (2004: Table 2.1) places Cedar Bank early in his Scioto-based Hopewell sequence, but the actual evidence for such assignment reduces to the presence of an exterior ditch, a construction choice that Byers claims to

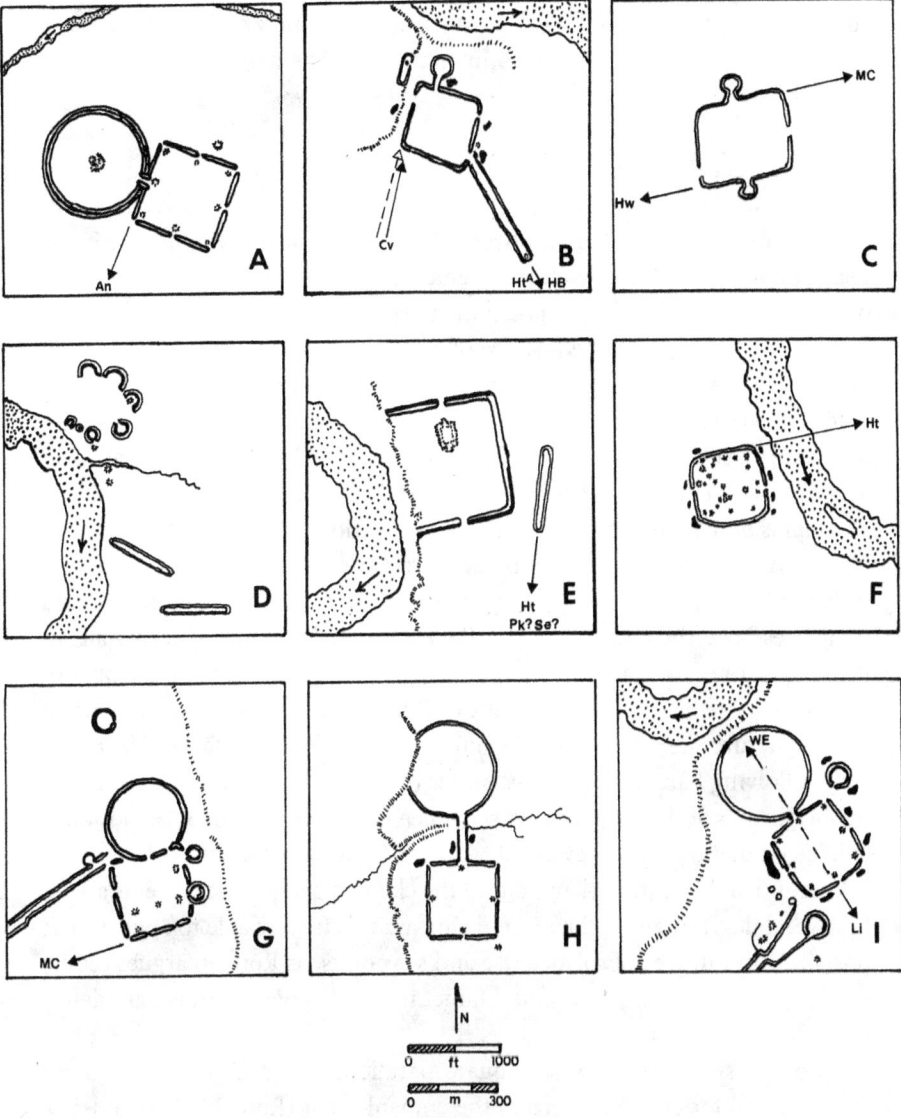

Figure 6.3. Scioto monuments based on plan maps by Squier and Davis (1998 [1848]) and incorporating revisions made by Marshall (1995). Key: A = Circleville; B = Dunlaps; C = Anderson; D = Blackwater; E = Cedar Bank; F = Mound City; G = Hopeton; H = Seal; I = High Bank.

be diagnostic of early Hopewell. The walls of the Cedar Bank enclosure do not align with other sites, but the nearby avenue, which may or may not be contemporary with the enclosure, brushes nearby Hopeton (Figure 6.3E) and, somewhat remarkably, goes on to intersect the distant sites of Piketon and Seal.

Mound City and Hopeton

Just over two kilometers apart on opposite sides of the Scioto, these two sites are best considered together. As Byers (2004) and others have suggested, evidence indicates that the two were interacting contemporaries over a century or more. The Mound City embankment encloses 25 mounds—the precise number is still not confirmed—most of which cover mortuary structures. The northern and southern walls are subparallel, the former aligning with the Hopeton site to the east (Figure 6.3F). Hopeton reciprocates. The southern wall of its square bisects Mound City (Figure 6.3G). Charcoal embedded in wall fill at Mound City yielded a date of A.D. 61 ± 96 (OWU-172). This reading provides a *terminus post quem* for embankment construction. A second date of A.D. 178 ± 53 (OWU-51) pertains to a cremation fire underlying Mound 10. As shown in Figure 6.4, the structure beneath Mound 10 and several other submound structures have their long axes paralleling the western and eastern walls of the enclosure. This shared orientation suggests either that the final embankment *or* a sub-embankment enclosure of some kind was already in place when these structures were built. Thus I would invert the sequence favored by Byers, who, following Baby and Langlois, places these "north" trending structures at the beginning of the Mound City sequence (Byers 2004: 516–517). Nor am I convinced that the two gateways at Mound City influenced the positioning of submound architecture. All but one of the claimed gateway alignments are off by several degrees, and if the Mound City architects were able to align corner posts within 1 degree of solstice rise and set points, as Romain argues (2000: 152–157), then certainly they could target intrasite targets with equal fidelity, *if* that had been the intent.

Two dates for the Hopeton Square parallel Mound City: A.D. 20 ± 60 (Beta-96598) for charcoal beneath the embankment (Ruby 1997: 5) and A.D. 210 ± 50 (Beta-159033) for a burned post that should "be contemporaneous with the start of wall construction" (Lynott and Weymouth 2002: 6). This latter statement implies that a short interval lapsed after a post fence or similar partition was dismantled and then subsequently covered by an earthen wall. (This interpretation withstands the additional Hopeton dates tabulated by Carr and Chase [2004] in their Appendix 4.1.)

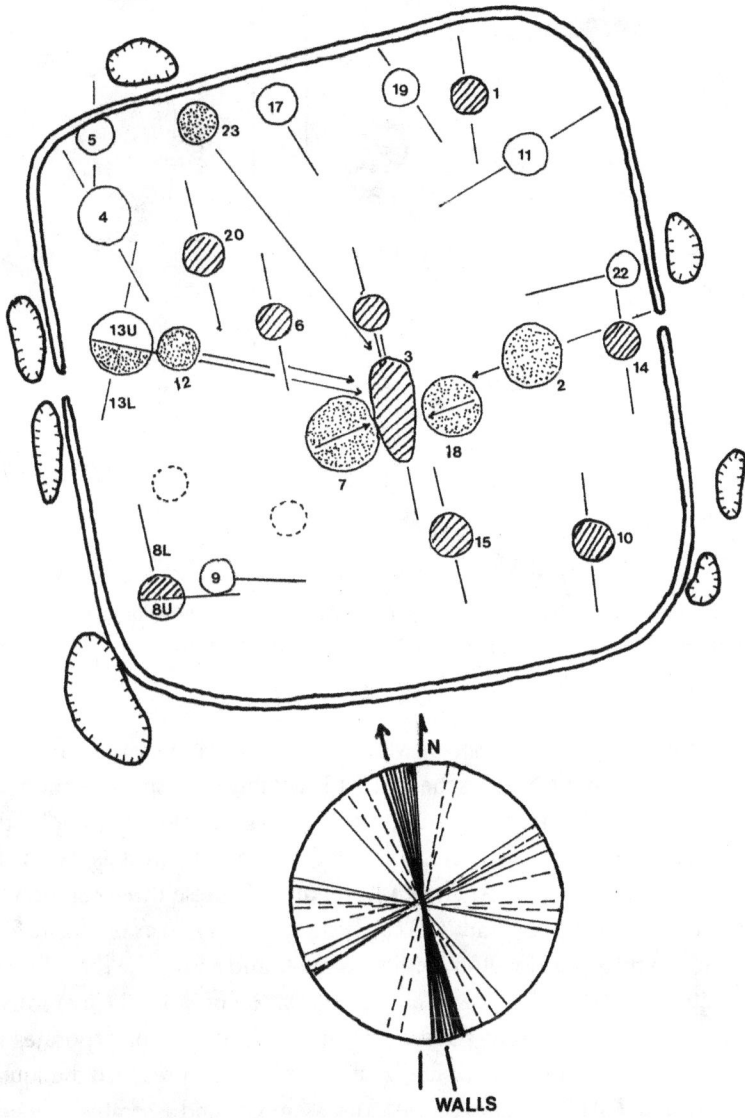

Figure 6.4. Orientation of submound structures at Mound City. Based on Brown 2004: Figure 2. Hatched mounds: the long axes parallel the monument's eastern and western walls; stippled mounds: long axes oriented toward Mound 3.

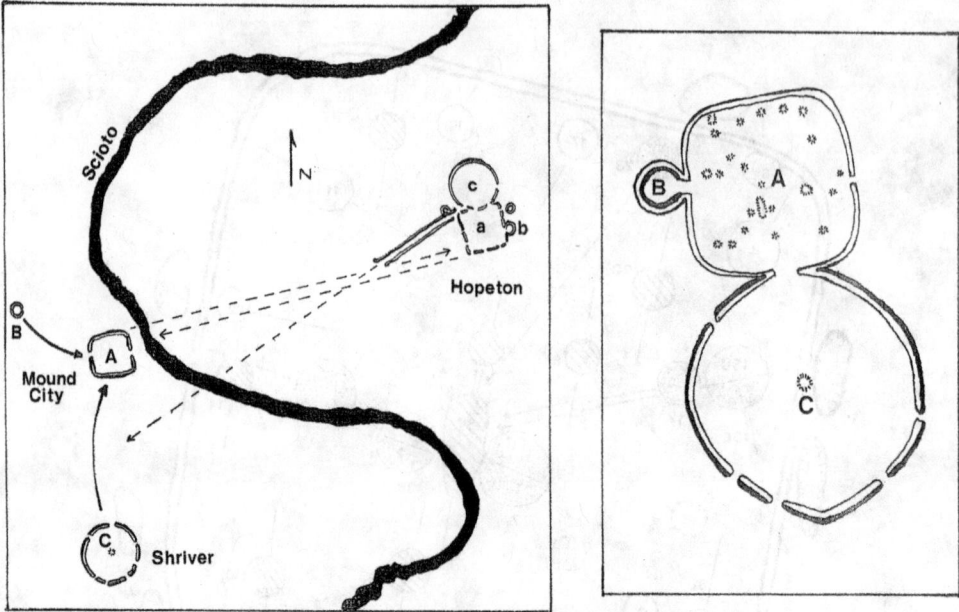

Figure 6.5. Left: Hopeton and Mound City; right: chimerical composition based on conjoining the A, B, and C components of the Mound City cluster.

In coordinating the histories of Mound City and Hopeton, Byers (2004: 47–50) advances an ingenious scheme that I will follow in spirit, if not in details. First, Byers insists that Mound City proper was part of a site complex that incorporated an earlier Adena circle situated to the northwest as well as the Shriver Circle to the south. As shown in Figure 6.5, these three components (which Byers labels "A," "B," and "C") can be transposed into a composite form that closely mimics the Hopeton configuration found across the river. Indeed, the Hopeton Works can be viewed as a juxtaposition of Mound City monads. Its square abuts the medium-sized circle to the north and incorporates the small Adena circle on its eastern side. That is, both circles preceded the square. It is as if Mound City and Hopeton were disassembled and assembled versions respectively of the same plan. I find this arrangement much more plausible than Byers's claim that the Mound City enclosure came to act as an "infix" for the Hopeton circle and square, thus anticipating a triadic form. The latter argument rests on a faulty claim that the Hopeton avenue targets Mound City. In fact, as seen in Figure 6.5, no such targeting is evident. An orientation to winter solstice set, however, remains a possibility (Romain 2000: 118).

Piketon

There is little to add to the reports of Squier and Davis (1998 [1847]: 88–90) and Thomas (1985 [1884]: 491–493). Gerard Fowke (1892: 77) questioned the artificial nature of Piketon's "Graded Way," but regardless of natural or cultural origins, Piketon was targeted by both Hopewell and Baum sites and apparently had magnet status in the Hopewell landscape.

Seal

Again, little is known about this monument beyond the plan initially prepared by Squier and Davis (1998 [1848]: Plate XXIV) and later rechecked by Thomas (1985 [1894]: 489–491). Seal is a classic dyad with a small, gated square connecting to a medium-sized circle that is situated upstream across a ravine descending toward the Scioto (Figure 6.3H). The major axis of the site is close to true north; however, this cardinal orientation could be incidental to the intent of the builders. Following a suggestion made by Jim Brown, I would view Seal as a beacon that pointed up the Scioto mainstream. In fact, the Junction Group, so named because of its location at the confluence of Paint Creek and North Fork, falls on the Seal azimuth (Figure 6.6). As the Junction Group is likely to be of Adena vintage, this alignment would be, in effect, time-regressive. Seal was also targeted by two alignments: one emanating directly from the nearby "graded way," at Piketon, the second channeled through Piketon from distant Cedar Bank. Byers (2004: 573) assigns Seal to his terminal phase of Scioto Hopewell, but strong support for this placement is wanting.

High Bank

According to Hively and Horn (1984), all eight lunar standstills and four solstices are marked in the High Bank Octagon. If so, perhaps not many orientations were left over for intersite alignments. Apparently this was not so. The major axis of the square inscribed by the octagon extends to Liberty Works to the southeast and, following a positioning argument to be discussed shortly, to Works East to the northwest (Figure 6.3I). Several radiocarbon determinations apply to contexts superposed by the High Bank Circle. Recovered from beneath the northwest wall, two of four charred oak samples yield tightly clustered dates of A.D. 20 ± 40 and A.D. 60 ± 40 (Greber 2002: Table 1). For a single burned oak post superposed by the south wall, however, age estimates range from 10 B.C. ± 40, through A.D. 120 ± 30, to A.D. 210 ± 60 (Greber 1999: Table 1). The latter trio perhaps intimates the chronological latitude accompanying samples taken from long-lived trees. No chronometric evidence is presently

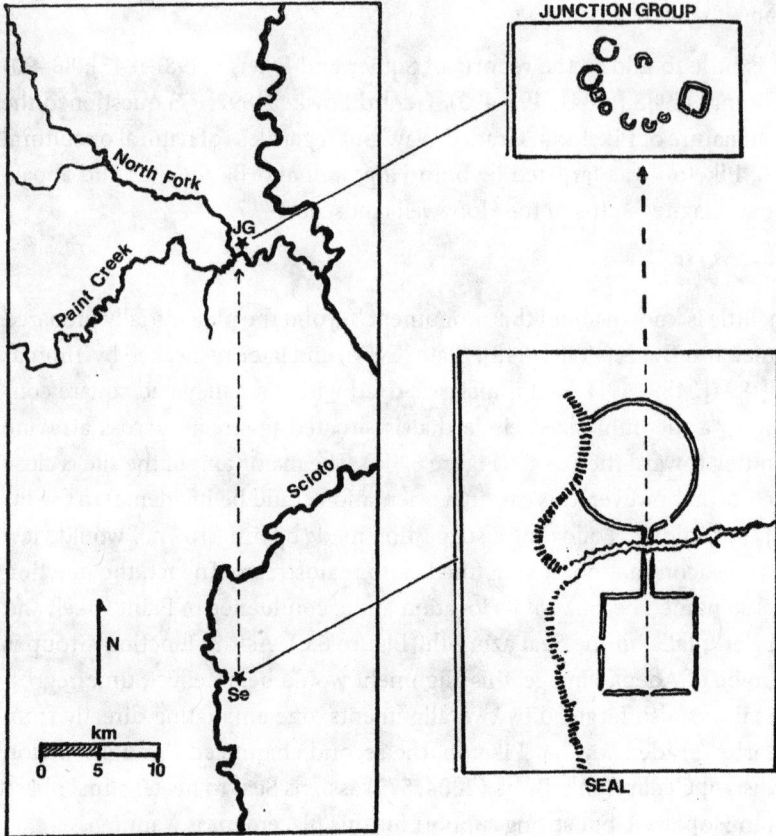

Figure 6.6. Projected alignment of the major axis of Seal with the Junction Group.

available for the High Bank Octagon. As shown in Figure 6.2I, a facsimile of this octagon can be generated by connecting the corners of two superposed squares representing the minimum and maximum extremes of the small-sized mode (for example, Seal and a "straightened-out" Anderson).

Frankfort

This earthwork is a characteristic triad in having a medium-sized square affixed to a large circle that, in turn, joins a medium circle (Figure 6.7A). As noted by Squier and Davis (1998 [1847]: 60), the square embankment was probably completed after the circles were already in place. This sequence is the general rule when construction sequence can be inferred. In other respects, however, Frankfort is distinctive. The arrangement of its three major units resembles a dyad to which a small circle had been added as afterthought. In

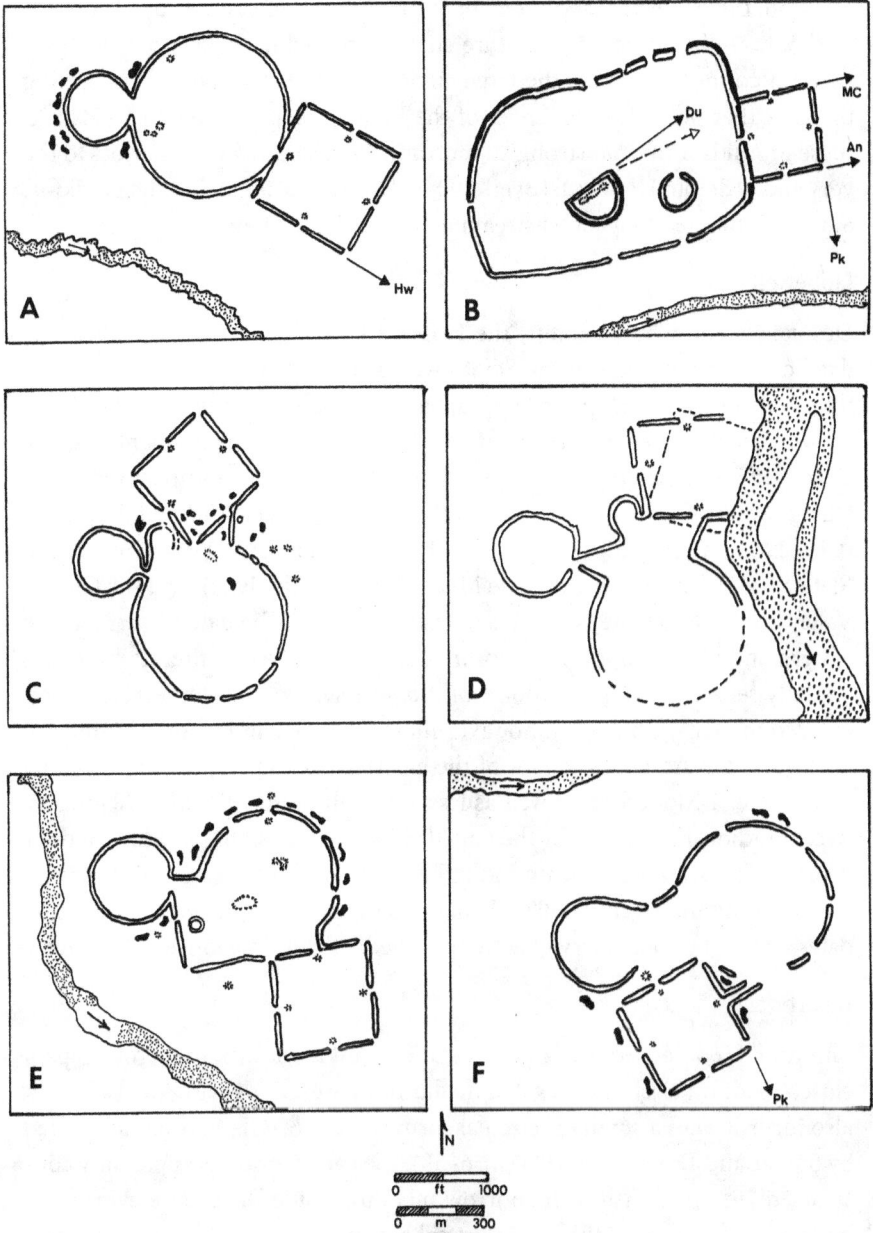

Figure 6.7. Scioto monuments (continued from Figure 6.3). Key: A = Frankfort; B = Hopewell; C = Liberty; D = Works East; E = Seip; F = Baum.

addition, the downstream placement of the square conforms to dyad conven-
tion but, among triads, is a feature shared only with Seip. Except for passages to connecting units, the large circle at Frankfort is unbroken, lacking
the gaps that puncture the circles of the Liberty, Seip, and Baum triads. On
these grounds, I find no strong support for Byers's dating of Frankfort to the
very end of Scioto Hopewell (Byers 2004: 522). The major axis of the Frankfort
Square is directed to its downstream neighbor, the Hopewell site.

Hopewell

Despite its eponymous status, the Hopewell site is atypical. In contrast to
dyadic and triadic sites of the Scioto which intimate underlying blueprints,
the final site plan of Hopewell appears as a cobbled arrangement reflecting a
lengthy and complex history (Figure 6.7B). The major embankment, vaguely
D-shaped and ditched on three sides, resembles other enclosures found over
a large swath of Ohio and Kentucky. These include Peter Village in Kentucky
(Clay 1988), Colerain on the Great Miami (Squier and Davis 1998 [1847]:
Plate XIII-2), Turner on the Little Miami (Willoughby 1922), and the Cherry
Valley enclosure at the Newark site (Lepper 1998). The gated square at the
eastern end of the Hopewell enclosure was clearly added to the latter and ap-
parently served as an orientation workhorse. Its major axis targets Anderson
and Mound City, while its minor axis intersects a distant Piketon. Within the
enclosure, the straight segment of the elevated D-shaped precinct that sur-
rounds mega-Mound 25 as well as lesser tumuli points directly to Dunlaps.
Recent radiocarbon dates for the famed obsidian deposit of Mound 11 and for
Altar 1 and Burial 260 beneath Mound 25 all center in the early third century
A.D. (Cowan and Greber 2002; Greber 2003). It is likely, however, that these
dates sample but one flurry of activity embedded within a longer site history.

Liberty

This triad is composed of a large circular embankment with numerous gaps, a
closed medium circle, and a gated medium square. Along with Works East, it
also incorporates a small subcircular form (Figure 6.7C). As originally noted
by Squier and Davis (1998 [1847]: 56–57), the earthwork was apparently constructed "in great haste." The borrow pits dug inside the square evince this
haste and may indicate that, in a reversal of usual practice, the large circle was
finished after the square was already in place. The square is innocent of intersite alignments. Radiocarbon determinations for Liberty pertain primarily to
the Edwin Harness mound. The DIC dates reported by Greber (1983: 91) are
not particularly constraining, while more recent Beta estimates suggest two
modes centering at about A.D. 150 and A.D. 300 (Greber 2003). Presumably the

later date would be more applicable to the hurried raising of the surrounding embankment.

Works East

Upon initial reading of the map prepared by Squier and Davis (1998[1848]: Plate II), I situated the now-destroyed Works East complex at the spot marked "1" in Figure 6.1. At this position and based on the site plan reconstructed by Marshall (Figure 6.7D), the Works East Square aligns with High Bank. I now think that this placement is in error and that a more likely location is on the next river bend to the west (2 in Figure 6.1). This relocation is supported by the 1906 USGS map in which a floodplain elevation, almost certainly the "singular ridge" noted by Squier and Davis (1998 [1848]: 59), is indicated. Only the more westerly position of Works East is compatible with this reference point.

In terms of form and proximity, Works East is a sister (or perhaps daughter) site to Liberty. Unfortunately, this earthwork has no surviving features comparable to the mounds associated with other triads, nor is it known whether the substantial erosion that cut away large sections of the circular and square embankments took place during or after the time when the Scioto Ceremonial Zone was an active entity. If the builders of Works East were indeed witnesses imbued with an inviolate "sacred earth principle," as imagined by Byers (1998), then the scouring of this monument by a turbulent river could well have been an unsettling omen, a cosmic portent of a world gone awry.

Seip and Baum

It could be said that Seip, a full-fledged triad enclosing numerous features, and Baum, a neighboring triad lacking such features, are the Paint Creek equivalent of Liberty and Works East (Figure 6.7E and Figure 6.7F). Yet such pairing is not total. Following the approach taken by Marshall (1996), Figure 6.8 superposes the plans of the five major triadic sites. Liberty, Baum, and Works East have their major units centered according to similar scalene triangles, while Seip and Frankfort follow layouts resembling flattened isosceles triangles. Even if Baum were a successor to Seip, as both Greber (1997a: 216–217) and Byers (2004: 559) have suggested, it was laid out according to a plan shared with Liberty and Works East, not with its upstream neighbor. In this architectural departure, the construction of Baum may be another symptom of unsettled times.

Burials 16 and 32 from the mortuary structure underlying Seip Mound 1 have yielded three radiocarbon dates that tightly cluster at A.D. 310. The mound itself was accordingly built later. The next few generations (quite literally so, according to Byers's age set model) must have been frenzied ones at Seip. After

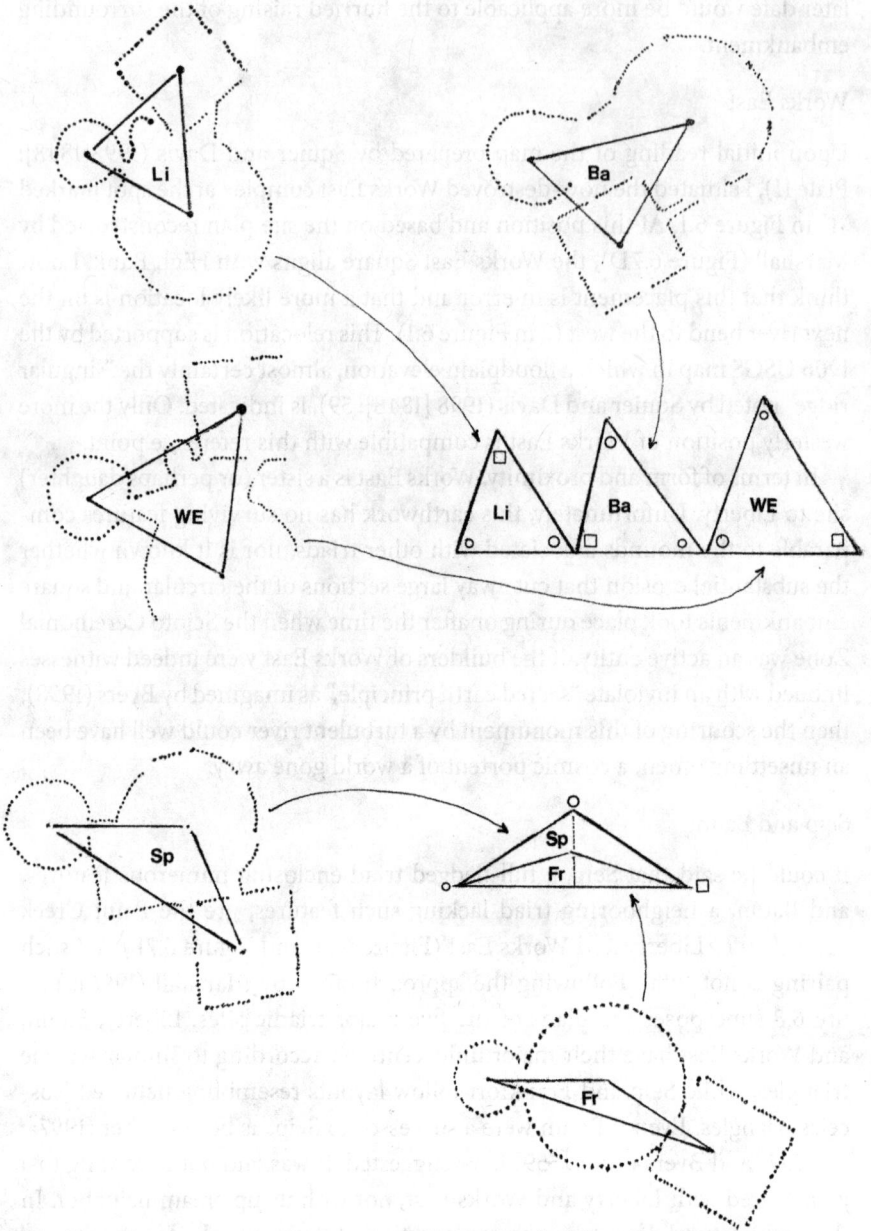

Figure 6.8. Triangles formed by connecting the centers of major triad unit earthworks.

the closure of Mound 1, also referred to as the Seip-Pricer Mound, mortuary activities continued at or shifted to the multiroomed structure found beneath Mound 2, also referred to as the Seip-Conjoined Mound (Byers 2004: 565–567). This latter mound, however, was never properly finished before approximately 50,000 m^3 of earth were exhumed from nearby borrows to form the large Seip circle and square (apparently in that order), while the Baum embankment, located a short distance downstream, was readied for projects that were never to reach full fruition (Greber 1997a). Uncannily, the minor axes of the Baum and Hopewell squares both converge on a distant Piketon. It is as if the contorted arrangement of the Baum Earthwork, unusual in that its construction preceded actual use rather than encompassing prior uses, was straining to deal with a landscape subject to new twists.

The Verity of Vectors

The preceding survey contextualizes 19 intersite alignments, the specifications of which are given in Table 6.2 and Table 6.3. It remains to be demonstrated if this frequency is "uncanny" or, in a statistical sense, sufficiently significant to support a claim for real patterning. Such an evaluation is more difficult than might be supposed. After struggling with several probability matrices, each incorporating somewhat varying assumptions, I turned to more statistically adept colleagues for help. Their advice was ambiguous. One shrugged and replied that the problem was really not statistical in nature and that I should just proceed to show that the purported alignments are warranted in terms of some independently derived model of monument usage. A second countered that the problem indeed was a statistical one, but of the intractable multiple-body sort. Stubbornly, and perhaps foolishly, undeterred, I offer the following.

First, it might be the case that alignments are epiphenomena of other undisclosed patterning in the data. For example, all of the considered earthworks border rivers, and in several cases their long axes parallel these river courses. Could such riverine entrainment account for the frequency of intersite alignments? Certainly it could if the Scioto and its tributaries followed straight courses. In fact, however, their courses display the sinuosity typical of kinematic regimes, and it can be shown that there is little correlation between the distribution of river bearings sampled at kilometer intervals and the orientation of riverside earthworks. Furthermore, six of the 19 alignments crosscut river drainages, while only four of the interdrainage alignments meet the requirement that an aligned embankment also parallel the course of the neighboring riverbank. In addition, all but one of the intradrainage alignments

(Anderson to Hopewell) are directed downstream. This asymmetry would not be generated randomly. Entrainment does not afford a general explanation for the observed alignments.

More challenging is to show that the overall pattern of alignments is improbable or, in less daunting terms, that reality is a bit weird. The approach taken here is to maintain the observed distribution of sites but to allow site orientation to vary. Sites can be imagined as spinners with four pointers in the case of squares, two in the case of avenues. It is evident that, on any one spin, one pointer falls in each quadrant in the case of squares or in each half-circle in the case of avenues. Thus one can tabulate for each degree of a quadrant or half-circle whether any target is hit over the full sweep of 360 degrees. That is, after giving each site a good spin, resultant vectors either intercept other sites or miss them entirely. The latter provision is adopted to handle the complication of "overshot" sites aligned with the vector in question or sites automatically intercepted because they occur at right angles to that vector. Thus only one hit is assigned to the Hopewell Square, which has its major axis targeting Anderson and its short axis Piketon. This ploy loses information but is tilted toward *overestimating* the probability of making any hit. It also nullifies the "edge effect" by which sites located at the periphery of the Scioto Ceremonial Zone have smaller target zones than do centrally located sites. These analytical simplifications, perhaps a bit extralegal, reduce a complex problem to a simpler one. At a determinable probability, each site targets at least one other site or none at all.

If these maneuvers pass muster, then the observed frequency of intersite alignments is unlikely to be a chance phenomenon. The probability of obtaining 12 hits for 19 site-spinners is less than .01. This result, obtained mechanically through the binomial theorem, is matched when the observed frequency is assessed against 100 randomly generated distributions. This significance of this patterning, however, remains moot until it sheds light upon the workings of the Scioto Ceremonial Zone.

Time Lines

Table 6.4 amplifies an earlier attempt to seriate the Scioto monument on the basis of shared and distinguishing features (DeBoer 1997). By seriation is meant arranging things in a series such that adjacent members in the series are as similar as possible. Such an arrangement may or may not represent change over time. Read from left to right, Table 6.4 probably tracks some temporal change. The order generally accords with the chronology worked out by Byers (2004: Table 22.1). The differences, a few of them clashing, largely stem from

Table 6.4. Features characterizing Scioto monuments, by size

	Se	MC	Ht	An	Du	Hw	HB	Cv	Li	Fr	Sp	WE	Ba
Number of major units	2	1	2	1	1	2	2	2	3	3	3	3	3
Minor circle diameter	-	-	Me	-	-	-	Me	-	Sm	Sm	Me	Me	Me
Major circle diameter	Me	-	Me	-	-	-	Me	Me	Lg	Lg	Lg	Lg	Lg
Size of square	Sm	Sm	Sm	Sm	Sm	Sm	Sm	Sm	Me	Lg	Lg	Lg	Lg
Gateway mounds	4	0	0	0	0	4	8	8	4	4	4	4	4
Acentric gateways	-	X	X	X	X	-	-	-	-	-	-	-	-
Associated "polyps"	-	-	X	X	X	-	-	-	-	-	-	-	-
Associated avenue	X?	-	X	-	X	-	X	-	-	-	-	-	-
Perforated circle	-	-	-	-	-	-	-	-	X	-	X	-	X
Downstream square	X	-	X	-	-	X	X	-	-	X	X	-	X
Upstream square	-	-	-	-	-	-	-	X	X	-	-	X	X
Ditch construction	-	-	-	-	-	X	-	X	-	-	-	-	-
Borrow pits	X	X	X	?	X	?	X	-	X	X	X	X	X

Notes: Small (Sm), medium (Me), and large (Lg) modes are defined in Table 6.3. Sites are ordered to maximize clumping of similar features.

the greater emphasis that Byers places on ancient dirt-moving protocols. We both agree that Works East and Baum and, by extension, other triadic earthworks are later than Mound City. The order of other monuments, however, remains less certain. Radiocarbon does not come to the rescue. Available dates are often *terminus post quem* age estimates that pertain to pre-embankment activities. The common occurrence of large posts beneath embankments, however, indicates that embankment construction may have followed years of activity conducted within periodically renewed palisades. Embankments could even mark the end of active site use, in which case, enclosure could signal closure. This is not to say that enclosed sites dropped out of the Scioto Ceremonial Zone. As we shall see, ancestors and monuments are never quite dead.

Let me return to some curious observations. Seal points up the Scioto to an earlier Junction Group. The north and south walls of the Hopewell Square, a late addition to that site, intercept the two decommissioned earthworks of Anderson and Mound City. Baum, perhaps representing the last gasp of the Scioto Ceremonial Zone, aligns with Piketon yet itself remains an untouched target. That targeted sites were in place before being targeted is not remarkable. Of greater interest is the finding that both chronology and alignments converge on a common scheme in which aligned embankments, or the post structures that they covered, target enclosures whose use as active centers had already ceased. From the perspective of linear time, these alignments act as memory-bound indices that point backward and, in this sense, inscribe their own history.

Let's see how far we can push the notion that the Scioto monuments congeal time lines or, to risk a neologism, paleotropisms. Given one-way temporality, late sites such as Baum or Works East were free to point to earlier sites but were themselves not available as targets. Accordingly, early and enduring targets such as Mound City should display a reversed pattern. On this premise, the upper chart of Table 6.5 sorts the Scioto monuments into three groups according to ratios of sent and received alignments. The higher the ratio of sent to total alignments, the later the site ought to be; the lower the ratio, the earlier. This perfect ordering, however, contradicts the very rule by which it was generated. It cannot encompass reciprocally aligned cases such as Mound City and Hopeton, nor does it create a sequence that is compatible with the formal seriation proposed in Table 6.4. For example, the formal seriation places all triadic works late. In contrast, an ordering based on sender-receiver ratios shunts both Liberty and Works East to the early part of the sequence.

The bottom chart of Table 6.5 faces this messiness by accepting local exceptions while preserving the overall time-binding trajectory from target to

Table 6.5. Two seriations of monuments incorporating ratios of sent:received alignments

Site	Sender (S)	Receiver (R)	Total (T)	S/T	R/T
Ba	1	0	1	1.00	0.00
Fr	1	0	1	1.00	0.00
Du[A]	2	0	2	1.00	0.00
CB[A]	3	0	3	1.00	0.00
Cv	1	0	1	1.00	0.00
(Subtotal)	8	0	8	1.00	0.00
Hw	4	2	6	0.67	0.33
HB	2	1	3	0.67	0.33
An	2	2	4	0.50	0.50
Ht	1	3	4	0.25	0.75
MC	1	3	4	0.25	0.75
Pk	1	3	4	0.25	0.75
(Subtotal)	11	14	25	0.44	0.66
Li	0	1	1	0.00	1.00
WE	0	1	1	0.00	1.00
Du	0	1	1	0.00	1.00
Se	0	2	2	0.00	1.00
(Subtotal)	0	5	5	0.00	1.00
Total	19	19	38	0.50	0.50
WE	0	1	1	0.00	1.00
Ba	1	0	1	1.00	0.00
Fr	1	0	1	1.00	0.00
Du[A]	2	0	2	1.00	0.00
(Subtotal)	4	1	5	0.80	0.20
Cv	1	0	1	1.00	0.00
HB	2	1	3	0.67	0.33
CB[A]	3	0	3	1.00	0.00
Li	0	1	1	0.00	1.00
Hw	4	2	6	0.67	0.33
An	2	2	4	0.50	0.50
(Subtotal)	12	6	18	0.67	0.33
Du	0	1	1	0.00	1.00
MC	1	3	4	0.25	0.75
Ht	1	3	4	0.25	0.75
Pk	1	3	4	0.25	0.75
Se	0	2	2	0.00	1.00
(Subtotal)	3	12	15	0.20	0.80
Total	19	19	38	0.50	0.50

Note: Both seriations sort into three sequent groups, most recent at top. The upper sequence is based on ratios alone, the lower on the principle that alignments are directed either to contemporary or earlier sites.

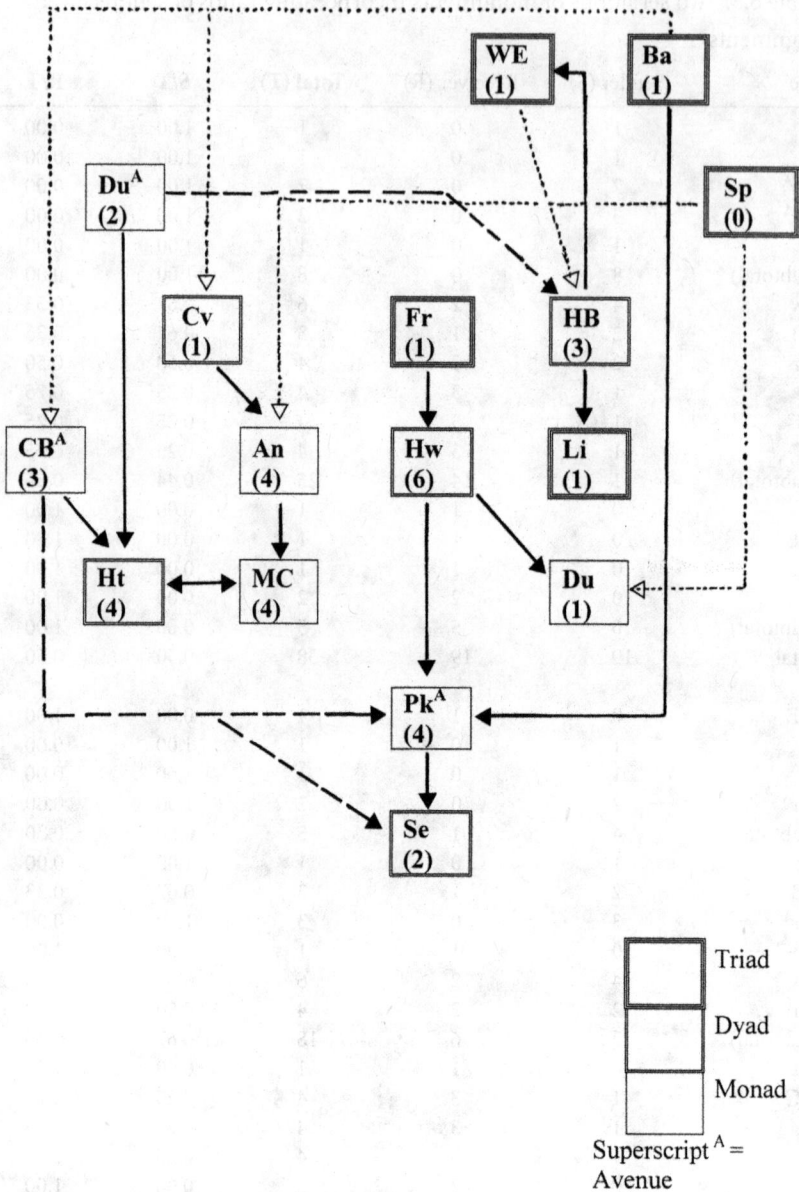

Figure 6.9. Seriation of monuments based on intersite alignments (latest at top). Solid lines = "hits." (Note the exceptional status of Works East.)

sender status. Such accommodation is inelegant but perhaps acceptable if it is allowed that history is as much inelegant patchwork as systematic unfolding. For two reasons, however, I am reluctant to stop with an airy truism. First, in its initial positioning, the Works East Square pointed to High Bank. This was a happy, if erroneous, outcome in that it allowed all triadic monuments to be placed late in the sequence—"right where they ought to be." A repositioned Works East, however, produces the awkward arrangement pictured in Figure 6.9 in which Works East receives the single arrow pointing forward in time. Such a flaw, although not fatal to the whole enterprise, is nonetheless bound to agitate the systematist. Second, and building on this consternation, is the very different scheme of intersite alignments developed by Hively and Horn in this volume. Of particular interest is their documentation of two cases in which three monuments fall on the same line, where "on the same line" pertains strictly to collinearity and does not entail the orientation of the embankments themselves. Seip-Anderson-Dunlaps comprises one such threesome, Baum–Mound City–Cedar Bank another. To these can be added another set not mentioned by Hively and Horn, namely, Baum-Hopewell-Circleville. All three of these sets include a triadic monument, either Seip or Baum, and in keeping with the weight of chronological evidence, I would argue that each of these triads was situated to align with the two preexisting monuments in order to constitute a collinear set. The troublesome Liberty–High Bank–Works East trio can then be viewed in a different light. Following a line-up of the kind emanating from Seip and Baum, Works East and the hastily constructed Liberty embankment, rather than serving as targets for a vector extended from the major axis of High Bank, were instead additions that created a collinear set having High Bank as a central member. With this special pleading, all triadic monuments, with the exception of Frankfort, are brought together into a system of collinear relations that contrasts with the earlier intersite system based on oriented embankments. This postulated shift is diagrammed in Figure 6.10A.

Although the skeptic may sense that this analysis now verges on a fanciful exercise in connecting the dots, there is yet another layering of order that can be detected in the Scioto landscape. In a 1995 presentation, James Marshall sensed this order: "Centers of these four works—Dunlaps, Cedar Bank, Hopeton, and Mound City—form a figure of giant, overlapping 3-4-5 right triangles. This requires these works to have been located and constructed at about the same time" (Marshall 1995b: 2).

Although I cannot verify the right triangles, these four sites, when treated as corner points, generate a quadrilateral form which is replicated at a much larger scale by connecting Seip, Frankfort, Mound City, and High Bank. As

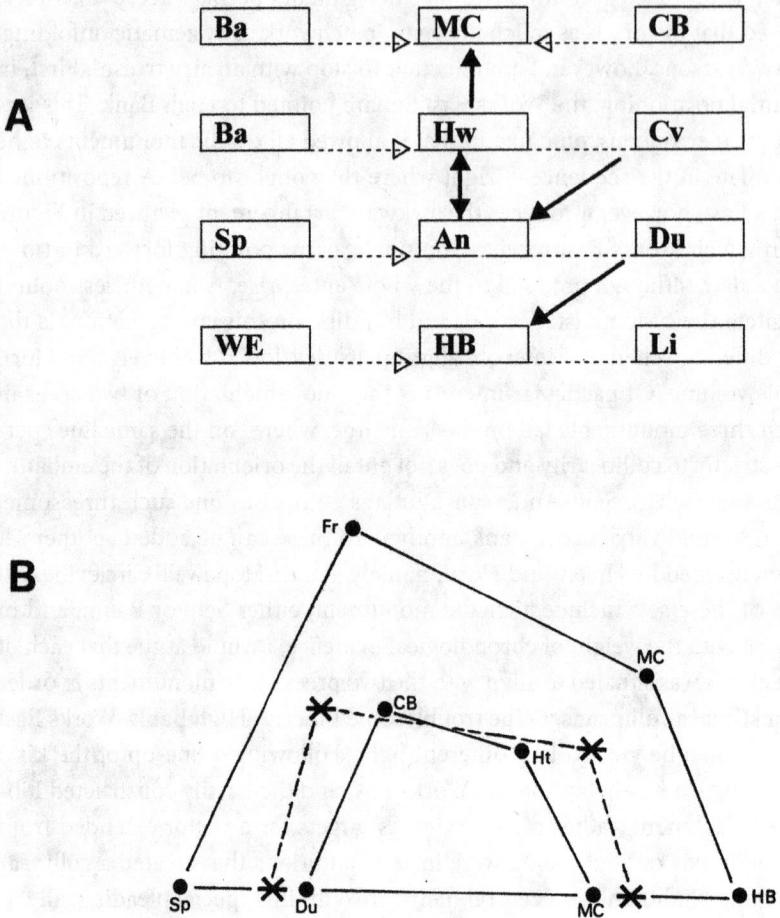

Figure 6.10. A: Alignments between sites: collinearity (dotted line); embankment orientation (solid line). B: Isomorphic projections based on two sets of Scioto sites and the bowl of the Big Dipper (stars) for comparison.

shown in Figure 6.10B, the match is indeed precise. It is likely that the smaller version provided the model for the larger projection with Mound City acting as a shared hinge point. The two triads of Seip and Frankfort are incorporated in this larger projection. The significance of this particular arrangement is unknown, but in a spirit of speculative levity one might sense a resemblance to the bowl stars of the Big Dipper (Figure 6.10B). This speculation is motivated by the central role that the constellation Ursa Major played in the astronomical thought of the Eastern Woodlands. In a classic monograph with the telling title *The Celestial Bear Comes Down to Earth*, Speck and Moses (1945) noted that the Big House used for staging the Bear Sacrifice Ceremony was regarded by the Delaware to be a sky projection upon the earth, one specifically modeled upon Ursa Major, a constellation that, as in the Old World, was identified with the a great bear. The same authors go on to offer a general claim that "ceremonial enclosures among eastern tribes from the Gulf of Mexico to the New England area are more or less vaguely conceived as portions of the sky-realm projected upon earth" (Speck and Moses 1945: 31). And the sky-realm involves more than sun and moon. The Scioto palimpsest, a veritable patchwork of multiple layerings, is sketched in Figure 6.11.

Ruins that Remind

> In every civilization without writing as such, the past of the society—its memory, its set of instructions, its sacred text—is literally embodied in every village plan, every domicile, in every person or group marked by a kinship term or by a taboo, in every person or group who exemplifies a ritual or who recalls a myth. The distinction between message and code in such a society is minimal.
>
> (Wilden 1980: 407)

The preceding analysis adds time lines to a corpus of claimed astronomical alignments. If these claims withstand scrutiny, then Scioto monuments, by referencing both linear and recurrent temporalities, come to resemble the redundant, overdetermined cultural terrain diagnosed by Wilden. A plenum of coordinated, yet strangely inert, matter needs to be recast in terms of a landscape filled with meanings that, however buttressed by omnipresent redundancy, are also subject to doubt. And much can be doubted. For starters, why time lines at all? That they reference the past or recruit the past into the present seems evident. Such practice is hardly novel. It is attested in Mesoamerica (e.g., Broda 1993) and finds a rather precise analogy in the ancient Chacoan landscape of the North American Southwest. As Van Dyke puts it, "The deliberate connection between two major structures separated by 150 years suggests that the road builders were making a conscious appeal to the past, constructing social memory for their own late 11th century purposes. . . . In these ways, we can see the Chacoans constructing a sacred geography, playing with visibility, directionality, astronomical alignments, and temporal references to construct their world as the center place" (2004: 84).

In the case of the Scioto Ceremonial Zone, it is tempting to view such "time bridges" (the phrase favored by Miller 2001: 504) as links to ancestors simply because the Scioto archaeological record, heavily biased toward burials, tells

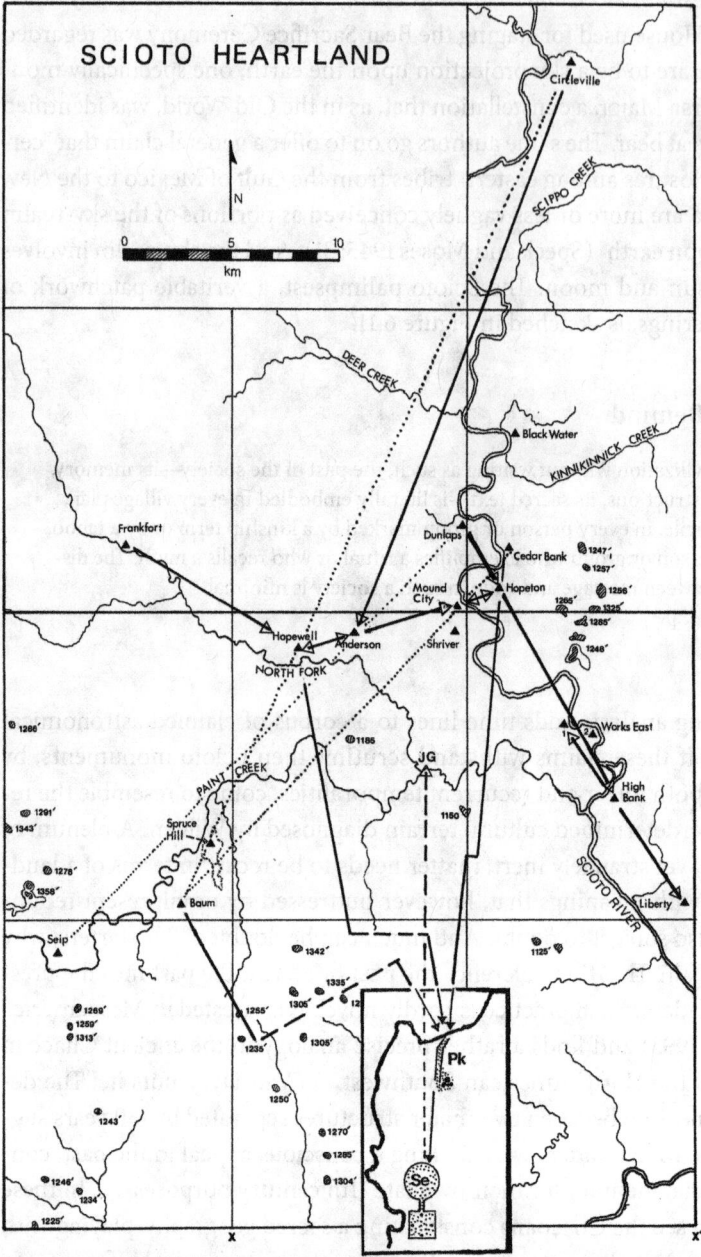

Figure 6.11. Schematic plan of intersite alignments. Solid lines = intramonument orientation; dotted lines = collinear alignments of Hively and Horn.

us more of the dead than of the living. Yet it would be a mistake to totally embrace such a focus. Many of the earthworks, of course, entailed mortuary activities, but many did not. Thus Mound City was cluttered with burial tumuli, while the Anderson enclosure was apparently vacant. The evidence does not support the notion that cemeteries were the selected targets of alignments. Thirteen of 150 vectors strike nonmortuary targets, while only 6 of 90 vectors hit cemeteries. In other words, 6 of 19 alignments were directed toward the dead. Alignments had a more encompassing role than serving merely as conduits to the bodily remains of powerful ancestors.

A second feature is obvious yet often passes without remark. In all dyads, excluding off-stream Circleville, the circular enclosure was situated upstream, the square downstream. Among triads, this seeming polarity also extended to Frankfort and Seip but was notably violated, or simply ignored, in the cases of Liberty, Baum, and Works East. Furthermore, with the exception of the problematic High Bank, no alignment emanating from a square, octagon, or avenue associated with a dyad transected the affixed circle. It is as if these ethereal alignments observed Byers's Sacred Earth Principle, or as the maxim was put by Snyder over a century ago "mounds were considered sacred . . . never again to be disturbed" (Snyder 2004 [1895]: 183). As the reader can glean from Figure 6.11, these two asymmetries worked in concert such that all alignments connecting sites within the same river valley (here, either the Scioto or the North Fork) pointed downstream. By implication, any power being sought was flowing upstream against the current, perhaps from Seal and its power-point companion, Piketon.

These patterns redirect attention to the debated significance of circles and squares. Particularly relevant are the differing views forwarded by Romain and Byers. While the former equates circle with earth and square with sky (Romain 2000: 170–172), Byers, in a 1998 paper, favored a reversed pairing (Byers 1998: 147). Ethnographic and archaeological comparisons can be marshaled to support either position. For the Alabama, the Middle Earth was a square-shaped island surmounted by a celestial hemisphere (Grantham 2002: 21). In Blackfoot ritual, the earth-associated beaver altar is round, the sky-associated pipe altar square (Harrod 1987: 73, 78), while among the neighboring Gros Ventre the earth pipe is associated with a square hearth, its sky counterpart with a circular mound (R. Flannery 1956–57: 90–91, 150). In Mound 9 at Turner, a Hopewell site in the Little Miami Valley, a rectangular basin filled with light soil was superposed over a circular basin with noticeably darker fill (Greber 1996: 162). These paired features could be symbolically decoded to indicate a dark circular earth below and a lighter celestial square above. Such a facile reading can also be extended to the monuments themselves. The large circle at Seip was composed of darker soil than its appended square (Greber 1997b 246). The outward faces of the High Bank circle as well as the Fairground Circle at Newark were of dark soil, while, in contrast, the square embankments at Hopewell, Anderson, and Hopeton incorporated fiery red earths. The pairing of a dark-light contrast with an earth-sky duality is compatible with, but not decisively supported by, North American ethnographic cases (DeBoer 2005).

At this point, earth-sky symbolism remains equivocal, a noncommittal opinion that Byers himself has recently adopted (2004: 95). This uncertainty, however, may not be so much a failure resulting from incomplete evidence as an insight into the workings of Scioto symbol systems. Recall that Kroeber concluded that, for his Arapaho informants, "a circle is a four-sided or four-ended thing—the rhombus, the rectangle, and the cross are all equivalents of the circle" (Kroeber 1983: 413). The Cheyenne also evince a "squared way" of looking at their circular ceremonial camps, or "big tipis" that in the nineteenth century rivaled large Scioto circles in scale (Moore 1987: 47). During the Cheyenne Massaum, or World Renewal Rites, the opening of the camp circle faced Bear Butte, a distant outlier of the Black Hills where both game animals and spirit allies remained sequestered until called by the shaman (Schlesier 1993: 58–59, Figure 7).

In a previous paper I argued that Scioto monuments, like Cheyenne camp circles, were modeled after domestic houses forms (DeBoer 1997). In a recent survey, Kent Flannery (2002) has again drawn attention to an architectural trajectory, commonly observed in archaeological sequences, in which rectangular structures supplant circular precursors, a shift often accompanying increasing degrees of sedentism and economic specialization. It has even been suggested that words for circle precede those for angled forms in human language acquisition (Burris 1979). Neglected in these discussions, however, is the symbolic dimension. In an overview of New World prehistory written from an art historical perspective, and thus largely ignored by archaeologists, Terence Grieder (1982) posited a major switch in earth-sky symbolism that can be tracked across the prehistoric terrain of both Asia and the Americas. In this symbolic flip-flop, a circular earth house or temple beneath a quadrilateral sky became a rectangular earth house or temple beneath a domed heaven. In Grieder's view, this switch in valence was a hallmark of what New World archaeologists call the Formative, a transition period in which underlying economic changes and social tensions were played out in extravagant and monumental displays (or, perhaps more aptly put, displacements). As I have suggested before (DeBoer 1997), and as Byers (2004) has analyzed in terms of contesting cults and clans, Scioto Hopewell is a precise exemplification of this tidal shift in which fixed meanings were being toppled or, to use a fashionable and gentler term, renegotiated. Consequently, the seemingly dyslexic proposition that "the sky is the true earth" (De Santillana and von Dechend 1969: 61) sheds light on human builders compelled to chart both earthly and celestial planes in their monuments. The upstream, unbroken circles of Scioto dyads are worlds apart from the large, perforated circles of later triads. The metaphorically disposed might even sense an unfolding cosmic drama in which these ruptured circles mark the last gasp of what some archaeologists call the Hopewell "climax."

Conclusion

> If a temple is to be erected, a temple must be destroyed: That is the law.
> (Friedrich Nietzsche, *On the Genealogy of Morals*, 1887)

The world is replete with temples of the conquerors raised over the rubble of the vanquished, but Nietzsche's law doesn't quite capture the Scioto situation. As far as can be told, no monuments were razed during Prehistoric times, although later nonbelievers occasionally buried their dead in mound tops or, as in the case of Hopeton, remodeled short segments of embankments (Lynott 2004). Even monuments otherwise retired from active service were not erased but incorporated into ongoing landscapes, not as nostalgic fixtures but as active components. The entire Scioto Ceremonial Zone, crisscrossed by time bridges and sky lines, was a sacred precinct—Nietzsche's temple writ large. The house-like structures uncovered at Seip (Baby and Langlois 1979) or at the Stubbs Earthworks (Cowan, Sunderhaus, and Genheimer 1999) were neither contemporary residences nor postmonument squatter settlements. These structures can be viewed more adequately as hostels for local visitors or foreign pilgrims drawn to the Scioto to witness or otherwise participate in ceremonial spectacles designed to set the cosmos right, to feast, dance, and socialize with other congregants, to outdo the performances of competing congregations, to be committed movers of earth when collective labor was required, to bury the dead, or, long after the heyday of a particular monument had passed, to revisit ancestors interred there. One can turn to the Yuchi ceremonial circuit to see a contemporary, if small-scale, version of a similar system in action (Jackson 2003) or to the regional, pantribal, world renewal rites of California brought to life by Buckley (2002: 215):

> In their classic forms, the major dances are the focus of great festivals that last for ten days and are attended by hundreds from throughout the region (thousands in the mid-nineteenth century). The medicine

men and their helpers prepare for the dances through additional long weeks of training, purification, and private ritual. Those who hope to attend are expected to prepare themselves as well. The metaphysics of renewal are accompanied by universal attention to the physics of social inter-relationships—the concrete side of returning the world to balance and beauty.

By A.D. 300, the Scioto stage was becoming saturated with astronomical and topographic alignments. It is as if generations of competing geometers had exhausted all the potential arcana of time and space congealed in the monuments. By about A.D. 400, either the world or its Scioto denizens declined to continue this joint project.

Acknowledgments

Many thanks to my Queens College colleagues Martin Braun, John Collins, Kate Pechenkina, and Sara Stinson for listening. None of them is responsible for the times when I did not listen.

COMMENTARY

Commentary on Bradley T. Lepper's "The Ceremonial Landscape of the Newark Earthworks and the Raccoon Creek Valley"

Commentary by Ray Hively and Robert Horn

Brad Lepper's paper begins with a poet's imagined lunar perspective on the distant past. We have tried to discover in a more prosaic manner what Kentucky poet Madison Cawein's "old moon" might tell us about its appointments with the Newark Earthworks and with the many related Middle Woodland earthworks in the valleys of the Scioto and Paint Creek.

Lepper rightly calls attention not only to the well-known geometrical earthworks at Newark that are the usual focus of attention—Observatory Circle and Octagon, Great Circle, and Wright Square—but also to their setting among less well known features of the site recovered from archival maps, narratives, and continued archaeological investigation. He places this more comprehensive, yet also more detailed, portrait of the earthworks into the context of the valley formed by the confluence of Raccoon Creek and the south fork of the Licking River. He also draws works near Granville into a larger map of Hopewell (and its Early Woodland predecessors), which, as he says, makes the question of vacant ceremonial centers "somewhat moot."

His conclusions about the extent of the "Newark" Works are consistent with our own current views of the Newark site. In forthcoming papers we will attempt to place the description of the Newark Works which we offered in "Geometry and Astronomy in Prehistoric Ohio" within this larger archaeological and topographical context (Hively and Horn 1982). We began this task in a recent paper (Hively and Horn 2006a). Both Lepper's work here and our current work raise questions about the chronology of the Newark and Granville Works that we cannot yet answer. With Lepper, we suspect the geometrically regular segments of the Newark Works were designed and built within a relatively short time span. But we also believe the specific locations of the major geometrical figures (Circle and Octagon, Great Circle and Wright Square, Oval and Salisbury Square) are tied into a network of higher altitude observation points on the surrounding Appalachian foothills. If this finding is supported by further research, the question of chronology will be still more acute.

In our chapter in this volume, we proposed a chronological scheme for the construction of major geometrical sites in the Paint Creek and Scioto valleys. At this stage of investigation, any such scheme is a more or less useful hypothesis. We will explore the possibility of something similar for the chronology of constructions at Newark. Certainly the problem is too complex to address in these remarks.

In light of our suggestions for the Hopewell Works in the Chillicothe region, Lepper's proposal that we regard the earthworks in the Newark-Granville region as landscape sacralized by human imagination, intelligence, and labor over perhaps thousands of years is plausible, if not compelling.

Commentary by Warren DeBoer (along with commentary on Hively and Horn's "Hopewell Cosmography at Newark and Chillicothe, Ohio")

For those of us who ventured into these matters skeptically, there is now an embarrassing surfeit of alignments encoded in the ancient monuments of Ohio. Some of these alignments track the recurring movements of sun and moon, some target prominent hills and other natural features, while others apparently connect monuments themselves. If most (some are likely to be fortuitous) of these claimed alignments are "real" in the sense of having been intentionally laid out by, let us say, an ancient cabal of priests with unexpected engineering skills, then we are confronted by one of the most culturally contrived landscapes of prehistoric North America. The challenge is to understand how these extraordinary fixtures, keyed both to landscape and skyscape, mesh with the larger world of Ohio Hopewell.

I am intrigued by Lepper's suggestion that the Newark "core" was designed and laid out during one human lifespan, albeit the life of some Hopewellian "Imhotep." The crux of Lepper's argument is that the hyper-coherent patterning of the Newark Circle-Octagon and allied monuments, although incorporating a lunar wait period of 18.6 years, reflects a unified plan and presumably a unitary project, the execution of which would be difficult to sustain for more than a generation. This hypothesis is not "outrageous," although its evaluation requires a degree of chronological resolution that radiocarbon dating is unlikely to provide. Nor does the hypothesis of a short chronology for construction at Newark necessarily conflict with the proposals that Hively and Horn and I have forwarded for construction sequences in the Scioto area. Our sequences, although partly conflicting with each other, are strictly relative chronologies and are silent on the actual duration of construction activity, although these matters of pace are obviously relevant to whether monuments were built in a burst of enthusiasm or in plodding increments. For the Scioto, I would bet on two or three rounds of frenzied activity, each witnessing the completion of several monuments. Any chronology, however, is complicated by the fact that the earthen constructions may cover earlier mound arrays or even woodhenge-like structures, the latter representing the active pose of the monuments.

As is often the case, the Hopewell site proper seems to stand apart from these scenarios. It behaves much like the Polecat ceremonial grounds of the contemporary Yuchi or the Stroke Smith grounds of the Cherokee. As the largest centers within their respective ceremonial circuits, both Polecat and Stoke Smith have unusual layouts and follow schedules that are often at variance with those of smaller centers. They also provide ceremonial specialists for these otherwise understaffed satellite centers (Jackson 2003: 149–150). One can imagine the Hopewell site bearing a similar aloofness (perhaps accentuated by Turner connections) while simultaneously orchestrating the workings of a Scioto ceremonial circuit.

After emphasizing that the Newark Works are part of an elaborately crafted landscape of pointers and reminders, Lepper expands his scale of analysis to address the relationship between Newark and the Scioto. He suggests that the contrastive emphasis on lunar or solar alignments in these respective regions corresponds to an opposition between the Lower and Upper Worlds that stratify so many Native American cosmographies. In this regard, it should be remembered that the night sky is often equated with the underworld, and the moon is a sibling sun. There is no need for "subtle" reasoning to find a celestial connection at Newark. The day/night, upper/lower, and sun/moon pairings are common ones and among some groups such as the Osage also partition society into moieties. Lepper and I are not reluctant to enlist the data of North American ethnography as a source of insight. Since Alison Wylie's capstone essay on analogy, we can put to rest those now weary 1970s debates on "ethnographic analogy" (Wylie 2002). As analogies invade all our arguments, I prefer the ethnographic kind, particularly those that point to unexpected connections and that ramify to shed new light on multiple matters.

Elsewhere I have discussed the quartered world and associated color symbolism that commonly occur both in Middle and North American cosmographies (DeBoer 2005). One of the interesting observations made in that paper is that while a standard, right-angled cross, whether engraved in shell or painted on a pot or in a codex, is often used to represent the world quarters, the four arms are simultaneously understood to signify the solstices (a fine example is given by Goss 2000). At the latitude on Chillicothe, the solstices subtend angles of about 62 degrees on eastern and western horizons, or 118 degrees to the north and south, a far cry from four right angles. Detecting this distinction is not a matter of quibbling over 1 or 2 degrees; such fine measurement misses the entire point. In addition, this concern over precision can easily lead to a "mystery of the ancients" syndrome in which we wonder how the ancients with rods, ropes, and birch bark maps could match our laser transits. These comments, of course, beg the reader not to dismiss my own arguments because they are based on primitive pencil and protractor technology.

In addition to the geometric niceties and astronomical alignments documented in their prior work, Hively and Horn now argue that many of the Hopewell monuments referenced salient topographic features as well as each other. The former point is important. I always thought that artistic license accounted for the striking match between horizon topography and foreground mounds as shown for the Hopewell site by Squier and Davis (1998[1848]: Figure 3) or, more recently, in the postcards sold at the Mound City bookstore that feature that site's tumuli against a Mt. Logan backdrop. Hively and Horn are persuasive in showing how these natural horizon markers, along with the positional vantages afforded by Mount Prospect in the case of the Scioto and Coffman's Knob or Geller Hill (Romain 2005b) in the case of Newark, could be used to accurately lay out cultural landscapes. Based on my own casual observations (not measurements), the Piketon trilobe is another site that should be checked for horizon concordances.

With respect to mutually referencing monuments, Hively and Horn develop a scheme in which triads of monuments are laid out on azimuths targeting minimum and maximum moon rises. This could well be, but it should be noted that there are other alignments that go unmentioned; for example, the foursome Baum–Spruce Hill–Hopewell–Circleville. My own scheme suggests a radically different basis for organization, one in which the orientation of monuments encodes not (only) celestial cycles but their own history in a far messier Middle World. Perhaps the monuments do both. The tentative construction scheme offered by Hively and Horn begins with Shriver–Mound City–Hopeton, posits High Bank as a medial pivot, proceeds to Liberty, and terminates with Works East–Seip–Baum–Frankfort. This general sequence can be accommodated with my own view of the chronology, although differences remain at the finer level of individual monuments. It should be fascinating as these perceived concordances and contradictions come to be investigated further.

I close with an entry from my notebook for June 2005: "Last day in Chillicothe. Three in the afternoon, purple cumulus piling up westward," followed by "bone trembling storm. Enough to make a true believer as Thunderers shoot their bolts at the Animal Lodge nestled deep within Mt. Logan." Across the highway, above to the left of the Arby's sign, the land is still speaking.

Rejoinder by Bradley T. Lepper to Commentary by DeBoer

DeBoer makes a useful point regarding my suggestion that the Newark Earthworks were designed and built within a single human lifespan. It is, of course, not presently testable given the current resolution of radiocarbon dating. I understood this but offered the suggestion for future testing when our chronometric reach no longer exceeds our grasp.

I take mild exception, however, to one aspect of DeBoer's further statement that any chronology of Hopewell ceremonial sites "is complicated by the fact that the earthen constructions may cover earlier mound arrays or even woodhenge-like structures, the latter representing the active pose of the monuments." It is unarguable that the chronologies of these sites could be complicated (Greber 2003), but I dispute the implied dichotomy between active and passive poses for the sites. The implication that the earthen monuments represent a "passive pose" in the history of Hopewellian monuments follows from assertions by Cowan, Sunderhaus, and Genheimer (2000), as well as others, that elaborate wooden architecture, like the great woodhenge at the Stubbs Earthworks, constitute the "active" use of the Hopewellian ritual spaces whereas the earthworks built over the sites of the wooden architecture represent a more passive "commemorative" use of the space.

I do not think the transition from woodworks to earthworks necessarily involved a change from active to passive uses of the monumental architecture. The transformation certainly signaled a significant change in how the ceremonial spaces were conceived and experienced, but I think the massive labor involved in building the earthworks was not merely a culminating performance of the sort envisioned by Bernardini (2004). That labor was, instead, an investment in a new phase of ritual activity that would have been, for a time at least, every bit as "active" as before. Even later, when all new construction had ceased and the sites were "abandoned," I doubt that local people regarded them as passive relics of a bygone era, commemorated but no longer actively revered (see Dillehay 1990: 226 and Mann 2005).

Commentary on Ray Hively and Robert Horn's "Hopewell Cosmography at Newark and Chillicothe, Ohio"

Commentary by Bradley T. Lepper

> The whole landscape a manuscript
> We had lost the skill to read
> A part of our past disinherited.
>
> (John Montague, *A Lost Tradition*, 1972)

Ray Hively and Robert Horn have opened up new vistas of complexity onto the Hopewellian ceremonial landscape. Whether considered as individual enclosures or as sets of interconnected elements arranged in intricate patterns across broad geographic expanses, Hively and Horn have revealed unexpected new layers of knowledge that the Hopewell builders encoded in their sacred architecture. Using the Newark Earthworks as a sort of Rosetta Stone, not the first time they have compared that archetypal key to otherwise indecipherable texts (e.g., Byers 1998), they proceed to "read" the landscape of the Hopewell heartland astonishing us with the vast scale of the cultural achievement.

At Chillicothe, as at Newark, the ancient architects linked earth, sky, and water in compositions of breathtaking grandeur. The theoretical chasm separating what the Hopewell monument builders demonstrably achieved and what other archaeological indicators of their level of social organization suggest they *should* have been able to achieve already was wide. In the light of Hively and Horn's latest work, it begins to look like the Grand Canyon.

Hively and Horn begin their chapter with the results of a statistical analysis that demolishes any credible argument that the lunar alignments they previously documented at the Newark Earthworks and High Bank Works might be the result of improbable coincidence. This was a necessary exercise and one explicitly called for by Anthony Aveni (2004: 254) in his assessment of studies in Hopewell astronomy. But this only provides robust corroboration of their previously published conclusions. Their chapter gets really interesting when they move on to a consideration of how the Hopewellian earthworks relate to their surrounding landscapes.

From my own explorations of the Raccoon Creek data (Lepper, this volume), I am absolutely convinced that the Hopewellian earthworks can be comprehended only within the context of their broader "cultural landscapes" (see Sauer 1925). Having established that the points on Newark's horizon marking the 18.6-year lunar cycle were integral to the architecture of the earthworks, Hively and Horn's explication of how those alignments originate and intersect at key hilltops that bracket the valley makes marvelous sense and I find myself in nearly perfect agreement. In saying this I am reminded of a line from Robert Bolt's play, *A Man for All Seasons*, in which King Henry VIII says to Thomas More, "Your taste in music is excellent! It exactly coincides with my own."

Hively and Horn strengthen the argument that there existed a close cultural connection between Hopewellian Newark and Chillicothe. Yet they also identify significant differences in the architecture and alignments, which may reveal accommodations to local topography or cultural differences between the local populations. What was the relationship between Newark and Chillicothe? Was it competitive or cooperative? Were two proto-polities competing to create the ultimate spiritual center? (If so, then Newark won!) Or are highly mobile groups of people (family groups or task groups?) periodically assembling at each site in a cyclical rotation perhaps governed by a lunar calendar? I find this latter view more consistent with the available data. In particular, it makes sense of the Great Hopewell Road as a conduit for pilgrims moving back and forth between these ancient North American Meccas. However, even if it can be established that this road physically linked these two regions, other explanations for its function are possible (cf., Bauer and Stanish 2001; Shaw 2001).

The construction sequence proposed by Hively and Horn for the various earthworks of the Scioto River/Paint Creek region is framed explicitly as a theoretical scenario with testable implications. Although the extant chronometric data on these sites can neither support nor refute the scenario, it is grounded in an elegant theoretical argument. (If it's not true, it should be.)

Given the close connections between the Scioto Valley and Newark, I wonder where Hively and Horn would place the construction of Newark in their temporal sequence. Are the Newark Earthworks the "prime object," in Kubler's (1962) terms, elements of which were copied at various times and with varying degrees of success in the Scioto Valley? Or is Newark the crowning achievement of the Hopewellian architects, the culmination of all the knowledge accumulated during the period in which the Scioto earthworks were being developed? Or are the developments in the two regions more or less simultaneous with each contributing in some way to inspire the other to ever more extravagant efforts?

One important implication of Hively and Horn's work, which they may not have recognized since it appears to undermine part of their original argument (see Hively and Horn 1982: S12), is that the Hopewell must not have intended for their earthworks to function principally as observatories. Hively and Horn make a compelling case that Newark was aligned to an ideal set of lunar alignments, based on a zero-degree horizon, rather than the actual alignments that would have been accessible to observers standing within the enclosures. Instead, the Hopewell builders embedded these cosmic rhythms in their architecture for more subtle reasons. The primary function of the alignments evidently was symbolic rather than calendric (Lepper 2004a). Regardless, the actual alignments are quite close to perfect and viewing the moonrise along the axis of Newark's Octagon is a powerfully dramatic experience (Mickelson and Lepper 2006), so perhaps the structures served different functions for different audiences. Simply experiencing the moonrise may have been enough for the majority of the pilgrims; but there may have been more esoteric motivations for those initiated into the deeper mysteries.

Rejoinder by Ray Hively and Robert Horn to Commentary by Lepper and DeBoer

Warren DeBoer is right that "other alignments go unmentioned" in our discussion. With an array of sites as dense as those in the Scioto and Paint Creek valleys, there are scores of alignments. The problem is deciding which, if any, were intended. We proposed two alignments of four sites along opposite sides of the old Paint Creek valley. We thought them deliberate only because eight sites were located along the bearing of the valley, with the two pairs of four aligned in parallel along opposite sides of the valley. DeBoer's foursome of Seip, Spruce Hill, Hopewell, and Circleville is perhaps plausible, especially with the support of the parallel pairs of four. The distance from Seip to Circleville is 68 kilometers; the sites are not intervisible. An additional interesting twist: Although the 24.7 bearing from Seip to Hopewell and Circleville is not solar or lunar, it is perpendicular to the 114.8 south minimum moonrise extreme. From the southwest corner of the "square" at Hopewell the bearing to the south minimum moonrise passes through High Bank. From the same point at Hopewell bearings to lunar extremes pass through the enclosures at Dunlaps and Cedar Bank, and within 1°.0 of a prominent circular enclosure on the North Fork of Paint Creek south of Hopewell. In addition, from the same point the azimuth to the winter solstice rise passes within 1°.0 of the enclosure at Liberty, and the azimuth to the summer solstice set passes through the enclosure at Frankfort. Did the builders intend these "alignments?" Here it is possible to see how convoluted and hazardous the assessment of alignments can be apart from those involving a simple geometrical design, and departures from it, as we believe happened at Newark. We have recently completed a comparative study of possible alignments among sites in the Hopewell core region and among an ensemble of closely related Roman Catholic churches in Mercer and Auglaize counties in Ohio where we know that no lunar alignments were intended. In that study we find that even where alignment patterns occur, as these among lunar and solar extremes defined by cultural sites and/or horizon features, or among related cultural sites, chance alignments are far more common than we expected (Hively and Horn 2006b).

Can ethnographic analogy provide an additional control on this proliferation of alignments? Perhaps, but we mistrust ethnographic analogy when the analogies are required to span a period of 1,000 years or more. Even the roughly 500 years between the "Trojan War" of Homer's epic and the epic itself obscured the Mycenaean world of the war. That Mycenaean world remained hidden until revealed by archaeology and then by the decipherment and translation of proto-Greek Linear B tablets in the mid-twentieth century. Where texts are lacking, efforts to reconstruct Early and Middle Woodland mappings of earth and sky may be as close as we can get, and that too is precarious. Ethnographic analogies between features of the Newark and Chillicothe sites and more recent Native American cosmographies are suggestive, but they are hard to control. Anthropologist Lewis Henry Morgan thought the walls of the High Bank Octagon once supported an adobe pueblo (Fowke 2002: 155).

With their work in the region of Chaco Canyon, researchers for the Solstice Project have described alignments that parallel some of Warren DeBoer's and our own among the Hopewell: solstices, lunar extremes, intersite alignments, and alignments along the bearing of structure walls (Sofaer 1997). At the level of mappings of earth and sky, detailed criticism and comparison of these findings will further the task of reconstruction. At this early stage of the inquiry cultural analogies between the Anasazi and the Hopewell would be as inapt as Morgan's Hopewell pueblos. Yet at present Chaco may be the closest "architectural" analogy to Ohio Hopewell at and near its core. As already is clear in works such as Colin Renfrew's (2001) "Production and Consumption in a Sacred Economy: The Material Correlates of High Devotional Expression at Chaco Canyon," we have much to learn.

Commentary on the Volume Introduction by Bradley T. Lepper

I agree with Byers and Wymer's argument that Hopewell archaeologists, especially, seem to be divided between those who focus on the mortuary/ceremonial sphere and those who focus on the more down-to-earth problems of technology and subsistence. I also agree with their assertion that maintaining this separation will be detrimental to a comprehensive understanding of the Hopewell "episode." As a result, I am pleased to be a part of this volume, which seeks to bridge this artificial divide.

I am, however, troubled by aspects of their review of how our discipline came to find itself divided into these more or less extreme positions. I disagree with their assertion that Binford, in particular, is to blame for dismissing socio-ideological aspects of human experience as "epiphenomenal" and "unimportant in understanding the larger picture of cultural evolution." I believe these views perpetuate a simplistic and fallacious postprocessualist critique of Binford's work that is not based on a close reading of what he actually wrote.

In the essay in which Binford proposed the now evidently contentious division of artifacts into technomic, sociotechnic, and ideotechnic, he wrote that while "archaeologists can *initially* only indirectly contribute to the investigation of social evolution," he considered "the study and establishment of correlations on the basis of behavioral attributes and structural types of material elements as one of the major areas of anthropological research yet to be developed" (1972: 24; emphasis added). Nowhere does he suggest that such efforts are less important than the more traditional archaeological focus on the technomic domain. Indeed, the whole point of the essay was to broaden the conception of archaeology to make it more anthropological in scope.

As a student during the period when processual archaeology was at its zenith, it appeared to me, at the time, that Binford and his co-workers were injecting a heady optimism into the field, not shackling us to a starkly limited view of the past. I was profoundly inspired by the following pronouncement from an essay by Lewis and Sally Binford:

> The position taken here is that different kinds of phenomena are never remote; they are either accessible or they are not. "Nonmaterial" aspects of culture are accessible in direct measure with the testability of propositions being advanced about them. Propositions concerning any realm of culture—technology, social organization, psychology, philosophy, etc.— for which arguments of relevance and empirically testable hypotheses can be offered are as sound as the history of hypothesis confirmation. The practical limitations on our knowledge of the past are not inherent in the nature of the archaeological record; the limitations lie in our methodological naïveté, in our lack of development for principles determining the relevance of archaeological remains to propositions regarding processes and events of the past. (1972: 95–96)

Clearly, the issue for processual archaeologists, or at least for the Binfords, was not the relative importance of the "cognitive-normative dimension" but its relative inaccessibility to archaeological methods of inquiry. In this light, the so-called privileged status of "functional" over "symbolic," "concrete" over "abstract," and so on arises directly from the accessibility of the various categories of archaeological data. If abstract thoughts are not manifested in action with concrete expressions, written documents or monumental earthworks for example, then they are not accessible to archaeological study. And the Binfords made it crystal clear that they regarded the accessibility question as subject to developments in archaeological method and theory. Therefore, if processual archaeologists have neglected the cognitive domain, and I do not dispute that many have done so, it was not because Binford regarded it as of no consequence but because they had not figured out how to get an empirical handle on it.

The challenge facing Hopewell archaeologists, regardless of their theoretical orientation, is how to make reliable linkages between the material record left to us and the intangible cognitive aspects of the culture that produced that record. It will be up to readers of this volume to decide whether the contributors have succeeded in meeting that challenge.

SECTION 3

The Earthworks and Their Material Cultural Relations

Both authors in this section are addressing what we can learn about the possible symbolic principles, the ritual proscriptions and prescriptions, of the Hopewell world by analyzing the configurations of earthwork enclosures in southwestern Ohio. Robert V. Riordan accomplishes this by paying close attention to the detailed construction phases of one hilltop enclosure and possible associations among groups of earthworks, while A. Martin Byers explores the relationship between the Turner and the Hopewell sites based on assessing the style and configuration of their earthwork design, mortuary rituals, and the domestic-ceremonial duality. Riordan begins with describing the results of his recent excavations conducted at the Pollock Works and outlining the multistage construction sequence and utilization of the enclosure. He places this hilltop "edifice" in its unique landform space and explores how this enclosure could be linked to the nearby rectangular Bull Works. He utilizes the discoveries made at the Pollock Works to delve into the underlying symbolism encoded in its creation and how this may reflect ritual principles understood by Hopewell populations and represented in other earthworks and their possible pairings.

Riordan notes that the Pollock Works represents a small, geologically isolated landform that had been intentionally remodeled and reconfigured through a series of construction phases by Hopewell builders to create a space distinctive, visually and physically, from the surrounding landscape. Most important, Riordan is revealing that by studying in detail the smaller, less "flamboyant" Hopewell constructions in more remote areas we can gain unique insights and a different perspective to examine the underlying principles which guided Hopewell landscape modification. The Hopewell did more than just build geometric enclosures on the wide valley floors and broad terraces of the major river systems. Thus Riordan's contribution is a valuable addition to a possible integration of implications derived from the hilltop enclosures found in topographically distinct settings with analyses conducted with the more "prominent" geometric earthworks. Riordan uses his discussion of the Pollock Works to also address intriguing ideas about the relationship of elevated circular enclosures (that world—astral) with paired lower elevated noncircular enclosures (this world) found in a number of earthwork groupings, such as the nearby Turner Earthworks.

Byers, also utilizing insights from the Turner Earthworks (as well as other sites), addresses the "central puzzle" that has perplexed archaeologists—the apparent contradiction between populations who lived in largely "invisible," small, scattered habitation sites yet produced earthworks on a monumental scale. He rightfully points out that this goes beyond simply the "ceremonial versus domestic" duality apparent in such a contradiction to note that this also represents what could have been competition between the needs of survival (e.g., domestic concerns) and the energy and time invested in the ceremonial. Byers discusses one way that Hopewell populations could have handled such potential antagonism is for them to have utilized a dually structured kinship/cult sodality system of communities with individuals having memberships in both mutually autonomous groups. He also intriguingly asserts that one mechanism that may have balanced the polluting survival pursuits of everyday life with the labor and time that would have gone into the sanctifying ceremonial activities is for groups separated geographically to have created alliances. Thus these intervalley alliances could be drawn upon for additional labor to help with building earthworks, as well as promoting the exchanges of exotic resources and goods, and such relationships would have been cemented through mutual ceremonies. One such alliance that he proposes is between the Turner and Hopewell sites and their respective participating populations (as well as Newark with the southern Chillicothe works).

Byers then leads us to consider the potential "ground-truthing" independent data sets that could verify his proposal. He explores the linkage between Turner and Hopewell in both the earthworks' construction and configuration and what he terms "mortuary residue." Both aspects, however, must be carefully assessed since each population would also interpret the "overarching" world view about proper world renewal ceremonies with their own unique interpretive ideology and rituals. This section also concludes with a lively exchange between Riordan and Byers about interpreting the Hopewell's built environment, revealing that we have come an extensive way in our conceptualizing of the principles that guided their constructions and illustrating that we still have a long road to travel.

7

Enclosed by Stone

Robert V. Riordan

That the earthwork constructions of the Hopewell culture make symbolic references to the world as the Hopewell understood it is by now virtually an article of faith among the archaeologists who research them. While this does not necessarily imply that we have always or often successfully placed ourselves in Hopewellian moccasins, nonetheless, we do regularly try them on for size and offer what we are pleased to identify as new insights. Although I believe, as Flannery and Marcus (1993) have cautioned, that cognitive insights diminish rapidly as the distance widens between historical and archaeological data, I am still hopeful that well-grounded speculations about the Hopewellian mindset may occasionally strike near their mark.

I propose that a small, geologically isolated limestone plateau in southwestern Ohio was intentionally remodeled with embankments to cause it to better resemble, and thereby to more properly *become*, an elevated space that was considered to be divorced from its surrounding landscape: a hilltop effigy, if you will. This notion came about because of one excavation trench, four stone-faced embankments, and one particular stone.

The Site and the Trench

The trench was located on the exterior side of one of the embankment sections at an Ohio hilltop enclosure known as the Pollock Works (Figure 7.1). My students and I have worked there for many field seasons, during which time we have investigated the site extensively, digging trenches in embankments as well as units located inside and outside the enclosure.

Pollock's landform encompasses a 5-ha ovoid space that slopes downward toward the west, demarcated by vertical cliffs 3 to 15 m high on the south, east, and north that blend into a broad talus on its western side. Embankments composed of earth and stone 3 m high were erected as a barrier wall across this western slope, stretching between the outcropping cliff on the south and

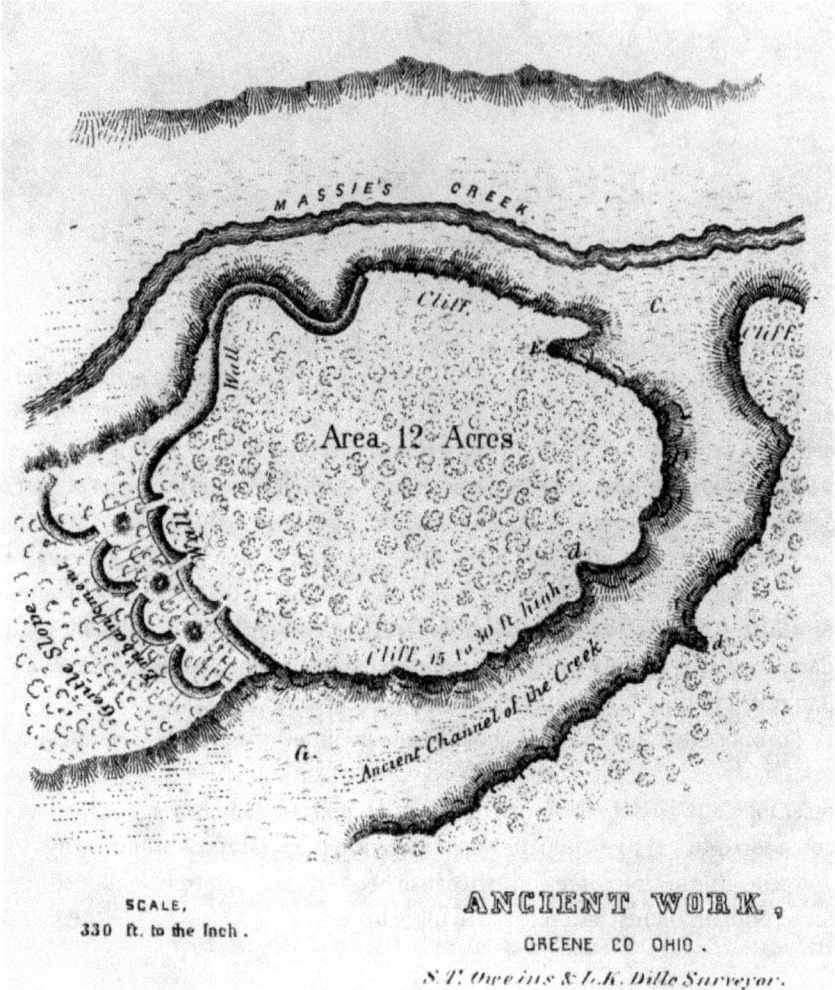

Figure 7.1. The Pollock Works (Squier and Davis 1848: Plate XII, No. 3).

the 7-m-high creek bluff on the north (Figure 7.2). The barrier is penetrated by two major openings, the north and central gateways, as well as a third (south gateway) that is just a shallow depression on top of the barrier embankment where it meets the exposed cliff of the plateau to the south. A low embankment less than 1 m high continues along the cliff south of the south gateway for more than 30 m. Three small mounds were reported by Squier and Davis (1848) to have been present, one just outside (to the west of) each gateway; in addition, two to four low earth crescents were also reported to have existed outside the enclosure and to have formed part of its western approach. Recent mapping and the development of a computerized model of the site indicate that despite Squier and Davis's depiction of four crescents, there was room for only three. In any event, both the crescents and mounds have been destroyed, the mounds apparently gone even prior to Squier and Davis's review of the site (Davis 1847). The cause of this was due to both limestone quarrying, conducted just west of the enclosure in the nineteenth and early twentieth centuries, and burning the stones of the mounds for agricultural lime.

Another major feature of the site, which I have labeled its perimeter wall, is a low embankment formed of soil behind an exterior pile of limestone that was 1 m or less in height. Depicted in the early plats as having surmounted the bluff above Massie's Creek between the main (barrier) wall segments on the west and the exposed limestone cliff on the northeast, it is not visually apparent today except for a short section just east of the north gateway. Soil has eroded from higher on the plateau and has piled up behind this low wall, in most places completely masking its presence. Excavation, however, has clearly demonstrated its continued existence and its structure.

It has been proposed that the enclosure's embankments were built in five major stages, with construction occurring over a span of about 100–150 years. This sequence will be briefly recapitulated here, but it can be found in greater detail in an earlier article (Riordan 1995). Stage 1 consisted of a low embankment, possibly incorporating a central gateway opening, that connected the outcropping cliff where the south gateway is now located with the creek bluff directly to the north. Stages 2 and 3 consisted of soil mantles added to this embankment, raising the height to over 2 m, leaving openings at the central and north gateways. Stage 4 was a wooden fence or stockade built on top of the embankments and along the previously undisturbed edge of the bluff above the creek ending on top of the cliff that outcrops in the north-central part of the landform. This edifice was burned down, an embankment was then constructed above its remains on the bluff edge, and a final 40–50 cm of soil was also added to the top of the barrier wall segments. Stone was used to face the exteriors of the perimeter wall and barrier wall segments, and a stone pavement was deposited through and outside of the central gateway, probably to mark it as the primary entryway into the enclosure (Riordan 2006).

The trench of interest in this article was designated "U" and in 2001 was dug 1.5 m wide and 6 m long into the exterior side of the 12-m-wide embankment segment between the north and central gateways (Figure 7.2). The vertical profile of the trench, at its point of deepest penetration into the embankment (the 9 East profile in the trench's coordinate system), showed that 2.4 m of soil lay piled above the original surface. None of our other trenches dug in any of the four segments of the north-south barrier wall had been extended to reach the extreme exterior end of an embankment. We had always assumed that all

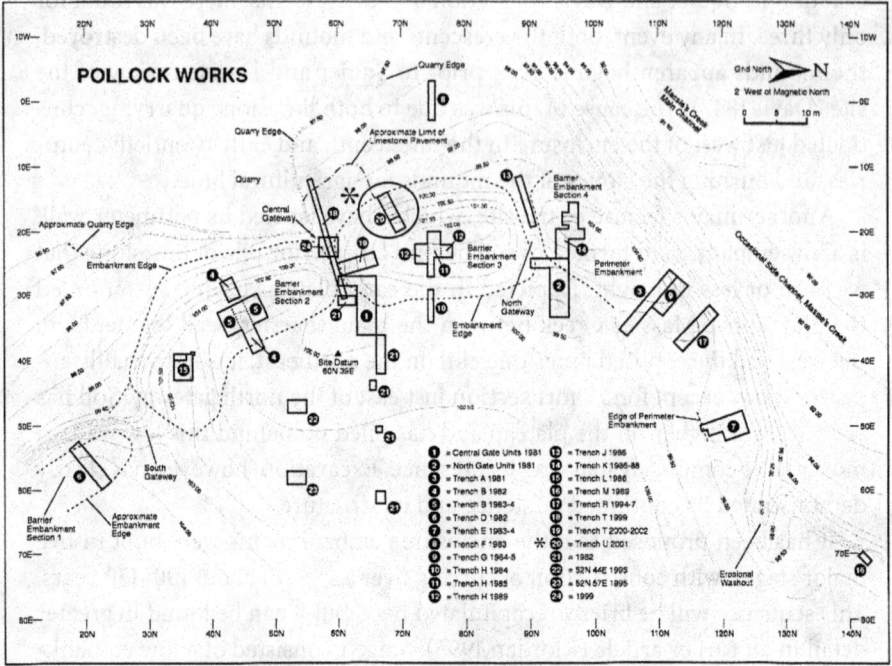

Figure 7.2. Excavation units at the Pollock Works with Trench U indicated.

the stone on the embankment exteriors had been placed as part of the fifth and final building stage at the enclosure (Riordan 1995).

We wanted to find the point of juncture where the exterior stone met the piled soil of the embankment and fully expected that it would not be found in the first few horizontal meters (beginning at the extreme exterior end). We began removing rock from the surface of the first 4 m of the trench (denoted as 3–7 East in the trench grid coordinates), and constantly found more rocks below those we removed. The first four horizontal meters of the embankment slope were formed solidly of piled rocks. The interface between soil and stone that we sought was found in the middle of the last 2-m section of Trench U, between 7 and 9 East (Figure 7.3). Since we were able to document the transition from stone to soil by fully revealing the profile walls on both sides of the trench between 7 and 9 East, it was decided not to remove any more stone from the exterior 3 m.

Very unexpectedly, however, the trench profiles revealed not only that the builders had used limestone to face the last (fifth) construction stage of the embankment but also that stone had been used to face the exterior of each of the three previous stages that had involved soil deposits to the embankment.

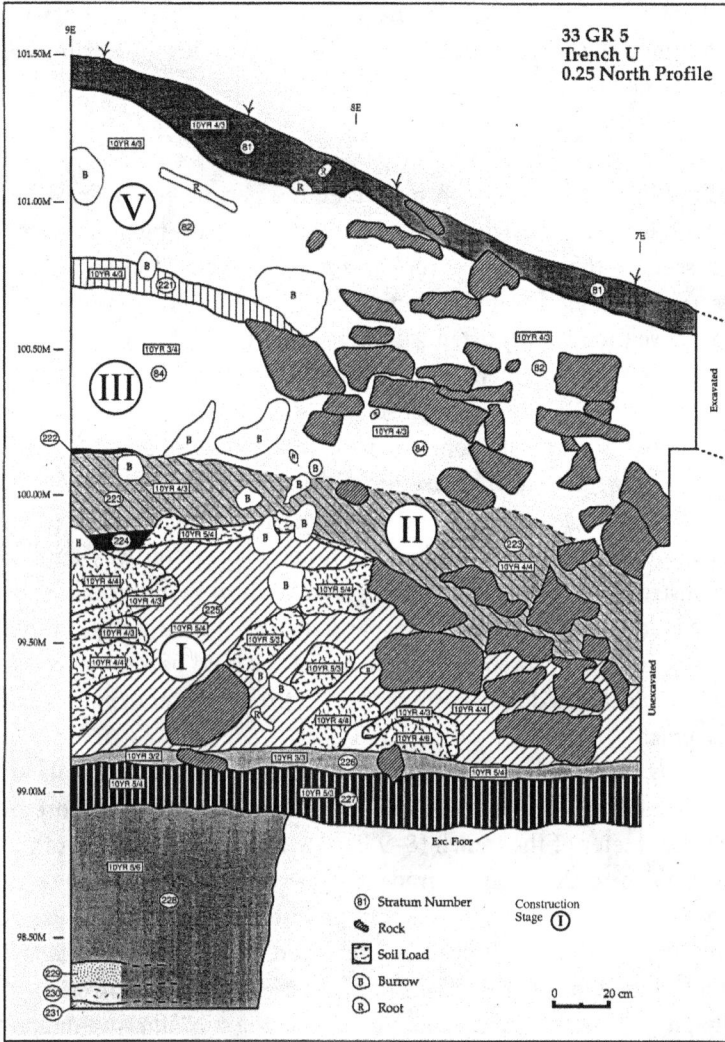

**33 GR 5
Trench U
0.25 North Profile**

Figure 7.3. Trench U, Pollock Works, 0.25 North Profile.

(The fourth construction stage was the wooden fence, or stockade.) The rock-bound face of the barrier embankment segment therefore grew ever higher, as added layers increased its height from approximately two-thirds of a meter to almost 3 m (Figure 7.3).

This discovery (which is critical to the argument I summarize in this chapter) indicates that at any time both during and after the extended period of construction, Middle Woodland viewers who approached the Pollock earthwork were consistently confronted by a stone-faced wall. Initially it was very low and probably virtually unnoticeable until one was almost upon it, but with time and additions the embankment grew to become a substantial physical and visual barrier.

The Stone

The several trenches that have been dug along the perimeter wall have revealed substantial exterior piles of limestone at the edge of the bluff, above the steep 7-m descent to the water. This rock was placed, we continue to believe, to help preserve the embankment by limiting the downslope erosion of its soil. This reasoning we then simply extended to explain why the barrier wall sections also had a similar placement of stone on their exterior faces.

Just west of the barrier embankment segments, outside the enclosure, the landform continues to gradually slope down to the west, but for several meters beyond the foot of the Trench U excavation the slope is virtually negligible. It is also true that the clayey soil employed in wall construction is very resistant to short-term erosion. There probably is no functional reason why an embankment constructed only of earth would not have survived in this place just as well as one made with earth and stone, particularly in its early stages when it was less than 2 m high. Moreover, a close look at the kind of rocks encountered when Trench U was dug may support an entirely different explanation for their placement.

As noted above and depicted in Figure 7.3, the interface between soil and piled stones was found between 7 and 8 East of Trench U, while almost all of the innermost meter of the trench (8–9 East) was soil, from the top of the embankment down to the original grade. All the stone was removed from this 2-m portion of the trench (7–9 East) in order to secure good profiles of the interface. The weights of all the stones removed were recorded. This had been previously done in other trenches to give some concrete expression of the effort that it had taken to move and pile stone at the site. Since we did not remove all the stone from the outer 4 m of Trench U, however, the total human effort could not be as accurately estimated as elsewhere, but enough was removed to clearly reveal the range of variation in what was present.

Some 1,400 stones were counted and weighed from the entire trench, 70 percent of them coming from the last 2-m segment (7–9E), in which all were removed and weighed. The total weight of stone removed from the entire trench was almost 4.6 tons and the average stone weighed almost 3 kg. Of particular interest and potential significance, however, is the number of *large* examples that we encountered. One hundred and twenty rocks weighed 10 kg or more, including 78 that were between 10 and 20 kg, 21 that were between 20 and 30 kg, and 21 that weighed more than 30 kg.

Most of these rocks had angular surfaces and had probably been pulled or quarried from near the base of the exposed limestone in the gorge upstream. Obtaining them would have involved a one-way trip of something like 0.5–1.0 km to the embankment building site. The most notable example was a 127 kg monster that took three of our crew to move, which they accomplished by staggering a short distance *downslope* with it from the place where it had been lodged in the embankment. Remember, this stone had been originally transported from a source as much as a kilometer away, with part of that route having been of necessity *upslope*. Why? The question occurred to us even as we struggled to move it. The effort to move and place such stones did not seem reasonable if it had been done only to prevent erosion. Had that been the only concern, then surely the builders would have preferred to carry, say, 12 stones that each weighed 10 kg over one that weighed 127 kg, even if it had meant making a few more trips. The nagging question "Why did they do this?" continued to fester until an alternative solution, one radically different from the functional explanation, occurred to me a few months later.

The finds at Trench U suggested that rock had always been an important element in the work, even before the embankments had been built to a height and steepness of slope where erosion might have been a valid concern. Instead, I believe that the original intention of the builders was to create an immediate aesthetic and symbolic effect, and that this was then repetitiously expressed in the subsequent building program. Stone was used to both define the western side of the landform and suggest to viewers that the enclosed space was to be considered as separate and distinct from its surroundings, that what had been constituted was an elevated, rocky place. Whether this created landscape was made to emulate one or more existing models (e.g., Fort Hill?) or represented the pursuit of an idealized form is unknown. It seems that the plateau itself must have been selected for its distinctive and locally unique geographic characteristics and that, once discovered, its gradual western slope was deliberately modified with rock-faced embankments that were joined to rocky cliffs, forming a space that was enclosed by stone.

Interpretation

Recent works by Byers (2004) and Romain (2000: 167; 2004) have sought to explain the meaning of the several earthworks that repetitiously link circles and rectilinear forms. Both authors believe that they may signify a cosmological symbolic dichotomy of this world/otherworld or earth/sky, although they disagree on the actual referents. Most of the examples they reference are the enclosures built on broad floodplain terraces. Some of these examples contain rectilinear and circular forms that are connected by short parallel-walled hyphens, as, for example, at High Bank, Dunlaps, Seal, and Newark; while others have tangential polygonal and/or circular forms, as at Hopeton, Liberty, Frankfort, and Circleville. These conjoined geometric earthworks occur primarily in south-central Ohio, where they were constructed on broad river terraces. Southwestern Ohio contains many fewer examples of elaborate polygonal earthworks, but the earthwork tradition there almost surely arises from the same belief system and iconic tradition. I suggest that Middle Woodland earthworks in southwestern Ohio encode some of the same meanings as are found in Scioto and Paint Creek earthworks but that they express it in an analogous rather than a homologous manner. One of the chief differences between the two regions is that in southwestern Ohio the earthwork builders seem to have routinely used the natural topography to emphasize symbolic relationships.

This requires us to adopt a wider view, a landscape perspective of the earthworks that goes beyond the consideration of individual figures. A case in point may occur in the narrow valley of Massie's Creek (Figure 7.4). A mile to the west of Pollock there is a second enclosure known as the Bull Works (33GR3), which was depicted by Squier and Davis (1848: Plate 34, No.3) as a rectangle with outlying arcs and mounds (Figure 7.5). It was built in the first location downstream that offered a spot wide enough to hold a figure that large (it enclosed about 8 acres), and it is in a section of the valley that is over 15 m lower in elevation than the highest point within the Pollock hilltop. This same earthwork could as easily have been built on expansive uplands to the north, south, or west of Pollock, which are all about equal in elevation or higher than the Pollock plateau, but the builders instead selected the lower valley. I think that this was intentionally done, that Pollock and Bull were contemporaneous, and that they constituted a linked pair of earthworks that was always intended to be considered together rather than in isolation.

In contrast to the rectilinear plan of Bull, I believe that the Pollock Works probably satisfied Hopewellian notions of a circular enclosure. The plateau can be circumnavigated via a fairly easy and rapid walk following a roughly circular path, while always walking below its cliffs and walls. That its actual shape, dictated by the landform, was more ovoid than round was probably an unimportant distinction to an earthbound Middle Woodland perspective. Pollock's barrier embankments, always faced by stone, were therefore an expedient way of completing the circuit of the hilltop while emphasizing its elevated characteristic. In a symbolic pairing, I prefer to view Pollock, round and elevated, as having represented the astral or solar sphere, while the

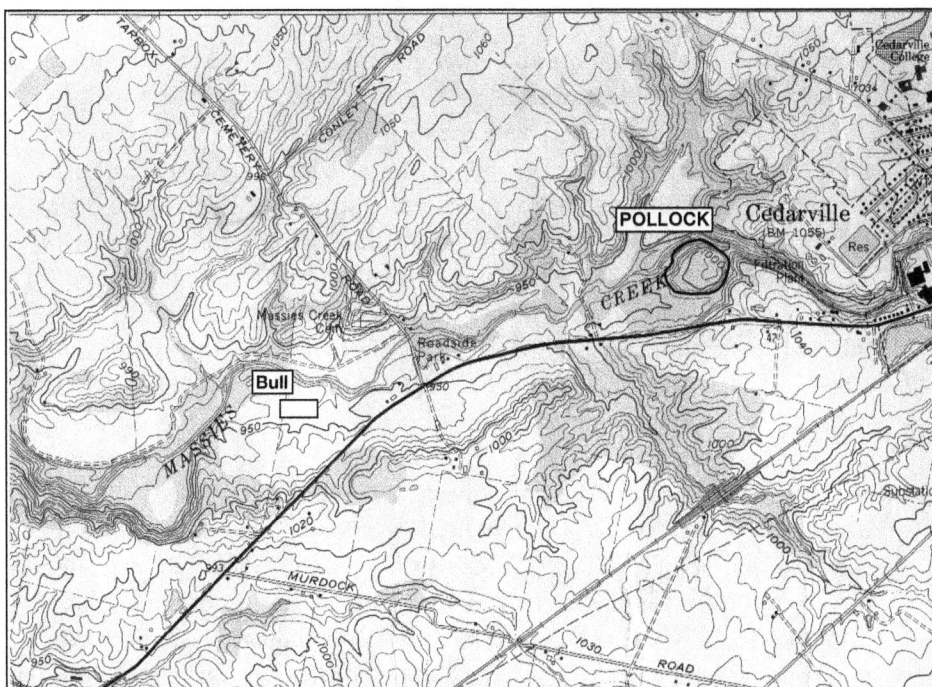

Figure 7.4. The Bull and Pollock works (USGS Cedarville 7.5-minute quadrangle).

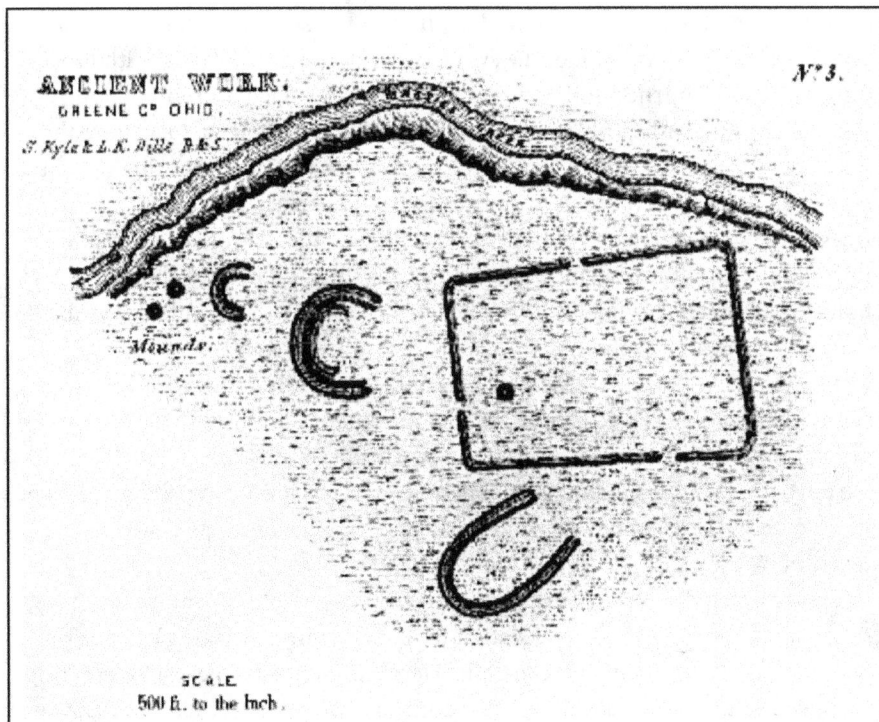

Figure 7.5. The Bull Works (Squier and Davis 1848: Plate XXXIV, No. 3).

rectangular Bull Works, rooted on lower ground and figuratively overlooked by Pollock, represented *this* world.

The identification of Pollock with the solar sphere might find archaeological support in the remnants of the burned wooden structure that constituted the fourth major building stage at the site. This structure, which I have interpreted as a stockade, was built on top of the third soil mantle on the barrier wall segments and on top of what was until then the unaltered edge of the bluff above Massie's Creek. From what we have seen of its remains, it was never substantially repaired, probably existed for only a short time (measured as no more than a few years and perhaps considerably less), and its builders burned it down just before they added the final layer of soil to the barrier segments and built the perimeter wall along the bluff. I have previously suggested that the construction and destruction of this feature may have satisfied a military need—Pollock as a refuge—and that its destruction allowed the site to be reconverted into a sacred place (Riordan 1996). I have alternatively suggested that the stockade's destruction may have constituted an event of ritual theater, perhaps in keeping with the tantalizingly suggestive finding that similar events may have occurred at three or more other elevated enclosures in southwestern Ohio (Riordan 1998: 83–84). At Pollock, the archaeological facts include locally variable but generally very considerable amounts of burned soil that were associated with the carbonized timbers of the structure and which I attribute to the lower portion of the structure having been plastered with mud. The presence of burned soil deposits indicates prolonged and intense burning. It has recurrently struck us how difficult it must have been to achieve the uniform combustion of this structure, and it seems evident that this was an effort that had to have been very purposefully undertaken. Furthermore, if the trees in the space between the Bull Works and the Pollock Works were cleared, it would potentially also have been visually striking and possibly highly symbolic to have been able to illuminate the portion of the enclosed plateau visible from the direction of the Bull Works. A burning western perimeter at Pollock could have served to reinforce the identification of the earthwork as an astral representation. Accomplishing the burning of the Pollock stockade in a visually significant manner, as opposed to a less visible slow smolder, would perforce have been a singular event but one with a high potential for audience involvement, the memory of which would likely have long persisted in the local community.

I also contend that the pairing of earthwork shapes and the intentional use of topographic differences in elevation to make a symbolic statement was repeated elsewhere in southwestern Ohio. Here are some possible examples. The highly elevated Fortified Hill enclosure in Butler County (Squier and Davis

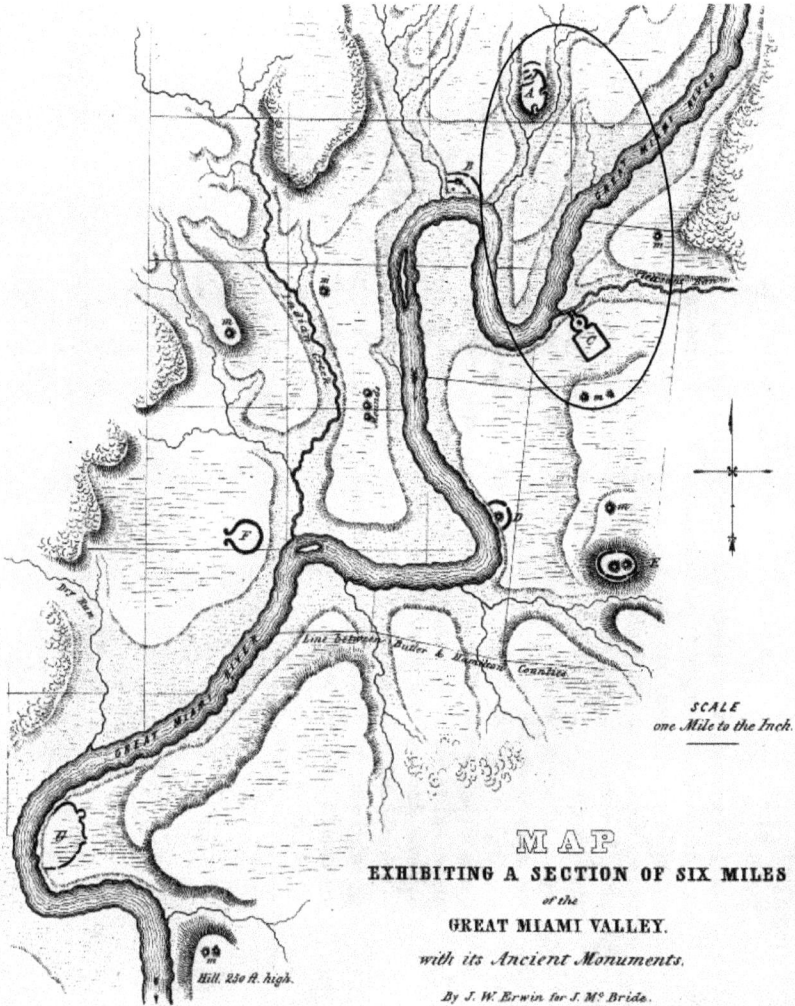

Figure 7.6. Pleasant Run and Fortified Hill (Squier and Davis 1848: Plate III, No. 2).

1848: Plate 6) is just northwest of and across the Great Miami River from the Pleasant Run Works (Squier and Davis 1848: Plate 30, no. 1). Pleasant Run had a short hyphen, or set of parallel-walled embankments, on its northwest side that pointed in the general direction of Fortified Hill. A person can walk below the latter following a circuitous route, and while not round, to an earthbound perspective Fortified Hill could have been considered a fully bounded hilltop and therefore, like Pollock, equivalently circular. Pleasant Run, with its square at river level a couple of hundred feet below, completes the earthwork pairing (Figure 7.6).

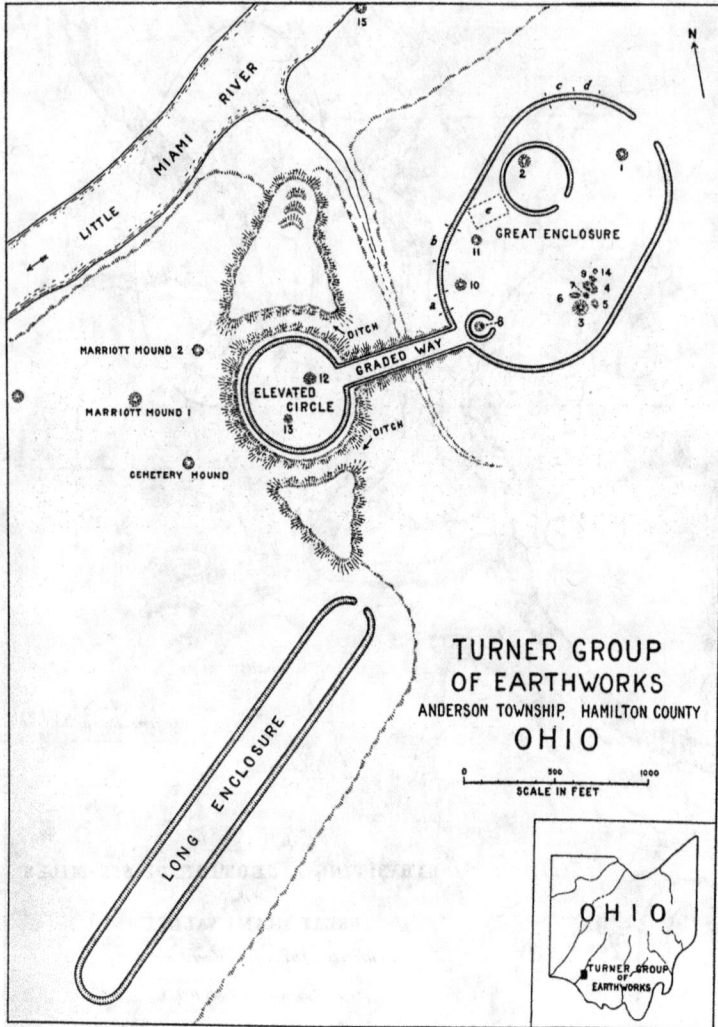

Figure 7.7. The Turner Group of earthworks (Willoughby 1922: Plate 1).

Near the confluence of the Little Miami and Ohio rivers are two more possible examples. The Turner Earthworks (Figure 7.7) include an elevated landform that was circularly enclosed and connected via a graded way to the lower ellipse. At nearby Milford (Figure 7.8) an elevated circle was connected via a parallel embankment connection to a flattened circle into which a rectangular figure was intruded. Note that in these examples the circular elements are elevated with respect to rectilinear or elongated oval forms.

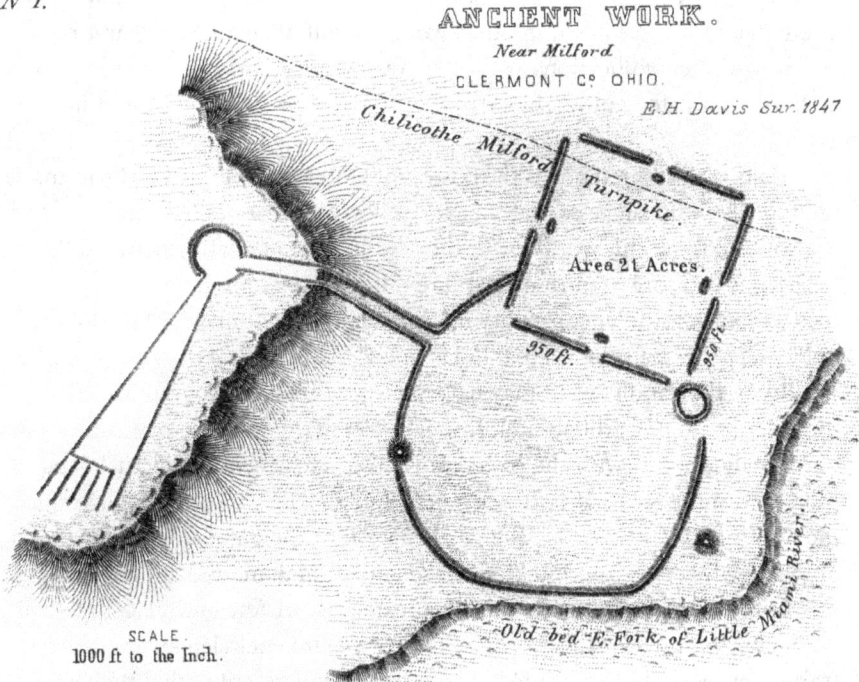

N°1.

ANCIENT WORK.

Near Milford.

CLERMONT C° OHIO.

E.H. Davis Sur. 1847

Chilicothe - Milford

Turnpike.

Area 21 Acres.

950 ft.

950 ft.

-Old -bed -E.-Fork- of- Little Miami River-

SCALE.
1000 ft. to the Inch.

Figure 7.8. Milford (Squier and Davis 1848: Plate XXXIV, No. 1).

Fort Ancient may constitute yet another case (Squier and Davis 1848: Plate 7). The South Fort, for all its irregularity of outline, is isolated from everything and elevated with respect to everything nearby except for the narrow neck of land in the adjacent Middle Fort. Like Pollock, it can be circumnavigated via a roughly circular track by always walking—with great difficulty, given the degree of slope—below its walls. Entering the South Fort from the Middle Fort, one must walk up and over an embankment, which may have served to emphasize its spatial coherence and conceptual distinction from the North Fort. The North Fort has, on the other hand, both a large number of rectilinear embankments and is substantially and directly connected to the immediately adjacent uplands. In line with the reasoning previously advanced, the North Fort with its several rectilinear embankments could have been the lower/this world enclosure that was paired with the isolated solar/astral enclosure of South Fort.

It is generally believed that the South Fort predates the North Fort, but we know that the embankments of both parts of the enclosure contain multiple stages of construction and that their chronology is virtually unknown. It is entirely possible that an early version of the North Fort was in existence soon after, or even contemporaneously with, an early version of the South Fort. There need not have been, in other words, a gulf of centuries separating the building of the two portions of the earthwork, and it may be that a symbolic architectural statement was being incorporated very early in the building program.

The above interpretation is the reverse of that recently proposed by Romain (2004b: 78), who suggests that the North Fort is an astral representation and the South Fort is "this world," with the Middle Fort mediating between them. What may be more important than the differing referents is that we are both trying to match similar concepts with this earthwork. Romain, following Connolly and others, also notes that the artificial extensions of the streams to the vicinity of the parallel walls may have served to create a geographic isolate of the entire complex (2004b: 77). I offer a second hypothesis, one that is not necessarily at odds with the one expressed above. The gradual enclosing of more and more space at Fort Ancient may indeed have conceptually united the South and North Forts. The construction of the parallel walls northeast of the North Fort involved their encircling of a small mound at their extreme northeast end. In this scenario, the whole of the Fort Ancient enclosure could then have represented this world, while the distant encircled area was the astral/upper world representation. If so, then it will be noted that the circular (solar) element is not elevated. It is believed that Fort Ancient was under active, if episodic, construction for several hundred years and that the parallel walls were probably the last site element to be built. Its construction may have occurred after the elevation distinction went out of vogue in southwestern Ohio. By then it may have been more significant to morphologically echo what had been built at Milford and/or Turner. It might finally be noted that, while it is entirely possible that both these scenarios about Fort Ancient are completely wrong, in a large and architecturally evolving site it is also possible that both could be correct.

Conclusion

Recent archaeological work at the Pollock Works has been interpreted to suggest that its natural topographic characteristics were combined with construction elements intended to create repetitiously an elevated, rock-bound, and conceptually circular space. Pollock is believed to have been complemented by the siting and rectilinear form of the nearby Bull Works. Together, they may have constituted a single architectural and symbolic statement: Pollock, elevated and circular, symbolic of the astral sphere, and Bull, rectilinear and lower, as this world.

Four earthworks within 50 miles of one another in the Little Miami River drainage, Turner, Milford, Fort Ancient, and Pollock plus Bull, are thought to have all employed natural elevation to emphasize their symbolic accounts, which may be seen as a local tradition at work. The chronology of these cases is incompletely known, but construction has been shown to have occurred at both Pollock and Fort Ancient by the mid-first century A.D. Turner seems the most idealized of the set, and it contained the archaeological residue of an elaborate mortuary ritualism not known from the others. Possibly Turner was a later, more elegant expression of the symbolic equation that had been earlier and more crudely expressed by the Bull-plus-Pollock configuration. Alternatively, Bull plus Pollock may represent the subsequent translation of the ideas of Turner expressed in a frontier setting by people who used the local geography to make the best of what they had.

8

The Turner-Hopewell Axis

Exploring Interaction through Embankment Form and Mortuary Patterning

A. Martin Byers

This chapter addresses a central puzzle of the settlement pattern of the Woodland period of the Eastern Woodlands, in particular as it is manifested in the Early and Middle Woodland periods of the Central Ohio Valley region. This is the contrast between the monumental earthwork locales, often associated with a rich mortuary residue, and the nearly archaeologically invisible domestic-habitation locales. The best known account of this earthwork-habitation dichotomy treats it as the binary expression of a social system based on kinship-based communities having exclusive proprietorial corporate territorial domains. The earthworks thus are interpreted as the symbolic as well as material expression of the corporate nature of the community and the habitation locales, usually distributed as a clustering of small, almost ephemeral sites loosely dispersed in the region surrounding the earthworks, as the gardening-based kinship domestic groups (see Dancey and Pacheco 1997; Prufer 1964, 1965, 1997a, 1997b). Corresponding to this earthwork-habitation dichotomy is a fairly well-defined separation of artifacts and facilities according to ceremonial and domestic categories. The ceremonial artifacts and facilities, in the form of a complex set of items such as copper, shell, lithic, and ceramic artifacts and facilities such as mortuary-related log-cribs, "altars," and charnel structures, are almost exclusive to the earthwork locales. The domestic-type artifacts and facilities, in the form of post holes, middens, hearths, and utilitarian ceramics and lithics, are prevalent in the habitation locales.

The earthwork-habitation dichotomy manifests two sets of distinctly different material interests. The habitation sites display a range of interests that might easily be identified with the pursuit of everyday life, the routines of raising a family, providing and preparing food, and being prepared to move when required, for example, in terms of seasonal demands. In contrast, the earthwork sites display interests that have conditions of satisfaction that reach beyond the everyday concerns of the domestic sphere since the sites have a strong mortuary component associated with raw materials procured from great distances and all this is framed by constructions in timber and earth that clearly involved the mobilization of labor resources well beyond those available in the locally dispersed set of domestic habitations. In short, it is not simply that the earthwork-habitation dichotomy displays a strong division of the material cultural assemblage into two contrasting categorical sets but that these presuppose equally strongly contrasting social interests and concerns.

When the contrasting interests are taken into account, the notion that the earthwork-habitation dichotomy manifests a unitary kinship-based community becomes somewhat strained since it is easy to note that the demands of the activities encompassed by the earthworks involved long-distance travel, intergenerational mortuary cycling, and major collectively organized labor and these activities would subtract from the effectiveness of the activities demanded by the domestic sphere. It is not that this could not be done, since it is obvious that the labor for both spheres of interests was procured, organized, and applied. However, it strains credulity to believe that if the same organization was responsible for both the earthworks and the habitations, that it would be able to dispassionately allocate labor and time to the contradictory activities of both spheres.

Of course, it might be argued that this could easily be the case if, in fact, the community was structured hierarchically into dominant and subordinate kin groups. In these terms, it would have to be assumed that the subordinate made up the majority dispersed in the domestic habitation sites and the dominant made up the minority occupying the earthworks. It would then be necessary to argue that the earthworks can be characterized as being among the material conditions of satisfaction of the interests of the dominant kin groups such that the latter would set priorities favoring earthwork-related activities, including their construction and the production of the whole panoply of facilities associated with them, in particular the mortuary materials, even though the latter would necessarily require reducing the labor directed to fulfilling the needs of the majority in their pursuing everyday survival. The problem with this is that since all the known habitation locales are materially similar, namely, ephemeral and basic, indicating that none of them would be candidates for elite residence, the only known locales that would be candidates for the latter would be the earthworks themselves. However, it is now generally accepted that the structures and facilities associated with these were distinctly not domestic but ceremonial in nature (Dancey and Pacheco 1997; Greber 1976, 1979a, 1997a).

Therefore, there is no residential data that would support the structuring of the society in terms of dominant "elite" and subordinate "commoners."

If it is agreed that the earthwork-habitation dichotomy grounds a social system that embodies a distinct and to some degree contradictory division of interests, there is another structuring that would easily account for this without having to invoke an elite/commoner or dominant/subordinate contrast. I have argued elsewhere that the earthwork-habitation dichotomy manifests a duality of companionship and kinship (Byers 2004: chap. 10). In these terms, two parallel and relatively autonomous social institutions are manifested in this dichotomy. I have postulated that these complementary organizations are based on complementary cultural structures/principles of kinship and companionship and, therefore, are constituted as dual social structures that I have termed generically "clans" and "sodalities." If the habitation locales and the earthwork locales are characterized in these terms, as the manifestation of clans and their constituent family groups, on the one hand, and same age/same gender sodalities, on the other, then there is no difficulty accounting for the differences of interests that each type of locale entails. Even though the earthwork-based labor and scheduling needs of the sodalities would necessarily intervene in the deployment of labor to fulfill the needs of the kinship-based domestic groups responsible for the habitation sites, and vice versa, since the same people would be members of both, there would be an ongoing process of mutual inter-organizational accommodation.

I call this the Dual Clan-Cult Sodality model of the Woodland period of the Central Ohio Valley (Byers 2004).[1] Critical to this model is the principle central to the ethos, autonomy. It operated at every level: individual, group, and intercommunity. The model characterizes the two types of social groups constituting the community, clans and sodalities, as relatively autonomous. In social structural terms, I have defined groups according to two types of relationships: *relative autonomy* and *mutual autonomy*. Clans and sodalities are relatively autonomous in the sense that their respective social natures are defined in complementary relation to each other. A sodality is what a clan is not, a group of (usually) same-age/same-gender companions; and a clan is what a sodality is not, a group of unilaterally related kin. Two or more groups of the same social nature are mutually autonomous when they relate to each other. Therefore, two or more sodalities will stand to each other as mutually autonomous. When two or more autonomous groups are structurally related, that is, when they stand to each other as having complementary or mutual rights and duties, they constitute a heterarchy. If these groups are relatively autonomous, that is, clans and sodalities, they constitute a complementary heterarchy. In these terms, therefore, a dual clan-cult sodality community of the type postulated for the Ohio Middle Woodland would constitute a complementary heterarchical community. If two or more allied groups are mutually autonomous, for example, sodalities, then they constitute a mutualistic heterarchy (Byers 2006b).

In a social world where agentive autonomy was central to the ethos, decisions would entail ongoing negotiation and consensus among all relevant parties, whether these decisions were made in the context of a complementary heterarchical community or a mutualistic heterarchy of cult sodalities. These parties could well be and, in fact, it could be anticipated that they would be unequal along different dimensions, for example, senior as compared to junior, male as compared to female, wealthier and larger compared to less wealthy and smaller, and so one. However, while such inequalities would be recognized, because each party was autonomous, each would be recognized as responsible for his/her/their decisions and actions, and, therefore, no party could transform its material or social advantages into dominance over the other. Groups of unequals could cooperate through negotiated consensus, each being recognized as responsible for its own traditional area of endeavor. Hence, clans would not intervene in the affairs of the cult sodalities, or vice versa.

The Dual Clan-Cult Sodality model, therefore, potentially resolves many problems and puzzles in the archaeological record, particularly in terms of the settlement pattern of the Woodland period of the Central Ohio Valley. One of the most central puzzles that it can be useful to account for is the earthwork-habitation dichotomy. As I suggested above, it dissolves this puzzle by supporting the view that this manifests the parallel existence of two relatively autonomous social groups, cult sodalities and clans respectively. These would have had different and to some degree contradictory interests. However, for the most part the imperatives of these different interests would have been kept in check by the fact that participants in the cults were also clan members. These different and to some degree contradictory interests, the pursuit of ceremonial ritual and the pursuit of everyday survival, partly account for the baroque-like richness of the former, requiring long-distance procurement and exchange as well monumental construction, and the Spartan-like nature of the latter, focused on minimizing the labor required to sustain family reproduction. I have also argued that part of the contradiction in these two pursuits was overridden by the central cosmological and ethos premises that underwrote this social world, namely, that it was believed the natural world was immanently sacred and that, consequently, in intervening in the natural order, practices of an everyday subsistence and settlement nature simultaneously intervened in and polluted the sacred order. Hence domesticity was, in general, polluting. In contrast, the ritual performed in the earthwork context and mediated through mortuary practice was sanctifying, thereby counterbalancing the polluting costs of the pursuit of survival with the rectifying benefits of world renewal ritual.

This Dual Clan-Cult Sodality model also accounts for another puzzle in the settlement patterning, this being the variation in the earthworks themselves. If these are understood as the context of world renewal ritual performed by autonomous cults sharing the same basic cosmology and the same goal, to reverse the pollution caused by domesticity and resanctify the world through mortuary-mediated world renewal ritual, there is no difficulty understanding why the form of the earthworks could vary intraregionally and over time. As mutually autonomous groups, each mutualistic cult sodality heterarchy responsible for a given monumental earthwork locale would determine what would count as an appropriate earthwork form by which the renewal ritual was most effectively performed and each would determine what mutualistic alliances with other cult sodality heterarchies that they might make in order to enhance this capacity. Therefore, it is not at all surprising that the region south of the Ohio River was dominated by Adena-style earthworks during the early and middle Middle Woodland while the Hopewell-style earthworks prevailed north of the river. The peoples in both regions would have been organized as complementary heterarchical communities and each would have its associated systems of mutualistic cult sodality heterarchies jealously guarding its own and contrasting formal architectural traditions, what we have come to term Adena and Hopewell. Nor is it surprising that the Hopewell style varied within its own region with ridge-top and quasi-geometrical earthworks predominating in southwestern Ohio and the geometrical earthworks in the center. These differences probably mark alternative ideological forms that the different autonomous cult sodality heterarchies of each regional zone would promote, each believing that its forms were "correct" while seeing those of the cult sodality heterarchies in the more distant zone as being less or even marginally adequate.

Of course, this claim suggests that since many of these earthwork-based groups coexisted they were probably perfectly aware of each other. As I have already suggested, one way that the incipient contradiction between the labor needs of the habitation and earthwork spheres of clans and cult sodalities could be resolved would be for the latter to set up alliances with each other. Not only could their members be allocated in a staggered manner so as to bolster the labor needs of each cult sodality heterarchy while not overly straining the labor requirements of the clans of the complementary heterarchical communities to which they belonged, they could act as way stations in long-distance exchange networks in the pursuit of exotic resources for specialized craft production, thereby enhancing the labor, the material resources of ritual, and so on. This means that we could expect to find that the material patterning of distantly spaced earthworks linked in different ways, reinforcing the likelihood that they were allied in higher order types of mutualistic heterarchies.

There are several interrelated lines of evidence that could ground this claim. There are the forms of the earthworks themselves. Everything else being equal, earthworks that shared the same form or, at least, shared major formal principles, would tend to be more closely related ideologically than those that did not. We also know that across the Ohio Hopewell the timber structures, the mortuary facilities, and the artifacts did vary. Again we could argue that those earthworks that shared in these areas, either in an emulating manner or in a functionally equivalent but formally different manner, were probably more closely related ideologically than those that did not. Finally, mortuary residue is common to many of these earthworks. If these were important media of world renewal as well as various mortuary events, from funerals to mourning to spirit release and rebirth rites, then those earthwork locales that shared mortuary residue that was patterned in a very similar manner would tend to be more closely related ideologically than those that did not.

In these terms I will argue below that at least one major set of intermutualistic heterarchical alliances can be discerned in the earthwork record. According to the above criteria, this was mediated primarily but not exclusively by two major earthwork locales: Turner in the Little Miami Valley and the Hopewell site on the periphery of the middle Scioto Valley. I call this the Turner-Hopewell axis. I believe that other equivalent axes existed and that, at a higher intermutualistic heterarchical level, there was similar interaction among the earthwork alliances that made them up.

The Turner-Hopewell Axis

In Shetrone's (1926) extensive report on the excavations he conducted of the Hopewell site, he presented a summary overview of the variation in the attributes of the major Ohio Hopewell earthwork sites as known at that time. These included Tremper, Mound City, Seip, Liberty Works, Hopewell, and Turner. He pointed out that while many attributes were shared by most of these sites, Hopewell and Turner stood apart by the dominance of extended burials over cremated burials. In a similar comparative spirit Willoughby (Willoughby and Hooton 1922) pointed out that, while certainly formally different, the embankment earthworks of Turner shared some attributes with nearby Milford and Camden and that the forms of these latter two were clearly echoed in the complex "geometricals" of the central Scioto drainage. In short, in the first quarter of the twentieth century, several prominent archaeologists raised the issue of the variable distribution of Ohio Hopewellian attributes across the major embankment earthwork sites with the possibility in mind that these might serve to underwrite historical and cultural processes that delineated intersite relations. Pursuing this thinking, I presented above the thesis that the Ohio Hopewell episode was characterized by an arm's-length relation sustained between at least two (probably more) networks of embankment earthwork groups and that these were articulated along two primary axes anchored by major sites. One network was distributed primarily across southwestern Ohio and was articulated around the Turner and the Hopewell sites, forming the Turner-Hopewell axis, and the other was distributed across south-central and central Ohio and was articulated around the major sites of the central Scioto drainage, particularly those around present day Chillicothe of Ross County, and the Newark site of Licking County, forming what will be termed here the Newark-Chillicothe axis (see Lepper, this volume). The Newark-Chillicothe axis has already been implicated in the recent work by Bradley Lepper on the Great Hopewell Road thesis (1996, 1998), this being the claim that a single set of effectively straight, cross-country parallel embankments connected the Newark site with the Chillicothe zone near High Bank. I argue below that these two axes interfaced in the North Fork/Paint Creek region with the Hopewell site and its associated Frankfort site on the North Fork being the eastern anchor of the Turner-Hopewell axis and Seip and Baum on the Paint Creek being the western anchor of the Chillicothe-Newark axis. Hence, these four sites acted both to separate and link these two axes and their associated networks.

Presupposing the claim that the North Fork/Paint Creek zone served as the interface between two networks of Hopewellian cult sodality heterarchies is the claim that the particular cult sodality heterarchies responsible for the North Fork sites and the Chillicothe sites had closer relations with their more distant axial anchors, the Turner and Newark cult sodality heterarchies, respectively, than they had with each other as near neighbors. Indeed, it would suggest that these near neighbors related to each other in a more competitive than cooperative manner, possibly each attempting to outdo the other in terms of the magnitude of the material and mortuary media of their world renewal ritual. In short, the Ross County "core" of monumental Ohio Hopewell locales cannot be characterized in unitary and cooperative terms but in dual, arm's-length, and competitive terms.

Embankment Earthwork Forms

There are two lines of evidence that can be summarily presented to support this claim, the first being the variation in the embankment earthwork forms and the second being variation in the mortuary records of the relevant earthwork sites. I have argued elsewhere (Byers 1987, 1998, 2004) that the major embankment earthwork of the Hopewell site is a classic Ohio Hopewell C-form, having a contiguous ditch on the "outside" of the embankment. It is important that while Cedar Bank on the central Scioto and the Granville site near Newark, and a few other sites, are also C-forms, this type of earthwork is most prevalent in southwestern Ohio, northwestern Kentucky and southeastern Indiana. Along with the table-top embankment earthworks, such as Fort Ancient and Miami Fort, I have defined these two types as making up the Miami Fort tradition (Byers 2004). These two types stand in contrast to the "geometrical" earthworks, a form dominant in the central Scioto region, as well as being found at Newark, Marietta, and Portsmouth. These earthworks can be treated as variations on a single configuration, which I have termed the "Circle-Rectilinear" or "C-R" configuration. I have argued that the C-R configuration comes in two versions, the High Bank C-R configuration and the Paint Creek C-R configuration. The latter is exemplified by Seip and Liberty Works, as well as Frankfort, Baum, and Works East. I treat these two types as defining what I have called the Chillicothe tradition (Byers 2004). It is claimed here that the Chillicothe-Newark and Turner-Hopewell axes articulate these two contrasting Ohio Hopewell traditions.

I will postulate that the Hopewell site mediates the interface between these two traditions. In these terms, it is important to note that its formal embankments combine elements of both traditions. Its main embankment is a C-form, and it has two subsidiary earthworks, the small circle and the small square, that together display the Paint Creek C-R configuration. This combination of C-form and C-R configuration can be interpreted in different ways. However, I see it as a historical development. First the C-form was constructed and then the circle and square were added. In fact, the open side of the C-form overlooking the creek bottom was closed by means of a low stone wall, probably at the same time as the addition of the circle and square. I suggest that this history of add-on construction acted as a nominal recognition by the Hopewell site cult sodality heterarchy of the C-R configuration motif. This makes the added-on set of C-R components the expression of an ideological strategy of accommodation to the presence of the nearby earthworks of Seip and Liberty Works, classic examples of the Paint Creek C-R configuration type.

Turner cannot be classed in a straightforward manner as either a C-form or a table-top ridge earthwork, the two defining types of the Fort Miami tradition, despite its being near two of the best known expressions of the table-top type, Fort Ancient and Miami Fort. However, it would be a mistake to conclude that this earthwork had no parallel to its neighbors or with the Hopewell site. For example, there are a number of attributes it shares with the Hopewell site, the most prominent being that both sites incorporate an upper and a lower terrace level. The back of the Hopewell C-form embankment runs along the edge of the upper terrace overlooking the site and then the two main arms run down to the lower terrace and stop short of the edge. Turner displays the same dual-level configuration since the smaller circle of the Turner site is built on the remnant of the nearby upper terrace and it is connected by the constructed ramp, sometimes referred to as the "sacred way," to the Great Enclosure on the lower terrace.

Willoughby (Willoughby and Hooton 1922) also commented that this dual-level arrangement is displayed at the nearby Milford site, which also had a connecting set of parallel embankments. Interestingly, this latter site, along with the near neighbor Camden site, also displays the circle and rectilinear components similar to those that are found at the Hopewell site. All this suggests both a chronological order and ongoing social relations among these four sites. Finding variants of the C-R configuration making up Camden and Milford, as well as several other sites in southwestern Ohio, suggests significant interaction between the latter region and the central Scioto drainage. However, the attributes of these variants indicate an indirect relation with the source, a relation mediated through local traditions. Another site that is a variant of the C-R configuration, of course, is the Hopewell site itself. Therefore, it is suggested that this distribution of variant C-R configurations from the Hopewell site westward connects the latter site more to the southwest region of Ohio than to its near neighboring C-R configuration sites making up the central Scioto region. The fact that the main and original component of the Hopewell site is its C-form embankment, a form that is dominant in southwestern Ohio, simply adds to the sense that the Hopewell site does not seem to "belong" where we find it. That is, its dual-level C-form links it strongly to the southwestern region of Ohio, and its having variant circle and square components, similar also to those found in the latter region, acts to set it apart from nearby Seip, Baum, and Liberty Works, despite sharing the C-R configuration as such.

In fact, as pointed out above, the Turner site also seems to be "out of place." It displays neither the C-form pattern nor the C-R configuration of its near neighbors of Camden and Milford. However, it does have a complex patterning that may be a variant of the C-R configuration. In this case, instead of a rectilinear configuration, it was an oblong, the Great Enclosure, suggesting a

Circle-Oblong (C-O) instead of a Circle-Rectilinear pattern. The C-O configuration suggests a variant of the C-R configuration that would be equivalent to the variant C-R configuration added on to the Hopewell site. The upshot of this brief comparative analysis of the embankment forms suggests that the Hopewell site, despite its location in the "heartland" of the C-R configuration, had greater ties of affiliation with Turner and its related sites in southwestern Ohio than it did with its own near neighbors of Seip, Baum, and so on. Support of this claim can be made by a comparative analysis of the mortuary and related patternings of the Hopewell and Turner sites in contrast to the mortuary pattern of Seip, Liberty Works, and Mound City.

Mortuary Pattern

The mortuary patterning of the Hopewell site sets it apart from its near neighbors. In the case of Seip, Liberty Works, and Mound City, almost all mortuary deposits were cremations. These deposits marked the end of a complex regime of postmortem manipulatory practices. In contrast, the majority of the mortuary deposits of the Hopewell site, about 70 percent, were extended burials. It is important that a similar dominance of extended over cremated deposits characterizes the mortuary deposits of the Turner site. This similarity sets the mortuary patterning of these two sites apart from the patterning of the mortuary deposits of the other major Ohio Hopewell sites. However, it is not enough to confirm that the Hopewell site was itself related more closely to Turner in terms of their mortuary patternings than it was to its near neighbors of Seip, Liberty Works, and Mound City since the Hopewell site also had a significant proportion of cremations associated with artifacts and features that were similar to those found at its near neighbor Chillicothe tradition sites. What is necessary is to argue that the overall patterning of the mortuary deposits of the Hopewell and Turner sites share similarities that would reinforce the view that these two sites were more closely related to each other than the Hopewell site was to its near neighbors.

This is not an easy task to argue since, other than sharing the same prevalence for extended over cremated deposits, the details of the actual mortuary patternings of the two sites do differ significantly; however, it appears that they differ possibly in a similar way that their embankment forms differed. That is, while directly observable forms were different, these may simply have been equivalent expressions of similar abstract commitments. In this regard, it is useful to focus on two broad aspects of the treatment of the deceased, the mortuary depositional feature and the associated burnt deposits. Although the burnt deposits are not "mortuary" in the narrowly defined sense, that is, these did not involve the dead directly, it will be assumed that the burnt deposits were part of the overall mortuary process of these two sites. Since these burnt deposits were similar across both sites in terms of associated features (e.g., "clay basins"), richness and variety of contents, complementary nature of paired deposits, and so on, it will be assumed here that they also implicate a strong parallel in the mortuary practices of these two sites (Byers 2004; Greber 1996; Greber and Ruhl 1989).

What strongly contrasts between the mortuary data of both sites, however, is the burial feature itself that is found dominant in each site. Most extended burials of the Hopewell site were found in the well known timber-built "vaulted chambers" on the floors of Mounds 23 and 25, and on simple prepared earth platforms on the floors of the lesser mounds. At Turner, however, with few exceptions, all mortuary deposits, whether extended or cremated, were found in elaborately prepared stone-lined pits, a few of these being found on the floors of several of the mounds, and the majority being found in the two major burial places inside the Great Enclosure. This analysis will focus on the "vaulted chambers" of the Hopewell site and the "stone-lined pits" of the Turner site.

Despite the clear differences between these two mortuary features, timber-built "vaulted chambers" and "stone-lined pits," I argue that they had the same symbolic-functional meaning, serving as laying-in crypts. I have given a fuller characterization of the "vaulted chamber" as a laying-in crypt in Byers (2004). This crypt allowed the deceased to be subjected to a series of incremental mortuary rites. These constituted what I have termed the funerary–mourning–spirit release–world renewal ritual mortuary process. As implied by the terminology, it is postulated that this ritual cycle served both mortuary and world renewal needs through the medium of sacrificially releasing the different spiritual aspects of the deceased associated with the different components of the body (flesh, bones, organs, and so on) in order to both release the free or personal soul of the deceased so it could travel the Path of Souls (the Milky Way) to the land of the Dead and release the other multiple living souls of the body in order to enhance the re-creative capacity of the cosmos. I will not repeat the full argument that is found in Byers (2004) with regard to the Hopewell site mortuary patterning. Instead, I will focus on the Turner patterning, arguing that just as the vaulted chamber of the Hopewell site served as a laying-in crypt mediating the incremental series of mortuary/world renewal rites, so the "stone-lined pits" of the Turner site served in an equivalent manner, with the possibility that they served an additional function as terminal world renewal altars. I have called this the Laying-In/World Renewal Crypt model of the Turner site. As laying-in crypts that were reused for a series of mortuary/world renewal events similar to those mediated by the vaulted chambers of the Hopewell site, these stone-lined pits should display evidence to this effect, particularly marked by stray burial artifacts, reconstruction, additions, and so on. A careful reading of Willoughby's report (Willoughby and Hooton 1922), in fact, gives strong empirical support to this proposition. For example, Grave 5 contained a female who was classed by N'omi Greber (1976, 1979a) as the highest-ranking burial of Turner largely because of the variety, quantity, and elaborateness of distribution of the mortuary artifacts found in association. These artifacts included an ocean shell container, several copper ear spools, bladelets, a copper "plate" or band, several pearl inlaid bear's teeth, a galena lump, a copper blade, a copper bead, and so on. Greber commented particularly on the elaborateness of the distribution of these materials and used this as well as their relative quantity and variety as grounds for assigning the female high social standing. However, there is another interpretation that can be given. Rather than this elaborate distribution marking high standing, it marks the accumulated residue of repetitive usages of the same feature. Indeed, this is the interpretation that I have given to this same deposit and its "elaborate" artifactual associations.

In this regard it is important to note that the deceased was placed on a set of flat stones that formed the floor of the pit. As Willoughby describes these data, a number of the artifacts were found *under* these stones, in particular, several bladelets, a copper blade, one broken ear spool, or at least two halves or disks or an ear spool, one partial copper-covered bead, and a thin copper band. Furthermore, the broken ear spool disks were under one stone, the copper band under another, and the broken ear spool disks under yet another (Willoughby and Hooton 1922: 16–17). The distribution of the other artifacts, those found on top of the floor stones along with the deceased, was also complex in that some were in more or less direct contact with the body—for example, copper ear spools with the bones of the hand, as well as set beside the head—while others were distributed away from the body, particularly in the corners at the feet or at the knees, for example, the galena piece, the conical stone item, and the bear teeth ornaments.

Clearly, both the dispersed nature of several broken artifacts and the fact that these were *under* the floor stones suggest that they should be considered as the result of mortuary activities that were separate from, prior to, and probably unrelated to the mortuary activities that generated the distribution of materials on top of the stone floor. In fact, this latter distribution suggests the unwitting by-product of the removal of one or more deceased as part of the same type of mortuary process suggested above. This suggests that the complexity of the distribution of artifacts *on* the floor stones, in particular, those found in the corners and broken, was also the by-product of a series of placements and removals of deceased individuals *prior to the final disposition of the female deceased,* the latter being simply that last of this series that had been mediated through the stone-lined pit of Grave 5. In short, this elaborate distribution supports the conclusion that this stone-lined pit had a complex history of mortuary usage and reusage, as postulated under the Laying-In/World Renewal Crypt model.

This claim is supported empirically by analyzing other stone-lined pit mortuary deposits, many of which display distributions similar to that in Grave 5, namely, "stray" items almost incidentally accumulated in the corners, signs of deliberate bone breaking, the accumulation of burials within the same pit but separated by stratification, and so on. Furthermore, just as in the case of Grave 5, several stone-lined pits show a history of modification indicating changes in use. That is, these features were not "single-use" graves, the type of feature that would terminate a funerary burial. Instead, they display a range of material indications of reusage, multiple usage, and, in general, a rich history of intensive ritual functioning, all of which would be expected under the Laying-In/World Renewal Crypt model.

A similar, although less obvious type of patterning is displayed in the "vaulted chambers" of the Hopewell site, suggesting that despite their formal differences, these two types of features, stone-lined pits and vaulted chambers, were simply local variants of the same general type of mortuary feature, here referred to as a laying-in crypt or, more completely, a laying-in/world renewal crypt altar. The term "altar" is deliberately used since the nature of the ritual that they mediated is postulated as more properly characterized in postmortem sacrificial terms than in personal, funerary terms. That is, although different in physical properties, these formally different features are equivalent in terms of symbolic pragmatics in that they were used to mediate equivalently complex ritual regimes in both sites, each regime exploiting the dead as symbolic capital by which to sustain postmortem sacrificial offerings in the performance of world renewal rites (Byers 2004).[2]

Conclusion

Despite the tangible differences of the Hopewell and Turner sites in both their earthwork and mortuary forms, a careful comparative analysis has demonstrated that the two groups responsible for these locales shared similar formal attributes in regard to their earthworks and shared similar mortuary activities aimed at achieving world renewal goals. It is true that these varied in the particular forms of the material features that were used to this end. However, these differences suggest that, from the perspective of the Turner cult sodality heterarchy, rather than the Hopewell site cult sodality heterarchy being alien, it was recognized as a close "cousin" that, located on the distant "frontier," had to accommodate to the demands of its near neighboring cult sodality heterarchies at Seip and Liberty Works. The Hopewell site cult sodality heterarchy, as well, could then act as the bridge by which Turner and its own near neighbors could sustain interaction with the Chillicothe tradition of the central Scioto sites sharing the classic monumental embankment C-R configuration. In short, the differences between Hopewell and Turner can be adequately accounted for in the above terms, as the attempt on the part of the Hopewell cult sodality heterarchy to maintain a working "rapprochement" with its near neighboring cult sodality heterarchies while maintaining a symbolic and real social closeness with the Turner cult sodality heterarchy.

It has been shown that the Dual Clan-Cult Sodality model can accommodate variation and continuity at different levels. The earthwork-habitation dichotomy, for example, can be easily understood in terms of this model as the expression of complementary heterarchical communities, these being communities based on relatively autonomous clans and cult sodalities. Each of these groups had separate but overlapping interests. Clearly, the interests of the clans would tend to limit their geographical reach since their main concern was reproduction and the pursuit of survival, both constraining their socio-ecological strategies to the rather local region. However, the cult sodalities had a broader reach, given the state of the cosmos as their main concern. Therefore, we can expect more long-distance interaction linking the mutually autonomous cult sodalities in different regions. These alliances constituted cult sodality heterarchies and the great earthworks were both built and used by these groups as monumental contexts in which to perform ongoing mortuary-mediated world renewal rituals. As argued above, I have shown that the formal patterning of the earthworks and their associated mortuary deposits in different regions of the Central Ohio Valley reinforces the claim that these were interacting over distances and across generations.

Notes

1. In Byers 2004, although I referred to the earthwork-based groups as cults, I characterized their social nature in terms of companionship and, therefore, as sodalities. I will now refer to them as cult sodalities and, of course, this means that the Dual Clan-Cult model needs to be retitled to the Dual Clan-Cult Sodality model.

2. I use the term "postmortem human sacrifice" to refer to the nature of mortuary deposits that were the result of postfuneral spirit release rites. As noted earlier, the mortuary process I have postulated entailed an incremental sequence of rites in which

the deceased served centrally. The first was probably of a funerary nature directed to releasing the personal soul to enable it to travel to the land of the dead. Subsequent rituals involved releasing other spiritual powers of the deceased, sometimes referred to as living spirits: the spirits of the flesh, the bones, and so on. I have postulated that these spiritual powers were effectively sacrificial offerings made to the cosmos. This is why I have termed this total mortuary process a form of postmortem human sacrifice. This characterization of the process also warrants my referring to the vaulted chambers and the stone-lined pits as sacrificial *altars*.

COMMENTARY

Commentary on Robert V. Riordan's "Enclosed by Stone"

Commentary by A. Martin Byers

Robert Riordan has significantly advanced our understanding of Ohio Hopewell monumentalism as it was manifested in the southwestern sector of Ohio. His work nicely illuminates what I have called the "hermeneutic spiral method" (Bhaskar 1978: chap. 3; 1979, 11–28, 164–169; Byers 2004: 106–107; 2006a: 20–23). This method assumes that human reasons, meanings, and social conditions are a critical part of the causal conditions that generated the archaeological record. In emphasizing the particular way that stones were used in the construction of Pollock, Riordan points to how we can reconstruct the social conditions of this activity and, therefore, opens up postulating possible reasons for the building of such monumental constructions by peoples who had only the use of their own muscle power. Noting the size of the stones and the distances they had to be carried made him rethink his original explanation, and instead of treating their use as erosion stoppers (i.e., a use that would be practical in Western cultural terms), he started to treat them as having symbolic purpose that reached beyond Euro-American notions of practicality. His reinterpretation led me to realize how we could use the stones as a measure of the qualitative nature of the labor expended to move them. We can certainly measure the magnitude of earth-digging labor required to build earthworks and average this in terms of manpower work days, but the labor required for building with stone, rather than earth, has another advantage in that it allows for estimating the qualitative nature of this labor and, therefore, the cultural value it may have had for those who carried it out. Riordan's description of the difficulties his own field crew had with moving some of the stones indicates that even when shared, the labor involved would approach the maximum levels of normal human capacity. When seen as being performed as a form of sacred activity, it is reasonable to interpret the material labor as the performance of a type of ordeal ritual, possibly a rite of passage by which the laborers achieved a new social status and recognition. This then allows postulating a particular type of social structure that would make such ordeals possible and intelligible, for example, the type that is well researched by anthropologists of historically well-known Native American peoples. This illustrates how Riordan's use of the hermeneutic spiral method opens up new ways of interpreting more data to verify the likely existence of these social conditions and so on.

Therefore, Riordan's paper has shown not only that reconstructing this cognitive-normative dimension from objective data is possible but also that it is a critical part of expanding our understanding and accounting of the archaeological record. His work has shown that we must break out of the interpretive limitations that are imposed by our own cultural framework and be willing to treat the data as the residue of activities that were the conditions of satisfaction of the collective strategies of the responsible builders while still knowing that their collective intentionality would be different from our own, although certainly not totally foreign since, of course, it was a collective intentionality of a human community (see Hancock, this volume). While this means using objective data to ground a model of a social reality that was distinct from the data themselves, his work shows that by treating these data in symbolic terms, they can be used as media that logically and necessarily link the patternings of stones, water, natural topography, and distance, on the one hand, and the possible beliefs, motives, purposes, and intentions of those responsible, on the other. This linkage is effected by human material *and* cognitive-normative capacities as realized in pragmatic or action-constitutive symboling. In short, while the material data have an objective ontological status and the cognitive-normative reality has an intersubjective ontological status, the reaching out archaeologists must perform is not really to go beyond the data to a social reality, one emergent from subjects interrelating, that is, intersubjective, since the data must be treated as an expressive and necessary part of the realization and reproduction of that social reality. Furthermore, as Riordan's interpretation of Hopewell monumentalism illustrates, this interpretive exercise is far from being merely unsupported speculation. This is because of the nature of the hermeneutic spiral method. Although we are, of course, limited in our model construction by our imaginative capacities, the method allows us to make theoretically informed and empirically grounded rational choices among the alternative imagined worlds—social models—and since these models are always presented as approximate and not absolute models of the social causal conditions of the archaeological record, our current choices among alternatives are themselves corrigible, making the method an open-ended process of knowledge formation, reformation, and correcting—in short, a hermeneutic spiral. Therefore, rational judgments can be contingently definitive without being necessarily absolutist.

Furthermore, each theoretically elucidated and empirically grounded choice opens up new avenues for research to expand our understanding and this new research might well recursively act to force us to modify the older model. For example, Riordan has argued that while the protocols underwriting construction in the Little Miami drainage are similar at one level to the protocols manifested in equivalent construction in the Scioto drainage, he also notes that they are different in that the latter seem to be more attuned to symmetry and "accuracy" while the works in the Miami drainages, such as Bull Works, Pollock Works, and even Fort Ancient, manifest a lesser concern with symmetry. He attributes this difference, probably correctly, to the greater topographical constraints under which the latter worked. There just are not very many broad, level valley bottom regions in the Miami drainages, while these are much more common in the central Scioto. However, there may be more to it than this. In my paper in this section, I have argued that the core component of the Hopewell site embankment earthwork on the North Fork in the Scioto drainage has more attributes relating it to Turner in the Little Miami Valley than it does to its own near neighbors in the Paint Creek, such as Seip and Baum. Only later in its history was its main C-form embankment supplemented by a stone wall closing its open side and a circle and square similar in form but smaller in size to those making up Seip and Baum. Since, in fact, the main terrace on which the Hopewell site was built was easily large enough to accommodate the total C-form, extending the embankment to the upper terrace was deliberate, and adding the circle and square, I have suggested, was probably expedient as part of ameliorating relations with near neighbors. If this assessment is accepted, it implies that the original builders may have preferentially chosen the North Fork largely because it had a distinctive topographical arrangement of the secondary and primary terraces that may have allowed them to construct the primary embankment to incorporate two distinct levels, thereby replicating the lower/upper distinction that Riordan has noted seems to be basic to the Miami drainage constructions. Thus what may have started as a topographic necessity in the Miami drainages became a symbolic pragmatic rule and may have been emulated in the Scioto drainage as an important part of the strategy in choosing the locale for the construction of the Hopewell site earthwork.

This combination of an initial dual-leveled construction with a later addition of circle and square suggests a distinction that can be a temporal marker. As Riordan notes, Camden and Milford manifest the same circularity/rectangularity: high/low patterning that he identifies for Pollock and Bull Works. However, they also incorporate a closer approximation to the circle-square symmetry, a characteristic of the Scioto drainage. In short, just as I claim the set of circle and square was a relatively late addition made to the Hopewell site, so the building of the embankments of Turner, Camden, and Milford, each incorporating or adding a form of symmetry characteristic of the earthworks of the Scioto drainage, may have been rather late events. With further research, this hypothesis could be tested as valid or, alternatively, rejected. More important, it would also start to allow us to work on postulating the possible *quality and nature* of the Miami-Scioto interrelations and their historical development. Peoples differing on rules and protocols making up collective construction strategies while sharing the same cosmology and ethos would tend to stand to each other in a somewhat hostile attitude since each likely would consider the other's material features to be less than felicitous forms for constituting the equivalent ritual (see Byers's "Heartland" chapter, this volume).

However, if this characterization is accepted, it raises one troubling aspect I have with Riordan's interpretive approach. This is his largely taken-for-granted assumption that monumental constructions are symbols in a manner similar to words. This seems to be why he favors speaking of the monumental constructions as statements: "The pairing of earthwork shapes and the intentional use of topographic differences in elevation to make a symbolic statement was repeated elsewhere in southwest Ohio." But the analogy of monumental constructions as statements is misleading. Statements convey information; monumental earthworks are among the constitutive material components of a social world. Thus we can use the monuments as empirical data to ground our propositional statements, that is, models, about the cultural conditions that made them possible, but surely the people who built them were doing much more than making statements about their world. Since they could do this in ordinary speech about the world as represented by the monuments, it follows that the purpose of these constructions goes well beyond the level of making a statement.

I have argued that the symbolism of the Hopewell earth (and stone) works must be seen as expressive and pragmatic rather than as referential (or designative) and descriptive (Byers 2006: 34–35). Pragmatic expression is expression that is action constitutive. It is action constitutive because expression manifests intentions—for example, an angry expression often means the intention to *strike out to satisfy ones anger*—and when this expressive behavior is mediated by material symbols, it manifests both the action intentions of the user and the authoritative source that, in the understanding and perception of all the relevant parties, transforms the expressive behavior itself into a particular social act. An example of a pragmatic expressive artifact would be our court warrant. By officers of the court using warrants while physically seizing the persons named in them, they simultaneously transform their physical behaviors to count as and be the legal acts of arrest rather than the illegal acts of assault. Seen in this warranting or symbolic pragmatic view, the Pollock stones that are surplus to any actual anti-erosion needs have an action-constitutive meaning akin to our court warrants. As I suggested above, in this case they can be treated as constituting the labor behaviors into ritual ordeals, and by extension, the walls that they capped were transformed into action-constitutive symbolic pragmatic monuments of any subsequent rites performed in their context, including the deliberate and thorough burning of the timber curtain wall.

This does not deny that the designative moment is an important part of symbolism—the alignment of the Newark Octagon with the turning points of the lunar cycle certainly makes the latter the probable object of these alignments. However, it is the symbolic, pragmatic, expressive moment that explains the purpose of these monumental symbols since they express the likely sacred intentions and social roles of the builders/users. The designative or referential meaning of the monuments is important because it specifies the source of the power of the monuments. Therefore, rather than Pollock being a statement merely conveying information about the world that it designates, for example, the essential powers of the astral sphere, as an expressive symbol, it would be taken by the users as expressing and thereby presencing these powers (albeit, a reified form of expression much like we reify the symbolic pragmatic force of the court warrant as "literally" presencing the authority of the judge). This reified expressivity transforms their experiencing of their own behaviors performed in its context as the ritual acts they intended. Riordan's symbolic interpretation of his empirical data can be easily modified in these expressive or symbolic pragmatic terms, thereby firmly grounding the intelligibility of Ohio Hopewell monumentalism in the pragmatic strategies of these cultural prehistoric populations.

Rejoinder by Robert Riordan to Commentary by A. Martin Byers

When one strays into the realm of symbolic interpretation, it is important to remember how quickly an elaborate castle so carefully crafted in the air can be slighted. I am pleased that Byers, when he evaluated my construction, found it to have at least some firm archaeological foundations. I concur with Byers that the stones in the Pollock embankments lend themselves to our being able to make observations about the qualitative differences in individual contributions of labor to the construction project in a way that heaped soil does not. While the addition of stones weighing tens of kilograms probably was an ordeal for those involved, most of the stones in the embankments are small. Thus facing an embankment with stone could have been an important participatory rite. And the statuses and egos of some who contributed may have been enlarged by the size of the stones they moved—and based on the sentiments expressed by certain males in my field crews, I can envision that an aspect of competition was probably at work here. I think that the many thousands of small stones that were piled up are a more important part of the story: They can reasonably be taken to signify the contributions of many more younger, older, and weaker people than those few athletes who moved our signature monster stone. They may be taken to demonstrate that it took a village to build Pollock. Earthwork construction itself, and not just the addition of stones to them, was an activity that built communities.

As I move from piling stones to coupling earthworks, I fully appreciate that my argument gets airier (some might prefer "cloudier"). In an earlier draft of my essay, I had noted (but then finally omitted) that in the Scioto Valley the Shriver Circle and Mound City constitute a pair of separate but nearby rectilinear and circular earthworks that are not connected by parallel walls. Were they a conceptual pair? There are many obvious and important differences between these sites and Pollock plus Bull, including the absence of an elevation difference, but perhaps the morphological similarities speak to an underlying Hopewell earthwork semantic that existed across southern Ohio. I also appreciate the connection Byers makes between Hopewell and the southwestern Ohio earthworks. For many years, he has championed a connection between the builders of the Hopewell site and people in southwestern Ohio, in contrast with those who hold a localized view of the Scioto-Paint earthworks. The fact is that Hopewell's builders did trouble themselves to incorporate the edge of the adjacent and much higher terrace as part of the enclosed C-form (in Byers's terms), something unnecessary if the purpose of the embankment was simply to define an impressive amount of ceremonial space on an already very wide landform. Instead, they chose to increase their labor in order to incorporate an elevation difference into the enclosure, and that is in symbolic similarity with what occurred in southwestern Ohio.

I take Byers's point about my use of the term "statement" when referring to the builders' intent concerning Pollock and other earthworks. I do believe that the building of the Pollock Works, as it has been revealed by the archaeological program my students and I have conducted there, involved elements that had little relation to everyday practicality and much to do with its ability to facilitate, ameliorate, and/or demonstrate its builders' spiritual and social needs. The stones piled on the embankments' external faces are the objects that ground my essay. They are an obviously integral component of the earthwork and what it meant to its builders, but without an archaeological investigation that took the time to examine them in some depth, I would not have recognized that I needed to work them into an interpretation of what I think Pollock may have been about. My point is that, while my own expressed interpretation might be close to or very wide of the mark set by the builders, we do still need hard data on construction practice, sequence, and chronology from many more such sites. While destructive practices have removed the opportunity to gain information from a significant portion of the corpus of Ohio Hopewell earthworks (although some "destroyed" sites may still preserve important and recoverable data below the ground), the preservation of many others can, on the other hand, ensure that some ambitious future projects are still possible. Our earthworks of the air may yet find better and more grounded interpretations if archaeologists will return to them in order to conduct the necessary research.

Commentary on A. Martin Byers's "The Turner-Hopewell Axis: Exploring Interaction through Embankment Form and Mortuary Patterning"

Commentary by Robert V. Riordan

A. Martin Byers alludes in his article to several of the issues he developed at length in his recent (2004) book on the Hopewell while elaborating on the connections he perceives between the formal plans and material residues of the Hopewell and Turner Earthworks. I am not yet willing to accept all of Byers's assumptions about the Hopewell, in particular, that they conceived the world as immanently sacred and that renewal ritual—if that is what the material residues at ceremonial sites like Hopewell and Turner actually represent—

was necessarily aimed at ameliorating the polluting effects caused by the daily living of lives. The Dual Clan-Cult model he proposes is, on the other hand, an ingenious reading of the material record and one that, given his assumptions, works well as an interpretation of Ohio Hopewell. He notes that it can usefully explain the regional differences in earthworks, since he views each cult as autonomous and free to make decisions about: "What would count as an appropriate earthwork form by which the renewal ritual was most effectively performed. . . . Therefore, it is not at all surprising that the region south of the Ohio River was dominated by Adena-style earthworks during the early and middle Middle Woodland while the Hopewell-style earthworks prevailed north of the river."

The idea that people of different traditions might find different "appropriate" means of concretely expressing their socioreligious beliefs is something to which almost everyone can subscribe. What the Dual Clan-Cult model does not explain is why the societies in southern Ohio that built and then maintained the earthworks and their associated properties should have expended so much more effort and time on them than did other contemporary societies. It is well to remember that construction was only one aspect of a society's involvement with an earthwork; they would also have spent considerable time in actually using it for the purpose(s) for which it was designed, and they likely also felt obliged to maintain it, or at least some portion(s) of it and perhaps also the facilities that were enclosed by it, to a certain standard. Was the imbalance in effort attributable to ideology, differences in population size and its organization, different forms of leadership, or all three? It has been observed by several authors that the effort of constructing large earthworks, when spread over time, makes them less costly than they might seem when the ultimate finished product is considered in isolation, but nevertheless, many of these sites did involve huge amounts of labor, labor that was not expended by their contemporaries in Kentucky, or in Illinois for that matter. My own efforts at disassembling portions of several earthworks during the course of undertaking archaeological excavations have underscored for me the sheer magnitude of the construction efforts that these sites represent, especially given the technological base that produced them. A question I pose to Byers is, Why did the members of the proposed sodalities of Ohio Hopewell invest so lavishly in earthworks and their related panoply when, presumably, those in sodalities elsewhere did not feel that same compulsion? That naturally leads to a second question: What did those others do with all their free time? Would he see this as due to a fundamental difference in ethos between Ohio societies and their contemporaries elsewhere? If so, why was Ohio Hopewell so different from its contemporaries?

In Byers's world of dual clans and cults, which denies the existence of Hopewellian elites, we are left adrift concerning the identification of just who *was* responsible for designing the earthworks, motivating the troops into episodes of construction, and maintaining the integrity of the design over the span of decades. Such direction could have been the province of particular groups, but such special knowledge could also have been the basis for elitism.

I find merit in Byers's observations concerning the possibility that a Turner-Hopewell tradition existed and in the implication that Hopewell was closer ideologically to the southwestern Ohio centers than those near the confluence of Paint Creek and the Scioto River. In particular, but not surprisingly given the sentiments expressed in my article, I think the connection involving the incorporation of elevation differences at Turner and Hopewell may serve to emphasize a distinction between Hopewell and the other nearby Chillicothe-area earthworks such as Seip and Liberty Works. In my article I focus on the incorporation of elevation differences as a means of linking earthworks not physically connected but in close geographical proximity to each other. I am not certain that circular and rectilinear forms necessarily needed to be pure expressions to have been satisfactorily "appropriate" to the Hopewell. The preponderance of extended burials at Turner and Hopewell, contra the situation at other Chillicothe-area earthworks, is probably a more important similarity than the material differences that exist between the mortuary facilities present at the two sites.

Byers is undoubtedly correct in emphasizing the possibility of subregional traditions whose builders were in full awareness of the kind of expressions developed by other builders. The bearers of each tradition no doubt believed in their own interpretation as being the most satisfactory, but the location of Hopewell, and the sheer substantiality of its construction and the apparent duration of its use, set in close geographic proximity to the distinctly different earthworks of the Paint-Scioto drainages more likely evidences a situation of peaceful rapprochement rather than a resented intrusion.

Byers mentions briefly that historical developments may have resulted in additions to Hopewell. He emphasizes the importance that time depth may have played at this and other sites, although he—like everyone else—is unable to do much more than note the fact. Archaeological research has been insufficiently focused on the tedious necessity of unraveling the chronologies of site development for us to do more than speculate on the directions such developments took. At Hopewell, for instance, was the large square an appendage to the large enclosure? Probably, but it would be nice to know that with certainty, and also how much later it was built. Similarly, I speculate along with many others on the chronology of the developments at Fort Ancient. Contrary to Byers's statement, I see Fort Ancient as more than a "table-top" affair and propose that it should be regarded in the same category as Turner and Milford. Its parallel walls may, in fact, constitute an effort at homology with the elongated walls at Milford and those connecting the circular and elliptical enclosures at Turner.

Rejoinder by A. Martin Byers to Commentary by Robert V. Riordan

I can certainly agree with Riordan that ongoing usage of the earthworks was a significant component of the ritual that they mediated and that this usage involved constant, probably scheduled and additional building. Therefore, I have no difficulty accepting his observation that large amounts of construction labor were required. Indeed, in this regard the Scioto earthworks are deviant from most other Ohio Hopewell earthworks in that what I have termed the Paint Creek C-R configuration seemed to be a one-shot affair, and instead of adding more layers or making lateral extensions, the earthwork would be abandoned and a new one built. However, the other embankment earthworks, such as High Banks, were accretional, along the lines that Pollock and Fort Ancient were accretional. Is it possible that the symbolic pragmatic meanings of the two forms, the Paint Creek and the High Bank C-R configurations is the distinguishing factor?

That these earthworks were monumental symbolic pragmatic devices mediating world renewal ritual reiterates my commitment to the claim that Riordan is reluctant to recognize, namely, that the cosmology of the peoples responsible for these earthworks was what I have termed an immanentist one and, therefore, informed them that the world was immanently sacred. My reason for this commitment is fairly straightforward. I assume that the earthwork builders/users acted strategically and, therefore, were rational. Hence, to explain these monumental earthworks it is necessary to specify the type of collective belief(s) that would have had to exist to make it rational and possible for foragers and gardeners, possibly mobile for much of the year, to build these monuments. In short, without positing an immanentist type world belief I cannot make these material phenomena intelligible. Of course, I have also marshaled significant empirical data to support this claim, in particular, that critical patterning exists that is most coherently explained as the outcome of significant proscriptive or avoidance construction actions, and such avoidances presuppose the belief that the earth was immanently sacred.

However, Riordan is quite right to raise the issue of the spotty distribution of Hopewellian earthworks. He questions why the Ohio Hopewell invested so lavishly in earthworks and their related panoply when, presumably, those in sodalities elsewhere did not feel that same compulsion. I will call this question 1. His follow up questions are equally germane, of course, namely: (2) "What did those others do with all their free time?" and (3) Does this absence of earthworks count as "a fundamental difference in ethos between Ohio societies and their contemporaries elsewhere?" Finally, assuming the response to the third question is yes, he then asks (4) "If so, why was Ohio Hopewell so different from its contemporaries?"

These are hefty questions and deserve a much longer response than I can give here. However, I will sketch out some responses. First, the questions presuppose an interpretive background that I found myself struggling to break from when writing my book, *The Ohio Hopewell Episode*, this being what I have called the Monistic Modular Polity model. This presupposes what I have termed the Exclusive Territorial/Proprietorial Domain paradigm as its "deep" structural premises. The reason I had to struggle is because the central premises are effectively those of my own culture and, of course, as I have argued, my North American archaeological colleagues who share the same culture have generally projected these premises onto the prehistoric data. In short, implicated in this distinction between those regions with and those without earthworks is the notion that the communities in these regions were modular polities, and because of the presence/absence of monumentalism, it follows that the two polities must have been structured differently. It is this modular polity perspective, therefore, that is presupposed by his questions. However, I have claimed that this perspective as a general background framework leads to a serious distortion in our understanding prehistoric Native North American societies. A more appropriate perspective is what I have termed the Polyistic Locale-Centric Community model, along with its auxiliary Dual Clan-Cult Sodality model. Presupposing these models is the Inclusive Territorial/Custodial Domain paradigm and this characterizes the tenurial relations a community had with its land in custodial rather than unitary proprietorial terms. The result is to characterize communities as caught up in an open network of alliance and interactions.

I cannot review the whole argument that these models represent, although my discussion in this book of the cultural traditions of the "Heartland" does give a sketchy overview (Byers, this volume). However, the upshot of this argument would be that, because territories were inclusive instead of exclusive, those living in regions not displaying earthworks would not have been excluded from fully participating in the earthworks in those regions where they proliferated. Hence, labor would regularly be drawn from all the nonearthwork regions, and this labor would be in the form of full members of the cult sodalities who, I have argued, were responsible for these earthworks. This brief explanation at least points to answers for questions 1 and 2 above. In regard to 1, since there were no social and only sacred boundaries, for the responsible cult sodalities (or alliances of such cult sodalities that I have referred to as cult sodality heterarchies), the operating scope of their earthwork construction and usage strategy embraced all those regions from which they drew their participating members. The population of nonearthwork regions, therefore, would have been represented in those cult sodalities where their family and clan members were participants. This means, of course, that, with regard to question 2, the latter had to travel farther than those fellow members who lived in the earthwork regions and, therefore, would have even less time to waste. These two answers, of course, also answer question 3, since treating the Ohio Middle Woodland period as having a complex social system consisting of an open network of intercommunity relations would mean having an equally broad sharing of the same cosmology and ethos. This inclusionary view, of course, stands in strong opposition to the modular perspective that is at the heart of the Vacant Center/Dispersed Hamlet view current in the literature, and, as I noted above, the questions that Riordan raises make sense only in that conceptual scheme or framework. However, answering question 4 requires a little more background, although the answer is already implicit in Riordan's recognition that, while the construction traditions of the central Scioto and the Miami River drainages were different in form, they would have been mutually understood by parties from both regions—although this understanding may also have been less than mutually sympathetic. That is, it is quite possible that each sector perceived the formal earthwork traditions of the other as constituting somewhat infelicitous expressions of what would count as a proper earthwork for mediating ritual.

This distinction in form between the two regional earthwork traditions, however, probably expressed a shared cosmology and ethos and, therefore, the variation operates at the level I have referred to as ideology (discussed in more detail in my "Heartland" chapter, this volume). I think it is legitimate to extend this ideological view so as to answer question 4, "Why was Ohio Hopewell so different from its contemporaries?" True, Ohio Hopewell is distinguished from, for example, Illinois Hopewell, in that the latter pretty well lacks any significant embankment earthworks, while the two are parallel in sharing a similar and rich Hopewellian mortuary and associated artifactual record. Why? I would speculate at the moment that, in fact, the two Hopewellian regions shared almost the same deep cosmological and ethos perspectives while differing partially at the ideological level. I have defined ideology in my "Heartland" chapter (this volume) as relating to all those rules and protocols and their rationales that govern the forms that activities and their outcomes must display in order to fulfill the collective strategies of groups. Ideologies tend to vary rapidly over time and space while at the same time reproducing, instead of transforming, the cosmology and ethos that make the ideological variation possible. Hence, while the ideological strategies of the cults of southwestern and of central and south-central Ohio embraced earthwork construction as a necessary medium of ritual while varying ideologically in terms of forms, the cult ideological strategies of Illinois may have largely rejected embankment earthwork construction as inappropriate contexts of ritual while embracing a form of mortuary and associated artifactual usage that was fairly similar to the Ohio region.

These answers to Riordan's questions, of course, are simply the logical implication of the Polyistic Locale-Centric Community model and require further empirical verification. As always, much more could be said on this matter, but I believe that most of the questions that Riordan has thoughtfully raised have been addressed, and as with all good questions, their answers have stimulated the need for new research.

SECTION 4

The Hermeneutic and Phenomenological Perspective

In this section, John E. Hancock's chapter addresses issues concerning the role and meaning Hopewell earthworks may have played within these ancient societies and, equally important, what the remnants of these built landscapes mean to the people of here and now. Hancock directs a unique endeavor, the EarthWorks multimedia project, which has utilized new digital imaging technology to generate interactive visual images of a number of recreated earthworks for modern audiences. Hancock comments that his recent foray into exploring Hopewell earthworks has "forced [him] to revisit some core questions of [his] discipline [of architecture]." In the same light, his unique training and perspective provokes exceptional nuances and insights for archaeological discourse and the understanding of such a remarkable built environment. His chapter, in the search for meaning, also discusses how the dialogue in which we participate in our own scholarly discourse deeply influences (and perhaps inhibits?) our own personal and professional understanding of the earthworks and the role they played within Hopewell societies (and continue to play today).

Hancock introduces us to the core concept of hermeneutic phenomenology and, as archaeologists and researchers, how our understanding
of this concept ought to force us to come to terms with the subtle understanding of interpretation itself (going beyond, as he notes, Ian Hodder's
own writings about the issue). At the core of his discussion is a fundamental concern: How do we come to understand the meaning of human
works (and the work of works) within communities and how can we apply
such insights into understanding the role of earthworks within an ancient
long-vanished society? Understanding such architecture, Hancock points
out, and the possible meanings they held for those within the ancient
communities that built them (or for people today), requires more than
simply utilizing the "scientific method," for there is a difference, he notes,
between "compiling information" and giving meaning to the objects of
that information. Such works encoded a thick web of interrelated meanings, both recognized and unrecognized, and mediated the relationships
between and among the community members who created the work. Thus
one of the key challenges of his EarthWorks project is to create a visual and
interactive medium that is "vivid for the modern mind" and to provoke
modern audiences into discovering multiple layers of meaning for themselves. Ultimately Hancock's words are extremely effective in revealing that
our own present-day cultural bias of seeing and constituting the world in
bifurcated "either/or" (sacred/secular, habitation/nonhabitation) terms is
not the world of the Hopewell earthwork builders, for clearly theirs was a
more complicated integrated realm of different spheres of understanding.

If Hancock addresses that it is not simply the "thing" itself but the creation of the "thing" that imbues meaning for communities, then A. Martin
Byers in this section's chapter extends this concept to include the meaning that people give to their place within the larger physical and social
environment. Byers provides us with a more sophisticated understanding
and interpretation of meaning than is currently in vogue in archaeological
discussion. He delves into how meaning is put into action/practice by humans—meaning at both an individual level (an individual's "place" within
society and the shifting roles that occur through age changes and social
expectations) and meaning at a larger societal level (kinship, tenure and
land rights and obligations, proscriptions and prescriptions for "proper" or
"improper" behavior). Thus, as he notes, poaching and hunting may both

result in the killing of an animal, but the killing behaviors constitute very different meanings, that is, actions, and, therefore, very different social responses on the part of community members. In essence, in his view all action is symbolically constructed (even the "practical" business of survival).

Byers uses the vehicle of analyzing and critiquing Berle Clay's Woodland "Heartland" model to introduce to the archaeological community a more powerful consideration of the concepts of cosmology, ethos, world view, and ideology (concepts often collapsed, as he notes, into some vague ethereal otherworld domain "over there" in archaeological discourse). He reveals how archaeologists can use these concepts as analytical "tools" for investigating and interpreting the duality of settlement—ceremonial distinctions between peoples within a region (e.g., differences and similarities among Hopewell sites or between Hopewell and Adena) as well as changes that occur in the archaeological record across time. He proposes that ceremonial sites (earthworks) and settlements (hamlets) are manifestations of the Hopewell (or contemporaneous Adena folks) "putting into practice" (ideology and world view) an underlying cosmology and ethos—that is, practice is the medium by which ideology is "written" into action. Thus ideology and world view may more readily change over time, but fundamental shifts in cosmology and ethos are slower to occur. Byers's discussion can thus have profound implications for recognizing and interpreting what differences within and across regions and time may mean in social as well as cultural terms.

9

The Earthworks Hermeneutically Considered

John E. Hancock

The literature of Woodland archaeology occasionally has ventured into the field of architectural theory. Recourse to general views about the nature of architecture, the means of its creation, and its role in the social world would seem indispensable to figuring out what the earthwork builders were up to on the hilltops and river terraces of southern Ohio. After twenty years as an architectural theorist, historian, and educator, my first encounters with the earthworks forced me to revisit some core questions of my discipline: how architecture arises from a cultural world and how it can best be interpreted and visualized. So alien and uncanny, these ancient works raise ontological and epistemological questions: What are we as humans across time? What are the essential capacities of works of architecture? How can something as enigmatic as Newark be commensurable with more familiar human spatial ideas today? So vast and subtle, they also raise perceptual and conceptual questions: How can our modern eyes and minds get hold of them? What means of spatial representation can turn them into graspable visual experiences comparable to those we hold of more familiar cultural landmarks? Ultimately, can they "say" anything to us, challenge our own suppositions, or help us see things anew?

What I offer here are three distinct vantage points on these issues. First, as a reader of philosophy, especially hermeneutic phenomenology, I will begin by questioning the dualistic logic of scientific discourse—the scientific versus humanistic approaches to knowledge, or those peculiarly modernist constructs the "objective" and "subjective" views of reality—and explain how these bifurcations limit our understanding of human existence and human-made things. Second, as an architect and scholar of architectural theory, I will explore the earthworks in terms of their roles as "works" both in the life and world of their makers and in their capacity to open up ideas and challenges for us today. And finally, as director of the multimedia EarthWorks project (Hancock 2006), I will discuss the special problems of visualizing the "Hopewell sacred landscape"—given our modern minds and our time-bound space conceptions (Giedion 1971) plus the extreme size, continuing degradation, and obscuring

Figure 9.1. The Hopewell Mound Group site today. Photo by author.

forest cover of the sites—and our methods for helping modern audiences to "see" what the ancient builders saw, or more precisely, what they imagined.

Although these viewpoints are all outside archaeology, I hope to offer some general "interpretive" views on the meaning of architecture, in its world and against its horizons, as well as some "rendered" views of the earthworks themselves. I hope that our almost completely differing terminologies will not overly obscure what I have to say.

Phenomenology and the Lifeworld

The issues posed by this conference are at the core of the theory and philosophy of interpretation, not just in archaeology but in consideration of all human societies and all human-made works. How we examine and make truth claims about a distant society, or the things it created, is naturally conditioned by our presuppositions about the nature of human existence itself: how it is that we, as humans, are (and how they were) in relation to things, artworks, tools, ceremonies, food, nature, each other, and so on. This is why we must begin with philosophy, opening up the questions of how we understand ourselves fundamentally to exist and to encounter phenomena, and how we interpret or represent things.

For the most part, since Descartes, modern science has presupposed our human existence and interpretive situation within the "subject-object dichotomy." This metaphysical view imagines that all truth claims arise from the encounter of a "subject" (we are in the act of thinking and observing) with an "object" (a thing is out there on its own in the physical world and presented for our examination). We (subjects) examine things (objects) and gather data necessary to create knowledge about them. Seeing ourselves in this way, we cannot avoid the "dichotomy" between the subjective and the objective: One class of knowledge arises from the subject (human viewpoints with their societal, historical, emotional, personal, or spiritual contingency), while another arises from the object itself (its fixed characteristics and properties that can be circumscribed, specified, and sometimes even quantified into predictive laws). This dichotomy is most visible to us as an epistemological condition, characterizing our conscious assumptions about knowledge and its validity. But it also operates as a broad, implicit ontology in which the fundamental nature of what it means to exist within human life, either in a distant society or our own, is to be "subjectively" encountering "objects."

Scientific method is of course essential for archaeological practice, as for many aspects of architectural practice. Its techniques of circumscribing and examining objects and subjects are capable of assembling "accurate information" on which we will always rely. But the ontology that it presupposes and implies fails to grasp human existence in a universal sense and the relationships among things, meanings, motives, and environments that are inherent in it. A century of phenomenological critique has shown why this is true, exposing behind and beneath either "objective" or "subjective" knowledge something more fundamental, a "lived world" of relationships in which human existence is embedded, prior to any conscious or specific act of examination. Consider this glass of water on the podium here: Is it an "object" to be grasped through measuring its weight or capacity, tracing the history of its manufacture, and so on? This is how we would attain "objective truth" about it. Or am I instead only creating it in my subjective consciousness, as a "personal" or maybe "cultural" construct? No, clearly neither of these describes my relation to the glass, at least before I brought it to attention just now. Beneath and prior to either of these possible views, I was simply, habitually, and unreflectively reaching for it in order to quench my thirst or out of a certain nervousness, already taking it for granted as part of an uncontemplated background world of everyday things and relations. Such a world of unthought, unseen relations and meanings, what phenomenology calls the "lifeworld," is always already understood, simply by our living, before any conscious act of analysis or contemplation, including scientific investigation, even begins. These "background" relations are too thick and complex to ever be stated as "objective" truths, and also too concrete and pervasive to be merely "subjective" contingencies.

Here is the ontological point: All things and experiences are "always already among" the tightly woven fabric, the structures and relations, of the lifeworld. This is as true for us, as it is for those whom we study. Methods presumed to be "objective" give us information about things, but artificially extract them out of this lifeworld, and prevent us from understanding the fundamental role of those same things in the world. (We might presume weight and manufacture to be the "truth" of the water glass since they can be factually verified, but then we will have completely missed its more embedded place in the lifeworld.)

We ourselves, like the Hopewell we would interpret, are always already situated within a world and among traditions, aims, tasks, beliefs, and practices which for the most part are nonexplicit and prereflective. We are in our own such world continuously, even while being scholars or scientists—going about our daily habits and activities, depending on traditions, presupposing meanings and relationships, and relying on equipment like a projector or a glass of water within easy reach. This inexhaustible lifeworld, even as it does not come to our attention, is the basis of the intelligibility of all things; it grants prior meaning to all conclusions. The scientist's explanation of the "sunset" (the earth rotates and light is refracted) can only come about and remain comprehensible within and upon the already-experienced foundation of "real sunsets" in the lived world (Luijpen 1966: 11) which are already saturated with emotional, historical, cultural, bodily, spiritual, poetic, and many other kinds of interwoven and simultaneous meanings. The sunset (or the obsidian blade or the earthwork), as an object of science, is always dependent on its prior reality as a "phenomenon" showing itself forth from within a richly contextual world, already together with all mortal concerns and among all beings.

Phenomenology is concerned with things "showing themselves as themselves" (Heidegger 1962: 51), while still among the relationships of the lived world, and constructs its knowledge of them accordingly. Yet this does not in any way suggest that this everyday background of experience is all that the lived world ever consists of, or that all things are forever relegated to obscurity in such a world. On the contrary (and this is its special virtue for architectural theory), this insight brings attention to the kinds of conditions under which entities arise out of their prereflective background and enter our conscious attentiveness, intentions or aspirations. Would I ever be prompted to actively take up my water glass for attentive examination? Certainly if it breaks or leaks, or when it becomes a communion chalice or is installed in an art gallery with a plaque. Or when it becomes a "find" during some future archaeological excavation!

This returns us to my earlier point about the limits of objective science, because the ways and conditions in which entities come forward as objects of scientific inquiry do not necessarily correspond at all to the ways that they do so (or did so) within the everyday contexts of the human lifeworld. Things come to presence as objects, emerging into reflective consciousness, under very special circumstances. To observe how this "emergence" occurs within a distant culture is one thing (through art or ritual for example, or through the uncanny size or precision of an earthwork), to attend to how we artificially cause it through our methods and theories is another. The interactive complexity of negotiating these "emergences" across time, the interplay between the "foregrounding" of works within past culture (as a matter of purported intention), and our "foregrounding" of them today (as a matter of plausible interpretation), requires that we take one more step philosophically, into "hermeneutics"—the understanding of interpretation itself.

Hermeneutics and the Fusion of Horizons

This requires a more complex and less circumscribed approach to our interpretations, particularly when these phenomena are the product of a past human society (like earthworks, rather than sunsets). Here we may turn to hermeneutics, which offers us a way of "communicating" with lived worlds beyond our own by turning the ontological insights of phenomenology into a process for creating knowledge about specific societies, situations, texts, and works. In this light, I could have titled my paper "Interpreting the Earthworks," since that is generally what "hermeneutics" means. Yet from Heidegger, Hans-Georg Gadamer (1994; Palmer 1969), and the growing numbers of their commentators come more specific and powerful points that can contribute to the questions before us here: In opening ourselves to "phenomena" from an ancient situation, we have opportunities to grasp a "world" and not merely objects or data. More radically, we can also open up a dialogue with past human conditions. By presupposing a fundamentally shared humanity (we, like they, already know something of rain and death and toil and community, for example), and the fundamental idea of a lifeworld (we, like they, exist within a thick weave of relations), we are able to project valid questions into the past, and bring refreshed insights forward into the present. At its best and most powerful, this process of interpretive "negotiation" puts our present conventions and understandings "at risk," by means of the challenging "otherness" of what is studied.

In light of phenomenology, the everyday life of the builders of the earthworks would likely not have had them standing apart over and above their own complex of social and environmental relations, over and above the flow of nature and the sacred and the social, and the practical forces of survival and so on, to "view" it. Nor would they have made or ever encountered circumscribed "objects" apart from this complex flow of multidimensional existence. Instead they "lived" their world, in all its interpenetrating, inexplicit complexity. If we can glimpse, however faintly, such a world, we improve our ability to understand them and their works as phenomena beyond a mere compiling of information about them.

Close as it may sound, this hermeneutic process touches a more fundamental ontological ground than a "contextualist" view like Ian Hodder's (1986: 150–151), however broadly or thickly described it might be. His short review of hermeneutics emphasizes the interactive-contextual process of uncovering meaning, as conveyed even from distant corners of the human world. Texts or evidence are not mainly seen as a physical system, or as subject to covering or predictive laws, but as processes of ongoing human thought, action, tradition, and understanding. Specific data and larger contexts, details and wholes, must be understood in a circular process of questioning in pursuit of the meaning of a situation, a meaning not limited to its actors' intentions because another circular process links them with their multiple contextual situations, and again with those of ourselves, the interpreters. Valuable as far as it goes, in advocating a more richly contextual view and explaining the expansive circularity of the process, Hodder's account stops short of the ultimate outcome of hermeneutic thought, its challenge to the present by bringing forward a powerful "communication" from past works. So how do we prepare ourselves for this radical encounter?

Insofar as we might situate the Hopewell's works as arising from within a lifeworld (our ontological insight about their "context"), we are obviously no longer dealing with "objects" being perceived by "subjects." Nor are we left with the false choice between "objective" or "subjective" methods—or their general caricatures as "true facts" versus "fuzzy concepts." Instead, any number of more encompassing clusters of interrelationships emerge that are capable of grasping, unifying, and structuring more of the world of human existence, purpose, activity, works, and meaning. For example, beyond both the "objectivist subsistence" and "ceremonial symbolism" theories that were posed for this conference, would stand the more encompassing idea of "human community." Both kinds of practices, that is, the toil of food production and shared meaningful ceremonies, are undertaken and subsumed within a form of community life. Built up of course in cyclical dialogue with confirmations from the data, such an interpretive idea gets us closer to the deep, ontological background, the mode of being of humans, where further connections or commonalities can be unfolded: The ceremonies are in part about subsistence activities such as planting or consecrating food and would necessarily evoke the rain and the soil and the times of the seasons, among many other things. Astronomy then, for example, is no longer seen as an abstract branch of physics in which the Hopewell had expertise but as a linking process between the heavens and the earth, food production and the seasons. Explored reflectively, this collection of intertwined themes is then capable of presenting us with new insights about our own human existence: the role of food in ritual, or how we are distanced from the weather, the earth, or seasonal markers, in our modern, technological world.

Aspects of life and existence intertwine, better approximating the unity that Indra Kagis-McEwen (1993: 17) has called "compact, mythical experience." In this way our encounter with these ideas and possibilities, and these places, moves beyond objective or subjective and becomes interpretive (hermeneutic) since an idea like "human community" calls up richer comparisons with ourselves, even reminding us that we (no matter how objectively we may deliberate over our field data) return home at night to the world in which the sun actually sets and we belong to real human communities ourselves. The Hopewell stand with us, as fellow humans, rather than merely with the "higher mammals." In Gadamer's terms, their horizon resembles ours, perhaps faintly at first but increasingly the more deeply we excavate the "ground" of human ontology or Being. Knowledge improves as we work in dialogue, with both our specific data and our broad human themes, toward a "fusion of horizons" (Gadamer 1994: 306–307). Our own ontological context poses questions and concepts that enable us to see more deeply into a human lifeworld that in turn illuminates and challenges our own existence and assumptions. We have ventured into the past not in order to merely "verify" something about them but to "learn" something from them as fellow humans.

How Works "Work" within a World and Horizons

So what is the impact of all of this ontological and interpretive theory? If the nature of human "Being" is to be "always already among" the largely inexplicit things, meanings, and relationships of the lifeworld, and if our way to knowledge is an "interpretation" of "the appearing of phenomena" within such a world and between our shared horizons, then what can we say about works of architecture, our principal aim? Evoking "theory" in its original, ancient, concrete sense, let us return to the works themselves. With help from their readings of continental philosophy, a number of recent architectural history and theory scholars have been exploring how works of architecture can be

Figure 9.2. The Great Circle at Newark, Ohio. Photo by author.

interpreted as arising from and revealing such a world (Perez-Gomez and Stephen Parcell 1994; Norberg-Schulz 1980a, 1980b; Mugerauer 1995).

Just as you are seeking in this symposium to dismantle worn-out divisions, distinctions, and definitions, we architectural historians are also rejecting methods from the hypertaxonomical nineteenth century, and the hypertech-nological early twentieth. Hermeneutic thought has begun to light a path be-yond earlier interpretive conventions that generally bracketed off works of architecture into various one-dimensional, circumscribed views, such as se-miotics, period styles, biography, typology, or formal aesthetics. Unlike works of painting or concert music, always predefined within a contemplative con-text, architecture needs to begin with the more fundamental question of how it emerges within our everyday unreflective existence. Whether it is by the conscious volition of its designers or otherwise, the means of this all-impor-tant "coming to presence" is missed entirely by merely undertaking an "aes-thetic" analysis or by assuming that "subjects" are contemplating "objects."

If the way we exist as humans is a "being-in-the-world," amid a largely unreflective set of everyday practices and traditions, then the nature and func-tioning of works created from within such a world must be seen anew. This is Heidegger's task in his essay "The Origin of the Work of Art" (1971: 15–87). He explains that the role of such works is to reveal, to make visible and explicit, the "world" in which the societies stand, to bring forth the "earth" to visibility, and to open up who and what a person is within that world, and upon that earth. All of this, without the "work," tends to concealment and inexhaustibility. In a famous passage he says, "The Greek Temple signifies nothing" (1971: 41). In other words, decoding some kind of correspondence symbolism will not be the path to understanding the work, or its world. He continues: "It is the temple-work that first fits together and at the same time gathers around itself the unity of those paths and relations in which birth and death, disaster and blessing, victory and disgrace, endurance and decline acquire the shape of destiny for human being. The all-governing expanse of this open relational context is the world of this historical people."

Soaked as we are in our conventions of circumscribed, quantitatively driven discourse, we moderns must be careful here. This is not merely some soft poetic reverie, but a precise and fundamental description of what "works" of architecture are "at work" doing, which is giving visibility and structure to the inexhaustibly complex network of things, meanings, and relationships, that constitute "being-in-the-world" for a particular society—bringing forward into explicitness those thick, invisible, traditional, habitual, intertwined patterns of everyday existence, toil, experience, community, and meaning.

In my years of teaching on classical temples, I have tried to unpack the significance of Heidegger's paragraph. But here we may take up another sort of temple, like the Woodhenge at Stubbs, or perhaps an earthwork, our name for it already evoking a construction "worked" intentionally by humans to some set of aims and already "working" toward us by projecting shared human volition, aspiration, meaning, knowledge, craft, social unity, and orders of various kinds. It arose from within a world—a full context of life and Being, where the sun and moon rose and set, where ritual practices were planned, enacted, and remembered, where community life was sustained, and conversations and arguments happened, where ancestors were remembered, and natural phenomena both felt and explained, and where the rain fell and the haze lifted. The work points to, mimics, frames, and foregrounds the surrounding landscape; it marks an act of clearing, and it both anticipates and remembers an act of gathering, two of the most primordial human gestures. It also reaches for eternity in its form and its material. It mediates the collective intentions of the community, telling them who they are within all stages of its construction and use.

As an intentional act, a spatial construct, and the scene of human community, the timberwork or earthwork brings the Hopewell "world" into explicit visibility, revealing it out of its concealing background of earth and forest, subsistence and everyday toil. This is the "work" of architecture, to create, through its massive embodiment of volition and order, form and focus, impact and detail, an attentiveness to the structures of meaning that operate in a given society and a constitution of the activities it was intended to contain. Heidegger suggests the Greek *aletheia*, or "unconcealment" (1971: 51), to evoke this process of "truthing" whereby a work of art or architecture sets forth a "world"— all those social relations and shared understandings, practices, meanings, and so on—and "earth," the primordial and impenetrable background upon and out of which human constructs are set up.

Hermeneutic phenomenology radically reconceives human existence, not as the projection of consciousness or cognition toward circumscribed objects, nor even toward a world, as implied in the unfortunate expression "world view," but as "being-always-already-within-a-world-of-relations." This moves us beyond the distinction between scientific and humanistic approaches, beyond the tension of objective and subjective, and potentially even beyond the tension of past and present insofar as we come to understand the interpretive power of Gadamer's "fusion of horizons" by which concepts, habits, and patterns in our own human existence can be thrown open to fresh critical reflection through their exposure to the "otherness" of the past (Hancock 1995).

My living room affords me an unobstructed view of the eastern horizon. Since learning the workings of the Newark Octagon, and its marking of the angles of the moonrise through an 18.6-year cycle, I have noticed details in the relations among the moon, the sun, the horizon (and points on it like water towers), the times of day and of the month, and the weather, that would never have come into focus without that ancient work having prompted them. The builders of Newark have shown me my "world and earth" in new ways. I have also taken new questions back to them, about how they did it, after confronting the obscurity and complexity of the lunar cycle, and sensing the immense difficulty of its direct observation. So besides Hively and Horn's measurement data showing that Newark was a lunar marker, other themes emerge that have influenced our treatments and our reconstructions: As artificial horizons, the earthworks would have required vast clearings; as sighting instruments, they required huge dimensions and almost certainly pole markers; and as records of a community's knowledge, they required many accumulated generations' shared observation, vision, and sense of purpose.

So works of ancient architecture are not merely symbols or signifiers, nor merely pragmatic or engineering constructs, nor merely evidence of the "world view" of some extinct culture. Notwithstanding the necessity to attend to these specific properties as part of our gathering of evidence about them, works of architecture "work" in the fullest sense by revealing a lifeworld of human community, and that community's being on the earth and under the

Figure 9.3. The Turner Earthworks, Hamilton County, Ohio. Reconstruction by CERHAS, University of Cincinnati.

sky, together in their purposes, memories, practices, and aspirations. This is the path to "understanding" the work, as distinct from what could be called "compiling information" about it. And this is the starting point for our identification with the work's makers as our fellow humans, through whom we can refract our own humanity and our own relations with such fundamental things as ritual, community, monument, world, and earth.

Visualizing Works and Worlds

By now I am sure it is clear that my vantage point here is not only as a theorist of architectural works but also as a producer of public education media. We seek to deliver to audiences broad thematic insights in the humanities, as well as the archaeological knowledge on which these insights so largely depend in the case of the Hopewell. We aim to instill a sense of human identification and an opportunity for our audiences to think in fresh ways about their own natural and cultural world, and the role of themselves (and of their own rituals and monuments) within it.

In the course of producing public education media on this topic, we have had to confront the problems of "visualizing" these works, and to some extent, this world. Since all distant cultures capture and hold their place in the public imagination primarily through memorable architectural images (think of the Egyptian pyramids, the Great Wall of China, or the French cathedrals, for example), vivid images of the sites became a necessity. But the earthworks' size and invisibility created extra challenges, and there was no imagery extant in any medium that provided memorable, mentally comprehensible images of these places, much less their "working" as architecture or their capacity to reveal a world. The excellent drawings of Squier and Davis (1848), and their many talented collaborators, cannot really suggest the grandeur, subtlety, and wonder that are essential to these places. Nor can visits to actual sites, since even after all the inevitable pointing, squinting, and gesturing, most visitors are unable to conjure up the overall imaginative idea or the spatial experience of what had been built there.

We addressed these challenges in the EarthWorks project by using digital media to create vivid representations of the earthworks, in which audiences could interactively explore multiple topics and stories about the sites, their builders, and their meanings for us today. Influenced by the hermeneutic conception of "being-in-the-world," we sought to immerse our audiences within a human experience of landscapes, laden with meaning. Our visual animations and interpretive treatments do three things.

First, they bring these architectural works forward in vivid, atmospheric settings that connect them to our own experiences of forested valleys, open clearings, and rivers that reflect a flash of sunlight. The hills, horizons, and tall, thick forests help anchor the otherwise incomprehensible scale. The rebuilt mounds and walls are shown as fresh dirt to give them maximum definition and clarity as marks of human order and imagination. Most of the animation cameras imitate bird flights, because the size and conceptual order of the works are beyond ordinary human perception. The goal in all this was to make these monuments work vividly in the modern mind and to suggest as high a respect for their beauty and precision as possible.

Second, our script treatments juxtapose various disciplines and cultural perspectives, suggesting the open-ended "capacity" of the works to evoke multiple meanings. Many topics open up at interactive choice points, presenting many voices and ideas. The moon, for example, appears at the Newark Octagon but then leads in several directions: Hively and Horn discuss how they discovered the Octagon's alignments, Linda Poolaw describes the Lenape story of female ancestors dancing around the full moon, a narrator explains the complex lunar cycles, and Anthony Aveni connects astronomical observations by ancient societies with everyday life needs like subsistence. A breadth of interpretive space is opened up, offering wider appreciation of the earthworks and the Hopewell, and also a deeper insight and questioning about ourselves.

Finally, the stories unfold layer by layer within a predominantly spatial environment, with enough sensual impact to suggest a human lifeworld experience. The medium's quasi-realism draws in viewers just enough that the stories about a world can take hold, yet at points of more distanced reflection, such as the choice screens, it is clearly a guided journey, an artificial construct. This captures the structure of interpretation itself in that the audience is both immersed and distanced, both in the past and in the present, both believing and questioning. Particularly in the many interview segments, we recognize that a filtering process is involved, as a variety of disciplinary and cultural perspectives pose open-ended insights and metaphors, from David Cave on "ritual excessiveness" to James Brown on the "order of the cosmos on earth" to architect William Taylor on the "uncanniness" of Newark and a stealth fighter, to Bradley Lepper suggesting Newark was a "giant ritual machine." Together they expand the capacity of these ancient works to reveal a world—the Hopewell world but, ultimately, also ours.

Phenomenological hermeneutics, though unfootnoted in our media exhibits, helped us by emphasizing that especially for ancient societies, the lifeworld is an experientially lived unity. The sky, the earth, the haze, the seasons, those reflections on the river, dwellings, forests, game animals, and the circle of the horizon, like the circles of the earthworks, are embedded in a meaningful whole, in which a community of people found themselves sharing in struggles, aspirations, interpretations, and meanings: life and death, "disaster and blessing." We conceived our on-screen imagery and multivoiced perspectives to evoke, as much as an artificial medium can, such an immersive, integrated, experiential world and the vivid power of human-made works to rise up out of such a world and bring it to consciousness. Among the many questions of representation and media deployment, we were in search of methods conducive to letting these ancient, alien places challenge and confront us—with new ways of seeing the landscape or the natural world and new questions or new insights about what it means to live and die as humans, in our communities, among our tasks and works, on the earth and under the sky.

10

The "Heartland" Woodland Settlement System

Cultural Traditions and Resolving Key Puzzles

A. Martin Byers

Recently, R. Berle Clay (2002: 165–166, 171–172, 176–179, 183–184) has high-lighted three central characteristics of the Woodland period of the Central Ohio Valley, a region he refers to as the "Heartland." These three are *cultural pluralism, monumental architecture* (as the context of "event-centered" ar-chaeology), and the particular nature of the *population dispersal*. In terms of cultural pluralism, he rejects the view that the Early and Middle Woodland periods of the Heartland can be usefully treated in the monolithic cultural-historical categories of Adena and Hopewell. For example, speaking in taxo-nomic terms, he has even more recently stated that there is no cultural entity termed Adena—and presumably he would apply the same claim to Hopewell (Clay 2004: 108). Instead there is a complex of autonomous cultural entities dispersed across the Central Ohio Valley so that this region manifests a com-plex patchwork of multiple cultural variants that were quite localized, while, in addition, being variably linked into the mortuary and earthwork-based com-plexes that have been termed Adena and Hopewell. The monumental earth-works, he claims, mediated fluid interaction among dispersed domestic-based kin groups that built and used them cooperatively as mortuary centers (Clay 1991: 32). These mortuary practices served an additional strategy, namely, to mediate intercommunity alliances by which the participants secured access to each others' territories to minimize the consequences of subsistence shortfalls as a result of the dispersed domestic-based populations (Clay 1992: 80; 1998: 14, 16). Hence he has both recognized and attempted to account for probably the most puzzling feature of the archaeological record of this region and time, the radical contrast between monumental earthworks and the dispersed and nearly archaeologically invisible domestic settlements of the population.

While I can certainly agree with his presentation of the puzzle, I believe that his interpretation is too closely wedded to some basic and, in my view, invalid assumptions that prevail in North American archaeology. He correctly recognizes that, either tacitly or explicitly, human populations always relate symbolically as well as materially to their environments. Indeed, he accounts for the great earthworks and their associated mortuary and ritual content by causally connecting them to ecological imperatives, namely, people having adequate access to subsistence resources in the pursuit of survival. His postulating the mortuary practices as the medium of achieving this pursuit implicates a symbolic constitution of intergroup relations since it is the symbolic nature of the mortuary practices by which groups ally to gain and concede access to resources in their mutually exclusive territories.

However, to recognize this symbolic role of mortuary practices is to recognize what is basically a particular type of land tenure. Tenure defines the rights and duties that parties have toward the land that they use. These are exercised when tenure holders exploit the resources so that, in an important sense, the regular practices of hunting, gathering, and even ongoing residing realize human-land relations that are simultaneously symbolic and material. The rights, duties, obligations, and ethical principles that underwrite and integrate a social system constitute what can be termed the "deontic sphere of culture." If ecological practices are the realization of ecological relations in and through behavior, then in these terms, such practices are simultaneously symbolic as well as material engagements that humans have with the environment.

Therefore, I think that Clay and I agree in these general terms; that is, humans constitute their tenure of the land by means of constituting symbolic-material relations and these relations are constructed on the basis of agreements, promises, alliances, and so on, and certainly, it is defensible to claim that mortuary practices can be recruited as a major symbolic medium by which such solemn agreements and commitments among groups are constituted. In this case, the logical relation between mortuary practices and alliances would be that the mortuary ritual would *presence*—rather than merely "refer to"—the ancestors as the authorities by which the alliances were both legitimized and regulated (see Carr 2005: 323–324 for a similar argument). Hence presupposed in his approach are several interconnected levels of cultural and social structures: the ecological, economic, sociokinship, political, and, of course, religious-cosmological.

All this is implicated in Clay's insightful analysis, and I fully agree with the need to take a multidimensional perspective. Where I disagree is with the widespread assumption among North American archaeologists that tenure is largely equivalent to exclusive territorialism. That is, the tenure holders, usually postulated to be a kinship-based corporate group, have exclusive control of lands occupied by, in this case, the kinship-based community. This clearly is

Clay's view since for him the point of the earthwork-centered mortuary events is to ensure that the loosely related groups are able to sustain mutual access to *one another's territories and these are mutually exclusive* (Clay 1992: 80; 1998: 14, 16). As noted above, Clay is certainly not alone in this regard. Exclusive kinship-based proprietorial corporate territorialism is pervasively articulated in the North American archaeological literature. Indeed, the seminal studies of the relation of mortuary practices and territorialism by Douglas Charles and Jane Buikstra (1983: 120–121; also see Buikstra and Charles 1999: 211–214, 222) were explicitly grounded on this premise and this was not put forward as an empirical proposition but as an axiomatic characterization of tenure arising from the natural tendency of humans to aggressively compete in conditions of rising resource scarcity.

In contrast, I will present an alternative theoretical premise on which to construct my critique of Clay's claims of the Heartland settlement patterns. I claim that prehistoric native North American tenurial systems were firmly grounded on inclusive tenure. Significant ethnographic validity to the proposition of inclusive tenure is easily noted by reviewing the human-land interactions among historically known native North American peoples. These immediately reveal the nonexclusive and nonproprietorial nature of their human-environment relations. For them the world was immanently sacred, and, of course, sharing was the central axiom. I have argued in detail (Byers 2004: chap. 6; 2006b: chap. 2) that the relation between immanent sacredness and resource/land sharing is not incidental but logically necessary and empirically grounded in the patterning of the Ohio Hopewell earthworks, in particular, the anomaly of what I have termed the Feature A/Observatory Mound complex of the Newark Circle-Octagon. In my view, according to the formal rules that determined what would count as a proper earthwork form, this complex should not exist. Its very existence implicates a change of plan that required leaving in place preexisting embankments. Such avoidance practices, I have argued, presuppose proscriptions against dismantling embankment earthworks, even when such dismantling would ensure proper symmetries of form, clearly a significant value in Ohio Hopewell monumentalism. From this I concluded that the earthwork was immanently sacred and it took on this property from the first step of construction. Since the source of this sacredness was the land itself, it follows that the world was immanently sacred. This "sacred earth principle," as I have termed it, prevented Ohio Hopewell from dismantling embankment earthworks—except, possibly in what they perceived to be dire circumstances (Byers 2004: 8–9, 96).

If this belief could ground a strong deontic proscription against dismantling the earthwork, it implicates the notion that all disturbing of the natural order was taken seriously since immanent in that order were the sacred powers that sustained it. Hence, the sacredness of the land and all of nature is immanent in the material world that humans occupy and constitutes the world as a living entity. As such it cannot be treated as divisible and allocatable among human groups. Ownership of land as Euro-Americans conceive it was inconceivable to the Middle Woodland groups. Rather, those groups habitually occupying a region would constitute themselves as *custodians*, and as such, they would care for the land. Therefore, the social core in a region that would ensure stability would be an alliance of groups devoted to being the care givers. This alliance would be responsible for the performance of ritual that renewed the land on behalf of everyone.

Elsewhere I have called this notion of sharing the land *custodial domain* and the groups that collectively take on this responsibility as custodial corporations (Byers 2004: 144–148). I propose it as an alternative way of looking at the very same archaeological settlement record of the Heartland that Clay has. I also accept Clay's three points outlined above, namely, cultural pluralism, monumental earthworks as the locales of significant mortuary-mediated events, and demographic dispersal. I also second the deontic implications that his outline of juxtapositioning these attributes entails, while respectfully disagreeing with his premise of exclusive tenure and its related notion of proprietorial domain. Instead, I will replace the latter with the inclusive tenure premise and its related notion of custodial domain.

Ecological Practices and Symbolic Pragmatics

Accepting that tenure is a culturally constructed (i.e., a constituted human-land relation) entails recognizing that ecological practices are performed according to both practical imperatives and deontic rules. Since they are performed in accordance with the accepted rules and protocols of the particular type of tenure that prevails in a community as well as in terms of practical needs of a people given the objective opportunities of the local environment, the regular ecological behaviors they carry out are constituted as social as well as material practices (Ingold 1987: 130–164). This means that the type of tenure that prevails in a community or a regional group of communities presupposes the fundamental framework of deontic principles that is at the core of those communities and, of course, this core of rights and duties is an essential part of the cultural tradition, the social system, and the technology of the region, thereby entailing that the settlement pattern of a region manifests a total way of life. Furthermore, since rules and standards can only exist as the contents of the collective understanding of a community and they can only be manifested through tangible behaviors, it follows that these behaviors are always symbolically mediated. Additionally, these behaviors would have been mediated by tangible conventional signs, so that even practical tasks have an irreducibly *expressive symbolic moment*.

I have argued elsewhere that in nonliterate communities the clearest mode of manifesting deontic rules in ecological practices would be in the stylistics of subsistence tools (Byers 1999; 2004: 64–67; 2006b: 38–39). That is, the style of the tools, for example, the spears used in hunting, would constitute the latter as both killing tools and as licences or warrants of the killing process itself. This is an important claim. I am saying that the user is seen and takes herself or himself unproblematically to be hunting rather than, for example, poaching. The difference between hunting and poaching as social activities, of course, is not in the objective transformations that these behaviors bring about since the latter are effectively identical. The difference is constituted by means of the symbolic moment since it is this moment by which the deontic dimension is manifested in the material behavioral intervention itself. By displaying the proper styles, the killing behavior is constituted *as* hunting rather than *as* poaching and the individual is thus constituted *as* a hunter rather than *as* a poacher. Hence, in counterfactual terms, without the use of the appropriate styles, predatory killing becomes poaching and the predator would be perceived as a poacher. Land use would also be governed by basic deontic principles and rules. Thus clearing the land for planting would never be a neutral, objective exercise but would always have a strong deontic symbolic component built into it making the clearing as much a ritual as a material practice. Again, this ritual would be mediated through the stylistics of the tools, and these would presuppose a division of labor that would constrain who could perform it. In other words, only those having specific social identity, for example, only males of a certain age category, might be able to do the clearing while only females of a certain age category might do the planting and harvesting. Built into the ecological practices would be an irreducible and complex rule-governed moment that constituted the action nature of the behavior. For the prehistoric Native Americans I have used the term "midwifery" ritual to refer to this moment on the grounds that typically the destructive nature of the material intervention is always taken to have also a reproductive nature (Byers 2004: 136–169; 2006b: 56–58). The term "midwifery ritual," therefore, claims that warranted killing always manifests a destructive as well as procreative/reproductive cycling of life and death.

Of course, if the community practices exclusive tenure, then, if this predatory behavior is done according to the rules of exclusive tenure, it is a form of hunting and not poaching since it counts as the exercising of proprietorial rights; in these circumstances, poaching is the ignoring of these rights. However, if the community practices inclusive tenure, then defining hunting and poaching must be done differently since inclusive tenure means that no one can deny another access to resources that they need. Rather, poaching becomes a form of inappropriate killing, and it is viewed as inappropriate often because of the assumption that the person is intending to hoard rather than share the animal kill. Inclusive domain is roughly equivalent to the notion of public domain in our own culture and in the latter case what defines appropriate behavior are rules that everyone "must" follow. Style becomes critical here in a way that is different from its importance in an exclusive regime. Whereas the latter marks the user as a proprietor, the former marks the user as a responsible agent who knows how to treat the resources and how to share them. This is well illustrated by Polly Wiessner's study of arrow styles among the San of Southwest Africa (1983: 269). She showed separate groups of adult male San—a group of !Kung, another of G/wi, and a third of !Xo—the standard range of arrows that each group used: "A discussion ensued from one small group [of !Kung San] about what they would do if they found a dead animal with such an arrow [G/wi or !Xo styled] embedded in it in their own area, saying that they would be worried about the possibility that a stranger was nearby about which they knew nothing at all." What is particularly revealing is that it was the possible *social conduct* of the person responsible for an arrow bearing unrecognized *style* that concerned them most. This person was assumed not to have the know-how to conduct himself properly. The onus to prove otherwise was carried by that person: "Although afraid of !Kung strangers as well, they said that if a man makes arrows in the same way, *one could be fairly sure that he shares similar values around hunting, landrights, and general conduct*" (Wiessner 1983: 269, emphasis added). In the concern expressed, there is no hint of a concern that the strangers might be poachers acting in ways consistent with proprietorship; to them poachers were those who did not know proper sharing etiquette.

Treating stylistics as an expressive symbolic medium is based on the view I term "symbolic pragmatics." This claims that even the most instrumental-type activity, such as the basic forms of ecological practices, is symbolically constituted, and the above discussion of hunting, poaching, garden clearing, and midwifery ritual illustrates this very well. It also illustrates that "what" will count as poaching or hunting will be determined by the deontic sphere or rights and duties, standards and principles, and that these are an essential part of the cultural traditions of a people. In these terms, it follows that material culture is simultaneously an instrumental and a symbolic medium and the symbolic moment is mediated by the conventional moment of material culture, what is often called the style. Treated in deontic, constitutive terms, styles can become a primary entry into the cultural traditions of a people via the symbolic pragmatic route.

An analogy is useful at this point in order to clarify precisely how symbolic pragmatics works. I have argued that in a literate society licences and warrants are symbolic pragmatic devices by which the legitimate bearers transform their behavioral interventions into the type of social activity they intended (Byers 1999; 2004: 68–70; 2006b: 38–39, 46). This "warranting mode" is the symbolic moment mediated by warrants and licences. I believe that warranting is universal among physiologically modern human populations. Therefore, in my view, just as we can apply such notions as licencing and warranting to our own behavioral engagements with our own social *and* natural worlds, thereby constituting these engagements as the types of social activities we intend, as archaeologists we should assume that prehistoric societies are no different in this regard. Of course, in a literal sense, a warrant is a written document and therefore we must speak analogically when applying the same notion to the stylistics of preliterate societies. Hence, if styles are treated as the symbolic media of warranting ecological practices, then the latter also entail relevant notions of tenure and this means that subsistence and settlement practices and the archaeological patterning that they generate make it impossible to deny the deontic aspect of ecological practices. That is, deontics, in the sense of rights and duties, anchored on collective notions of the world (cosmology) and the moral, ethical, and juridical principles of a people (ethos), are always manifest in the ecological strategies of a people and the latter underwrite the settlement patterning.

The Dual Clan-Cult Sodality View

Below, I characterize the earthwork-habitation relation in terms that are quite different from Clay's. Nevertheless, I fully agree with his cultural pluralism claim. In this regard, he is arguing that despite the widespread distribution of the stylistics of the material records that we have classed as Adena and Hopewell, the cultures of the populations responsible for it were highly variable, as manifested in what he claims to be locally distinctive forms of ceramics, as well as the great variation within that aspect of the archaeological record specifically identified as diagnostic of Adena and Hopewell. How can this be? The answer that I propose is that we are not dealing with unitary kinship-based communities dispersed across the landscape but with dualistic kinship- and companionship-based communities. I propose that the kinship component of each community is anchored in the domestic habitation settlement pattern and the companionship component of each community is distributed differentially across the multiple earthwork-mortuary locales. That is, the domestic habitation sphere, on the one hand, and the Hopewell and Adena earthwork spheres, on the other, are not complementary "everyday" and "high cultural" expressions of a set of unitary mutually exclusive but "loosely" dispersed communities. Instead, they are the simultaneous manifestation of a dual, open-networked system of two relatively autonomous groupings based on complementary principles of kinship and companionship, what I have referred to generically as clans and cult sodalities—termed the "Dual Clan-Cult Sodality model" of the Central Ohio Valley Woodland (Byers 2004: 223–237). Hence, the dispersed and almost archaeologically invisible domestic habitations are structured by kinship and the equally dispersed but archaeologically very visible earthwork locales are structured by companionship based on the principle of same age/same gender. For the prehistoric dual clan-cult sodality communities of the Heartland, therefore, those who participated in the cult sodalities did so as companions making up age sets, not as groups of kin belonging to specific clans or extended (or nuclear) families. Hence, the majority of the male (and possibly female) adult population of each community had a dual social life based on responsibilities in both the domestic kinship sphere and the ceremonial cult sphere.

The age sets of companions would constitute a local autonomous cult sodality based on an enabling hierarchy structured by seniority. These autonomous sodalities were allied with similar cult sodalities to constitute a regional alliance having custodial responsibilities of caring for the land in its region. Ritual would necessarily become highly similar, while also, of course, having its regional variation since each cult sodality alliance was autonomous. These same cult sodality members, of course, also belonged to their own clans and these were responsible for their own domestic arrangements. Hence, the material goods used in the latter sphere, serving domestic needs, including domestic-based or kinship-based ritual needs, would be consistently different from the range of goods used in the cult sodality sphere. Indeed, I have argued elsewhere that, as symbolic pragmatic devices, the artifacts of the cult sodalities and those of the domestic spheres might have to be systematically isolated from each other to avoid sacred pollution, thus grounding the clear archaeological boundary that is generally recognized in the literature, namely, that the elaborate Adena and Hopewellian material cultures are essentially exclusive to the earthwork locales themselves, very little being found in the domestic habitation sites. In these terms, I have argued that the well-known distribution of the Middle Woodland Hopewell bladelet, found in both zones, is the outcome and expression of this separation. Since individuals belonged to both cult sodalities and clans and were required to attend to ritual in both organizational spheres, the development of the bladelet as an easily made, distinctive, and disposable symbolic pragmatic device constituting slicing and scraping behaviors as ritual served to ensure that individuals performing such ritual in the cult sodality sphere would not carry back these used tools to the clan sphere to use unwittingly in clan ritual, or vice versa, thereby polluting one or the other context (Byers 2004: 227–239).

Thus what I call the Dual Clan-Cult Sodality structure immediately resolves two of the central puzzles that Clay has targeted above, namely, the simultaneous existence of monumental earthworks and dispersed populations. However, this leaves a major question unanswered. How can material cultural variation occur in the same region that is marked by material invariance? How can the same people maintain and realize in practice two different forms of cultural expression, one that displays intraregional variability, the domestic sphere, and one that displays much less variability, the cult sodality sphere? In short, how can Clay's cultural pluralism be explained in the context of monumental earthworks; and even more pressing, how can the continuity of this settlement bifurcation be explained, an attribute that, if we accept Clay's claims, characterized the Woodland period of the Heartland for almost two millennia, approximately 1000 B.C. to A.D. 900? The answer to this question requires characterizing cultural traditions in a manner that would allow us to understand how cultural continuity and cultural change can occur simultaneously and over the *longue durée*.

Cultural Traditions, Intentionality, and Prehistoric Archaeology

When prehistoric archaeology moves away from the behavioral moment or aspect of culture to the cognitive-normative aspect, culture is usually spoken of as the set of beliefs, values, and attitudes shared by a people and constituting their cultural traditions. When giving a religious reading, terms such as "cosmology" and "ideology" or "ethos" and "world view" are often used. Typically, an archaeologist will favor the use of one or two of these terms over the others to speak generally about the cultural cognitive-normative aspect, without clarifying why the one or two used are favored over the others. Indeed, if practice is a guide, it almost seems that we might have a superfluity of terms for the concept(s) being expressed and that one or two could be usefully dropped. In fact, I consider this terminological ambivalence as revealing an absence of any adequate theoretical grappling with what these terms are being used to articulate and how these cultural phenomena might be related. The purpose of this section is to directly address the nature of cultural traditions since it is by understanding cultural traditions more realistically that I can return to the problem of material cultural plurality and continuity as outlined above and easily resolve it.

Intention and Intentionality

Before delving into cultural traditions, it is helpful to briefly look at what is probably one of the most undertheorized concepts used in archaeology, *intention*, followed closely by *intentionality*. These concepts' undertheorization is most clearly demonstrated by the terms often being used synonymously, with the latter simply being used to refer to an aggregation of intentions. I want to briefly touch on these two concepts because I consider cultural traditions to be emergent forms of collective intentionality, and to understand how I am treating cultural traditions, it is helpful to understand how I treat intentionality.

The term "intentionality" is used by most philosophers to refer to "that property of many mental states and events by which they are directed at or about or of objects and states of affairs of the world" (Searle 1983: 1). Seen in this sense, an intention is only one form of intentional state. In fact, Searle argues that we have four major basic forms of intentional states, that is, mental states that are characterized by being directed to objects, actions, processes, and states of affairs in the world. These are beliefs, desires, perceptions, and intentions. He argues that each type can logically be structured into a psychological attitude and a representational content of the attitude. He represents this structuring as Bel(r), Des(r), Per(r), and Int(r), respectively. The representational content "r" specifies what the intentional state is about. The psychological attitudes are characterized by "direction of fit." Since an intentional state is directed at the world, then its direction of fit is going to either "fit" the mind-to-world (M-W) or "fit" the world-to-mind (W-M). Each form has its specific "direction of fit," and this simply specifies how an intentional state achieves "fitness" or, as Searle refers to it, its "satisfaction."

For example, my belief Bel(r), which I express by saying, "I believe that Caesar's army crossed the small Italian river called the Rubicon," has M-W direction of fit, and its representational content (r), "Caesar's army crossed the small Italian river called the Rubicon," simply specifies what the belief is about. If my belief "fits" or "corresponds" to the way the world was, in other words, if there really was a person who was named Caesar and who crossed this small Italian river, the Rubicon, then I can say that my belief is true, that is, a belief that "fits" the world is what we term true. If this event did not occur, then the belief is false. For example, if instead of my belief specifying "the small Italian river" and specified "a small river in Greece," it would not achieve "fit" and would be false. But by modifying it to "fit" or "correspond" to the world, I can easily correct this. For the belief to be true, it is the "responsibility" of the belief holder to fit the idea to the world, thus, M-W direction of fit.

Now let us say that while Caesar may have initially equivocated, he nevertheless did desire/want/need to cross the Rubicon in order to achieve his political goals. He may have expressed his desire, Des(r), to his men by saying, "I want the army to cross the Rubicon." Although expressed in different words (not to mention a different language), this utterance by Caesar had the same representational content (r) as my above belief about what Caesar did. Therefore, the question is, what makes Caesar's utterance of his desire, Des(r), different from an utterance of the belief? That is, could it not be said that the want/desire is simply a certain type of belief? According to Searle, the answer is no. The difference is in direction of fit. Beliefs have M-W direction of fit and desires/wants/needs have W-M direction of fit. We say that the belief is true (i.e., satisfied) if the Caesarian event occurred, but we do not say that the desire/want/need was true (it may have been real, but that is a different matter.). Rather, we say that Caesar's desire was fulfilled, carried out, and so on; in short, it was satisfied when his army crossed the Rubicon. Caesar's world came to fit the content of his desire/want/need. By the way, according to historical narratives, Caesar would have had to express his desire to his men in order to get them to cross the Rubicon. He necessarily had to perform a directive speech act, an order to his army. Directives, such as orders and commands, are "raw" social power manifested and exercised through the medium of symbols. That is, symbolically mediated acts are real because they make a real difference in the social world. If Caesar failed to order his army to "cross the Rubicon," then his career trajectory and Western history would have been different! In any case, notice that while both the representational contents (r) of the above expressed belief and expressed desire are the same, they critically differ in terms of psychological attitude because they have opposite and complementary directions of fit: M-W and W-M, respectively. Expressing the (r) of a belief in words constitutes an assertive speech act, "I believe that X"; expressing a desire with the same (r) constitutes a directive speech act, "I order you to do X." Hence, as intentional states, beliefs and wants differ in terms of direction of fit and expressing them in speech constitutes different speech acts: assertives and directives, respectively.

Perceptions and intentions are equivalently complementary to each other. "I see X" means that the representational content of my visual experience "fits" the world, that is, M-W direction of fit; and to say, "I intend to do X" or "I promise to do X" means that I must behave in a specified manner, that is, do X, in order to fulfill my intention, that is, W-M direction of fit. Again, notice that the expression through the use of word symbols of promises, agreements, alliances, and the like, are real social acts. Searle classes these as "commissive speech acts." They bind parties together in deontically entrenched relations and are constituted by "mere" symbols. Promises make real differences in the social world. But this raises a problem. If both a belief and a perception can have the same content and the same M-W direction of fit, for example, "I believe that X exists" and "I see an X," and if a desire and an intention can also have the same content and the same W-M direction of fit, for example, "I want my army to cross the Rubicon" and "I intend to have my army cross the Rubicon," then it would seem that there are really only two basic forms of intentionality, beliefs and desires, and that these differ only in direction of fit.

Searle, however, argues that this is not the case. While beliefs/perceptions and desires/intentions form a complementary parallel pair of intentional states, perceptions and intentions also have intentional causality while beliefs and desires do not. "I want" only becomes "I intend" when I add the intentional causal factor. I can want or need many things and never *intend* to act so as to achieve them. But to say, "I intend to do X" or "I promise to do X," Int(x), and actually *mean it*, I have to formulate an intention "to do X." The Int(x), here, has causal force, and in this case the causality has M-W direction of fit. That is, for my Int(x) to be satisfied, fulfilled, I must materially behave so as to change or "fit" the world in conformity with the representational content of my intention. When I do this, I can say that I have performed a particular action. The same is the case for perceiving, except the direction of causality is the opposite, W-M. That is, the world physically causes my visual experience. Hence, intentions and perceptions are similar in that they entail causality but this causality has complementary directionality. I will satisfy my intention when I see my behavior X as changing the world as I intended, and I will have a "true" visual experience when I see the object that causes it as an X that conforms to my knowledge of the world.

To review: Beliefs and perceptions share the same intentional property of M-W direction of fit, and desires and intentions share the same intentional property of W-M direction of fit. However, these two pairs cannot be collapsed into simply beliefs and desires because the beliefs and desires have no property of intentional causality while perceptions and intentions do; and the direction of causality of perceptions and intentions are complementary opposites: Perceptions have W-M direction of causality and intentions having M-W direction of causality. The objects of the world are the material cause of my perceptions of them; and exercising my intentions in behaving causes my behaviors to change the world in ways specified by the contents of my inten-

Table 10.1. Schematic order of logical structure of four basic intentional forms

Intentional state	Direction of fit	Direction of causality
Beliefs	M to W	None
Desires	W to M	None
Perceptions	M to W	W to M
Intentions	W to M	M to W

Source: Derived from Searle 1983: 91, 97, and passim.

tions, if these behaviors are successful; and when these are properly mediated with warrants according to the rule and protocol contents of my intentions, they constitute my behaviors as the actions I intended. Table 10. 1 might be helpful.

Cultural Traditions

I use the term "cultural tradition" to speak about the cognitive-normative sphere of a cultural community, and I treat this as a collective form of intentionality. Just as Searle structures individual agent's intentionality into four basic states as collective forms of intentionality, I also characterize cultural traditions into four basic states. For this reason, I consider all four terms—cosmology, ethos, world view, and ideology—necessary to adequately characterize this collective cognitive-normative sphere. Hence, Table 10.1, laying out the structure of beliefs, desires, perceptions, and intentions, also articulates the structural nature of the cultural traditions of a community, that is, its cosmology, ethos, world view, and ideology. The primary difference, however, is that these cultural traditions are based on human reflexivity and therefore incorporate the awareness that "everyone"—at least all "normal" persons—shares the same beliefs, values, perceptual experiences, and (action) intentions. This is what makes them collective forms of intentionality.

Cosmology is one aspect of a cultural tradition, and it can be understood as the total set of world beliefs that characterize a given tradition. Since a people relate to two worlds simultaneously, the natural and the social, cosmology can be further structured as having two related collective belief sets, one characterizing the natural world and one characterizing the social world. I will use the term "cosmology" to refer to both sets of beliefs and the term "sociality" when referring to only the beliefs that constitute the social world of the people. I have already alluded to the notion of ethos, this being the deontic sphere of ethical and moral standards, values, and attitudes in relation to the social and natural worlds. "World view" refers to ongoing perceptual experiencing of the world that a people have in virtue of their cosmology and ethos. By this I mean something more than a generalized "viewing" or situating of a people in their cosmos. The latter is important but it is part of the cosmology, expressed as beliefs about the relation that humans have with the world around them. By the notion of world view, I intend to speak of the character of the ongoing flow of collective perceptual experiencing of the natural and social world that a people have in virtue of their cosmology and ethos. For example, a local mountain may be characterized as sacred in the local cosmology and, therefore, the way the people visually experience this mountain will be different from their visually experiencing neighboring mountains that, in all objective aspects, seem pretty well the same in appearance. However, the former may be assiduously avoided except on certain crucial ritual days, while the others may be regularly visited for exploitative purposes. I am suggesting that the character of the perceptual experiencing of the mountains and, therefore, of they way they are materially related to, will vary in virtue of the special place that the "sacred mountain" plays in the cosmology. World view, therefore, refers to the character of the ongoing perceptual engagements that a people have with the natural and social worlds in virtue of their cosmology, sociality, and ethos.

Ideology, as I use this term, has a similar immediacy in the experience of the people. While world view refers to the ongoing perceptual experiencing a people have of their environment, both natural and social, ideology is tightly tied into the ongoing practices by which a people engage physically with their world. All practices, as I define them, are intentional behaviors. However, to be a practice—an institutionalized social action—it must conform to the specifications as stipulated by the rules and protocols that make up the content of the collective (i.e., publicly recognized) intentions with which it is performed. The shared rules and protocols constitute the content of their ideological postures. As I argued above, hunting is distinct from poaching in terms of its deontics and these are manifested in material symbols, namely, the stylistics of the material cultural hunting gear. The stylistics are the manifestation of these rules. Hence ideologies as collective intentions are not simply prescriptions and proscriptions that have some abstract, transcendent existence; these rules and protocols are the contents of the collective intentions that specify how behaviors are to be performed so as to be the social practices they are intended to be, both by the agents responsible and by the relevant others constituting the agent's social context. Presupposing any ideology, of course, are the cosmology and related ethos that are the source of the world knowledge and deontic principles that make the rules and protocols intelligible and possible. Seen in these terms, it becomes clear that all our active and perceptual and behavioral engaging (world view and ideology) with the world is informed by cosmology and ethos.

As I treat it, therefore, a cultural tradition is constituted and structured into these four basic states and these are mutually and relatively autonomous in the sense outlined above for the four basic states of intentionality, that is, none is reducible or collapsible into the other. Hence they are autonomous, and yet an ethos can only exist in relation to a cosmology, and an ideology always presupposes and can only exist in relation to a cosmology, and so on. In short, these states are not absolutely but only relatively autonomous; however, they are integrated into a structured whole—the integrated view of cultural tradition. As I noted above, however, many archaeologists tend to use only one or two of the above terms to cover what I have treated as four relatively autonomous collective cognitive-normative states making up a cultural tradition, favoring, for example, world view or ideology (Byers 2006: 76-80). This effectively treats a cultural tradition as a largely unstructured, amorphous cognitive-normative sphere treated as an inextricably "blended" set of beliefs, attitudes, and values (or what could be termed the "fused view" of cultural traditions). This fused or "blended" view leads to speaking of a cultural tradition as an amorphous "package" of "ideas" as if for a community to have a particular set of ideas, for example, world beliefs (cosmology) it must also have all the particular collective values and attitudes (ethos), collective perceptions (world view), and collective intentions (ideology) that "go along" with that particular set of ideas.

This fused view has important implications in understanding the problem of cultural pluralism in the "Heartland" that Clay outlined since it would suggest that any modifying of the ideological rules entails modifying the whole "package" of values and beliefs also. In effect, if cultural traditions are treated as "fused" packages, the only way a people can change their cultural tradition is to replace the old with a new tradition. Therefore, assessing the significance of variation in the archaeological record becomes highly problematic. In particular, it makes cultural pluralism of the sort Clay has noted for the Early and Middle Woodland periods of the Central Ohio Valley difficult to comprehend. Precisely what does the simultaneous existence of Hopewellian and Adenan earthworks in the same region and in overlapping time mean? Does this count as two different cultural traditions or variations on the same basic cultural tradition? If the fused view is accepted, then it must be the former since in terms of the fused cultural tradition view differences in material expression entail differences in cultural traditions.

In contrast, by treating a cultural tradition in terms of the integrated view outlined above, we can account for the Adena and Hopewell patternings as being simply surface structural variants, that is, alternative but equivalent ideological expressions of the same cultural tradition and, therefore, basically they differ *only at the ideological level*. In other words, despite their ideological differences, they probably share the same cosmology and ethos and, for the most part, have the same world view. Of course, in terms of the participants in the two earthwork systems, each likely perceived the earthworks of the others as probably inadequate media of ritual practices and this, of course, means that by faulting each other for their formally different and, therefore, mutually "inadequate" earthworks, they necessarily understand each other.

The integrated view illuminates a very important characterization of a cultural tradition. A collective intentionality implicates a dual and emergent structuring of these four collective cognitive-normative states into deep and surface structural forms. In these terms, in general, cosmology and ethos are deep structures of a cultural tradition, and these states would tend to be its *most stable* spatio-temporal components; while ideology and world view are surface structures of the same tradition and would tend to be its *least stable* spatio-temporal components. This is because, as noted above, any modification of an ideology presupposes a stable cosmology or a cosmology that, while also possibly being modified, retains much of its essential content. Also, since an ideology is realized in actions and their outcomes, recognizing the action nature (or pragmatic nature) of the behaviors is an interpretive exercise that either reproduces or transforms the ideological rules of the parties involved and for this interpretation to be possible, the beliefs and values have to be relatively stable. The ideology can change but this tends to reproduce rather than transform the cosmology/sociality and ethos that made the ideology and its changes possible. Hence, it is likely that cosmology and ethos will remain largely constant within a region and from generation to generation while the world view and ideology will largely co-vary.

Because ideology as collective intentions is realized in concrete action and its material media, ideological stances are always collective strategies of real groups. These groups prefer performing actions as specified by their ideological stances since these constitute for them the most authentic conditions of satisfaction of these stances and, therefore, count in their view as the most felicitous material mode of discharging their sacred duties. Since a community can have a range of ideological stances while sharing the same cosmology and ethos, it is very useful to call the different parties that bear and promote them "ideological factions." The ideological position of a community or group is manifested in the symbolic pragmatic component of its material culture and the overall patterning and its variation in time/space maps the shifts in the community's ideological position as the preferences of one faction gain greater expression than those of competing factions. Hence, changes in ideological forms can be used by the archaeologist to assess the shifting balancing of power among ideological factions. For example, I have argued that during its history of development the Hopewell site on the North Fork of the Paint Creek started as a major C-form embankment and that later in its history, geometrical forms were added to the older embankment form (Byers 2004: pt. 4). I have suggested that this maps a shift in factional dominance in time with the earlier times being dominated by radical factions that promoted large scale construction projects by which world renewal ritual would be enhanced while the later times were dominated by more conservative factions that believed "small" is good or "smaller" is better.

It is important to note that since social positions and the relations they constitute are an intrinsic constituent component of social actions, a parallel deep and surface structuring can be applied to the social system. Social structures, such as kinship, class, and ethnicity, can remain stable—like cosmology and ethos—reproducing rather than transforming over time. In contrast, as the social postures of the more stable organizations, social factions are ephemeral social phenomena and they will largely vary as part of the ideological variation. In this sense, therefore, social systems are also organized in terms of deep and surface structures. Thus this surface/deep structuring of social systems and their associated cultural traditions resolves the cultural plurality question that Clay raises. Only if a fused perspective is taken does the variation that Clay notes, both in terms of domestic and nondomestic ceramics and in terms of earthworks and mortuary variation, mark fundamental cultural and social differences. Seen in terms of the integrated view of cultural traditions and social structures, these variations are surface structural differences and presuppose a fundamental continuity and sharing across the region and through time of the basic deep cultural and social structures. In the former case, these would be cosmology and ethos; in the latter case, they would be the fundamental social structural axes of clan and cult sodalities.

The Woodland Heartland Patterns (Re)Interpreted

I can now reinterpret the archaeological record of the Woodland Heartland in terms that modify but also reinforce the insights that Clay has made. In deontic ecological terms, I would postulate that the three characteristics of the archaeological record of Early, Middle, and Late Woodland periods in the Heartland as sketched out by Clay, namely, cultural pluralism, monumental earthworks, and dispersed populations, are the marks of a social system manifesting a cultural tradition characterized by an immanentist cosmology and ethos and realized in a regional social system based on two fundamental or deep social structural axes, those of kinship and companionship. Now this does not mean that such a regional social system necessarily must generate a settlement pattern of the Ohio Hopewell type. What it does mean is that if such a settlement pattern is generated, it could only be the outcome of a social system that was grounded on an immanentist cosmology and ethos and mutually autonomous kinship and companionship structures.

What is shared by Hopewell and Adena is the same type of settlement articulation modal posture, what I have termed the "bifurcated posture." This is manifested as the monumental ceremonial locale/dispersed hamlet settlement pattern. This is a surface social structural expression in which the relatively autonomous deep structural components of communities—clan (kinship) and cult sodality (companionship)—sustain spatial arm's-length separation, thereby generating dispersed kinship-based domestic hamlets and major monumental companionship-based ceremonial locales, respectively. Clay's recognition of the continuity across the region and through almost 2,000 years of dispersed domestic populations committed to a mixed foraging/cultivation regime is fully consistent with the ethos associated with an immanentist cosmology. As argued earlier, the core ecological value of such an ethos would be to pursue survival by minimizing the degree of material intervention, that is, "living lightly on the land" would be a strong deontic proscriptive or avoidance principle. Of course, this proscription must always be exercised in practical contexts. Thus gardening must be carried out in order to sustain the material needs of the population, but the proscription promotes a minimalist stance. It also promotes an obligation to rectify the pollution caused by the unavoidable disorder that this settlement process generated. Therefore, as the level of environmental intervention increases, the need to escalate world renewal ritual also increases.

Paralleling the archaeologically demonstrated intensification of gardening through the Early and Middle Woodland periods is the continuity and escalation of earthwork ceremonial locales and their associated mortuary-mediated ritual. Thus the expansion of earthworks and mortuary practices from Early Woodland Adena into the Middle Woodland Late Adena and Ohio Hopewell is fully consistent with an immanentist cosmology and ethos. While everyday ecological settlement and subsistence practices can systematically pollute the world, thereby also promoting a dispersed settlement pattern as a minimalist strategy, world renewal ritual performed in the context of monumental icons that presence the sacred powers of the cosmos can rectify or reverse this polluting and thereby resanctify the cosmos. Hence a complementary kinship-companionship relation of domestic-based clans and earthwork-based world renewal cult sodalities, respectively, can be understood as the working out of a settlement and subsistence strategy (surface structure) having a strong component of prescriptions and proscriptions by which occupying populations sustained their pursuit of survival while simultaneously resanctifying the land they occupied. I have argued elsewhere (Byers 2004: 139–140, 177–184; 2006b: 107–120) that central to this ecological strategy of world renewal would be the practice of using the remains of the dead as sacrificial media by which to return the spiritual power they embody in their flesh and bones to reenliven the cosmos. In these terms, the earthworks constituted the mortuary-mediated behaviors as a range of world renewal postmortem sacrificial offering rituals to the multiple sacred aspects and components of the cosmos.

Conclusion

What is presupposed by the work of the contributors of this volume is the Intelligibility Factor of the Hopewell assemblage, in particular, of the embankment and mound earthworks. By this I refer to the basic reasons, motives, and social structures that informed and enabled the great Ohio Hopewell earthworks of the Middle Woodland period to be built. I believe that the nature and content of this intelligibility should be made explicit, and this is what I have attempted to do in this chapter by arguing that the earthworks served as critically important symbolic pragmatic devices by which world renewal ritual was constituted, as described above. Laying out the cultural and social structures underwriting the intelligibility factor, the factor that made their existence possible, has required using a very broad brush. I have had to deal with a range of topics here in a somewhat superficial manner, although I have addressed all of them elsewhere in considerable detail and I intend to further the process in coming publications (Byers 1999, 2004, 2006b). I have advanced the symbolic pragmatic view and linked this to my notion of integrated cultural traditions, showing how ideological change governing construction practices can modify and vary across space and time while the cosmology and ethos that made these practices possible can remain rather stable. This directly relates to the three aspects of the Heartland Woodland period archaeological record that Clay outlined (2002: 165–166, 171–172, 176–179, 183–184) and, therefore, it seems appropriate to close by commenting on his own conclusions.

Clay notes that we should not confuse the complexity of the Hopewell earthworks with a complexity of social structure and, instead, we should think of the Middle Woodland, and by extension the total historically reproduced Heartland social system of the Woodland period, as based on simple social structures integrated in complex relations: "However complex, the earthwork/ mound complexes of Hopewell grew out of a series of event-like 'happenings.' I visualize these . . . as products of somewhat fluid ceremonial groups that came together for a variety of activities including, importantly, mortuary ritual. . . . Confounding earlier interpretations of Hopewell, complexity in *social structure* of Heartland social groups should perhaps be replaced by complexity in the *social relations* between relatively simply structured social groups" (2002: 183).

This is an insightful comment, and it directly links my view to the central problematic that he himself raises, this being the radical contrast between the physical complexity and monumentalism of what he refers to as corporate/ceremonialism and the near invisibility of the dispersed habitation system. While I fully agree with his highlighting this dichotomy, the key difficulty I have with his resolution of it is that it hinges on an inadequate characterization of both the Adena and Hopewell of the Heartland region. In effect, he is claiming that these monumental constructions were primarily the outcome of largely ad hoc or effectively contingent events performed by fluidly organized ritual groups, the type that might occur when widely dispersed and rather small domestic populations largely incidentally aggregate. I am thoroughly unconvinced that these monuments were under the custodianship of "fluid" ceremonial groups. As I noted above and as I have fully argued elsewhere, the earthworks were the custodial responsibility of companionship-based sodalities constituted as world renewal cults that had considerable organizational continuity in that they extended beyond the lives of their individual members. These collectives perceived themselves as having sacred duties of world renewal to perform. In parallel with these central purposes would be the complementary purpose of the domestic sphere, the main source of sacred pollution arising out of the pursuit of organic survival, to sustain what I have termed a "proscriptive settlement and subsistence strategy," one that ensured their "living lightly on the land," and this principle was lived through the medium of dispersed settlement and the optimization of mobility/sedentism. Thus domestic clan-based dispersed habitation units and ceremonial companionship-based cult sodalities were mutually dependent and relatively autonomous with respect to each other. The cult sodalities, through their pursuit of mortuary mediated world renewal postmortem human sacrificial ritual, acted to ensure the continuity of the sacred powers of the cosmos through their ongoing ritual sanctifying and resanctifying of the cosmos, the primary condition that made everyday survival possible.

Hence, rather than the "corporate/ceremonial" earthworks being the context and medium of "fluid ceremonial groups," they were the sacred locales of custodial groups having a rather well-defined system of ritual practices, scheduling, promotion, and so on. Rather than being social groups that were "simply structured," it is more likely that, at least for the Middle Woodland period Ohio Hopewell, they were internally complex organizations with permanent congregations, what I have referred to as ecclesiastic-communal cult sodalities, having both senior and junior age grades cross-cut by the laity/clergy structure. Nor does this mean that the parallel system of clans on which the domestic habitation sites were grounded was itself any less complex. Instead, this system likely was also relatively complex internally. Why it manifested such an ephemeral archaeological signature arises not from its being "simply structured" but from the proscriptive deontic ecological strategy that promoted "living lightly on the land," thereby generating a mixed subsistence and dispersed settlement process that, if Clay is correct, was sustained for 2,000 years, if not longer. Hence, while Clay suggests that our view of the "complexity in *social structure* of Heartland social groups should perhaps be replaced by complexity in the *social relations* between relatively simply structured social groups," I would reconstrue this by claiming that the Heartland social system was complex in *social structure* as two formally different types of networks consisting of relatively autonomous social groups—clans and cult sodalities.

COMMENTARY

Commentary on John E. Hancock's "The Earthworks
Hermeneutically Considered"

Commentary by A. Martin Byers

There are many points that Hancock raises which I endorse, the central one
being that Enlightenment-inspired science has promoted the subject-object
dualism. This has in turn promoted the view of the isolated scientist, the
observer, assessing the world of objects independently of preexisting understandings or, as Hancock puts it, of a preexisting lifeworld. Hence, observation
of the objective world is an unmediated or direct mode of gaining understanding. The point of this empirical science was to establish the causal laws that
governed the objective world. Paralleling and motivating this development
was the Enlightenment value of establishing the truth of the lawlike claims
and that this could be done only if there were no "prejudgements" coming
between the observer and that which she or he observed. Therefore, Enlightenment objectivity had two aspects: an ontological, this being the commitment to the view that the object world existed independently of the observer,
and an epistemological, this being the commitment to the notion that only
direct or unmediated observation would establish the truth status of the lawlike claims.

Of course, the notion that we always experience the objective world from
within the context of our cultural traditions and social context, a lifeworld,
contradicts this Enlightenment epistemology. However, there is an important

shared commitment; this being that, whether experienced in a mediated or unmediated manner, there really is a world that exists independently of its observation. Therefore, both epistemological perspectives commit their holders to a correspondence theory of truth; that is, claims about the nature of the world are true if they correspond to or "fit" the world as their claims describe it. It is the subliminal or unwitting effect that the different epistemologies have on their ontological commitments that I want to discuss briefly. The unmediated approach promotes an ontology of tangible objects to the degree that, in the extreme, only that which is observable can have "real" existence. Hence the ontological status of the world is reduced to what the observer can perceptually experience. When applied to the reality articulated in the notion of the lifeworld, this object-world-equals-tangible-world logically leads to denying the existence of the lifeworld since, of course, this is a world of subjective and intersubjective being, a world constituted of collective human intentionality. The essential properties of this world are cognition, human-human relations, and human-object relations, all of which are intangible, only manifest in the expressive media of subjects. These media can be understood as intrinsic and extrinsic in nature. Intrinsic expressive media consist of the bodies of subjects and their kinesic capacity to express their subjective states. Extrinsic expressive media, of course, consist of what archaeologists refer to as material culture. Architectural features are among the most outstanding modes of such extrinsic expressive media.

If I understand Hancock's perspective correctly, then, it would follow that to account for the Hopewell earthworks we must treat them as expressive media of the Hopewell lifeworld, a proposal with which I am in accord since I consider his concept of the lifeworld to be equivalent to what I have called a cultural tradition. When using this perspective, we can no longer afford to isolate our study of the earthworks from the study of the material residue of subsistence and settlement practices. As he puts it, the "builders of the earthworks would likely not have had them standing apart over and above their own complex of social and environmental relations, over and above the flow of nature and the sacred and the social, and the practical forces of survival and so on, to 'view' it."

This accords with the central theme of my own contribution to this section. However, there are several problems I have with his elucidation of the notion of lifeworld, the central one being that, assuming it equates with my concept culture tradition, I find that the lifeworld concept tends to be more a fused than an integrated form of collective subjectivity or awareness. I argued in my contribution that a cultural tradition is constituted as an integrated set of four, relatively autonomous forms of collective intentionality. While certainly respecting the notion that the lifeworld exists as a largely preconscious background of humans engaging with their world, both social and physical, I have also emphasized our effortless reflexivity which allows us to continually bring aspects of this preconsciousness to discursiveness as the content of our world viewing and intentional acting. I detect an important difference, therefore, with Hancock's lifeworld concept in that, presupposed by this concept is the view that human self-awareness is something that must be effortfully worked at. In fact, this effortfulness is the reason he suggests earthworks were constructed. Following Heidegger in this regard, he argues that the purpose of architecture as art "is to reveal, to make visible and explicit, the 'world' in which the societies stand, to bring forth the 'earth' to visibility, and to open up who and what a person is within that world, and upon that earth. All of this, without the 'work,' tends to concealment and in exhaustibility."

I also find a certain irony in Heidegger's stressing the perceptual role of art/architecture as an expressive sign to articulate the totality of the lifeworld since it echoes the Enlightenment stress on the observer's stance. Of course, I also understand that he is reversing the consequence by saying that treating art/architecture as an expressive sign dissolves objectivity and through articulating the collective lifeworld, it enhances the observer's sense of community. However, there are two problems here. First, the claim that art is needed in order to achieve this greater awareness simply highlights the fused-like nature of the lifeworld concept and this would tend to reduce the human subject to being more determined than autonomous in her or his awareness and action. Second, there is still an Enlightenment residue in that this emphasis of art and architecture as a perceptual medium still privileges the observer's stance. Even though the Heideggerian observer's stance has the opposite effect, the problem when applied to other lifeworlds is that it imposes the privileging of perception as the purpose of art/architecture. An immediate problem emerges if we are to account for the Hopewell earthworks in these terms since, of course, if the purpose of the earthworks is to articulate and bring fully to consciousness the multiple relations of humans to humans and humans to the sacred world, then where did the determination and capacity to build the earthworks come from? The degree of consciousness these earthworks are to bring about is required in order to motivate and organize the construction process itself.

Treating the lifeworld in my integrated cultural tradition terms allows focusing on the action perspective that DeeAnne Wymer and I emphasized is at the heart of archaeological interpretation and avoids this quandary of explaining the earthworks in terms of their presumed articulatory consequences. As we argued there, collective practices such as earthwork construction are among the necessary conditions of satisfaction of the collective intentions (ideology) with which they are performed. In this view, material practices are emergent phenomena in that they are symbolically constituted. Therefore, the point of constructing earthworks would be to constitute the collective material behaviors by which they were built and the subsequent nonconstruction collective behaviors mediated by them as the types of social practices intended. This certainly does not deny that the earthworks would articulate fundamental principles of the lifeworld in ways that were probably unintended, such as committing the initiates who may have been the primary laborers to the principles by which their being constructed were made intelligible. It also certainly does not deny the relevance of perceptions in the process since, of course, for collective strategies to be satisfied, everyone has to perceive that the behaviors and their material outcomes conform to what would count as felicitous forms of the types of social activities intended.

Rejoinder by John E. Hancock to Commentary by A. Martin Byers

I agree with Martin that, to a substantial extent, we agree: Humans living in communities share in a complex, mostly collective, intricately interrelated world of experience, action, habit, meaning, intention, and so on, and that our "pictures" of how this world is "put together" of course affect how we will interpret their creations, and any activities or beliefs that we may infer from those creations.

Martin finds my descriptions of the lifeworld to imply more of a "fused" than an "integrated" picture of human existence, though I think my "woven fabric" metaphor can accommodate the layers and interactions which he has elucidated and which I respect greatly. I also embrace the notion that the earthworks are "intentional outcomes" (things people *made*—"works" of architecture), not merely "objects of experience" (things people perceive—*how* they "work"). Further clarifying this dual nature of the "work" may also supply my answer to Martin's key question, "Where did the determination and capacity to build the earthworks come from?"

Human works are created within an already ongoing cultural world context in which traditions and institutions (and prior works) are already influential and already structuring perception, conception, and intention. There was no intention ex nihilo to build an earthwork, apart from such an already-in-place world involving, yes, an integrated (or woven) "cosmology, world view, ethos, and ideology," but also that rested upon the unreflective background from which these are brought forth into varying degrees of explicitness under various conditions (this variation being more a "weave" than a "fusion").

So the seeming "effortfulness" of this bringing forth of meaning, that Martin mentions in his critique, would be true if we had to create every intention anew or account for it fully in some self-sufficient and atemporal causal model. But we humans are already immersed in a temporal world, that is already awash in meanings, that are already structured by influential works, that are therefore already enabling our volition and our creativity.

All traditions of monumental or sacred architecture have emerged along such continuities, and the works that stand within them (those French cathedrals again, for example) are always both "intentional acts" (works), and "meaningful experiences" (at work). The fact that new works are always thus influenced within ongoing, interwoven institutional and stylistic contexts, does not reduce their makers to mere "determinism" nor does it "fuse" the lifeworld, since, as Martin has so ably shown with his examples of "warrants," artifacts emerge as meaning bearers within our lived reality in multiple, subtle, and complex ways.

My goal here has been more interpretive than explanatory. My recourse to ontological insights was meant to open the possibility that even works from a distant, alien time can emerge for us as bearers of meaning, and can illuminate our shared humanness. This can be most effectively accomplished if we do justice in our accounts and representations to their extraordinary beauty and power, and to their settings within the human and natural world, as well as to the research data on which our knowledge about them so largely depends.

Commentary on A. Martin Byers's "The 'Heartland' Woodland Settlement System: Cultural Traditions and Resolving Key Puzzles"

Commentary by John E. Hancock (with commentary on the
volume introduction)

I am sure to be using Martin's integrated, four-layer description of "cosmology, ethos, world view, and ideology" with my architectural history students in the years to come. (I have even been persuaded that in this carefully crafted arrangement even the term "world view" has some merit!) Essentially it maps on to my messier lists of "traditions, aims, tasks, beliefs, and practices" that constitute a lifeworld. But it seems to have some implications even beyond what Martin so admirably enumerates: The first is that because of its subtlety it calls into question our use of the familiar overarching naming conventions, and the second is that it only silently presupposes both the unreflectiveness and the general humanness that are the massive ontological foundations enabling any given cultural formation to exist, or to be interpreted by another.

First, once we've shed this much light on the complex structures within our human cultural traditions, we will need to abandon the practice of naming them "categorically" as we do. As an architectural historian, I have resisted terms such as "romanesque" and "Gothic" (and even "postmodern") to describe buildings or the periods or cultures that made them. The building techniques and cultural histories of eleventh- to twelfth-century France always seemed too complex. Certain monasteries, for example, had distinctive blends of "romanesqueness" and "Gothicness" that defied their being put into one box or the other. Instead, they reflected a particular institution building within a certain flux of intentions, and with the favored conventions, practices, techniques, and opportunities of their time, which more often than not were multifarious and in transition.

So except in survey textbooks, architectural historians have largely stopped using such terms as categorical "period styles" or "cultural epochs," instead attending to the comingled intentions and innovations of individual works and places. In this approach, "style" as a methodological tool is closer to Dee-Anne and Martin's sense, where design conventions are intentionally directed toward situating a work in a meaningful world of relations. As an "internal quality" or characteristic of an artifact in its context, this is quite important. But as the name of a "category" of works, or a whole cultural milieu, or a circumscribed period of time, words such as "Gothic" become untenable. And so should, by the same token, "Hopewell." Would "being Hopewell" correspond to being French, being Catholic, being medieval, being Burgundian, being Benedictine, or being from a particular house like Cluny? Or any combination of these? The brilliance and utility of Martin's four-layer system, and his clan-cult sodality model, is that it can help us sort this out; though a consequence of working with such richly differentiating interpretive ideas is that the umbrella terms stop being helpful or important to our interpretations of works, people, and places.

The methodological breakthrough here is a switch from "putting things in categories" to "distributing characteristics across phenomena." A site or object is no longer "Adena" or "Hopewell" but may have some "Adena-ness" and/or some "Hopewell-ness." This way of thinking can also help us temper the dichotomies this conference began with: "Tools" and "artworks" for example, or "pragmatic" and "symbolic" world views or functions, are not categories into which we must sort things but characteristics that can be and usually are distributed across things in varying blended measures. Martin's examples of useful objects as "warrants," made in such a way as to do their jobs but also clarify roles and protocols, indicate well how these blends occur. This also reminds us to question other categories such as "art" or "religion," "agriculture" or "the sacred" (all derived from modern institutions) and to grasp that as circumscribed categories these are largely irrelevant to our considerations of ancient societies.

Second, even after we have so elegantly mapped the workings of integrated cultural traditions, they are for the most part, as Gadamer so famously said, "like water to a fish." From cosmology through ideology, the constructs of any particular society are rooted in deeper relationships and characteristics, in varying degrees both unreflective and universally human. Presuppositions about what this universal human ontology consists of, both explicit and implicit, cannot be avoided, and saturate all the interpretive and methodological constructs in our human sciences and in this volume. Deep notions of community, competitiveness, coping with the natural order, hunger, toil, consciousness, volition, love, fear, aspiration, and so on are always already at work in any human activity, and in any interpretation of such activity. And in these deep, precosmological relations is also, as I emphasized in my chapter, that blanket inattentiveness that saturates everyday existence.

I raise these "deep" notions with more of an architectural than a philosophical motive: In order to expose the fundamental nature of the work of artistry, from the crafted blade for killing (as Martin has shown) to the monumental axiality that marks the moonrise. The work's "work" is to uncover and make visible for explicit consideration the cosmology, ethos, world view, and ideology of the people and, in the greatest works, to root these culture-specific relations in a wider universal humanity. Grasping the role of artifacts and monuments in culture needs to begin at the beginning: How they enable the "world" to be "experienced" or "viewed" or perceptually registered at all. It is artistic or ritual elaboration or excess that breaks through the everyday lifeworld with layers of attentiveness and explicit consciousness, bringing into focus both the shared meaningful practices and the physical form and arrangement of things.

The project of hermeneutics is to bring increasing layers of this shared humanness into focus as the backgrounds or horizons of our interpretive activities as scholars. Not only do the cultures we study have distinct cultural traditions and processes (Martin's integrated-not-fused model), and the capacity to operate among multiple life goals and complex networks (Martin's clan-cult sodality model), but these cultural systems are also built upon and within deeper, more universally human conditions that we all always already presuppose and share. DeeAnne questions how we are to judge the plausibility of our theories. Mainly, it is by whether they "explain experience" better than rival theories. However, our experience of the "data" as such (the stuff we dig up) is only part of the picture. We are always also layering in our background experiences of multiple contexts, both narrow scholarly and broadly human ones, all the way to our most fundamental and inexplicit assumptions about the nature of human existence itself. The hermeneutic approach is to open out across these multiple contexts and backgrounds (the horizons that are making interpretation possible in the first place) and to search and explore their resonances and implications.

Finally, to return briefly from the general to the specific: The vastness of the earthwork complexes which, as we have learned in making our media programs, makes them nearly invisible, also made them extremely resource- and labor-intensive for both construction and maintenance. Martin's imputing to their builders a "sacred earth" ethic, and a "minimalist" intervention strategy, seems at odds with such gargantuan enterprises, obviously organized over multiple generations, and directed against the "natural" conditions of the forests, hilltops, streams, and slopes of the region. The entire north half of Fort Ancient was scraped away to the clay subsoil, while waterways were aggressively extended, springs moved, streams disrupted, ponds built, ravines filled, and so on, as Patricia Essenpreis and Robert Connolly have shown. Vast prairies were maintained at geometric sites such as Newark through huge expenditures of cutting and burning. Everywhere were huge projects entailing the cutting, filling, hauling, burning, and burying of vast quantities of stone, soil, clay, and timber.

It seems apparent that these projects were cosmological "intensifications" of the natural environment: completing water boundaries, leveling artificial horizons, foregrounding iconic hills and valleys, memorializing temples and the dead, and so on. And the scale was obviously important: to provide more accurate back-sights for astronomical positions or more sympathetic or "worthy" idealizations of the region's landscape forms and vistas. But it seems implausibly disproportionate to interpret such vast and aggressive rearrangements of the earth's surface as propitiations for the disruptiveness of domestic gardening. The clan-cult sodality model might instead suggest that in the world of the cult sodalities a far greater project, with a far larger frame of reference, was in play.

Rejoinder by A. Martin Byers to Commentary by John E. Hancock

My integrated view of a cultural tradition as structured into relatively autonomous forms of collective intentionality I have labeled cosmology, ethos, world view, and ideology plays an important role in my contribution to this book. It particularly pleases me that John Hancock has found it useful in his own work. Of course, it requires much more development, in particular, extending and elaborating the nature and role of ideology. However, even in its current form, I have found it very useful as a medium for constructing plausible models of the collective intentionality that is presupposed by the archaeological record we term Ohio Hopewell, as well as other archaeological records.

Hancock has astutely highlighted an apparent implausibility in my claim that there is a connection between gardening and earthworks. As he points out, some of the earthwork constructions are so massive in their areal extensions that their actual formal appearance is incapable of being fully experienced from the normal person-on-the-ground perspective. Therefore, as he notes, "it seems implausibly disproportionate to interpret such vast and aggressive rearrangements of the earth's surface as propitiations for the disruptiveness of domestic gardening." He then closes his excellent commentary by suggesting that the "clan-cult sodality model might instead suggest that in the world of the cult sodalities a far greater project, with a far larger frame of reference, was in play."

Hancock's skepticism is warranted since he has zeroed in on two inadequacies in my development of this chapter, inadequacies arising largely from the constraints of space. First, I did not elaborate the relation between monumental earthwork constructions and the rich mortuary residue that is so often identified with them and how this combination relates to the settlement and ecological practices of the people who occupied the region. In short, I did not sufficiently develop the causal linkage between "domestic gardening" and earthwork construction and use. Second, I did not fully clarify just how inter- and intracult factionalism and competition can generate activities that appear to surpass and even contradict the primary purposes of these groups, thereby promoting a massive degree of landscape modification that, as he notes, makes my claim about everyday gardening as the motivational source apparently implausible. Unfortunately, space prevents me from fully addressing these two shortcomings. I am convinced, however, that there is a sociocausal relation between ecological practices and ceremonial practices and that the Central Ohio Valley peoples took themselves to be facing an ecological crisis as a result of increasing intensity of traditional gardening practices, as well as the expanding of their traditional foraging practices. In effect the settlement pattern can be understood as the outcome of radical changes in ecological strategy.

I have an excuse for the first inadequacy since, in fact, I addressed this in another chapter of this book and, therefore, there would be no reason to re-address it in this chapter. Unfortunately, because of the organization of the book, Hancock did not have access to this chapter before writing his commentary. What is important to keep in mind, however, is the particular nature of the cosmology and ethos that I have postulated for the prehistoric inhabitants of this region.

As I argued, the collective beliefs and values constituting these deep structural traditions, that is, the cosmology and ethos, presuppose and make possible the collective perceptual experiences, that is, their world view, that the participants in these social systems had of their world, both natural and social. And, of course, the same deep structural traditions of cosmology and ethos presuppose and make possible the collective intentions, that is, their ideology, whereby the regular behaviors that the same participants performed were constituted for them as the types of social activities that they were. The experiencing of living in an immanently sacred world will thus necessarily interconnect ecological and religious practices. For example, I am committed to the position that what material behaviors will count as appropriate exploitation of resources in such a world will be different from those behaviors that will count as appropriate in a transcendentally sacred world. In the former, clearing the land for small gardens will be perceived quite differently than in the latter and different rules will apply. In a transcendental world where personal and corporate property will prevail, clearing is an act of proprietorship. Either the owner does this in person or else commands that a laborer does it. Hence, any person(s) who clears a piece of land and does(do) not own it, will be treated as squatters, in effect, as "poaching" the property of the owners. Squatters will be disdained and, at best, might be tolerated if they subordinate themselves to the owners through accepting that the latter control the non-owner's labor on the land. Such labor will count as recognizing the role of the owner and will be publicly expressed through rituals of rental payment, usually manifested as the transfer of the products of the tenants' labor to the owner's storage bins.

In contrast, in an immanently sacred world, "squatting" is the normal practice and it expresses a standard set of attitudes and values toward the land. In this world, occupying the land expresses the value of "living lightly on the land," and this requires caring for the land, and so on. This is why I spoke of such tenure as custodial usufruct. In short, each type of cosmology and its associated ethos will implicate a different valuation of land and, under the special conditions of scarcity, the differential tenure, proprietorship or custodianship, will translate into unique monumental architecture. Of course, the limitations of this article make it impossible to elaborate in any detail on the relation of gardening to Ohio Hopewell monumental architecture that Hancock has correctly and insightfully raised. As I also noted above, some of these issues are addressed in chapter 8 of this book (see Byers 2004: chap. 6; 2006: chap. 3).

SECTION 5

Critical Methodology and Epistemology

DeeAnne Wymer's chapter addresses the questions of where our ideas about the Hopewell come from and how we assess or ought to assess these ideas. She is very sensitive to the claim that most Hopewellian archaeologists would make, that prehistoric archaeology is a social science and, therefore, we are responsible to warrant our characterizations and explanations of the archaeological record. As she argues with regard to the Hopewell, this requires generating and testing ideas, expressed as theories and models, about a prehistoric social world that may have been and, indeed, in all likelihood was, profoundly different from any social world that has been experienced by modern-day anthropologists. Therefore, we are faced with a heavy burden of explaining an archaeological record while being able to rely on only some of the current anthropological theoretical knowledge since much of the patterning of this record, particularly the great earthworks and mortuary features, may have been generated by a people whose cultures have no direct analog today.

She argues that we must tackle this problem by recognizing the indivisible integration of the cognitive/symbolic and the instrumental so that we can no longer proceed by neatly maintaining the symbolic and instrumental spheres as mutually separate, a division that conveniently allowed for each to be pursued by its own specialized groupings of archaeologists. In this regard, she recognizes the importance of the postprocessual approach while, at the same time, in a processualist vein, cautioning us that, as social scientists, we are not "doing" archaeology to discover ourselves but to reconstitute the real social world of those who actually did the work that resulted in these sacred landscapes. Of course, this does not deny that we can also discover or rediscover our own cultural backgrounds and, through insights we gain in doing archaeology, come to better appreciate or even critique it in its own terms. There is no doubt that one of the valuable spin-offs of doing "good archaeology" is to gain a greater understanding of one's own social world (see Hancock, this volume). However, she cautions that this achievement should not become the raison d'être of our work, for if it does, deliberately proceeding in this way will probably lead to a distortion of the past social reality through projecting a romantic view of our own social world onto the archaeological record.

Hence she comes out strongly in favor of pursuing realistic understandings of the archeological record through drawing on current social and anthropological theory to construct and test alternative models of prehistoric social worlds, and through using the current data at hand, accumulating new data through further fieldwork, and "reexcavating" the past through reevaluating the museum and archival data. She concludes that, while no model will be absolutely adequate, rational, albeit contingently adequate, scientific conclusions can be achieved through objective theoretical, methodological, interpretive, and empirical debate. She ends on a very positive note for the future of Hopewellian studies.

11

Where Do (Hopewell) Research Answers Come From?

DeeAnne Wymer

The dispersed hamlets generated by the subsistence and settlement practices of Ohio Hopewell are, importantly, partly the outcome of the pursuit of survival. The Ohio Hopewell embankment and mound earthworks are, importantly, partly the outcome of the pursuit of the sacred. How do archaeologists deal with what seem to be two opposite spheres of activity carried out by the same regional population? (Personal communication, April 2004)

Current research in Hopewellian studies, manifesting a resurgence in the field, has focused on "typical" processualist interests (e.g., settlement patterns and subsistence) as well as Hopewell ritual and cosmology. Recent excavations at earthwork complexes and habitation sites, as well as new analyses of archived museum collections, are revealing unexpected information while fresh perspectives offered by symbolic/cognitive archaeologists are illuminating our theoretical landscape. However, it often seems as if two theoretical camps face each other across a great chasm. But simply acknowledging that Hopewellian cosmology influenced all facets of their culture, or that Hopewell peoples needed food to survive, does not adequately inform either theoretical emphasis, and I would suggest that merely acknowledging that both perspectives are useful or necessary does not do justice to the potential of truly integrating both paradigms into a new type of approach.[1]

Given my specialization in paleoethnobotany, as well as my recent work in the ritual utilization of plant (and animal) resources by the Hopewell, I find that I straddle both—the world of the "scientifically-oriented/data driven" processualist archaeologist and the world of the symbolic/cognitive postprocessualist/contextualist archaeologist. I thus believe that I can offer a unique perspective, and indeed, this chapter is a very individual journey into the nature of what we are trying to do as a profession through the vehicle of Hopewell research. Hopefully, some of the suggestions and musings I offer in this chapter could perhaps offer solutions to bridge that theoretical divide.

Symbolic/Cognitive Archaeology: A Cautionary Tale?

> I suggest that, as a discipline, we encourage those who are gifted in creative dia-
> logue to think great thoughts: to brainstorm, unconstrained by the rigor of normal
> scientific methodology; to look at the world from all angles, both the obvious and
> the less obvious; and to put forward interesting propositions, providing enough
> information for others to determine whether a dialogue should be pursued. I
> certainly would not hope to turn the entire discipline into storytellers, but we need
> our share! The key is that they recognize that the pursuit of knowledge is not over
> once they have promulgated their story. (Redman 1991: 303)

When working within the domain of Hopewell archaeology you simply can not ignore the fact that symboling, ritual, ceremony—the ideological—imbued their entire world and thus their entire archaeology. Certainly within the past decade there has been a literal explosion of publications, conferences, and popular interest in this aspect of Hopewell archaeology. Some of the research drawn from this "postprocessual/cognitive" perspective is compelling, and some of it leaves me less than satisfied and at times exasperated. In the creation of this chapter, particularly while reading background material and the other chapters my colleagues fashioned for this volume, I focused on trying to pinpoint and illuminate where my dissatisfaction specifically lies while, as well, trying to understand what aspects of these approaches appeal to me as a scholar and why they do so.

Hence I came to the central question of any discourse and of any scholarship: How do we know when our ideas are valid? Although it may have become unpopular to admit that Lewis Binford is correct when he demands, oftentimes stridently, that the essential core of what we do as archaeologists is "inference justification" (Binford 1983, 1987, 1988, 1989, 2001), he is, in essence, correct. We do not excavate social systems, ceremony, symbol, or world view; we "dig up stuff." It is upon these material remains, whether artifact or altered landscape, that we depend in order to validate our assumptions and test our ideas about how the Hopewell world worked and the larger questions about cultural change and transformation.

Even those who wish to explore the nature of the Hopewell social system and ceremonial/ritual lifeways must ultimately face the issue about "standards of evidence" (Brown 2006). All too often I have found that the literature in this domain begins with some essential fundamental assumptions concerning some aspect of the Hopewell world and then builds an ever increasing elaborate schema based upon those ideas—without ever truly, to my satisfaction, validating the first principle assumptions. Although, in a philosophical sense, you can not empirically demonstrate an assumption,[2] nonetheless assumptions must be valid in terms of the relevancy with respect to the subject data as well as the larger body of currently confirmed knowledge we have about the world that those data represent. Thus in the domain of philosophy an assumption is a statement that is generally accepted as true. However, the problem still remains: If that acceptance is based on invalid ontology about the nature of things, then the entire conclusion and suite of ideas generated from those first principles is built upon a rather unstable or, to be more precise, "irrational" foundation (see, for example, the discussion below about the problems faced by "crop circle" researchers when their guiding assumption, namely, that only supernatural or extraterrestrial forces could have created such complex designs, had to be reassessed). If we become complacent in our first essential assumptions, and the premises drawn from them, this may very well inhibit us from truly exploring those first ideas and, perhaps, further inhibit us from drafting alternative ideas about the way that things work. It seems apparent that major paradigm shifts in scholarly disciplines (the "ah ha" factor) have indeed occurred when established principles are reexamined or new ones are postulated.[3]

One of the most glaring illuminations of an inherent weakness in the arena of the validation of ideas came early in the history of the development of post-processual archaeology. Why are the ideas of professional archaeologists about the past more accurate and valid than those of individuals who propose that space aliens built the world's pyramids or that Stonehenge is a psychic battery storing ritual energy? (See discussions in Hodder 1991; Renfrew 1989; Shanks and Tilley 1987, 1989.) Although Hodder and Shanks and Tilley addressed the issue, their words were not effective in answering such a fundamentally important question.[4] How do we know our ideas are valid?

The province of "sacred geometry" perfectly illustrates this dilemma. Some of the recent work in this field consists of discerning numerous patterns linked to solar, lunar, and stellar alignments, to cardinal directions, and to geometrical patternings apparently embedded within the Ohio Hopewell earthworks and then proposing grand unifying ideas that link these data to the Hopewell world view (Marshall 1996; Romain 1994, 1996; some of the discussions in this volume as well—and please note that this is not denying that much of this work is quite good and very insightful). With enough points on the landscape, whether earthwork or natural terrain, it is all too easy to play the game of "connect the dots" (and, of course, this is not to imply that the scholars who delve into this domain do not recognize and acknowledge this problem; see DeBoer, this volume, as well as the insightful comments by Hively and Horn in the Commentary section for section 2, this volume). Patterns can indeed be discovered, but the crucial question is what caused the patterns?

This was the intrinsic criticism surrounding the rather interesting "crop circle phenomenon" (and the "face on Mars" or cold fusion claims) (Hoagland 2001; Taubs 1993). Individuals who proposed that crop circles were the result of a purposeful alien intelligence discovered intriguing correlations in the formations, including mysterious mathematical equations, musical scales, sublime messages for encouraging world peace, oddly deformed plant structures in the wheat, strange energy fluctuations, and so on (Anderson 1991; Cropcircleconnector.com 2005; Kollerstrom 2002; Levengood 1994; Levengood and Talbott 1999; Nickell 2000; Silva 2002).

We now know that several quirky artists (Doug Bower and the late Dave Chorley) came forward in 1991 to confess to having created some of the most famous of the crop circles in England; and other nocturnally inclined folks have also admitted to the cereal highjinks (see Anonymous 1999; Circlemakers.org 2006; Schnabel 1994a, 1994b). In fact, an embarrassing number of the crop circles were lovingly crafted by students, artists, and debunkers. However, in the days following the appearance of the circles, they found that their creations were being touted to a gullible popular press by crop circle researchers as being "genuine" examples of an alien intelligence or the results of a secret government weapon testing program (see, for example, numerous web site discussions, such as http://www.skepticreport.com/mystics/crapcircles.htm/ and http://www.amtsgym-sdbg.dk/as/ufo-2001/cirkleri-uk.htm/; Anonymous 1999; Ridley 2002; Roberts 1999; Whittaker 2000). After making statements along the lines of "such formations are too complex to have been created overnight by humans!" these "cropologists" soon experienced consternation after rather gleeful debunkers unveiled videos showing their night time activities. The debunkers had simply utilized ropes and boards to produce patterns "too complex to have been created by mere humans." Eventually all of this led to formal contests (also occurring during nighttime hours) to award prizes to teams producing the most elaborate and beautiful crop circles (see Whittaker 2000). Various web sites now illustrate how to create your own crop designs (see, for example, "How to Draw a Crop Circle," http://www.amtsgym-sdbg. dk/as/ufo-2001/cirkleri-uk.htm/; Circlemakers.org 2006).

Thus the "artifact of patterns" found within and among the British crop circles by cerealogist researchers, who based their work on the *assumption* of supernatural or alien cause, was due to a number of factors: (1) they found the results they wanted to find (sensu "wishful science"; Sagan 1996), (2) they discovered connections among an infinite suite of possible correlations (any number of points can be found and/or created among the circles and geometric forms of the crop circles), and (3) some of the patterns they discovered were undoubtedly due to the fact that humans do pattern things, such as musical and mathematical equations, ratios, and fractal designs (apparently nonrandom repetitions were merely the result of individuals applying a set of simple geometric forms and procedures to create the designs). Psychologists call the tendency humans possess to incorrectly infer accurate causation (or perhaps infer causation in random events when there is no "real" or "purposeful" causation) as "unobserved" or "hidden" causation (see the interesting discussion in Marks and Kammann 1980 and Flew 1987). The danger of medical researchers unintentionally finding positive results verifying the efficacy of drugs or appropriate treatments is, of course, the major reason that double-blind studies are conducted (as well as to account for the placebo effect). Unfortunately, archaeologists cannot conduct blinded studies so alternative methods and means to counteract the natural human tendency to fall into the trap of "wishful thinking" must be creatively developed.

Do not mistake the above discussion as suggesting that the current archaeological research focusing on elucidating earthwork alignments or patterns and associations among and between various earthworks is simply misguided archaeological "cropology." Rather, the lessons learned from the field of pseudoscience, such as the crop circles, are case studies intended to caution us that we must recognize the danger of falling prey to the all-too-human frailty of finding what we wish to discover. In fact, as noted above, I find some of the most interesting, illuminating, and thought-provoking research in Ohio Hopewell archaeology are the studies trying to elucidate the significance and purpose for the earthwork construction and accompanying mortuary features. The chapters in this volume, for example, are excellent examples of the promise of such investigations (as well as work conducted in Illinois; see Charles, this volume, and Van Nest 2006; also Charles and Buikstra 2006).

A unique aspect of these analyses and the intriguing work now being conducted into the domain of the symbolic/cognitive (or the integrated view of cultural traditions, that is, of cosmology–ethos/world view–ideology in Byers's terms) is that these models and ideas can ultimately encompass test implications that can be "ground-truthed," or independently evaluated in the archaeological record. My Binfordian-processualist soul insists that the various ideas put forth about the Hopewell can at least be empirically investigated. How can we operationalize and evaluate ("test" if you will) some of the proposed models with independent data in the archaeological record? How do we assess the ideas sparked from this remarkable journey into the understandings of an ancient peoples and their place in their landscape (symbolic and physical)? The philosopher Philip Kitcher described this important criterion in his discussion about the nature and importance of testable hypotheses as the "observable consequences" of an idea (Kitcher 1989, 1995; see also Klemke 1988 and Salmon et al. 1992).

I believe this is indeed possible. For example, Byers (2004) proposes a pivotal concept—the sacred earth principle—in which, due to the ritual/symbolic nature of the act of creating an earthwork, embankment construction, in addition to being an act of building, was also directly intervening into the sacred order of the cosmos. Of importance, he notes the rather anomalous nature of the Observatory Mound embedded within the "end" of the circle segment of the Newark Earthwork's Octagon-Circle complex and suggests that the "Observatory Mound Complex is the material manifestation of an avoidance practice" (Byers 2004: 86). In other words, the builders of the circle originally began at the southwestern end of the circle with the construction of two parallel embankments (incorporated into the odd formation now known as the Observatory Mound) heading off into the opposite direction of the current Octagon's parallel walls. Byers proposes that, for some unknown reason, the builders could not continue in this direction, but since the very act of building was sacred (and the earth utilized in the construction was thus imbued with ritual significance), simply stopping and dismantling the segment and beginning anew was not an option. Thus this initial parallel embankment feature was incorporated into the eventually completed earthwork. "To dismantle them [construction segments] at any step in the construction process, including the very first, would have been tantamount to 'dismantling' that which they represented, the cosmos," Byers notes (2004: 87). This principle can be empirically verified by future excavations (if possible) at the Observatory Mound and, potentially, could be explored at other earthworks as well. However, in his review of my chapter prior to publication Byers made an extremely salient point that I thought best to incorporate into this section in his original words. He noted, "Remember, however, I had to build a framework of rules determining what would count as a proper earthwork in order to frame that anomaly—in fact, even to recognize it as an anomaly—so the Sacred Earth principle was not snatched out of the air or simply analogically borrowed from what we know about Native American thought. I treat it as theoretically generated and empirically grounded." His point is extremely valid (see also discussions in Byers 1996 and 1998).

Many ideas within Byers's work and other authors (such as in this volume) should also have "empirical consequences" that with enough imaginative ingenuity could be evaluated or "ground-truthed." Some theoretical offerings could also be explored and evaluated through different data sets (see discussion below). For example, Byers notes, "Everything else being equal, earthworks that shared the same form or, at least, shared major formal principles, would tend to be more closely related ideologically than those that did not" (page 235, this volume). Thus if there are special relationships among and between specific earthworks (such as the geometric earthworks of Hopewell-Turner, Hopeton–Mound City, and others; see Byers this volume), it would seem reasonable to find a matching similarity in artifact styles, unique mortuary features, radiocarbon dates, construction techniques, and habitation sites (and the objects within those sites) as well as many other potential correlations. In other words, we should be able to test the underlying principles that apply to earthworks and the symbolic world with artifacts, mortuary structures, even domestic structures, since the same underlying cosmology-ethos/world view–ideology cultural tradition should structure the patterns for these segments of the archeological record as well (see also Byers 2006a; Byers, chap. 10, this volume).

Additionally, there are some practical hurdles that researchers investigating this realm must address. I suspect that it is all too easy to forget that we view the river valleys and uplands of the Hopewell world through a twenty-first-century perspective. This was brought home to me during excavations at the Brown's Bottom 1 site in Chillicothe, Ohio, during the summers of 2005 and 2006—a site that Pacheco, Burks, and I have proposed is a Hopewell habitation site (Pacheco et al. 2006). As I stood looking across the vast open agricultural fields that now covered this beautiful bottomland adjacent to the Liberty Earthworks, with the gentle breezes sweeping down through the valley, my mind's eye clothed the landscape in a darkly forested environment. My research into creating what the original environment had been like for many Hopewell sites and localities, from the Newark Earthworks to the heartland of south-central and southern Ohio, suggests that the majority of these areas had been covered with dense rich forests (see Wymer 1996, 1997). Thus if there had indeed been either celestial alignments or alignments between particular and among various earthworks (with some researchers suggesting purposeful alignments that spanned some great distances; see section 2, this volume), how could sightlines have been created through these forests? Even to create a simple circle or rectangle (such as those of the classic sites such as Newark, Mound City, Hopeton, Liberty, and the many others) would have entailed a fairly significant amount of land clearance. And how indeed could the Hopewell have lined up points on their landscape that were miles apart? The dilemma is not as simple as one may think. Even to utilize a high prominence of a hill is not straightforward in a practical sense since the crown of the hill would be covered in forest and bramble; to try to sight down into a point in the valley, therefore, would be very difficult. Today ours is a relatively clear environment that enables us to see for a great distance. The current landscape is not that of the world at the time of the Hopewell. Struggling to visualize the world of 2,000 years ago illustrated for me the importance of the work of John Hancock and the CERHAS project. Such computer simulations can have a profound impact beyond the simple beauty and educational aspect of their work (see Hancock, this volume).

I am not saying that the Hopewell were too dull-witted to have made such achievements—obviously they did create such masterpieces—but I wonder about the practical end of things. For example, after trekking through my own mountain forest this winter, I was struck with the thought that the easiest and perhaps the only way to view features of the terrain, whether cultural or physical, is to do so in the depths of winter when the foliage of the trees and the underbrush has largely thinned out and disappeared and the world is blanketed in snow. In fact, the only view of the setting sun on the horizon that I have as I sit here typing in my home is in winter. In the summer, the canopy is too dense for such a glimpse. I thus find it intriguing that during my analysis of organic material still extant on copper artifacts I discovered that one side of a breastplate from the Hopewell site (Mound 25, Burial 6) was entirely covered in small flowers (something like a small aster) that were beginning to set seed. The most likely season for the placement of this artifact within a mortuary ritual would have been late fall (Wymer 2001, 2002b, 2004). And certainly the lunar view across the Newark Octagon-Circle complex is most spectacular in fall and winter. Ironically, the latest research at Stonehenge in England suggests that the main importance of the megalith was to mark the shortest day in winter rather than as a summer solstice marker.

The Straightjacket of Historic Analogy?

Finally, my recent review of a series of new publications has revealed a significant and, I believe, troubling pattern within the application of interpretive archaeology to Hopewellian studies. Many authors relied upon ethnographic analogy to support their assertions about some aspect of Hopewell archaeology and to illuminate important features of the Hopewell world. Even in cases in which such an analogy was not necessary, the authors felt a need to legitimatize their discussions by referring to selected historically known myths and rituals (Lepper 1995, 2006). I found many researchers utilizing selections drawn from historic indigenous populations, from Mesoamerica to the Ojibwa and the Southwest (and, indeed, from across the entire world), describing various rituals and myths that have been "torn" from their cultural contexts and consequently used to support an interpretation of the Hopewell world view and modus operandi (see, for example, various chapters in Charles and Buikstra 2006 and discussions in Hall 1997). I do not disagree with the assumption that the earthworks do indeed reflect the Hopewell world view and that some of them encompass celestial alignments and cosmological ideals. But I am inherently suspicious of ideas that "Answer Everything and Are Always Correct." Was it not Popper (2002) who pointed out that the weakest arguments are those which, by their very nature, answer everything and thus can not be shown to ever be incorrect?[5]

I am not saying that these recent publications are not good. Much of the work is some of the best I have yet seen in Hopewell archaeology. However, the studies exemplify an underlying, inherent problem. If we become too comfortable with "plugging" the Hopewell into historically documented Native American myths, ceremony, ritual, and world view, we are not forced to truly develop and explore alternative ideas. We become complacent in our own mythology of what we want the Hopewell to have been. I am also not so foolish as to not recognize that there are clear connections across the ages in iconography and ethos, but the more that I delve into Hopewell research, the more I suspect that the Hopewell were in some ways clearly unlike any known historic group.

Why this trend toward the largely unquestioning use of analogy? I am not the first to note that the most powerful and persuasive of the work conducted by the postprocessualists focused on cultural critique and criticism of the historic present (such as museum exhibits) or the recent past (see comment sections in Binford 1989; Hodder 1982, 1987; Leone 1981, 1982; Leone and Potter 1988). The point is this: It is easier to explore the realm of the ceremonial, social structure, and individuals' manipulation of their culture's symbols when you already have a good sense of the overarching world view that structures these elements of a people. It seems that by ultimately tying the Hopewell in some way to the known historic present their world view is made visible, understandable, and we can thus begin to evaluate that world through their symbols whether in the form of artifact or their myths writ large upon the landscape (see Greber 2006). Thus we can only know the world from the world we already know. And this may lead us down a rather seductive, and ultimately dangerous, path. Is such use of simplistic anthropological analogy perhaps a substitute for the development of good theory? In fact, in his review of the first draft of this chapter, Byers commented that "such higher-level interpretive uses [of analogy] simply tends to be a substitute for good theory and, moreover, it presupposes that the explanations and characterizations of the cultural practices given by anthropologists and used by the archaeologist for analogical purposes are correct or at least adequate. This means archaeology simply replicates the ethnological sector of anthropology and, moreover, endorses rather than advances its claims." I found his remark more than salient, and it echoes my own concern with this increasing trend in Hopewell studies.

Problems with the Processual Perspective

> If hunting and gathering and other everyday practices are, like rituals, symbolically constructed, and if rituals presupposed both a given cosmology and ethos, then Ohio Hopewell settlement and subsistence practices drew on the same cosmology and ethos. Therefore, getting a good handle on the type of cultural traditions the Ohio Hopewell had is not only necessary to reconstruct the earthwork ritual, it also is necessary to reconstruct their subsistence and settlement practices and, therefore, their total social system. (Byers, e-mail comment to me during preparations for the original symposium)

It is also becoming increasingly clear that in order to address the really important questions about the Hopewell we cannot ignore the symbolic and ritual realm. Previous research, and certainly much of my own work, indicates that our understanding of the emergence of the Hopewell cultural pattern and the "demise" of the Hopewell (or rather the transformation of the population into the nucleated settlements of the Late Woodland) hinges upon understanding how the Hopewell social and symbolic systems operated. The more comfortable and familiar "forces" of evolutionary change, such as dramatic environmental and major subsistence reorganization, do not account for the origins or the "disappearance" of this remarkable archaeological culture—the "easy" answers from a superficial ecological or materialist perspective, for example, simply do not apply (Wymer 1987, 1992, 1993, 2002a).

We need to better understand how the kinship system of the Hopewell operated as well as how local groups were organized at the regional and interregional level and how the sociopolitical realm functioned (Byers, this volume; Greber 2006; Pacheco and Dancey 2006; Seeman and Branch 2006).[6] We need to better understand what "fueled" the Interaction Sphere, how goods moved throughout the land, and how this was integrated into local populations. We need, as well, to understand how the corporate combined with the ceremonial. And the pivotal key to all of this will be to comprehend the ceremonial/ritual world view of the Hopewell because it is that world view that structured what we deal with today as archaeologists—the archaeological residue of their material culture. These populations literally recreated and reformed their landscape in their ceremonial image, and those actions—clearing large areas of forest and carving and molding earthworks and mounds on an immense scale—undoubtedly set the stage for what was to come in subsequent periods.

As some authors have noted (see Sieg and Burks, this volume), Hopewell cosmology undoubtedly also structured the world beyond areas that may have been viewed as sacred. I wonder, for example, how the possible demarcation of sacred from secular (or the opposite for that matter—the incorporation of the sacred into the mundane) influenced location of domestic sites and garden locations. Of course, even to describe the Hopewell world in "oppositional pairings" (the sacred versus secular noted above) may very well be nonsensical in their social world since it is just as likely that the sacred imbued the secular. This dichotomy that we so easily fall into more than likely reflects our own Western industrial view of the world and illustrates the difficulty of breaking out of the trap of our own cultural milieu. We have given lip service, or rather a few lines on the page of publications, to noting the importance of this part of the Hopewell world, but truly, we have not integrated this aspect into our scientifically oriented ideas about cultural change and transformation.

A number of researchers have suggested that Hopewell cosmology and ethos (sensu Byers 2004; Byers, chap. 10, this volume), as the collective sociology,[7] structured the very fabric of individual Hopewell populations. It may be that spatially distinct Hopewellian populations constituted their ideologies and world views differently from one another, thereby accounting for the great variation in the material makeup of the ceremonial sphere; however, by sharing the same set of deep cosmological and ethos structures, they would not have compromised a pervasive common understanding across vast regions of what the world order ought to be. In short, perhaps the differences we see in the archaeological record between Hopewell populations—whether within one river valley, such as the Scioto "Heartland," or between the Illinois and Ohio centers—reflect each population's unique ideological expression and world view interpretation that was made possible by their sharing the baseline or broadly common deep structures of cosmology and ethos with most of the rest of the Eastern Woodland populations.[8] In essence, the Hopewellian artifacts and features, presupposed and made possible by this "baseline" or shared cosmology, are the material realization of what earlier Hopewell researchers recognized and termed as the "Interaction Sphere" (see Caldwell 1964). Such a shared cosmology, for example, is undoubtedly what made the extensive trade network possible, while it was ideological innovations realized in Hopewellian stylistics that made it necessary. And the apparent rapid "demise" or disappearance from the archaeological record of the famous hallmarks or diagnostic markers of Hopewell (mortuary and earthwork construction, trade in specific raw materials, among other things) suggests that there had been a relatively sudden change in the ideological structures that had made this manifestation of their shared cosmology and ethos possible. That is, perhaps while the deep structures of Hopewellian cosmology and ethos remained largely unchanged, the surface structural level of world view and ideology underwent a rapid and dramatic transformation, thereby pointing in the direction of explaining the "disappearance" of this remarkable Hopewellian phenomenon.

The various models proposed about earthwork creation and their cosmological implications can of course only be approximations of the reality that they are about. No model about the prehistoric past can ever really eliminate the approximative nature of our descriptive and explanatory attempts to account for what had been the very real and complex world of ancient peoples. However, we can rationally choose among alternative approximations (models) by assessing how well each explains the common set of data our models address. In any case, "absolute" truth is not what I think that most researchers are trying to achieve, nor is this the inherent value of such work. More important, the recent shift to a more sophisticated exploration of the Hopewell cosmos and ideology (as understood by the Hopewell in virtue of their cosmology and realized in their ideological strategies) forces us to cogitate and imagine differently—we do need theories/ideas about how to study and think about such broad landscape archaeology and the symbolic. Such new theoretical modeling is essential to drive the development and creation of new technologies and ways of verification (or negation) (Wylie 1999).

So Where Do Hopewell Research Answers Come from and Where Do We Go from Here?

Ideas and theoretical insights can come from anywhere (although, of course, in reality ideas typically are the result of applying prior understandings to new data), but how do we know if indeed we have the right of it? I have to agree with Seeman and Branch (2006: 107) that "without historical grounding we need to utilize multiple lines of inference" and that we must work between "several spatial scales." How do we do this? In the end all we really have as archaeologists to test the validity of our ideas, other than the material remains, are two key factors: context and pattern. This includes the context of the small-scale (individual artifacts, ecofacts, stylistic motifs, among others) and context on a "grander scale"—the context of an altered landscape (the use-life history of earthworks, for example, as well as the nature of an individual habitation site). And we have pattern, whether this is the pattern of ritually placed items in burial contexts from site to site, the statistical patterns of association of organic materials on copper artifacts, to the patterns of earthwork shape and placement on the landscape. We need to tie together these contexts and patterns at the micro and macro levels in better defined ways. It is, of course, theory and model development that drives data acquisition and new technological innovations (and is, indeed, a third vital factor to the two of context and pattern noted above), but eventually archaeological data must be utilized to ultimately support or negate among a realm of potential theories and explanatory ideas. We may never be able to truly and totally understand in a detailed way the Hopewell world view and ethos, but we may not need to do that if what we are looking for and assessing are changes in the patterns (whether small or large scale) across time. And of course it is our theoretical models that then give meaning to the changes that we see in the archaeological record.[9]

A Synthesis of Perspectives?

I sense that many of us have already come to the same conclusions, and I would like to offer some suggestions that build upon current work or perhaps highlight what may be useful areas to explore. In fact, much of what I am going to advocate is already underway:

1. We need to continue to investigate Hopewell archaeology at the intra- and interregional scale. I have always found exciting insights from comparisons and contrasts betwixt and between Ohio and Illinois Hopewell in terms of settlement and ceremonial distinctions and similarities. All too often we do not poke our heads out of our own river valleys to take a broader perspective of the Hopewell world. Why, for instance, did the Ohio Hopewell create such monumental earthworks while the Hopewell of Illinois (or other regions) did not? Such comparisons may also illuminate what avenues of research are perhaps not relevant. Yerkes's recent peculiar insistence in the literature (2002, 2006) that the Ohio Hopewell were fairly nomadic and that the Eastern Agricultural Complex was not important in their diet (calling the complex taxa merely collected weedy seeds, for example) not only ignores crucial elements of the Ohio data but also is oddly silent about the extensive information from Illinois clearly showing the nature of their settlements and their diet.

2. What constitutes a "local or regional" population for Ohio Hopewell? The recent work of individuals such as Greber (2006), Seeman (Seeman and Branch 2006) and Dancey and Pacheco (1997a and 1997b; see also Pacheco 1989, 1997; and Pacheco and Dancey 2006), to name a few, that have focused on trying to understand the settlement-sociopolitical (or corporate-ceremonial) juncture is breaking new ground and revealing important information and insights. Were the larger and more com-

plicated earthworks the ceremonial/ritual center for a dispersed and relatively small population? How large were these populations? What drew them to earthworks (and when?) for construction or alteration activities? What are the "linkages" between habitation and earthwork? How were the individual regions, such as Newark and Ross County, connected (Byers, this volume; see Greber 2006)?[10]

3. We will need to continue with excavations of Hopewell settlements (or reexcavations of sites such as McGraw) as well as larger GPS and GIS regional surveys of both earthworks and habitation sites (see Burks, Pederson, and Walter 2002; Burks and Pederson 2006; Dancey 1991; Greber 1999; Lynott 2001; Lynott and Weymouth 2002). I am also struck by the insights offered in appreciating the potential importance of "negative space" (sensu Sieg and Burks, this volume) or the Hopewell utilization of the region outside earthworks and earthwork clusters. The utilization of varying methods—including magnetometer, "traditional" pedestrian surface survey, aerial imaging, and excavation—in the Brown Bottom 1 explorations in Ross County revealed the advantage that combining several different techniques and technologies can offer in field research (Pacheco et al. 2006).

4. We should continue developing tighter chronological controls for Hopewell sites (both ceremonial and habitation). If, as postulated, there were links between individual earthwork sites, perhaps radiocarbon data might help to illuminate whether this was the case (although the apparent utilization of earthworks for long periods of time could hinder such assessments). Unfortunately, this potential database is hampered by the destruction of most of the earthworks and mortuary features, although recent excavations (see below) suggest that there may be ways of getting at materials suitable for radiocarbon dating. Also, advanced AMS technology has permitted dating of minute quantities of organic material still extant in museum collections.

5. I would encourage those who explore and evaluate possible earthwork alignments, whether celestial, horizon, or links between individual sites, to find ways to operationalize their ideas. Are there empirical consequences that can be assessed in the archaeological record or the physical landscape? Are there conditions or parameters that would invalidate some of these models? There are a number of individual researchers (see this volume, for example) who have suggested alternative models for the same suite of earthwork and natural landscape features (as well as intersecting concurrence for several lines of evidence). It would be interesting and perhaps useful to have a workshop or series of work-

shops bringing together the various researchers to explore their ideas as a group.

6. We need to return to "classic" Hopewell ceremonial sites for examination with new techniques, technologies, and insights. The work of Brown at Mound City, Greber at Harness and High Bank, Lynott and crew at Hopeton, and the continuing investigations at Mound City, Fort Ancient, Newark, and the Stubbs Cluster are revealing a fascinating and subtle complexity to the creation, alteration, and use of these special places (Burks, Pederson, and Walter 2002; Burks and Pederson 2006; see also Sieg and Burks, this volume; Riordan, this volume). It is clear, especially with the development of new technologies, that there is much more to learn about how the Hopewell utilized the spaces within earthworks and mortuary areas (Connelly 1996, 1998; Cowan, Sunderhaus, and Genheimer 2000; Essenpreis and Moseley 1984; Genheimer 1997; Pickard 1996; Riordan 1995).

7. We need to reassess archived artifacts and paperwork in museum collections from the famous excavations of sites such as Putnam, Mills, and Shetrone (Mills 1907, 1909; Putnam 1885). Asking the right questions and using the appropriate theory, combined with new technologies, such collections may be untapped sources of information (Greber 1996; Greber and Ruhl 1989). Certainly my own work with organic materials preserved on Hopewell copper artifacts revealed an unexpected world. What I am most excited about is that this research is disclosing intriguing patterns of association of organic materials among the copper artifacts and the sites (Wymer 2001, 2002b, 2004, 2006, and ongoing). Do the patterns that I find for this particular class of materials (organics) match any patterns among the iconography found on Hopewell artifacts as well as burial placement, treatment, and objects for the mounds and the internments? Do these patterns match earthwork creation, shapes, artifacts recovered at habitation sites, and other such factors?

8. One of the most fruitful avenues of research may be to combine field and museum research and then move from the micro to the macro levels. For example, I suspect there is great potential in reassessing archived materials (both artifactual and "paper") from the early excavations at selected sites and then linking these data with a reexamination of the relevant sites and with new excavations and technologies, such as that conducted by Greber at the Liberty Works site (1983). The next step could be to move from the micro to the macro level by linking all of this information to sophisticated regional surveys and exploration of the areas within and outside the earthwork complexes. Along with such

investigations must be the exploration of Hopewell habitation sites in the same general area. The use of new technologies also could include more unusual elements; the computer-generated imaging that we have seen created by John Hancock's CERHAS team, for example, may have a greater impact on generating new ideas than previously suspected.

9. Can we "test" some of our ideas about the Hopewell ritual world, the world of symbols and ceremony, going beyond merely noting the layout of their settlements and the foods they ate? I offer the following contemplation of a recent publication that tackles elements of the Hopewell trade network, the implied ceremonial/symbolic elements of the world view fueling the interaction sphere and touching upon the individual in the archaeological record. Warren DeBoer (2003) writes about a unique artifact resembling the horn of a bighorn sheep that was recovered from a burial at Mound City. The artifacts of Burial 12, laid out upon the floor of Mound 7 in a specific pattern, are remains that, DeBoer suggests, "can not be adequately viewed as 'grave goods' accompanying the central cremation. Rather, they comprised parts of a costume, or given their neatly piled arrangement, a sartorial composition. It is only surmise that this regalia pertained to the individual represented by the cremation" (2003: 98). I could possibly test this idea by examining the rather numerous copper artifacts from the burial for the presence of traces of leather or other materials. I have identified worked leather, and plant-based and fur textiles, on many of the breastplates from sites such as Harness, Turner, Seip, and Hopewell (Wymer 2001, 2002b; 2004; and current research). It would be interesting to see what a detailed microscopic inspection of the artifacts, including the copper horn, would reveal. Thus multiple lines of evidence (context and pattern) at "different spatial scales"—the configuration of the artifacts within this particular feature plus a microscopic examination of some of the materials—combined with perhaps a theoretical reassessment of the other features in the same mound (and the same for the other mounds within the earthwork) may offer a way to independently test our ideas.

10. We must also conceptually assess the sources of our ideas. "Teasing apart" the intricacies of theoretical structures is crucial, too, since different hypotheses can have the same deductive consequences and the recognition of what *are* valid (or essential) data is mediated by our theories (or even our unrecognized cultural biases). Thus for me the data clearly indicate that "space aliens" more than likely did not create England's crop circles, but cropologists can look at the same information and come to an opposite conclusion. In fact, as Byers noted in his first review of

this chapter, "I would also add that we need to rejoin our anthropological and sociological colleagues by becoming much more familiar with the new social and cultural theories that are animating those disciplines and revolutionizing their interpretations and understandings of human society and culture. I think we are woefully inadequate in this area and I would include many of the postprocessualists in this critique. Theory cannot be derived from data but can only be derived from theoretical critique itself." I use his words because he has so deftly stated the crux of the need for theory formation. We need our "story makers" as it were. Thus a priori model creation is as important as a posteriori model grounding in the empirical data.

Hopewell archaeology is at an exciting stage in this decade. I am impressed with the quality and nature of the work that is being conducted by so many scholars from so many different perspectives. I believe we can continue to tell the remarkable story of a remarkable people.

Where do Hopewell research answers come from? They come from hard-won data from the field, a reappraisal of museum collections and archived notes, an integration of differing expertise in new technologies and specializations, an understanding of the role that ceremony and symbol plays in any human society, critical theory development, and, ultimately, ourselves.

Notes

1. The development of this chapter has benefitted enormously from a series of delightful e-mail exchanges between Martin Byers and me as well as his extensive comments during a number of his reviews of the chapter. Given that we are attempting to create a more "interactive" format for this volume, I have decided to include a number of Martin's insightful and extensive comments and responses to points within my text in a series of endnotes. This not only allows readers to examine Martin's ideas (and prose) for themselves but also reveals the advantages of a literary dialogue and interaction between and among authors with very different approaches and expertise in our field. I also include a beautifully written, and more than perceptive, comment by John Hancock in note 3. After all, one of the greatest benefits brought to archaeological literature by the postprocessualist critique has been the insistence of a more self-reflective and recursive understanding of the craft of idea formation and dissemination.

2. "I am not convinced by this claim, at least in the absolute way you state it. Assumptions can be validated by theory and by comparison with other assumptions that may be made. Which assumption is then better supported by the data in the sense that it makes coherent a greater amount of the data than do alternative assumptions and even dissolves anomalies in the data that other assumptions have generated and cannot dissolve is the one we should, for now, go with. That is, assumptions are both theo-

retically validated and empirically verified relative to alternative assumptions, while still being only contingently correct, that is, all our assumptions, even when validated and verified, are still corrigible" (Byers's text comment).

3. In his review of my chapter, John Hancock made an extremely salient point in an e-mail exchange with me, and in the same vein as the Byers's comments, I wish to include his own words: "And finally the 'paradigm shifts' sentence on page 3, with reference to Thomas Kuhn, might more accurately read: 'have indeed occurred when established principles and theories become inadequate at explaining our changing experience, or accounting for new patterns that emerge in the data.' That experience and those patterns can come from anywhere, but it is the anomalies within this changing interpretive context that prompt the criticism of our theories, the invention of new and rival ones, and the growing authority of more effective ones. . . . It seems important to the thrust of the book that we not imply that new theories just somehow rise up in a vacuum or for the sake of novelty alone—that 'reexamination and postulation' take place within a context of changing experience and a certain arguable loss of functionality of the old theories." I am in absolute agreement with Hancock's perceptive view.

4. "Of course, their ideas were based on anthropological literature about the nature of human societies in contrast to a lack of such knowledge for those proposing that space aliens created England's crop circles" (Byers's text comment).

5. "I would say that every model can be shown to be incorrect in some way. However, it can only be shown to be incorrect or inadequate in comparison to another model (and the theoretical premises that it relies upon and expresses) addressing the same question or body of data. That is, we do not confront a model directly with the data but confront alternative models with the same data. If data are what make our models true, then the same data can make one model addressing them more adequate than another model addressing the same data. The one that is 'truest' or the one that 'fits' the data best is the one we go with, even though we assume that it does not fit these data completely and can be replaced by another model—in time. This reorients Popper's approach. Because it works from his premise that a model must be falsifiable, it assumes, therefore, that all models worth their name are inadequate as representations of reality. But this means that the model that is least falsifiable or has greatest resistance to being falsified—which means the model that invests the greatest coherence into the data—is the one we must logically go with, hoping that it will itself be replaced by being shown as more falsifiable than another" (Byers's text comment).

6. "I would add that we need to reconceptualize the nature of the social system and stop being imprisoned by our unitary view of Native American societies, as kinship based—this is not simply an archaeological problem but a broader anthropological problem" (Byers's text comment).

7. "I speak of cultural tradition as cosmology (collective world beliefs), ethos (collective second-order values, standards, and attitudes), world view (collective perceptual experiencing), and ideology (collective intentions). In this scheme, for lack of a better term, collective sociology (hate the term) would be that aspect of cosmology that has the social system as its complex object, the basic social structures, groups,

positions, roles, and so on. That is, the social system is a part of the cosmos (i.e., world), that part that delineates humans and their relations to each other and to all other components of the world. I do not know if this is totally coherent but I feel that the notion of collective sociology is necessary to round out the notion of cultural traditions" (Byers's text comment).

8. "Expressive interpretation? I agree with this basic sense. In my scheme, the cosmology and ethos as deep structures of a cultural tradition can be very widespread and stable in time and space, while the ideology and world view, as surface structures, can vary historically. The material features and artifacts manifest the processes of interaction, and such interaction, for example, monumental construction and use, is the realization in behavior of collective strategies, that is, ideology, with these material things acting as the conditions of satisfaction of the world view, that is, the way people perceptually experience the world, including the great features they collectively construct. Since these are the expression and realization of surface structures, they can vary across regions that share the same basic deep structures of cosmology and ethos. However, this variation will not necessarily be taken positively by different populations. The Ohio earthworks may have been perceptually experienced by groups from Illinois as polluting the world or as having lower polluting than sanctifying results because of their magnitude. I suspect that even within Ohio the different regions sustained some arm's-length constraint, each perceiving the earthworks of the other regions as somewhat less than felicitous media of ritual, and so on" (Byers's text comment).

9. "In fact, you might want to say that rather than assuming that we can ever 'truly and totally understand . . . ; our goal should be to understand better than we do now and hope that future archaeologists can surpass us. This keeps with the earlier claim you made. Remember also that context is itself a material pattern. It is not self-interpretive, and, therefore, must be interpreted. I think in my book I noted that just as we have the behavior/action duality so we have the locale/context duality. Behavior pattern then becomes a behavior process constituted as an action/activity, that is, a rule-governed behavioral process. Therefore, the realities we are trying to reconstruct through the patterns are the rules, relations, and larger structures that these patternings presuppose" (Byers's text comment).

10. I do want to note that Lepper's comments on my chapter perhaps missed the main thrust of my criticism of the utilization of Native American oral traditions and myths by archaeologists. I did not intend to mean that such sources are invalid or not useful but that we need to acknowledge the selectivity that can be involved in which particular myths/legends/traditions are chosen to support (or refute) an individual scholar's theory or idea. The selection of Native American historical or current myths or accounts, for example, may reflect an unknown bias on the part of the researcher to support their own ideas about the past. Also, and ironically, my assessment of the environment of the Newark Earthwork locality (based on historic records as well as the physical parameters of soil, slope, and the like) as most likely supporting a dense rich forest was utilized by me to argue that prehistoric humans had indeed had a profound

impact upon the biome of the region. That, in fact, the pollen data set we recovered during our excavations at the Great Circle was one data set that could be utilized to support the idea of deforestation and shift in ecological succession of the locality by the region's ancient human population. Certainly many of my publications and paper presentations have noted consistently that my view of the Hopewell as "managers of their environment" included a significant impact to their larger environments, including forest canopy density and succession, in the vicinity of earthworks as well as habitation sites.

COMMENTARY

Commentary on DeeAnne Wymer's "Where Do (Hopewell) Research Answers Come From?"

Commentary by Bradley T. Lepper

> To be sure, we hear not the voice of the prehistoric races and never shall, but may we not yet hear him speaking in the voices of our aboriginal Americans . . . ?
>
> By what we find buried in the earth we can reconstruct something of the manner of life of the prehistoric man. . . . But by confining our interpretations strictly to these remains, may we not be overlooking some valuable contribution from the lore of our first Americans? (Henry Roe Cloud, Winnebago tribal member and educator [1929: 563–564])
>
> Although archaeological science is the guiding principle, it is not the only light we shine on the shadows of the past. (Dorothy Lippert, Choctaw tribal member and archaeologist [2005: 278])

In 1992, DeeAnne Wymer and I codirected an excavation into Newark's Great Circle. When we reached the base of the earthwork and found an intact ancient soil profile, we made a bet as to what sort of paleoenvironment might be revealed in the soil samples we collected. Wymer felt the data would indicate the former presence of a dense white oak forest (see also Wymer 1996: 48) because that's what would have developed in the normal process of ecological succession. I argued that the environment would prove to have been a prairie. Historically, there had been a wet prairie around the large pond at the heart of the Newark Earthworks, and I thought this could have been a remnant of a much more extensive prairie that had been diminishing since the abandonment of the site. Ultimately, Linda Scott Cummings's analysis of pollen and phytoliths, combined with Tod Frolking's observations of the soil profile, established that the local environment had indeed been a prairie (Lepper 1998: 126; Wymer 1996: 48). Moreover, these results later were corroborated and amplified by Kendra McLauchlan's (2003) work at the Fort Ancient Earthworks. I figured I had won the bet. So imagine my surprise to find Wymer still assuming the landscape around the Hopewellian earthworks, including Newark, was covered with "dense rich forests," which would have made it difficult to build even a "simple" circle and might have precluded the ability of the inhabitants to observe astronomical phenomena occurring at or near the horizon. This interpretation, unsupported by the available data, appears to reflect a rigid adherence to a rather simplistic ecological model that denies humans a significant role in niche construction. Moreover, it suggests a knee-jerk skepticism that rejects evidence for purposeful alignments because of a priori assumptions about what the environment might have been like and what ancient people might have been capable of achieving in that assumed environment.

Why should Ohio's rich valleys have been dense, pristine forests in A.D. 100, when humans already had been occupying the region for more than 10,000 years? Early Woodland forager-gardeners as well as Archaic and even Paleoindian hunter-gatherers would have made significant modifications to the landscape, including the creation and maintenance of prairie habitat through periodic burning. So when the Hopewellian earthwork builders were looking for locations to erect their grand enclosures, surely one of their site selection criteria could have been the presence of already existing, anthropogenic prairies to minimize construction costs and, perhaps, to maximize the visible horizon for making ceremonially necessary astronomical observations.

In her now-classic analysis of the Ohio Hopewell econiche, Wymer (1996: 41) argued persuasively that Hopewell farmers had been sophisticated "managers of their environment," but she appears to apply that revolutionary idea only to the small scale of their garden patches. McLauchlan (2003: 561) documents pollen percentages at Fort Ancient that match, in some respects, assemblages from deposits associated with "extensive European-style agriculture, annually ploughed soil and road construction." Wymer is not seeing the absence-of-the-forest for the trees.

In her discussion of the "straightjacket of historical analogy," Wymer singles out my work as an example of studies by authors who feel a "need to legitimize their discussions" by appealing to more or less irrelevant or dubious ethnographic analogies. Needless to say, I was surprised by this characterization of my use of American Indian oral traditions. The traditions I referred to in the papers she cites are in no way intended to "legitimize" my discussions. As I indicated in one of these papers, my inclusion of these oral traditions primarily was an attempt to take seriously what, if anything, American Indians might have had to say about these ancient structures (Lepper 2006: 132). Wymer's dismissal of my use of these references as naive or misguided suggests a presumption that such oral traditions can have no role in elucidating the purpose and meaning of the earthworks. Intentionally or subconsciously, Wymer appears to relegate ancient American Indians to the role of relatively passive inhabitants of an imaginary "natural" wilderness, while excluding their descendants from an active role in the construction of their own history.

Certainly, oral traditions are difficult to verify and some archaeologists, such as Mason (2000), despair of gleaning anything of use to archaeology from these data. Nevertheless, a number of other scholars regard it as essential to incorporate American Indian testimony in our reconstructions of the past, when it can be construed as at all relevant (e.g., Cloud 1929; Echo-Hawk 2000; Renfrew and Bahn 1991: 369; Whiteley 2002).

I heartily agree with Wymer that the "use of simplistic anthropological analogy" should be avoided. And she also is undoubtedly right to observe that "the Hopewell were in some ways clearly unlike any known historic group." Analogies based on enthnohistoric or ethnographic data cannot possibly do justice to the rich and varied prehistoric record (e.g., Wobst 1978). Nevertheless, to suggest that American Indian oral traditions can have nothing to say that might aid in our understanding of Hopewell cultural phenomena is to imply that there is no historic connection between the Hopewell and the tribes that are known to have inhabited the eastern Woodlands. Such an assertion is tantamount to resurrecting the moundbuilder myth.

Wymer states that we "need to better understand what 'fueled' the Interaction Sphere, how goods moved throughout the land, and how this was integrated into local populations." This is one of the problems the pilgrimage model addresses (see Lepper 2006); and it is in no sense founded upon or legitimized by "simplistic anthropological analogy." It could not be, for there are no historically documented American Indian societies that engage in the construction and use of pilgrimage centers on the scale I infer for the Hopewell (e.g., Lepper 2006). It is based, fundamentally, on archaeological data combined with a cross-cultural analysis of pilgrimages. Moreover, there are independent archaeological data that can be used to test the model (see, for examples, Cowan, Sunderhaus, and Genheimer 2004 and Vickery 1996: 123). My use of American Indian oral traditions is not a substitute for developing and exploring "alternative ideas" as Wymer claims. It is, instead, one way of introducing alternative ideas to archaeological interpretation and respecting the testimony of the descendants of the people whom we are studying.

SECTION 6

Hopewell Settlement Patterns and Symbolic Landscapes

12

Coda

Still Seeking "Hopewell"

N'omi B. Greber

It is an honor and a responsibility to compose a coda for this collection of papers and conversations. Each chapter adds to our view of "Hopewell," and the conversations refine this view by providing a "whole that is greater than the sum of the parts," allowing synthesis of separate ideas. I hope that this approach in writing will encourage more actual conversations at meetings, such as the sessions on Oneota that took place at the 2007 Midwest Archaeological Conference. I look forward to participating with the authors in this volume and with other interested individuals in such sessions.

In the usual literary style, while reading a paper one can frequently hear the voice of the author, which allows an appreciation of the personal context for the ideas and information put forth in the writing. In the conversations in this volume, one more clearly hears the voice of each speaker and thus may possibly gain a glimpse of his or her "being-in-the world," a context eloquently described by John E. Hancock. We all speak from within our own culture and must work toward finding some entry into others. I urge readers to listen to all the voices herein. Although individual interests and research strategies appropriately vary, one can find useful and thought-stretching information from voices that speak in different dialects.

In this coda, an ending rather than a summary, I do not presume to provide a synthesis or overview of the presentations and the conversations. The editors, A. Martin Byers and DeeAnne Wymer, have ably written introductions and abstracts. Rather, I muse a bit about concepts of theory and data in general terms that, as the editors note, are integral to all archaeological research (see also Hegmon 2003). Then I consider a few examples of the relevance of these concepts to "Hopewell" studies, as inspired by the contributions herein. In particular, I consider where, when, who, and, more important, what distinguishes the "Hopewell" associated with various patterns perceived in the several material and abstract systems portrayed in this volume. My notes are not unique, in that they touch upon articulated views of the present authors and of many others including myself.

Frameworks for Thinking

In seeking to better understand the peoples we call Hopewell, we all must deal with basic dimensions of time, space, and peoples, both cosmological and practical. Time can be linear, from a beginning to an end, or at least on-going. This type of time appears to be the one that we tend to emphasize as we write about Paleoindian to Cultures in Contact. Or time can be cyclic, in either natural or cultural cycles: patterns in the sky or culturally determined anniversaries. Space includes the physical environment of rivers, hills, mead-ows, and perhaps the seashore, the home of a conch that was carried inland. These spatial elements provide natural divides. Or space, and divisions within it, may be cultural as determined by peoples using their material cultures and following their being-in-the-world. The latter may be illusive. We define pa-rameters of peoples from archaeological remains, ancient and modern texts and books, and the peoples we can see and listen to now. Time, space, and peoples can be measured (articulated) in concrete and abstract units.

> Theory: Systematically organized knowledge applicable in a relatively wide variety of circumstances; especially, a system of assumptions, ac-cepted principles, and rules of procedure devised to analyze, predict, or otherwise explain the nature or behavior of a specified set of phenom-ena. (*Heritage Illustrated Dictionary of the English Language*, Interna-tional ed., ed. William Morris [Boston: Houghton Mifflin, 1979], 1335)

Theories, whether called archaeological theories, models, frameworks, tax-onomies, or whatever, are not independent of data, that is, descriptions of elements from time, space, and peoples. We know from the physical sciences that Kepler could not have devised his "model" of our solar system without the data collected by Tycho Brahe. Einstein devised an intellectual revolution based on the astronomers' description of the universe known to them at the time. Darwin contemplated the marvels of the creatures he saw and collected, and devised a model of the path their ancestors had taken. His ideas are more likely to appear in archaeological discussions than those of Einstein. For ex-ample, as given in the introduction to the present volume, a general goal in ar-chaeological studies is "understanding the larger picture of cultural evolution." We should remember, as we borrow the term used in linear time by biology, that "evolution" also has a wider meaning of "change," even in cyclic time. A useful example of a definition of taxonomies that applies to other frameworks used in archaeology is set out in the first paragraph of a recent study of a "Post-Hopewellian Archaeological Unit."

> They become the language of explanation if they help increase our understanding of the data. Conversely, if our taxa do not provide useful insights, either because they were poorly conceived in the first place, or, more typically, because new data have introduced qualitatively different relationships, they should be changed or discarded. (Dancey and Seeman 2005: 134)

In all branches of human knowledge, when we devise some manner in which to "explain the nature or behavior of a specified set of phenomena," we begin with assumptions. An assumption may be useful or not useful to the reader; we cannot validate or prove it, but we can "disprove" it by finding data that contradict the assumption. This is not a superficial problem but lies at the root of all knowledge. We should be particularly careful when assumptions become accepted common wisdom. Remember, that about a century ago, kings and fields of corn were assumed to be required for building great physical monuments in the Central Ohio Valley. Today, we discuss "social integration" rather than forced labor. My predilection for emphasizing the role of data is illustrated in one of my favorite e-mail messages: "*N'omi, no more data. It stifles the imagination.*" Fortunately, "it" has not and will not. Plentiful new views and differing assumptions regularly (cyclically?) appear. New data can jolt current common wisdom and hasten new views. An example of this may come from recent reviews of widely accepted definitions of the beginning or ending time of Ohio Hopewell (e.g., Lynott 2007, Railey 1991, Richmond and Kerr 2005). Considerations of warrants, "Riverworlds," the design of sacred or secular spaces—all have begun with objects, whether tools, a physical environment, walls, mounds, or variously sized structures, found by archaeologists. Interpretations of the data begin in a view (theory? hypothesis?) devised by an inquiring mind. The same data have been interpreted in differing ways, and the usefulness of these genuine differences for answering particular questions of interest is determined by the reader (e.g., Greber 1976; Byers 2004; Clay 1991, 2003).

"Hopewell" Across the Eastern Woodlands

The easiest elements to start with when describing "Hopewell" are elements of space. Traditionally, units at different scales are used in accordance with the questions being studied: the Eastern Woodlands, the Middle Ohio Valley, the tributary valleys of the Ohio (most frequently those north of the river, but some recent studies include those on the south), and other regional spatial units scattered across the Eastern Woodlands, defined by a portion of a river valley or some other geographic parameter. Physical environments vary across these spaces as they likely did centuries ago. There is no single type of "Hopewell" physical space. Thus one can conclude that the local subsistence strategies also likely varied (Smith 2006: 501–502). The family spaces described by Doug Charles and Paul Pacheco from broadly separated locations have similarities, but the overall settlement patterns differ. This is apparently due in part to differences in the physical environments that may indicate differences in subsistence. However, it is also due to differing political, social, and economic elements that distinguish the Hopewell peoples of the lower Illinois Valley from those in the central Scioto. Some part of these differences may have its origin in the particular histories.

For example, a contrast exists between the suggested migration history of lower Illinois "Hopewell" into a "vacant" land and the apparent long-term usage of sites in the central Scioto, as seen in recent data from Hopeton and the Hopewell site (Lynott 2007; Weinberger and Pederson 2006) and apparently at Liberty and Seip (Coughlin and Seeman 1997; Greber 1995, 2003). Earlier work has established the long-term commitment to construction at the Fort Ancient and Pollock Works in the Little Miami Valley (Connolly and Lepper 2004, Riordan 2006). The intensity of site use likely varied through time. Some earthwork sites came to "carry the weight of history" as special spaces (Seeman and Branch 2006: 121). A migration into a new area by a group of people suggests a social cohesiveness that is not apparent across the local regions in the central Scioto. One should note that this is comparing several river valleys with one another.

Significant differences in the local archaeological materials occur not only in the lower Illinois and the central Scioto but also within other major geographic sections of "Hopewell." Clearly, the major earthwork walls that are heavily emphasized in this volume—enclosures that are located mainly in Ohio—do not occur in the known archaeological record from Illinois. They do in the land between, in Indiana at Mann (Ruby 1997b; Ruby and Shriner 2005). All these enclosure and linear earthworks vary in ground plan, construction materials and designs, and building and use time, and likely concomitantly they vary in "purpose" as seen in the builders and users conscious decisions and their being-in-the-world. In Ohio the community associated with a site could vary in size, composition, and type of relationship through time. Warren DeBoer, Ray Hively, and Bob Horn seek monolithic ideas that could indicate a strong common cultural thread through linear time in the

Scioto Valley. If found, this is still a different type of cohesion from that seen in a migrant group.

At any point in time, is the place of these enclosures in the settlement pattern comparable to that of the mounds that occur as earthworks in both areas and in other localities of the Eastern Woodlands? Mounds, just as enclosure walls, display variations in attributes. Were there differences between the total societal resources needed to plan and construct Newark Earthworks, Ohio, as compared to Mound House, Illinois? Clearly, the total physical requirements were greater at Newark, but a relatively simple social system of shared organizational leadership by generally autonomous social units, based on an agreed-upon time cycle, could exist independent of any individual leader. However, it is also likely that to begin the process, ground plans needed to be set by the right person(s) in the right place at the right time.

I have been struck by the similarities between a ceremonial-ritual-cemetery mound space in Illinois (Figure 12.1) and the classic space that Greenman excavated and used as a basis for his analysis of the Adena culture (Figure 12.2). Assuming a possible earlier time period for this Ohio Adena suggests a difference in linear time as well as differences between "Hopewell" material remains in Illinois and those in central Ohio. From a different perspective, variations between Illinois Hopewell and Ohio Hopewell have also been noted by James Brown (1979). New evidence also points to an earlier beginning of "Hopewell" in Illinois than in Ohio. Katharine Ruhl has suggested that the origins of the bi-cymbal earspool, one of the few items actually found across the Eastern Woodlands during Middle Woodland times, were in Illinois despite the vast number of these found in Ohio (Ruhl 2005). Recent studies have identified an Illinois site as the apparent source of the pipestone used to make a number of platform pipes found in a section of the Tremper Big House (Emerson et al. 2005). Traditionally, Tremper is placed earlier in time than the major central Scioto sites. Its enclosing earthwork is simple in design. Its several sectioned Big House and adjacent apparent work areas formed a style of ground plan different from that seen in the central Scioto. The imported pipes add to the suggestion that dimensions of time need to be considered in discussions comparing Hopewell peoples of the lower Illinois Valley and those of the Scioto Valley.

One (or more) person(s) walked from Illinois to the mouth of the Scioto River at some point in time carrying one (or more) gifts. It was Mauss (1967: 37) who pointed out that the giving and receiving of material cultural items as gifts generates and/or reproduces reciprocal social relations through constituting obligations for the interacting parties to strategically "repay" these

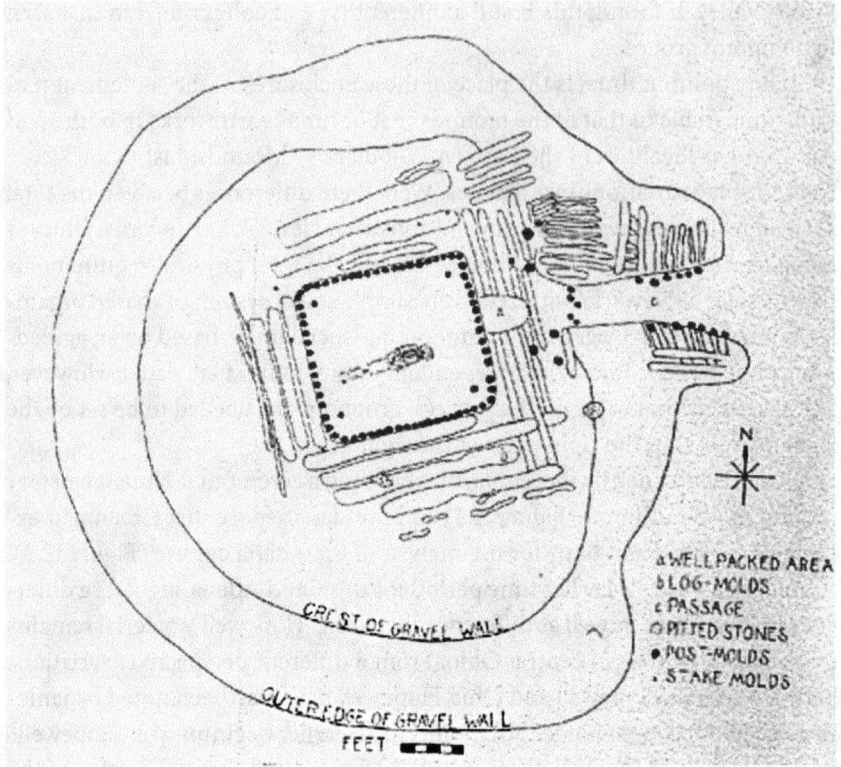

A

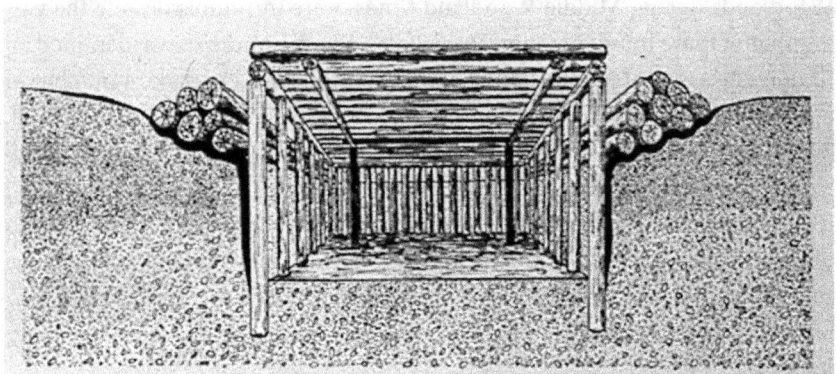

B

Figure 12.1. A: Plan of the floor and strata edges of the Coon Mound (Greenman 1932: Figure 6). B: Artist reconstruction of the central tomb (from Greenman 1932: Figure 22). Courtesy of the Ohio Historical Society.

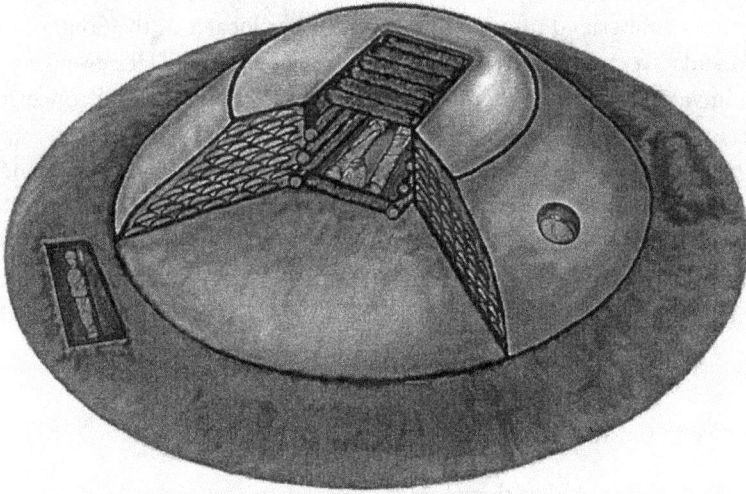

Figure 12.2. Artist rendition of a "typical" Middle Woodland Illinois mound (from Buikstra and Charles 1999: Figure 9). Reproduced with permission of Blackwell Publishing Ltd.

items. We do not know where the person(s) carrying the pipes, probably as gifts, began the journey. Perhaps Ohio, perhaps Illinois, perhaps elsewhere. The acquisition of the pipes more likely occurred during a peaceful encounter rather than in dealings with traditional enemies for ritually required items (Ford 1972) or while traveling to "far places" at the edge of the "known world" to secure powerful materials, such as obsidian or silver (e.g., DeBoer 2004; Cowan and Greber 2002; Spence and Feyer 2005). This does not mean that the pipes themselves did not have symbolic meanings attached to them. Prescribed songs, chants, and other specific ways in which they were to be used were likely separately acquired or emulated by the gift bearers. These rituals were then translated into ways appropriate to the local being-in-the-world at the confluence of the Scioto and Ohio rivers.

Another connecting journey between the lower Illinois and the central Scioto, some 45 miles upstream of Tremper, is suggested by a recent DNA study identifying a person interred in Illinois who was a possible relative of someone interred at the Hopewell site (Bolnick and Smith 2007). Migration is again an acceptable explanation in archaeology but not necessarily useful in describing the origins of Ohio Hopewell. The details of "Hopewell" peoples entering Ohio and forcing "Adena" peoples to move to the east coast have been refuted by data acquired since 1963 (Dragoo 1963: 282–294). I will make some additional comments on possible relationships among "Adena" and "Hopewell" peoples in the Middle Ohio Valley following a theoretical journey that continues eastward from Illinois through Indiana and the Ohio River valley, then along the Cumberland into Tennessee and other locales in the Southeastern Woodlands, to end in present day Georgia and Florida. "Hopewell" exists, again in variable forms, along the way. The observations of Ruhl concerning the technical and stylistic aspects of the copper earspools that were an important item in "Hopewell" describe what may be the ending time of the phenomenon at sites in the Southeast where the earspools fall at the far end of the Ruhl seriation (Ruhl 2005). On this particular path, the trend of "Hopewell" linear time appears to go from west to east, perhaps as an old-fashioned example of cultural diffusion. A more complicated time line would likely be found by taking a path crossing other areas north, south, and west of Illinois.

"Hopewell" in the Middle Ohio Valley

There is no question that the peoples living in the several tributaries of the middle Ohio River knew and interacted with one another, but the types of interactions likely varied, as did the specific combination of interacting groups or individuals through time. Questions have been raised for several decades concerning relationships between the archaeological materials labeled "Adena" and "Hopewell" (Swartz 1971). These include not only variations in interpretations of these remains, as suggested by Martin, but also suggestions by those now working with new data and reviewing old records that these two sets of archaeological materials represent a single cultural phenomenon in the Middle Ohio Valley. This phenomenon was expressed differently through time in local regions (e.g., Clay 2005; Greber 1991, 2005; Greber and Clay 1993; Richmond and Kerr 2005). One attribute that was shared across this space through time is the use of copper. The amount of the metal, the forms of the objects made, and their depositional context vary. For example, copper was used to emphasize the eyes of some animal effigies from Tremper, while pearls were more commonly used in the central Scioto major sites. The most unusual object I have seen is an effigy flared-end tubular pipe of copper from Connett Mound 7, The Plains, in the Hocking Valley (Greber 2005: Figure 2.3). The archaeological materials in this area traditionally have been labeled "Adena"—which would fit in well with a flared-end stone pipe. The limited number of radiocarbon dates from The Plains, however, fall within the traditional Hopewell era (Abrams and Freter 2005: 107). The ritual-ceremonial-social remains described by William Webb and his collaborators share themes with the central Scioto Hopewell sites, but with a less elaborate manifestation in the wider geographic area that includes the Hocking and the southern tributaries of the Middle Ohio River (Webb and Snow 1945, Webb and Baby

1957). One can chose to call a particular set of archaeological remains "Adena" or "Hopewell," but for a reader to have a useful understanding of the choice, it is necessary to append the geographical location of the materials. One must look to the history of each local space to find factors that influenced culture change and resulted in the differing archaeological remains found during Middle Woodland times.

By considering possible relationships among the sites traditionally included in Ohio Hopewell from the Great Miami to the mouth of the Muskingum, one can recognize both separate local expressions, even within the central Scioto region such as Mound City and the Hopewell site, and close ties at some points in time. An example of the latter, as I have much discussed, joins the five major earthwork sites with related ground plans (e.g., Greber 1997a: 219). The Hopewell site, frequently considered the type site for the widespread phenomenon that shares its name, might be called a "type" site because it has a bit of everything considered Ohio Hopewell (Greber and Ruhl 1989). However, in addition, there are excessive amounts of some things, including copper, that skew any distributional studies. Copper is an exotic, widespread, unevenly distributed raw material within southern Ohio. The quantity per site falls off significantly from that found at Hopewell Mound 25. The next largest amount is associated with Seip-Pricer, the second largest Ohio Hopewell mound (Seeman 1977). An unusual use of copper at these two sites strongly suggests close interactions.

The treatment, possibly postmortem, of two pairs of individuals, one pair interred in the westernmost structure covered by the Central Mound of Mound 25 and the other in a small structure (large tomb) adjoined to the larger section of the Seip-Pricer Big House, is recorded nowhere else in Ohio Hopewell. Folded copper pieces were placed into the nose opening of the skulls of the extended burials and rods of copper appeared to have been used as hair ornaments (Shetrone 1926; Shetrone and Greenman 1931). A line of copper earspools surrounded the Mound 25 interments, while lines of pearls were placed at Seip-Pricer.

The sense of the Hopewell site as a place has both a local side and a pilgrimage side. We do not know the home places of pilgrims; there were likely several such localities. Some visitors came from relatively nearby and others from medium to far distances. A range of separate ritual-ceremonial-civic activities and constructions occurred at the site. These constructions were eventually decommissioned and separately mantled by mounds ranging in size from the smallest to the largest Ohio Hopewell mound.

I interpret the space covered by Mound 2, the Great Flint Mound, as a possible example of interregional interactions involving the Hopewell site.

At some point in time, a person or persons brought gifts by walking from the Little Miami (possibly Turner) to the North Fork of Paint Creek. Stone constructions, both tombs and plaza walkways, are commonly found in the Little Miami but are few in the central Scioto. A unique stone grave was built on the ritual floor, and two carefully arranged layers of thousands of Wyandotte bifaces were deposited, and the total was covered by Mound 2. These bifaces were likely not chipped at the site but brought as finished pieces. The raw material (a.k.a Harrison County flint or Indiana hornstone) came from south-central Indiana and is relatively common in southwestern Ohio. It was likely one of the special materials appreciated by Ohio Hopewell peoples since it has been found in reasonable quantities not far from Flint Ridge, the source of high-grade and beautifully colored flint used extensively by Ohio Hopewell knappers. Perhaps the quantities of Wyandotte and Flint Ridge bladelets Pacheco describes from the Murphy IV site reflect the complementary nature of these materials. An earspool in the Ohio Historical Society collections that was probably recovered from Hopewell Mound 2 falls at the far end of the Ruhl seriation, possibly reflecting the work of a copper master at Turner (Greber 2003: 96–97, Figure 6.4; Ruhl 1992, 1996; Ruhl and Seeman 1998).

A closer symbolic cultural tie between Turner and Hopewell is reflected in the remarkable complementary pairs of deposits of objects and materials that contained the majority of artifacts associated with Ohio Hopewell. One pair of complementary deposits was found at Turner and two pairs were found at Hopewell (Greber 1996). A possible time overlap exists between the use of the lands within and about the enclosures at Turner and at the Hopewell site. This suggests that all pairs may have been placed in a "relatively" short span in the Hopewell era, even though the total time span and/or intensity in the use of each site likely differs (Greber 2003). The details of the paired deposits differ, and the design of the associated ritual-ceremonial-civic-social spaces at the two sites differs even more. In general, at Turner the designs of the floors beneath the single mounds found within the major enclosure have more in common than the wider range found at the Hopewell site.

Turner is unique among the Ohio Hopewell sites in having interments covered by a portion of the major enclosure wall (Willoughby and Hooton 1922: 6–13). At Turner the major buildings containing ritual facilities, such as clay basins and major deposits of symbolic objects, were physically separate from the largest known cemetery area (Willoughby and Hooton 1922; Greber 1996), while at Hopewell Mound 25 and other central Scioto sites such as Seip, large groups of interments shared a common activity floor with major artifact deposits. (As would be expected, since the Hopewell site includes the "range" of Ohio Hopewell manifestation, no interments were on the floor covered by

Shetrone Mound 17, where one pair of major deposits had been placed, but other small mounds covered extensive deposits and interments such as Mound 2 and Moorehead Mound 17.) At Turner the series of seven ritual structures containing ritual clay basins was covered by conjoined mounds. The construction, design, and deposition of ritual basins (specialized clay hearths that are a basic element in Ohio Hopewell ceremonial-rituals [Seeman and Greber 1991]) significantly differ at Turner (Greber 1996: 159–164). At least four pairs of ritual basins occur under Mounds 5, 7, and 9 that contrast in plan form (circle/rectangle) and in deliberate fill (dark/light). In addition, numbers of Turner basins were built and left in a stratified context (Greber 1996: Figure 9.8). No such superpositioning has been found at the Hopewell site. In the Scioto Valley, only at Mound City was a ritual floor and basin placed over another (Brown 1979). The two ritual basins holding the major deposits at Turner were in separate structures that were part of the major ceremonial area. They had a somewhat rectangular shape similar to those found in the central Scioto, but with unique trilobed shaped corners rather than simple rounded ones that are more common elsewhere (Greber 1996: Figure 9.9).

In general the artifact styles at Turner differ from those at Hopewell; however, this is not unexpected for any major (or even small) site. A more important difference between Turner and Hopewell is the difference in the overall site plan and use. As previously mentioned, within the major enclosure at Turner the designs of ritual spaces covered by separate mounds outside the central ceremonial area are more similar to each other than are those at the Hopewell site. As also mentioned above, unusual but similar mortuary practices occurred at Seip and Hopewell, significantly different from any at Turner, suggesting some type of close tie between neighboring Scioto tributaries. Various types of intraregional ties are also suggested in other material aspects of Scioto sites (Greber 1979a, 1979b, 1983, 1997a). Perhaps a technical study of the source of the material used in making the well-known figures found at Turner might suggest interregional interactions between Turner and the Mann site on the Ohio River in Indiana, west of Turner (Ruby and Shriner 2005).

Other connections between the Little Miami and the central Scioto would almost of necessity have occurred during the Hopewell era. Hints of a connection and another possible walk that may have begun in the Little Miami appear to me to be represented by the only stone tomb built within the larger section of the Seip-Pricer Big House. Again, this is a unique construction. The cremated remains within this tomb included an adult and a child (Shetrone and Greenman 1931: Burial 10, Figure 15; Greber 1976: Figures 6a, 16). Was this a "foreign" spouse who arrived through a different type of interaction from that seen in Hopewell site Mound 2? The paths along which persons walked from the Little Miami to the central Scioto during the Hopewell era were most likely a part of intersecting trails that joined areas of the Eastern Woodlands in a manner similar to those traveled in 1751 by Christopher Gist, a frontier guide. These trails tended to follow the uplands along waterways, likely using the rivers as maps but avoiding the marshes and other obstructions along the river banks. Traveling westward from the upper Ohio, Gist took parts of trails that intersected at Maguck, an Indian settlement near present-day Circleville, Ohio, less than 20 miles north of Mound City. From Maguck, trails went north to Sandusky on Lake Erie, westward to the Great Miami and passing near the headwaters of the Little Miami, southward along the east side of the Scioto to the Ohio River, and east toward Newark and beyond (Greber 2006: 101). Gist took the southward trail from Maguck toward Portsmouth at the mouth of the Scioto, where the Portsmouth Earthworks stretched for many miles along the Ohio River. Perhaps if he had continued westward he would have passed near the site of the Manring Mounds.

> Available environmental data fail to clarify the curious nature of this site location. . . . Probably more important in understanding the Manring site location than any relationship with the Mad river drainage is the site's relationship to other drainages. The upper reaches of 3 other drainages, the Little Miami River, Paint Creek, and Deer Creek, lie respectively within 3, 11, and 10 km of the site over easily traveled ground. The site thus lies at a point with easy access to the Great Miami, Little Miami, and Scioto drainages. (Seeman and Cramer 1982: 152)

Gist did not mention trails along the Muskingum that I assume were also walked by Ohio Hopewell people. At some point in time a person or persons with knowledge of the appropriate design for a major enclosure likely walked south from the great earthworks at Newark to Marietta, an Ohio Hopewell outpost on the Ohio River (Greber 1990; Pickard 1996).

The contrasting dualities described above and others used by authors in this volume, are included in one of my favorite frameworks for viewing Ohio Hopewell. Dualities in many forms are easy to find—perhaps too easy. The formal description of them as used in Levi-Strauss's *Introduction to the Science of Mythology* (1975) fits well with the many discussions of cosmology and symbolic landscapes and artifacts that occur in both older and more recent literature on Ohio Hopewell peoples in which authors, including myself, are looking for the results of both conscious and being-in-the-world behaviors. As an example, the cultural rules in the implementation of the copper/mica–red/white contrast appear to place the importance of raw material over that of object form. Effigies of human hands or torsos were made from either copper or mica. One custom I am still trying to understand better is the apparent accept-ability of interchanging circular and square shapes. For example, a rounded swastika design was carved on the back of the head of a human effigy pipe from Edwin Harness while a square outline was used for the two opposing copper cutout swastika forms from the Copper Deposit of Hopewell Mound 25. Could such an interchange occur in the design of single or neighboring enclosures?

End of Coda

Who were the Hopewell? They were a mosaic of rational, intelligent, gifted peoples scattered through space and time. They did not speak the same lan-guage or share identical forms of political and social organizations. Each group likely had its own version of acceptable religious practices and its own interpretations of the few nonperishable symbolic items that were made lo-cally, following widely shared forms. Their subsistence strategies, I assume, allowed them in their homes to make rational decisions in their own way by which to put the time and effort needed into their great celebrations and physical constructions that would maintain the balance of yin/yang, dark/light, upland/lowland, circle/polygon, empty/filled, clan/cult, domestic shrine/regional altar, private/public, ancestor/descendent, conscientiousness/being, family compound/great enclosure, earth/sky (what do we do with wa-ter?), or whatever expression of duality was important to them. They chose to work to ensure that the moon would complete its travels and the great hawks would return, and for some generations, a great cycle would repeat, perhaps with some modification, as the sun rises on a new world's order. We still have a limited understanding of what these worlds were and how they may have been connected through time and space. Which elements remained stable through the more than half a millennium of the Hopewell era? Which ele-ments changed, especially at each local level, to influence the rhythm of the rise and fall of activities across the Eastern Woodlands during the Middle Woodland time period?

As we break apart a monolithic "Hopewell" into elements separated in space, time, and material remains, we still seek to find an "Interaction Sphere" that somehow contains the "what" that defines the essence of whatever "Hopewell" was. That is, we apparently still sense a unity that we have not yet clarified but strive to recreate (Charles and Buikstra 2006). New archaeological data and technologies have identified both original sources and locales where people acquired apparently special materials, but we cannot yet tell the human gen-eration or generations in which the relatively few concrete nonperishable materials actually moved. It is increasingly clear that all objects and knowledge acquired local interpretations. The literal meaning may change as religious becomes secular or as esoteric knowledge such as concerns of events in the sky must be translated into the local physical and social environment (Hively and Horn 2006a). The details of the interactions have numerous possibilities, as noted by many authors (e.g., Ruby and Shriner 2005: 569–572; Chapman 2006: 527–528). A main difficulty in sorting out the most reasonable possibilities is the lack of a linear time scale at the fineness, not only of human generations but even to decades as suggested for interpretations of the acquisition of silver. Hopefully new technologies or the ability to better apply present technologies such as DNA testing will arise to help us gather data needed to evaluate the suggested theories.

> It is clear now that the distribution of Hopewellian [raw] materials and, occasionally, artifacts, was achieved through a wide variety of procurement mechanisms and interpersonal links, which by their nature were unstable over time, rather than through ongoing, structured exchanges among regional groups. This picture suggests that regions, even particular communities, should have experienced some fluctuations and even dislocations in their supply over time. (Spence and Fryer 2005: 730)

We each travel a different path toward the being-in-the-world of these peoples. I often wonder how we avoid the rocks and gaping holes in the paths; sometimes we do not. On our way we see many different horizons or vistas among the trees. Putting our experiences together we will likely provide a better approximation of that which we seek than can any single view. We need careful field archaeologists for data, creative storytellers for stretching our thinking and for fun. In other words, as DeeAnne quoted Charles Redmond, we need those who will "put forward interesting propositions, providing enough information for others to determine whether a dialogue should be pursued." It is dialogue we need.

References

Abrams, Elliot M., and Ann Corrinne Freter (editors)
2005 *The Emergence of the Moundbuilders: The Archaeology of Tribal Societies in Southeastern Ohio.* Ohio University Press, Athens.
Addington, James A.
1977 Archaeological Survey Report, LIC-Jo Ann Rd., Newark, Ohio. Manuscript on file. Ohio Department of Transportation, Bureau of Environmental Services, Columbus.
Anderson, Alun
1991 Britain's Crop Circles: Reaping by Whirlwind? *Science* 253: 961.
Anonymous
1999 Crop Circle Hoaxes. *Skeptic* 7: 12.
Anschuetz, Kurt F., Richard H. Wilshusen, and Cherie L. Scheick
2001 An Archaeology of Landscapes: Perspectives and Directions. *Journal of Archaeological Research* 9: 157–211.
Appy, Ernest F.
1887 Address before the Pioneer Picnic. *Newark Weekly American*, July 28. Newark, Ohio.
Asch, Nancy B., Richard I. Ford, and David L. Asch
1972 *Paleoethnobotany of the Koster Site: The Archaic Horizons.* Reports of Investigations No. 24. Illinois State Museum, Springfield.
Ashmore, Wendy, and A. Bernard Knapp (editors)
1999 *Archaeologies of Landscape: Contemporary Perspectives.* Blackwell, London.
Atwater, Caleb
1820 [1997] *A Description of the Antiquities Discovered in Ohio and Other Western States.* Transactions and Collections I, Archaeologica Americana. American Antiquarian Society, Worcester, Mass. Also in *Archaeologia Americana* 1: 105–267. 1997 facsimile reprint of original. Arthur W. McGraw, Chillicothe, Ohio.
Aveni, Anthony F.
2004 An Assessment of Studies in Hopewell Astronomy. In *Fort Ancient Earthworks: Prehistoric Lifeways of the Hopewell Culture in Southwestern Ohio*, edited by Robert P. Connolly and Bradley T. Lepper, pp. 243–258. Ohio Historical Society, Columbus.
Aveni, Anthony F. (editor)
2008 *Foundations of New World Cultural Astronomy.* University Press of Colorado, Boulder.
Baby, Raymond S., and Susan M. Langlois
1979 Seip Mound State Memorial: Non-Mortuary Aspects of Hopewell. In *Hopewell*

Archaeology: The Chillicothe Conference, edited by David S. Brose and N'omi B. Greber, pp. 16–18. Kent State University Press, Kent, Ohio.

Bachelard, Gaston

1964 *The Poetics of Space*. Beacon Press, Boston.

Bamforth, Douglas E.

1986 Technological Efficiency and Tool Curation. *American Antiquity* 51: 38–50.

Barton, C. Michael, and Geoffrey A. Clark (editors)

1997 *Rediscovering Darwin: Evolutionary Theory and Archeological Explanation*. Archeological Papers of the American Anthropological Association No. 7. American Anthropological Association, Arlington, Va.

Bauer, Brian S., and Charles Stanish

2001 *Ritual and Pilgrimage in the Ancient Andes: The Islands of the Sun and Moon*. University of Texas Press, Austin.

Becker, Marshall

1979 Priests, Peasants, and Ceremonial Centers: The Intellectual History of a Model. In *Maya Archaeology and Ethnohistory*, edited by Norman Hammond and Gordon R. Willey, pp. 3–20. University of Texas Press, Austin.

Beers, F. W.

1866 *Atlas of Licking County, Ohio*. Beers, Soule, New York.

Bender, Barbara

1985 Emergent Tribal Formations in the American Midcontinent. *American Antiquity* 50 (1): 52–62.

1998 *Stonehenge: Making Space*. Berg, Oxford.

Bender, Barbara (editor)

1993 *Landscape: Politics and Perspectives*. Berg, Oxford.

Bender, Barbara, Susan Hamilton, and Christopher Tilley

1997 Leskernick: Stone Worlds; Alternative Narrative; Nested Landscapes. *Proceedings of the Prehistoric Society* 63: 147–178.

Bernardini, Wesley

2004 Hopewell Geometric Earthworks: A Case Study in the Referential and Experiential Meaning of Monuments. *Journal of Anthropological Archaeology* 23: 331–356.

Bernhardt, Jack E.

1976 A Preliminary Survey of Middle Woodland Prehistory in Licking County, Ohio. *Pennsylvania Archaeologist* 46: 39–54.

Binford, Lewis R.

1962 Archaeology as Anthropology. *American Antiquity* 28: 217–225.

1968 Post-Pleistocene Adaptations. In *New Perspectives in Archeology*, edited by Sally R. Binford and Lewis R. Binford, pp. 313–341. Aldine, Chicago.

1972 Archaeology as Anthropology. In *An Archaeological Perspective*, by Lewis R. Binford, pp. 20–32. Seminar Press, New York.

1979 Organization and Formation Processes: Looking at Curated Technologies. *Journal of Anthropological Research* 35: 255–273.

1980 Willow Smoke and Dog's Tails: Hunter-gatherer Settlement Systems and Archaeological Site Formation. *American Antiquity* 45: 1–17.

1982 The Archaeology of Place. *Journal of Anthropological Archaeology* 1: 5–33.

1983 *Working at Archaeology*. Academic Press, New York.

1987 Data, Relativism, and Archaeological Science. *Man* (new series) 22: 391–404.

1988 Review of *Reading the Past: Current Approaches to Interpretation in Archaeology*, by I. Hodder. *American Antiquity* 53: 875–876.

1989 *Debating Archaeology*. Academic Press, New York.

2001 Where Do Research Answers Come From? *American Antiquity* 66: 669–679.

Binford, Lewis R., and Sally R. Binford

1972 Archaeological Perspectives. In *An archaeological Perspective*, by Lewis R. Binford, pp. 78–104. Seminar Press, New York.

Bird, M. I., and J. A. Cali

1998 A Million-Year Record of Fire in Sub-Saharan Africa. *Nature* 394: 767–769.

Bhaskar, Roy

1978 *A Realist Theory of Science*. Harvester Press, Hassocks, Sussex.

1979 *The Possibility of Naturalism*. Humanities Press, Atlantic Highlands, N.J.

Blank, John

1965 The Brown's Bottom Site. *Ohio Archaeologist* 15 (1): 16–21.

1972 *Archaeological Investigations in the Salt Creek Reservoir, Ohio: Season I, the Drake Terrace Site (33Vi11)*. Report of Investigations, National Park Service Contract number 14-10-5-950-39.

Bleed, Peter

1986 The Optimal Design of Hunting Weapons: Maintainability or Reliability. *American Antiquity* 51: 737–747.

Bloor, David

1976 *Knowledge and Social Imagery*. Routledge and Kegan Paul, London.

Blosser, Jack K.

1996 The 1984 Excavations at 12D29s: A Middle Woodland Village in Southeastern Indiana. In *A View from the Core: A Synthesis of Ohio Hopewell Archaeology*, edited by Paul J. Pacheco, pp. 54–68. Ohio Archaeological Council, Columbus.

Bogucki, Peter

1987 The Establishment of Agrarian Communities on the Northern European Plain. *Current Anthropology* 28: 1–24.

Bolnick, Deborah A., and David Glenn Smith

2007 Migration and Social Structure Among the Hopewell: Evidence from Ancient DNA. *American Antiquity* 72 (4): 627–644.

Bowser, Brenda J. (editor)

2004 Recent Advances in the Archaeology of Place, Parts I and II. *Journal of Archaeological Method and Theory* 11 (1–2).

Bradley, Richard

1993 *Altering the Earth: The Origins of Monuments in Britain and Continental Europe*. Monograph Series No. 8. Society of Antiquaries of Scotland, Edinburgh.

2000 *An Archaeology of Natural Places*. Routledge, London.

Braudel, Fernand

1972 *The Mediterranean and the Mediterranean World in the Age of Philip II*. Translated by S. Reynolds. Harper and Row, New York.

Braun, David P.

1987 Coevolution of Sedentism, Pottery Technology, and Horticulture in the Central Midwest. In *Emergent Horticultural Economies of the Eastern Woodlands*, edited by William Keegan, pp. 201–216. Center for Archaeological Investigations, Occasional Paper No. 7. Southern Illinois University Press, Carbondale.

1991 Are There Cross-Cultural Regularities in Tribal Social Practices? In *Between Bands and States*, edited by Susan A. Gregg, pp. 423–444. Center for Archaeological Investigations, Occasional Paper No. 9. Southern Illinois University Press, Carbondale.

Brinton, Daniel G.

1890 Folk-lore of the Modern Lenape. In *Essays of an Americanist*, by D. G. Brinton, pp. 181–192. David McKay, Philadelphia.

Broda, Johanna

1993 Astronomical Knowledge, Calendrics, and Sacred Geography in Ancient Mesoamerica. In *Astronomies and Cultures*, edited by Clive Ruggles and Nicholas J. Saunders, pp. 253–295. University Press of Colorado, Niwot.

Brose, David S.

1979 A Speculative Model of the Role of Exchange in the Prehistory of the Eastern Woodlands. In *Hopewell Archaeology: The Chillicothe Conference*, edited by David S. Brose and N'omi B. Greber, pp. 3–8. Kent State University Press, Kent, Ohio.

1990 Toward a Model of Exchange Values for the Eastern Woodlands. *Midcontinental Journal of Archaeology* 15: 100–136.

Brown, James A.

1979 Charnel Houses and Mortuary Crypts: Disposal of the Dead in the Middle Woodland Period. In *Hopewell Archaeology: The Chillicothe Conference*, edited by David S. Brose and N'omi B. Greber, pp. 211–219. Kent State University Press, Kent, Ohio.

1997 The Archaeology of Ancient Religion in the Eastern Woodlands. *Annual Review of Anthropology* 26: 465–485.

1982 Mound City and the Vacant Ceremonial Center. Paper presented at the 47th annual meeting of the Society for American Archaeology, Minneapolis.

1997 The Archaeology of Ancient Religion in the Eastern Woodlands. *Annual Reviews of Anthropology* 26: 465–485.

2004 Mound City and Issues in the Developmental History of Hopewell Culture in the Ross County Area of Southern Ohio. In *Aboriginal Ritual and Economy in the Eastern Woodlands: Essays in Memory of Howard Dalton Winters*, edited by Anne-Marie Cantwell, Lawrence A. Conrad, and Jonathan E. Reyman, pp. 147–168. Illinois State Museum Scientific Papers No. 30. Springfield.

2006 The Shamanistic Element in Hopewellian Period Ritual. In *Recreating Hopewell*, edited by Douglas K. Charles and Jane E. Buikstra, pp. 475–488. University Press of Florida, Gainesville.

Buckley, Thomas

2002 *Standing Ground: Yurok Indian Spirituality 1850–1990.* University of California Press, Berkeley.

Buikstra, Jane E.

1976 *Hopewell in the Lower Illinois Valley: A Regional Study of Human Biological Variability and Prehistoric Mortuary Behavior.* Scientific Papers No. 2. Northwestern University Archeological Program, Evanston, Ill.

1977 Biocultural Dimensions of Archaeological Study: A Regional Perspective. In *Biocultural Adaptation in Prehistoric America*, edited by R. L. Blakely, pp. 67–84. University of Georgia Press, Athens.

1980 Epigenetic Distance: A Study of Biological Variability in the Lower Illinois River Valley. In *Early Native Americans*, edited by David L. Browman, pp. 271–299. Paris, Mouton.

Buikstra, Jane E., and Douglas K. Charles

1999 Centering the Ancestors: Cemeteries, Mounds and Sacred Landscapes of the Ancient North American Midcontinent. In *Archaeologies of Landscape: Contemporary Perspectives*, edited by Wendy Ashmore and A. Bernard Knapp, pp. 201–228. Blackwell, Oxford.

Buikstra, Jane E., Douglas K. Charles, and Gordon F. M. Rakita

1998 *Staging Ritual: Hopewell Ceremonialism at the Mound House Site, Greene County, Illinois.* Kampsville Studies in Archeology and History No. 1. Center for American Archeology, Kampsville, Ill.

Bullard, William R.

1962 Settlement Pattern and Social Structure in the Southern Lowlands During the Classic Period. In *Ancient Mesoamerica*, edited by J. Graham, pp. 137–145. Peek Publications, Palo Alto, Calif.

Burks, Jarrod D.

2004 *Identifying Household Cluster and Refuse Disposal Patterns at the Strait Site: A Third Century* A.D. *Nucleated Settlement in the Middle Ohio River Valley.* Ph.D. dissertation, Department of Anthropology, Ohio State University. University Microfilms, Ann Arbor.

Burks, Jarrod D., and Jennifer Pederson

2006 The Place of Non-Mound Debris at the Hopewell Mound Group (33RO27), Ross County, Ohio. In *Recreating Hopewell*, edited by Douglas K. Charles and Jane E. Buikstra, pp. 376–401. University Press of Florida, Gainesville.

Burks, Jarrod D., Jennifer Pederson, and Dawn Walter

2002 Hopewell Landuse Patterns at the Hopeton Earthworks. Paper presented at the 67th annual meeting of the Society for American Archaeology, Denver.

Burks, Jarrod D., and Dawn Walter

2003 Hopewell Occupation at the Hopeton Earthworks: Combining Surface Survey and Geophysical Data to Study Land Use. Paper presented at the 68th annual meeting of the Society for American Archaeology, Milwaukee.

Burton, Kelli

2006 Putting Down Roots. *American Antiquity* 10: 33–37.

Bushnell, H.

1889 *The History of Granville, Licking County, Ohio*. Harr and Adair, Columbus, Ohio.

Butzer, Karl W.

1977 *Geomorphology of the Lower Illinois Valley as a Spatial-Temporal Context for the Koster Archaic Site*. Reports of Investigations No. 34. Illinois State Museum, Springfield.

1978 Changing Holocene Environments at the Koster Site: A Geo-Archaeological Perspective. *American Antiquity* 43: 408–413.

Byers, A. Martin

1987 *The Earthwork Enclosures of the Central Ohio Valley: A Temporal and Structural Analysis of Woodland Society and Culture*. Ph.D. dissertation, Department of Anthropology, State University of New York at Albany. University Microfilms, Ann Arbor.

1996 Social Structure and the Pragmatic Meaning of Material Culture: Ohio Hopewell as Ecclesiastic-Communal Cult. In *A View from the Core: A Synthesis of Ohio Hopewell Archaeology*, edited by Paul J. Pacheco, pp. 174–192. Ohio Archaeological Council, Columbus.

1998 Is the Newark Circle-Octagon the Ohio Hopewell "Rosetta Stone"? In *Ancient Earthen Enclosures of the Eastern Woodlands*, edited by Robert C. Mainfort Jr. and Lynne P. Sullivan, pp. 135–153. University Press of Florida, Gainesville.

1999 Intentionality, Symbolic Pragmatics and Material Culture: Revisiting Binford's View of the Old Copper Complex. *American Antiquity* 64: 265–287.

2004 *The Ohio Hopewell Episode: Paradigm Lost, Paradigm Gained*. University of Akron Press, Akron.

2006a The Earthwork/Habitation Dichotomy: A Central Problem of Ohio Hopewell. In *Recreating Hopewell*, edited by Douglas K. Charles and Jane E. Buikstra, pp. 62–73. University Press of Florida, Gainesville.

2006b *Cahokia: A World Renewal Cult Heterarchy*. University Press of Florida, Gainesville.

Caldwell, Joseph R.

1958 *Trend and Tradition in the Prehistory of the Eastern United States*. Memoir 88. American Anthropological Association, Washington, D.C.

1964 Interaction Spheres in Prehistory. In *Hopewellian Studies*, edited by Joseph R. Caldwell and Robert L. Hall, pp. 133–143. Illinois State Museum Scientific Papers No. 12. Springfield.

Calentine, Leighann

2005 The Spoon Toe Site (11MG179): Middle Woodland Gardening in the Lower Illinois River Valley. Master's thesis, Department of Anthropology, University of Missouri, Columbia.

Carr, Christopher

2004 The Tripartite Ceremonial Alliance among Scioto Hopewellian Communities and the Question of Social Ranking. In *Gathering Hopewell: Society, Ritual and Ritual Interaction*, edited by Christopher Carr and D. Troy Case, pp. 258–338. Kluwer, New York.

2008a Social and Ritual Organization. In *The Scioto Hopewell and Their Neighbors: Bioarchaeological Documentation and Cultural Understanding*, edited by D. Troy Case and Christopher Carr, pp. 151–288. Springer, New York.

2008b Coming to Know Ohio Hopewell Peoples Better: Topics for Future Research, Master's Theses, and Doctoral Dissertations. In *The Scioto Hopewell and Their Neighbors: Bioarchaeological Documentation and Cultural Understanding*, edited by D. Troy Case and Christopher Carr, pp. 603–690. Springer, New York.

2008c Settlement and Communities. In *The Scioto Hopewell and Their Neighbors: Bioarchaeological Documentation and Cultural Understanding*, edited by D. Troy Case and Christopher Carr, pp. 101–150. Springer, New York.

Carr, Christopher, and D. Troy Chase (editors)

2004 *Gathering Hopewell: Society, Ritual, and Ritual Interaction*. Kluwer, New York.

Carr, Christopher, and H. Haas

1996 Beta-Count and AMS Radiocarbon Dates of Woodland and Ft. Ancient Period Occupations in Ohio 1350 B.C.–A.D. 1650. *West Virginia Archaeologist* 48: 19–53.

Carroll, Sean B.

2005 *Endless Forms Most Beautiful: The New Science of Evo Devo and the Making of the Animal Kingdom*. W. W. Norton, New York.

Carskadden, Jeff, and Brain Donaldson

2008 A Hopewell Habitation Site near the Great Circle, Newark, Ohio. *Ohio Archaeologist* 58 (2): 47–50.

Carskadden, Jeff, and John Morton

1996 The Middle Woodland–Late Woodland Transition in the Central Muskingum Valley of Eastern Ohio: A View from the Philo Archaeological District. In *A View from the Core: A Synthesis of Ohio Hopewell Archaeology*, edited by Paul J. Pacheco, pp. 316–339. Ohio Archaeological Council, Columbus.

1997 Living on the Edge: A Comparison of Adena and Hopewell Communities in the Central Muskingum Valley of Eastern Ohio. In *Ohio Hopewell Community Organization*, edited by William S. Dancey and Paul J. Pacheco, pp. 365–401. Kent State University Press, Kent, Ohio.

Chapman, Robert

1981 The Emergence of Formal Disposal Areas and the "Problem" of Megalithic Tombs in Prehistoric Europe. In *The Archaeology of Death*, edited by R. Chapman, I. Kinnes, and K. Randsborg, pp. 71–81. Cambridge University Press, Cambridge.

1995 Ten Years After—Megaliths, Mortuary Practices, and the Territorial Model. In *Regional Approaches to Mortuary Analysis*, edited by L. A. Beck, pp. 29–52. Plenum, New York.

2006 Middle Woodland/Hopewell: A View from Beyond the Periphery. In *Recreating Hopewell*, edited by Douglas K. Charles and Jane E. Buikstra, pp. 510–528. University Press of Florida, Gainesville.

Charles, Douglas K.

1992a Shading the Past: Models in Archeology. *American Anthropologist* 94: 905–925.

1992b Woodland Demographic and Social Dynamics in the American Midwest: Analysis of a Burial Mound Survey. *World Archaeology* 24: 175–197.

1995 Diachronic Regional Social Dynamics: Mortuary Sites in the Illinois Valley/ American Bottom Region. In *Regional Approaches to Mortuary Analysis*, edited by L. A. Beck, pp. 77–99. Plenum, New York.

2006 Telling Tales of the Dead: Paradigm Compartmentalization or Dissociative Identity Disorder? Paper presented at the 71st annual meeting of the Society for American Archaeology, San Juan, Puerto Rico.

Charles, Douglas K., and Jane E. Buikstra

1983 Archaic Mortuary Sites in the Central Mississippi Drainage: Distribution, Structure and Behavioral Implications. In *Archaic Hunters and Gatherers in the American Midwest*, edited by James L. Phillips and James A. Brown, 117–145. Academic Press, New York.

1999 Centering the Ancestors: Cemeteries, Mounds and Sacred Landscapes of the Ancient North American Midcontinent. In *Archaeologies of Landscape: Contemporary Perspectives*, edited by Wendy Ashmore and Bernard Knapp, pp. 201–228. Blackwell, Malden, Mass.

2002 Siting, Sighting and Citing the Dead. In *The Space and Place of Death*, edited by H. Silverman and D. Small, pp. 13–25. Archaeological Papers of the American Anthropological Association No. 11. American Anthropological Association, Arlington, Va.

Charles, Douglas K., and Jane E. Buikstra (editors)

2006 *Recreating Hopewell*. University Press of Florida, Gainesville.

Charles, Douglas K., Jane E. Buikstra, and Lyle W. Konigsberg

1986 Behavioral Implications of Terminal Archaic and Early Woodland Mortuary Practices in the Lower Illinois Valley. In *Early Woodland Archeology*, edited by Kenneth B. Farnsworth and Thomas E. Emerson, pp. 458–474. Kampsville Seminars in Archeology No. 2. Center for American Archeology, Kampsville, Ill.

Charles, Douglas K., Steven R. Leigh, and Jane E. Buikstra (editors)

1988 *The Archaic and Woodland Cemeteries at the Elizabeth Site in the Lower Illinois Valley*. Kampsville Archeological Center Research Series, Vol. 7. Center for American Archeology, Kampsville, Ill.

Charles, Douglas K., and Juliana L. Shortell

2002 Pots as Tools: Using Sherd and Vessel Distributions to Examine Site Structure. Poster presented at the 67th annual meeting of the Society for American Archaeology, Denver.

Chaudhuri, Jean, and Joyotpaul Chaudhuri

2001 *A Sacred Path: The Way of the Muskogee Creeks*. UCLA American Indian Studies Center, Los Angeles.

Chidlaw, Benjamin

1829 Platt of an Old Fortification near Granville, Ohio. Manuscript on file. Walter Havighurst Special Collections Library. Miami University, Miami, Ohio.

Church, Flora, and Annette G. Ericksen

1997 Beyond the Scioto Valley: Middle Woodland Occupations in the Salt Creek Drainage. In *Ohio Hopewell Community Organization*, edited by William S. Dancey and Paul J. Pacheco, pp. 331–360. Kent State University Press, Kent, Ohio.

Clark, John E.

2004 Surrounding the Sacred: Geometry and Design of Early Mound Groups as Meaning and Function. In *Signs of Power: The Rise of Cultural Complexity in the Southeast*, edited by Jon L. Gibson and Philip J. Carr, pp. 162–213. University of Alabama Press, Tuscaloosa.

Clay, R. Berle

1988 Peter Village: An Adena Enclosure. In *Middle Woodland Settlement and Ceremonialism in the Mid-south and Lower Mississippi Valley*, edited by Robert C. Mainfort Jr., pp. 19–29. Archaeological Reports 22. Mississippi Department of Archives and History, Jackson.

1991 *Essential Features of Adena Ritual: A Lecture Delivered at Angel Mounds National Historical Landmark, Evansville, Indiana on 3 April 1990*. Research Reports Number 13. Glenn A. Black Laboratory of Archaeology, Indiana University, Bloomington.

1992 Chiefs, Big Men, or What? Economy, Settlement Patterns, and Their Bearing on Adena Political Models. In *Cultural Variability in Context: Woodland Settlements of the Mid-Ohio Valley*, edited by Mark F. Seeman, pp. 77–80. Midcontinental Journal of Archaeology Special Paper No. 7. Kent State University Press, Kent, Ohio.

1998 The Essential Features of Adena Ritual and Their Implications. *Southeastern Archaeology* 17: 1–21.

2002 Deconstructing the Woodland Sequence from the Heartland: A Review of Recent Research Directions in the Upper Ohio Valley. In *The Woodland Southeast*, edited by David G. Anderson and Robert C. Mainfort Jr., pp. 162–184. University of Alabama Press, Tuscaloosa.

2005 Adena: Rest in Peace. In *Woodland Period Systematics in the Middle Ohio Valley*, edited by Darlene Applegate and Robert C. Mainfort Jr., pp. 94–110. University of Alabama Press, Tuscaloosa.

Clifford, James, and George E. Marcus (editors)

1986 *Writing Culture: The Poetics and Politics of Ethnography*. University of California Press, Berkeley.

Cloud, Henry Roe

1929 Mythologies of Our Aborigines. *Ohio Archaeological and Historical Society Publications* 38: 561–567.

Connolly, Robert P.

1996 Prehistoric Land Modification at the Fort Ancient Hilltop Enclosure: A Model of Formal and Accretive Development. In *A View from the Core: A Synthesis of*

Ohio Hopewell Archaeology, edited by Paul J. Pacheco, pp. 258–273. Ohio Archaeological Council, Columbus.

1997 The Evidence for Habitation at the Fort Ancient Earthworks, Warren County, Ohio. In *Ohio Hopewell Community Organization*, edited by William S. Dancey and Paul J. Pacheco, pp. 251–281. Kent State University Press, Kent, Ohio.

1998 Architectural Grammar Rules at the Fort Ancient Hilltop Enclosure. In *Ancient Earthen Enclosures of the Eastern Woodlands*, edited by Robert C. Mainfort and Lynn P. Sullivan, pp. 85–113. University Press of Florida, Gainesville.

Connolly, Robert P., and Bradley T. Lepper (editors)

2004 *The Fort Ancient Earthworks: Prehistoric Lifeways of a Hopewell Culture in Southwestern Ohio.* Ohio Historical Society, Columbus.

Corbin, Juliet, and Anselm Strauss

2008 *Basics of Qualitative Research: Techniques and Procedures for Developing Grounded Theory.* Sage, Thousand Oaks, Calif.

Coughlin, Sean, and Mark F. Seeman

1997 Hopewell Settlements at the Liberty Earthworks, Ross County, Ohio. In *Ohio Hopewell Community Organization*, edited by William S. Dancey and Paul J. Pacheco, pp. 231–250. Kent State University Press, Kent, Ohio.

Cowan, Frank L.

1999 Making Sense of Flake Scatters: Lithic Technological Strategies and Mobility. *American Antiquity* 64: 593–607.

2000 A Mobile Hopewell? Questioning Assumptions of Ohio Hopewell Sedentism. Paper presented at the Center for American Archaeology Conference, Perspectives on Middle Woodland at the Millennium, Pere Marquette State Park, Grafton, Ill.

2006 A Mobile Hopewell? Questioning Assumptions of Ohio Hopewell Sedentism. In *Recreating Hopewell*, edited by Douglas Charles and Jane Buikstra, pp. 26–49. University Press of Florida, Gainesville.

Cowan, Frank L., and N'omi B. Greber

2002 Hopewell Mound 11: Yet Another Look at an Old Collection. *Hopewell Archaeology: The Newsletter of Hopewell Archaeology in the Ohio River* Valley 5 (2): 7–11.

Cowan, Frank L., Ted S. Sunderhaus, and Robert A. Genheimer

1998 Notes from the Field: An Update from the Stubbs Earthworks Site. *Ohio Archaeological Council Newsletter* 10 (2): 6–13.

1999 Notes from the Field, 1999: More Hopewell "Houses" at the Stubbs Earthworks Site. *Ohio Archaeological Council Newsletter* 11 (2): 11–16.

2000 Wooden Architecture in Ohio Hopewell Sites: Structural and Spatial Patterns at the Stubbs Earthworks Site. Paper presented at the 65th annual meeting of the Society for American Archaeology, Philadelphia.

2004 Earthwork Peripheries: Probing the Margins of the Fort Ancient Site. In *The Fort Ancient Earthworks: Prehistoric Lifeways of the Hopewell Culture in Southwestern*

Ohio, edited by R. P. Connolly and B. T. Lepper, pp. 107–124. Ohio Historical Society, Columbus.

Creswell, John W.
2007 *Qualitative Inquiry and Research Design: Choosing Among Five Approaches.* Sage, Thousand Oaks, Calif.

Crites, Gary D.
1987 Human-Plant Mutualism and Niche Expression in the Paleoethnobotanical Record: A Middle Woodland Example. *American Antiquity* 52: 725–740.

Crump, Thomas
1990 *The Anthropology of Numbers.* Cambridge University Press, Cambridge.

Dalan, Rinita A.
2008 A Review of the Role of Magnetic Susceptibility in Archaeological Studies in the USA: Recent Developments and Prospects. *Archaeological Prospection* 15: 1–31.

Dancey, William S.
1991 A Middle Woodland Settlement in Central Ohio: A Preliminary Report on the Murphy Site (33LI212). *Pennsylvania Archaeologist* 61 (2): 37–72.
1992 Village Origins in Central Ohio: The Results and Implications of Recent Middle and Late Woodland Research. In *Cultural Variability in Context: Woodland Settlements of the Mid-Ohio Valley*, edited by Mark F. Seeman, pp. 24–29. Kent State University Press, Kent, Ohio.
1996 Putting an End to Ohio Hopewell. In *A View from the Core: a Synthesis of Ohio Hopewell Archaeology*, edited by Paul J. Pacheco, pp. 394–405. Ohio Archaeological Council, Columbus.
2003 Overly: A Middle Woodland Settlement Near the Hopeton Earthworks, Ross County, Ohio. Manuscript prepared for publication. In possession of the author, Columbus, Ohio.
n.d. The Ohio Hopewell Bladelet Industry and the Question of Craft Specialization. Unpublished manuscript. In possession of author, Columbus, Ohio.

Dancey, William S., and Paul J. Pacheco
1997 A Community Model of Ohio Hopewell Settlement. In *Ohio Hopewell Community Organization*, edited by William S. Dancey and Paul J. Pacheco, pp. 3–40. Kent State University Press, Kent, Ohio.

Dancey, William S., and Paul J. Pacheco (editors)
1997 *Ohio Hopewell Community Organization.* Kent State University Press, Kent, Ohio.

Dancey, William S., and Mark F. Seeman
2005 Rethinking the Cole Complex, a Post-Hopewellian Archaeological Unit in Central Ohio. In *Woodland Period Systematics in the Middle Ohio Valley*, edited by Darlene Applegate and Robert C. Mainfort Jr., pp. 134–149. University of Alabama Press, Tuscaloosa.

Davis, Edwin H.
1847 Letter to Ephraim Squier. Ephraim Squier Papers. Reel 1. Library of Congress.

Davis, William M.

1926 The Value of Outrageous Geological Hypotheses. *Science* 63: 463–468.

DeBoer, Warren R.

1997 Ceremonial Centres from the Cayapas (Esmeraldas, Ecuador) to Chillicothe (Ohio, USA). *Cambridge Archaeological Journal* 7: 225–253.

2003 News Under the Sun. *Reviews in Anthropology* 32: 1–12.

2004 Little Bighorn on the Scioto: The Rocky Mountain Connection to Ohio Hopewell. *American Antiquity* 69: 85–107.

2005 Colors for a North American Past. *World Archaeology* 37: 66–91.

DeBoer, Warren R., and John H. Blitz

1991 Ceremonial Centers of the Chachi. *Expedition* 33 (1): 53–62.

Delcourt, Paul A., Hazel R. Delcourt, Patricia A. Cridlebaugh, and Jefferson Chapman

1986 Holocene Ethnobotanical and Paleoecological Record of Human Impact on Vegetation in the Little Tennessee River Valley, Tennessee. *Quaternary Research* 25: 330–349.

Deloria, Vine

2001 Power and Place Equal Personality. In *Power and Place: Indian Education in America*, edited by Vine Deloria Jr. and Daniel Wildcat, pp. 21–28. American Indian Graduate Center and Fulcrum Resources, Golden, Colo.

DeLorme Software Solutions

2002 3-D Topoquads 2.0 software. http://www.delorme.com/.

2004 XMap 4.5 software. http://www.delorme.com/.

De Saussure, Ferdinand

1966 *Course in General Linguistics*. McGraw-Hill, New York.

Dillehay, Thomas D.

1990 Mapuche Ceremonial Landscape, Social Recruitment and Resource Rights. *World Archaeology* 22: 223–241.

1992 Keeping Outsiders Out: Public Ceremony, Resource Rights, and Hierarchy in Historic and Contemporary Mapuche Society. In *Wealth and Hierarchy in the Intermediate Area*, edited by Frederick W. Lange, pp. 379–422. Dumbarton Oaks Research Center, Washington, D.C.

Douglas, Mary

1984 *Purity and Danger: An Analysis of the Concepts of Pollution and Taboo*. Ark Paperbacks, London.

Dragoo, Don W.

1963 *Mounds for the Dead: An Analysis of the Adena Culture*. Annals of Carnegie Museum, Vol. 37. Pittsburgh.

Dunnell, Robert C.

1978 Style and Function: A Fundamental Dichotomy. *American Antiquity* 43: 192–202.

1980 Evolutionary Theory and Archaeology. In *Advances in Archaeological Theory and Method*, vol. 3, edited by M. B. Schiffer, pp. 35–99. Academic Press, New York.

1982 Science, Social Science, and Common Sense: The Agonizing Dilemma of Modern Archaeology. *Journal of Anthropological Research* 38: 1–25.

Dunnell, Robert C., and Diana M. Greenlee

1999 Late Woodland Period "Waste" Reduction in the Ohio River Valley. *Journal of Anthropological Archaeology* 18: 376–395.

Echo-Hawk, Roger C.

2000 Ancient History in the New World: Integrating Oral Traditions and the Archaeological Record in Deep Time. *American Antiquity* 65: 267–290.

Emerson, Thomas E., Randal Hughes, Kenneth Farnsworth, and Sarah Wisseman

2005 Sourcing Squier and Davis' Mound City Pipe Cache. Paper presented at the 51st annual Midwest Archaeological Conference, Dayton, Ohio.

Essenpreis, Patricia S., and Michael E. Moseley

1984 Fort Ancient: Citadel or Coliseum? *Field Museum of Natural History Bulletin* 55 (6): 5–10, 20–26.

Fagan, Brian

1997 Comments on DeBoer's "Ceremonial Centres from the Cayapas (Esmeraldas, Ecuador) to Chillicothe (Ohio, USA)." *Cambridge Archaeological Journal* 7: 247.

Fahlander, Fredrik

2001 Archaeology as Science Fiction: A Microarchaeology of the Unknown. *Gotarc Serie C, Arkeologiska Skrifter* No. 43. Department of Archaeology, University of Gothenburg.

Farmer, Philip Jose

1984 *To Your Scattered Bodies Go*. Berkley, New York.

Farnsworth, Kenneth B., and David L. Asch

1986 Early Woodland Chronology, Artifact Styles, and Settlement Distribution in the Lower Illinois Valley Region. In *Early Woodland Archeology*, edited by Kenneth B. Farnsworth and Thomas E. Emerson, pp. 326–457. Kampsville Seminars in Archeology No. 2. Center for American Archeology, Kampsville, Ill.

Feld, Steven, and Keith H. Basso (editors)

1996 *Senses of Place*. School of American Research Press, Santa Fe, N.M.

Firth, Raymond

1975 *Symbols Public and Private*. Cornell University Press, Ithaca.

Flannery, Kent V.

1982 The Golden Marshalltown: A Parable for the Archaeology of the 1980's. *American Anthropologist* 84: 265–278.

2002 The Origins of the Village Revisited: From Nuclear to Extended Households. *American Antiquity* 67: 417–434.

Flannery, Kent V., and Joyce Marcus

1993 Cognitive Archaeology. *Cambridge Archaeology Journal* 3: 260–270.

Flannery, Kent V., and Marcus C. Winters

1976 Analyzing Household Activities. In *The Early Mesoamerican Village*, edited by Kent V. Flannery, pp. 34–47. Academic Press, New York.

Flannery, Regina (editor)

1956–1957 *The Gros Ventres of Montana*, 2 vols. Catholic University of America Press, Washington, D.C.

Flew, Antony (editor)

1987 *Readings in the Philosophical Problems of Parapsychology*. Prometheus Books, Buffalo.

Ford, Richard I.

1972 Barter, Gift or Violence: An Analysis of Tewa Intertribal Exchange. In *Social Exchange and Interaction*, edited by Edwin Wilmsen, pp. 21–45. Anthropological Papers No. 36. Museum of Anthropology, University of Michigan, Ann Arbor.

Forsyth, Jane L.

1966 *Glacial Map of Licking County, Ohio*. Ohio Department of Natural Resources, Division of Geological Survey. Report of Investigations No. 59. Columbus.

Foster, John B.

2000 *Marx's Ecology: Materialism and Nature*. Monthly Review Press, New York.

Fowke, Gerard

1892 Some Interesting Mounds. *American Anthropologist* 5: 73–82.

1902 *Archaeological History of Ohio*. Ohio State Archaeological and Historical Society, Columbus.

Frege, Gottlob

1993 On Sense and Reference. In *Meaning and Reference*, edited by A. W. Moore, pp. 23–42. Oxford University Press, Oxford.

Fritz, Gayle J.

1990 Multiple Pathways to Farming in Precontact Eastern North America. *Journal of World Prehistory* 4: 387–435.

Frolking, Tod A., and Bradley T. Lepper

2001 Geomorphic and Pedogenic Evidence for Bioturbation of Artifacts at a Multicomponent Site in Licking County, Ohio, U.S.A. *Geoarchaeology* 16: 243–262.

Gadamer, Hans Georg

1994 *Truth and Method*. Translated by J. Weinsheimer and D. G. Marshall. Continuum, New York.

Gehlbach, Don R.

1985 An Important Hopewell Workshop in Fairfield County, Ohio. *Ohio Archaeologist* 35 (3): 12–14.

Genheimer, Robert A.

1984 A Systematic Examination of Middle Woodland Settlements in Warren County, Ohio. Manuscript on file. Ohio Historic Preservation Office, Columbus.

1996 Bladelets Are Tools Too: The Predominance of Bladelets Among Formal Tools at Ohio Hopewell Sites. In *A View from the Core: A Synthesis of Ohio Hopewell Archaeology*, edited by Paul J. Pacheco, pp. 92–107. Ohio Archaeological Council, Columbus.

1997 Stubbs Cluster: Hopewellian Site Dynamics at a Forgotten Little Miami River

Valley Settlement. In *Ohio Hopewell Community Organization*, edited by William S. Dancey and Paul J. Pacheco, pp. 283–309. Kent State University Press, Kent, Ohio.

Gibbon, Guy E.

1989 *Explanation in Archaeology*. Basil Blackwell, Oxford.

Gibson, Jon L.

1996 *Poverty Point: A Terminal Archaic Culture of the Lower Mississippi Valley*. 2nd ed. Louisiana Archaeological Survey and Antiquities Commission, Anthropological Study Series No. 7. Department of Culture, Recreation, and Tourism, Baton Rouge.

2004 The Power of Beneficent Obligation in First Mound-Building Societies. In *Signs of Power: The Rise of Cultural Complexity in the Southeast*, edited by Jon L. Gibson and Philip J. Carr, pp. 254–269. University of Alabama Press, Tuscaloosa.

Giddens, Anthony

1984 *The Constitution of Society: Outline of a Theory of Structuration*. University of California Press, Berkeley.

Giedion, Sigfried

1971 *Architecture and the Phenomena of Transition*. Harvard University Press, Cambridge.

Gould, Stephen. J.

1977 *Ontogeny and Phylogeny*. Harvard University Press, Cambridge.

1986 Evolution and the Triumph of Homology: Or Why History Matters. *American Scientist* 74: 60–69.

1989 *Wonderful Life: The Burgess Shale and the Nature of History*. W. W. Norton, New York.

Grantham, Bill

2002 *Creation Myths and Legends of the Creek Indians*. University Press of Florida, Gainesville.

Greber, N'omi B.

1976 *Within Ohio Hopewell: Analyses of Burial Patterns from Several Classic Sites*. Ph.D. dissertation, Department of Anthropology, Case Western Reserve University. University Microfilms, Ann Arbor.

1979a Variations in Social Structure of Ohio Hopewell Peoples. *Midcontinental Journal of Archaeology* 4: 35–78.

1979b A Comparative Study of Site Morphology and Burial Patterns at Edwin Harness Mound and Seip Mounds 1 and 2. In *Hopewell Archaeology: The Chillicothe Conference*, edited by David S. Brose and N'omi B. Greber, pp. 27–38. Kent State University Press, Kent, Ohio.

1990 Preliminary Report on the 1990 Excavations at Capitolium Mound Earthworks. Presented to the National Geographic Society, Washington, D.C.

1991 A Study of Continuity and Contrast Between Central Scioto Adena and Hopewell Sites. *West Virginia Archaeologist* 43 (1 and 2): 1–26.

1995 Some Archaeological Localities Recorded in the Seip Earthworks and Dill

Mounds Historic District. Report to the National Park Service. Manuscript on file. Hopewell Culture National Historical Park, Chillicothe, Ohio.

1996 A Commentary on the Contexts and Contents of Large to Small Ohio Hopewell Deposits. In *A View from the Core: A Synthesis of Ohio Hopewell Archaeology*, edited by Paul J. Pacheco, pp. 150–172. Ohio Archaeological Council, Columbus.

1997a Two Geometric Enclosures in the Paint Creek Valley: An Estimate of Possible Changes in Community Patterns Through Time. In *Ohio Hopewell Community Organization*, edited by William S. Dancey and Paul J. Pacheco, pp. 207–229. Kent State University Press, Kent, Ohio.

1997b Comments on DeBoer's "Ceremonial Centres from the Cayapas (Esmeraldas, Ecuador) to Chillicothe (Ohio, USA)." *Cambridge Archaeological Journal* 7: 244–247.

1999 Combining Geophysics and Ground Truth at High Banks Earthworks, Ross County, Ohio. *Ohio Archaeological Council Newsletter* 2 (1): 8–13.

2002 A Preliminary Comparison of 1997 and 2002—Limited Excavations in the Great Circle Wall, High Bank Works, Ross County, Ohio. *Hopewell Archaeology: The Newsletter of Hopewell Archaeology in the Ohio River Valley* 5 (2): 1–6.

2003 Chronological Relationships among Ohio Hopewell Sites: Few Dates and Much Complexity. In *Theory, Method, and Practice in Modern Archaeology*, edited by Robert J. Jeske and Douglas K. Charles, pp. 88–113. Praeger, Westport, Conn.

2005 Adena and Hopewell in the Middle Ohio Valley: To Be or Not to Be. In *Woodland Period Systematics in the Middle Ohio Valley*, edited by Darlene Applegate and Robert Mainfort Jr., pp. 19–39. University of Alabama Press, Tuscaloosa.

2006 Enclosures and Communities in Ohio Hopewell: An Essay. In *Recreating Hopewell*, edited by Douglas K. Charles and Jane E. Buikstra, pp. 74–105. University Press of Florida, Gainesville.

Greber, N'omi B. (editor)

1983 *Recent Excavations at the Edwin Harness Mound, Liberty Works, Ross County, Ohio*. Midcontinental Journal of Archaeology Special Paper No. 5. Kent State University Press, Kent, Ohio.

Greber, N'omi B., and R. Berle Clay

1993 Reconciling Adena and Hopewell. Paper presented at the 58th annual meeting of the Society for American Archaeology, St. Louis.

Greber, N'omi B., Richard S. Davis, and Ann S. DuFresne

1981 The Micro-Component of the Ohio Hopewell Lithic Technology: Bladelets. *Annals of the New York Academy of Sciences* 376: 489–528.

Greber, N'omi B., and Katharine C. Ruhl

1989 *The Hopewell Site: A Contemporary Analysis Based on the Work of Charles C. Willoughby*. Westview Press, Boulder, Colo. Reprinted. Eastern National, Washington, Pa., in cooperation with Harvard Peabody Museum of Archaeology and Ethnology, 2000.

Greenman, Emerson F.

1932 Excavation of the Coon Mound and an Analysis of the Adena Culture. *Ohio Archaeological and Historical Quarterly* 41: 366–523.

Grieder, Terence

1982 *Origins of Pre-Columbian Art*. University of Texas Press, Austin.

Griffin, James B.

1952 Culture Periods in Eastern United States Archaeology. In *Man in Northeastern North America*. Papers of the Robert S. Peabody Foundation for Archaeology 3, pp. 37–95. Robert S. Peabody Foundation for Archaeology, Andover.

1996 The Hopewell Housing Shortage in Ohio, A.D. 1–350. In *A View from the Core: a Synthesis of Ohio Hopewell Archaeology*, edited by Paul J. Pacheco, pp. 4–15. Ohio Archaeological Council, Columbus.

Goss, James A.

2000 Traditional Cosmology, Ecology, and Language of the Ute Indians. In *Ute Indian Arts and Culture*, edited by William Wroth, pp. 53–72. Taylor Museum of the Fine Arts Center, Colorado Springs, Colo.

Hajic, Edwin R.

1990 Late Pleistocene and Holocene Landscape Evolution, Depositional Subsystems, and Stratigraphy in the Lower Illinois River Valley. Ph.D. dissertation, Department of Geology, University of Illinois at Urbana-Champaign.

Hall, Robert L.

1997 *An Archaeology of the Soul: North American Indian Belief and Ritual*. University of Illinois Press, Urbana.

Hancock, John E.

1995 Radical Hermeneutics and the Work of Architecture. Paper presented at the 83rd Association of Collegiate Schools of Architecture meeting, Seattle. Published in the Conference Proceedings, Association of Collegiate Schools of Architecture, Washington D.C.

2006 *EarthWorks: Virtual Explorations of the Ancient Ohio Valley* (Interactive Video CD-ROM), CERHAS. University of Cincinnati, Cincinnati.

Harrod, Howard L.

1987 *Renewing the World: Plains Indian Religion and Morality*. University of Arizona Press, Tucson.

Hegmon, Michelle

2003 Setting Theoretical Egos Aside: Issues and Theory in North American Archaeology. *American Antiquity* 68: 213–243

Heidegger, Martin

1962 *Being and Time*. Translated by J. Macquarrie and W. Robinson. Harper and Row, New York.

1971 The Origin of the Work of Art. In *Poetry, Language, Thought*. Translated by Albert Hofstadter, pp. 15–87. Harper and Row, New York.

Helms, Mary W.

1979 *Ancient Panama: Chiefs in Search of Power*. University of Texas Press, Austin.

Hewitt, John

1983 Optimal Foraging Models for the Lower Illinois Valley. Ph.D. dissertation, Department of Anthropology, Northwestern University, Evanston, Ill.

Higgs, Eric S., and Claudio Vita-Finzi

1972 Prehistoric Economies: A Territorial Approach. In *Papers in Economic Prehistory*, edited by Eric S. Higgs, pp. 27–36. Cambridge University Press, Cambridge.

Hill, N. N., Jr.

1881 *History of Licking County, Ohio: Its Past and Present*. A. A. Graham, Newark, Ohio.

Hirsch, Eric, and Michael O'Hanlon (editors)

1995 *The Anthropology of Landscape: Perspectives on Place and Space*. Clarendon Press, Oxford.

Hively, Ray, and Robert Horn

1982 Geometry and Astronomy in Prehistoric Ohio. *Journal for the History of Astronomy: Archaeoastronomy Supplement* 13 (4): S1–S20. Reprinted. *Foundations of New World Cultural Astronomy*, edited by A. Aveni, pp. 39–60. University Press of Colorado, Boulder, 2008.

1984 Hopewellian Geometry and Astronomy at High Bank. *Journal for the History of Astronomy: Archaeoastronomy Supplement* 15 (7): S85–100.

2006a A Statistical Study of Lunar Alignments at the Newark Earthworks. *Midcontinental Journal of Archaeology* 31: 281–322.

2006b Hopewell Corporate Centers and Ohio Pilgrimage Churches: A Cautionary Tale. Manuscript on file. Department of Physics and Astronomy, Earlham College, Richmond, Ind.

2008 The Case for Lunar Astronomy at the Newark Earthworks. Manuscript on file. Department of Physics and Astronomy, Earlham College, Richmond, Ind.

Hoagland, Richard

2002 *The Monuments of Mars: A City on the Edge of Forever*. Frog Books, Berkeley, Calif.

Hodder, Ian

1982 *Symbols in Action*. Cambridge University Press, Cambridge.

1986 *Reading the Past: Current Approaches and Interpretations in Archaeology*. Cambridge University Press, Cambridge.

1990 *The Domestication of Europe*. Blackwell, Oxford.

1991 *Reading the Past*. Cambridge University Press, Cambridge.

1992 *Theory and Practice in Archaeology*. Routledge, London.

Hodder, Ian (editor)

1982 *Symbolic and Structural Archaeology*. Cambridge University Press, Cambridge.

1987 *Archaeology as Long-Term History*. Cambridge University Press, Cambridge.

Hooge, Paul E.

1993 Preserving the Ancient Past in Licking County, Ohio: A Case Study. Ph.D. dissertation, Department of Art Education, Ohio State University, Columbus.

Hudson, Charles
1976 *The Southeastern Indians*. University of Tennessee Press, Knoxville.
Ingold, Timothy
1987 Territoriality and Tenure. *The Appropriation of Nature: Essays on Human Ecology and Social Relations*, pp, 130–164. Iowa City: University of Iowa Press.
1993 The Temporality of Landscape. *World Archaeology* 25: 152–174.
Jackson, Jason B.
2003 *Yuchi Ceremonial Life: Performance, Meaning, and Tradition in a Contemporary American Indian Community*. University of Nebraska Press, Lincoln.
Jones, Ben
1935 Old Timer Tells of Hoax. *Newark Advocate*, March 28, Newark, Ohio.
Justice, Noel D.
1987 *Stone Age Spear and Arrow Points of the Midcontinental and Eastern United States*. Indiana University Press, Bloomington.
Kagis-McEwen, Indra
1993 *Socrates' Ancestor: An Essay on Architectural Beginnings*. MIT Press, Cambridge, Mass.
Keeley, Lawrence H.
1982 Hafting and Retooling: Effects on the Archaeological Record. *American Antiquity* 47: 798–809.
Keener, Craig S., and Stephen M. Biehl
1999 Examination and Distribution of Woodland Period Sites Along the Twin Creek Drainage in Southwestern Ohio. *North American Archaeologist* 20: 319–346.
Kelly, Robert L.
1992 Mobility/Sedentism: Concepts, Archaeological Measures, and Effects. *Annual Review of Anthropology* 21: 43–66.
Kennedy, Roger G.
1994 *Hidden Cities: The Discovery and Loss of Ancient North American Civilization*. Free Press, New York.
Kent, Susan
1990 A Cross-Cultural Study of Segmentation, Architecture, and the Use of Space. In *Domestic Architecture and the Use of Space: An Interdisciplinary Cross-Cultural Study*, edited by Susan Kent, pp. 127–152. Cambridge University Press, Cambridge.
1992 Studying Variability in the Archaeological Record: An Ethnoarchaeological Model for Distinguishing Mobility Patterns. *American Antiquity* 57: 635–660.
King, Jason L., Jane E. Buikstra, and Douglas K. Charles
n.d. Time and Archaeological Traditions in the Lower Illinois Valley. *American Antiquity* (in press).
Kitcher, Philip
1989 *Abusing Science: The Case Against Creationism*. MIT Press, Cambridge, Mass.
1995 *The Advancement of Science: Science without Legend, Objectivity without Illustrations*. Oxford University Press, Oxford.

Klemke, E. D., Robert Hollinger, and A. David Kline
1988 *Introductory Readings in the Philosophy of Science*. Prometheus Books, Buffalo, N.Y.

Knapp, A. Bernard
1992 Archaeology and Annales: Time, Space and Change. In *Archaeology, Annales, and Ethnohistory*, edited by A. Bernard Knapp, pp. 1–21. Cambridge University Press, Cambridge.

Knapp, A. Bernard, and Wendy Ashmore
1999 Archaeological Landscapes: Constructed, Conceptualized, Ideational. In *Archaeologies of Landscape: Contemporary Perspectives*, edited by Wendy Ashmore and A. Bernard Knapp, pp. 1–30. Blackwell, Malden, Mass.

Kohler, Timothy A.
1997 Public Architecture and Power in Pre-Columbian North America. Paper presented at the international symposium, "Power, Monuments, and Civilization," Nara, Japan. Electronic document, http://www.santafe.edu/research/publications/wpabstract/199803022/.

Kollerstrom, Nick
2002 *Crop Circles: The Hidden Form*. Wessex Books, Salisbury, UK.

Konigsberg, Lyle W.
1988 Migration Models of Prehistoric Postmarital Residence. *American Journal of Physical Anthropology* 77: 471–482.
1990 Temporal Aspects of Biological Distance: Serial Correlation and Trend in a Prehistoric Skeletal Lineage. *American Journal of Physical Anthropology* 82: 45–52.

Konigsberg, Lyle W., and Jane E. Buikstra
1995 Regional Approaches to the Investigation of Past Human Biocultural Structure. In *Regional Approaches to Mortuary Analysis*, edited by Lane A. Beck, pp. 191–219. Plenum, New York.

Kozarek, Susan E.
1987 *A Hopewellian Homestead in the Ohio River Valley*. Master's thesis, Department of Anthropology, University of Cincinnati.
1997 Determining Sedentism in the Archaeological Record. In *Ohio Hopewell Community Organization*, edited by William S. Dancey and Paul J. Pacheco, pp. 131–152. Kent State University Press, Kent, Ohio.

Kroeber, Alfred L.
1983 *The Arapaho*. University of Nebraska Press, Lincoln. Reprint of original 1902, 1904, and 1907 eds.

Kubler, George
1962 *The Shape of Time: Remarks on the History of Things*. Yale University Press, New Haven.

Kut, Steven T., and Jane E. Buikstra
1998 Calibration of C-14 Dates in the Lower Illinois River Valley. Paper presented at the 63rd annual meeting of the Society for American Archaeology, Seattle, Wash.

Kuznar, Lawrence A.

2008 *Reclaiming a Scientific Anthropology*. 2nd ed. AltaMira Press, Lanham, Md.

Lankford, George E.

1987 *Native American Legends*. August House, Little Rock, Ark.

2004 World on a String: Some Cosmological Components of the Southeastern Ceremonial Complex. In *Hero, Hawk, and Open Hand: American Indian Art of the Ancient Midwest and South*, edited by Richard V. Townsend and Robert V. Sharp, pp. 206–217. Art Institute of Chicago and Yale University Press, New Haven.

Layton, Robert, and Peter J. Ucko

1999 Introduction: Gazing on the Landscape and Encountering the Environment. In *The Archaeology and Anthropology of Landscape: Shaping Your Landscape*, edited by Peter J. Ucko and Robert Layton, pp. 1–20. Routledge, London.

Lazazzera, Adrienne J.

2000 Hopewell Community Evolution: Evidence from the Ft. Ancient Site. Paper presented at the Center for American Archaeology Conference, Perspectives on Middle Woodland at the Millennium, Pere Marquette State Park, Grafton, Ill.

2004 Hopewell Household Variation at the Fort Ancient Site. In *The Fort Ancient Earthworks: Prehistoric Lifeways of a Hopewell Culture in Southwestern Ohio*, edited by Robert Connolly and Bradley Lepper, pp. 84–106. Ohio Historical Society, Columbus.

Lekson, Stephen H.

1999 *The Chaco Meridian: Centers of Political Power in the Ancient Southwest*. AltaMira Press, Walnut Creek, Calif.

Leone, Mark P.

1981 The Relationship between Artifacts and the Public in Outdoor History Museums. *Annals of the New York Academy of Sciences* 376: 301–314.

1982 Some Opinions about Recovering Mind. *American Antiquity* 47: 742–760.

1986 Symbolic, Structure, and Critical Archaeology. In *American Archaeology: Past and Future*, edited by David J. Meltzer, David D. Fowler, and Jeremy A. Sabloff, pp. 415–438. Smithsonian Institution Press, Washington, D.C.

1995 A Historical Archaeology of Capitalism. *American Anthropologist* 97: 251–268.

Leone, Mark P., and Parker Potter Jr. (editors)

1988 *The Recovery of Meaning: Historical Archaeology in the Eastern United States*. Smithsonian Institution Press, Washington, D.C.

Lepper, Bradley T.

1989 An Historical Review of Archaeological Research at the Newark Earthworks. *Journal of the Steward Anthropological Society* 18: 118–140.

1991 Early Archaeological Investigations in Licking County, Ohio. *Ohio Archaeologist* 40 (4): 6–7.

1995 Tracking Ohio's Great Hopewell Road. *Archaeology* 48: 52–56.

1996 The Newark Earthworks and the Geometric Enclosures of the Scioto Valley. In *A View from the Core: A Synthesis of Ohio Hopewell Archaeology*, edited by Paul J. Pacheco, pp. 225–241. Ohio Archaeological Council, Columbus.

1998 The Archaeology of the Newark Earthworks. In *Ancient Enclosures of the Eastern Woodlands*, edited by L. Sullivan and R. Mainfort, pp. 114–134. University Press of Florida, Gainesville.

2002 *The Newark Earthworks: A Wonder of the Ancient World*. Ohio Historical Society, Columbus.

2004a The Newark Earthworks: Monumental Geometry and Astronomy at a Hopewellian Pilgrimage Center. In *Hero, Hawk, and Open Hand: American Indian Art of the Ancient Midwest and South*, edited by Richard V. Townsend and Robert V. Sharp, pp. 72–81. Art Institute of Chicago and Yale University Press, New Haven.

2004b Granville Before History: The Granville Area Inhabitants before the Coming of the Welsh and the New England Yankees. In *Granville Ohio: A Study in Continuity and Change*, edited by Anthony Lisska, pp. 1–34. Granville Historical Society, Granville, Ohio.

2005 *Ohio Archaeology: An Illustrated Chronicle of Ohio's Ancient American Indian Cultures*. Orange Frazer Press, Wilmington, Ohio.

2006 The Great Hopewell Road and the Role of the Pilgrimage in the Hopewell Interaction Sphere. In *Recreating Hopewell*, edited by Douglas K. Charles and Jane E. Buikstra, pp. 122–133. University Press of Florida, Gainesville.

Lepper, Bradley T., and Tod Frolking

2003 Alligator Mound: Geoarchaeological and Iconographical Interpretations of a Late Prehistoric Effigy Mound in Central Ohio, USA. *Cambridge Archaeological Journal* 13: 147–167.

Lepper, Bradley T., and Jeff Gill

1991 Recent Excavations at the Munson Springs Site, a Paleoindian Base Camp in Central Ohio. *Current Research in the Pleistocene* 8: 39–41.

Lepper, Bradley T., and Richard W. Yerkes

1997 Hopewellian Occupations at the Northern Periphery of the Newark Earthworks. In *Ohio Hopewell Community Organization*, edited by William S. Dancey and Paul J. Pacheco, pp. 175–205. Kent State University Press, Kent, Ohio.

Levengood, William C.

1994 Anatomical Anomalies in Crop Formation Plants. *Physiologia Plantarum* 92: 365–364.

Levengood, William C., and Nancy P. Talbott

1999 Dispersion of Energies in Worldwide Crop Formations. *Physiologia Plantarum* 105: 615–624.

Levi-Strauss, Claude

1963 *Structural Anthropology*. Translated by Claire Jacobson and Brooke Grundfest Schoepf. Basic Books, New York.

1975 *The Raw and the Cooked: Introduction to a Science of Mythology*. Translated by John and Doreen Weightman. Harper Colophon, New York.

Lewis, Henry T.

1991 Technological Complexity, Ecological Diversity, and Fire Regimes in Northern

Australia: Hunter-Gatherer, Cowboy, Ranger. In *Profiles in Cultural Evolution: Papers from a Conference in Honor of Elman R. Service*, edited by A. Terry Rambo and Kathleen Gilogly, pp. 261–288. Anthropological Papers No. 85. Museum of Anthropology, University of Michigan, Ann Arbor.

Lewis, Herbert

2001 Boas, Darwin, Science, and Anthropology. *Current Anthropology* 42: 381– 406.

Lippert, Dorothy

2005 Remembering Humanity: How to Include Human Values in a Scientific Endeavor. *International Journal of Cultural Property* 12: 275–280.

Longacre, William A.

1964 Archaeology as Anthropology: A Case Study. *Science* 144: 1454–1455.

1970 *Archaeology as Anthropology: A Case Study*. Anthropological Papers of the University of Arizona No. 17. Tucson.

Lovis, William A., Randolph E. Donahue, and Margaret B. Holman

2005 Long-Distance Logistic Mobility as an Organizing Principle Among Northern Hunter-Gatherers: A Great Lakes Middle Holocene Settlement System. *American Antiquity* 70: 669–693.

Low, Setha M., and Denise Lawrence-Zúñiga (editors)

2003 *The Anthropology of Space and Place: Locating Culture*. Blackwell, Malden, Mass.

Luipjen, William A.

1966 *Phenomenology and Humanism: A Primer in Existential Phenomenology*. Duquesne University Press, Pittsburgh.

Lyman, R. Lee, Michael J. O'Brien, and Robert C. Dunnell

1997 *The Rise and Fall of Culture History*. Plenum, New York.

Lynott, Mark J.

2001 Recent Research at the Hopeton Earthworks, Ross County, Ohio. Paper presented at the 66th annual meeting for the Society for American Archaeology, Milwaukee.

2004 Earthwork Construction and the Organization of Hopewell Society. *Hopewell Archeology: The Newsletter of Hopewell Archeology in the Ohio River Valley* 6 (1): 1–5.

2007 The Chronology of Earthen Wall Construction at the Hopeton Earthworks, Ross County, Ohio. Paper presented at the Midwest Archaeological Conference, University of Notre Dame, Norte Dame, Ind.

Lynott, Mark J., and John Weymouth

2002 Preliminary Report, 2001 Investigations, Hopeton Earthworks. *Hopewell Archeology: The Newsletter of Hopewell Archeology in the Ohio River Valley* 5 (1): 1–7.

Mainfort, Robert C., and Lynne P. Sullivan

1998 Explaining Earthen Enclosures. In *Ancient Earthen Enclosures of the Eastern Woodlands*, edited by Robert C. Mainfort and Lynne P. Sullivan, pp. 1–16. University Press of Florida, Gainesville.

Malville, J. McKim, and Nancy J. Malville
2001 Pilgrimage and Periodic Festivals as Processes of Social Integration in Chaco Canyon. *Kiva* 60: 327–344.

Mann, Rob
2005 Intruding on the Past: The Reuse of Ancient Earthen Mounds by Native Americans. *Southeastern Archaeology* 24: 1–10.

Marks, David, and Richard Kammann
1980 *The Psychology of the Psychic*. Prometheus Books, Buffalo, N.Y.

Marshall, James A.
1995a Astronomical Alignments Claimed to Exist on the Eastern North American Prehistoric Earthworks and the Evidence and Arguments Against Them. *Ohio Archaeologist* 45 (1): 4–16.

1995b Chronology of Hopeton, Mound City, and Nearby Works in Ross County, Ohio as Determined from Alignments. Paper presented at the 41st annual Midwestern Archaeological Conference, Beloit, Wisc.

1996 Towards a Definition of the Ohio Hopewell Core and Periphery Utilizing the Geometric Earthworks. In *A View from the Core: A Synthesis of Ohio Hopewell Archaeology*, edited by Paul J. Pacheco, pp. 210–220. Ohio Archaeological Council, Columbus.

Marshall, Michael P.
1997 The Chacoan Roads: A Cosmological Interpretation. In *Anasazi Architecture and American Design*, edited by Baker H. Morrow and V. B. Price, pp. 61–74. University of New Mexico Press, Albuquerque.

Mason, Ronald J.
2000 Archaeology and Native North American Oral Traditions. *American Antiquity* 65: 239–266.

Mauss, Marcel
1967 *The Gift: Forms and Functions of Exchange in Archaic Societies*. Translated by Ian Gunnison. W. W. Norton, New York.

McAndrews, John H.
1988 Human Disturbance of North American Forests and Grasslands: The Fossil Pollen Record. In *Vegetation History*, edited by B. Huntley and T. Webb III, pp. 673–697. Kluwer, Dordrecht.

McLauchlan, Kendra
2003 Plant Cultivation and Forest Clearance by Prehistoric North Americans: Pollen Evidence from Fort Ancient, Ohio, USA. *Holocene* 13: 557–566.

Mellars, Paul
1976 Fire Ecology, Animal Populations and Man: A Study of Some Ecological Relationships in Prehistory. *Proceedings of the Prehistoric Society* 42: 15–45.

Merleau-Ponty, Maurice
1965 *The Phenomenology of Perception*. Translated by Colin Smith. Humanities Press, New York.

Michelson, Andrew M.

2000 The Salt Wall: A Probable Woodland Period Earthwork in Granville Township, Licking County, Ohio. Paper presented at November 17 meeting of the Ohio Archaeological Council, Columbus. Electronic document, http://www.ohio-archaeology.org/joomla/index2.php?option=com_content&do_pdf=1&id=35/; accessed January 5, 2009.

Mickelson, Michael E., and Bradley T. Lepper

2006 Observational Archaeoastronomy at the Newark Earthworks. *Mediterranean Archaeology and Archaeometry* 63: 175–180.

Miles, M. B., and Huberman, A. M.

1994 *Qualitative Data Analysis*, 2nd ed. Sage, Thousand Oaks, Calif.

Miller, Jay

2001a Instilling the Earth: Explaining Mounds. *American Indian Culture and Research Journal* 25: 161–177.

2001b Keres: Engendered Key to the Pueblo Puzzle. *Ethnohistory* 48: 495–514.

Mills, Lisa A.

2003 Mitochondrial DNA Analysis of the Ohio Hopewell Mound Group. Ph.D. dissertation, Ohio State University, Department of Anthropology, Columbus.

Mills, William C.

1902 Excavations of the Adena Mound. *Ohio Archaeological and Historical Quarterly* 10: 451–479.

1907 Explorations of the Edwin Harness Mound. *Ohio Archaeological and Historical Quarterly* 16: 113–193.

1909 Explorations of the Seip Mound. *Ohio Archaeological and Historical Quarterly* 18: 269–321.

1914 *Archaeological Atlas of Ohio*. Ohio State Archaeological and Historical Society, Columbus.

1916 Exploration of the Tremper Mound. *Ohio Archaeological and Historical Quarterly* 25: 262–398.

1917 Exploration of the Westenhaver Mound. *Ohio Archaeological and Historical Quarterly* 26: 226–266.

1922 Exploration of the Mound City Group. *Ohio Archaeological and Historical Quarterly* 31: 423–584.

Moore, John H.

1987 *The Cheyenne Nation*. University of Nebraska Press, Lincoln.

Moorehead, Warren K.

1886 The Fort near Granville, Ohio. *American Antiquarian* 8: 297.

1890 *Fort Ancient: The Great Prehistoric Earthwork of Warren County, Ohio*. Robert Clarke, Cincinnati.

1892 *Primitive Man in Ohio*. G. P. Putnam's Sons, New York.

1897-98 The Hopewell Group. *Antiquarian* 1: 114–120, 153–158, 178–184, 208–214, 236–244, 254–264, 291–295, 312–316; *American Archaeologist* 2: 6–11.

1900 Report of Field Work. *Ohio Archaeological and Historical Publications* 7: 126–136.

1908 *Fort Ancient: The Great Prehistoric Earthwork of Warren County, Ohio*. Phillips Academy, Department of Archaeology, Bulletin 4 (pt. 2).

Morgan, David T.

1988 Ceramics at the Elizabeth Site. In *The Archaic and Woodland Cemeteries at the Elizabeth Site in the Lower Illinois Valley*, edited by Douglas K. Charles, Steven R. Leigh, and Jane E. Buikstra, pp. 120–154. Kampsville Archeological Center Research Series, Vol. 7. Center for American Archeology, Kampsville, Ill.

Morgan, Lewis H.

1965 *Houses and House-Life of the American Aborigines*. University of Chicago Press, Chicago. Originally published 1881. *Contributions to North American Ethnology*, vol. 4. Government Printing Office, Washington, D.C.

Morgan, Richard G.

1952 Outlines of Cultures in Ohio. In *Archaeology of the Eastern United States*, edited by James B. Griffin, pp. 83–98. University of Chicago Press, Chicago.

Morrow, C. A.

1987 Blades and Cobden Chert: A Technological Argument for Their Role as Markers of Regional Identification during the Hopewell Period in Illinois. In *The Organization of Core Technology*, edited by J. K. Johnson and C. A. Morrow, pp. 119–149. Westview Press, Boulder, Colo.

1988 Chert Exploitation and Social Interaction in the Prehistoric Midwest, 200 B.C.– A.D. 600. Ph.D. dissertation, Southern Illinois University at Carbondale.

1998 Blade Technology and Nonlocal Cherts: Hopewell(?) Traits at the Twenhafel Site, Southern Illinois. In *Changing Perspectives on the Archaeology of the Central Mississippi Valley*, edited by Michael J. O'Brien and Robert C. Dunnell, pp. 281–298. University of Alabama Press, Tuscaloosa.

Mugerauer, Robert

1995 *Interpreting Environments: Tradition, Deconstrution, Hermeneutics*. University of Texas Press, Austin.

Munson, Patrick J., and Cheryl Munson

1990 *The Prehistoric and Early Historic Archaeology of Wyandotte Cave and other Caves of Southern Indiana*. Indiana Historical Society, Indianapolis.

Neusius, Sarah W.

1982 Early-Middle Archaic Subsistence Strategies: Changes in Faunal Exploitation at the Koster Site. Ph.D. dissertation, Department of Anthropology, Northwestern University, Evanston, Ill.

Nickell, Joe

2002 Circular Reasoning: The "Mystery" of Crop Circles and Their "Orbs" of Light. *Skeptical Inquirer* 26: 17–25.

Norberg-Schulz, Christian

1980a *Meaning in Western Architecture*. Rizzoli, New York.

1980b *Genius Loci: Towards a Phenomenology of Architecture*. Rizzoli, New York.

O'Brien, Michael J.

1987 Sedentism, Population Growth, and Resource Selection in the Woodland Midwest: A Review of Co-Evolutionary Developments. *Current Anthropology* 28: 177–197.

O'Brien, Michael J., and R. Lee Lyman

2000 *Applying Evolutionary Theory: A Systematic Approach.* Kluwer, New York.

Odell, George H.

1998 Investigating Correlates of Sedentism in Prehistoric North America. *American Antiquity* 63: 553–571.

Oestigaard, Terje

2004 Approaching Material Culture: A History of Changing Epistemologies. *Journal of Nordic Archaeological Science* 14: 79–87.

Pacheco, Paul J.

1989a Ohio Middle Woodland Settlement Variability in the Upper Licking River Drainage. *Journal of the Steward Anthropological Society* 18: 87–117.

1989b Spatial Distribution of Ohio Woodland Period Mounds in the Lower Muskingum River Drainage. In *Anthropology: Unity in Diversity,* edited by M. Sidky, James Foradas, and Paul J. Pacheco, pp. 20–33. Department of Anthropology, Occasional Papers No. 4. Ohio State University, Columbus.

1993 *Ohio Hopewell Settlement Patterns: An Application of the Vacant Center Model to Middle Woodland Intracommunity Settlement Variability in the Upper Licking River Valley.* Ph.D. dissertation, Department of Anthropology, Ohio State University. University Microfilms, Ann Arbor.

1996 Ohio Hopewell Regional Settlement Patterns. In *View from the Core: A Synthesis of Ohio Hopewell Archaeology,* edited by Paul J. Pacheco, pp. 16–35. Ohio Archaeological Council, Columbus.

1997 Ohio Middle Woodland Intracommunity Settlement Variability: A Case Study from the Licking Valley. In *Ohio Hopewell Community Organization,* edited by William S. Dancey and Paul J. Pacheco, pp. 41–84. Kent State University Press, Kent, Ohio.

Pacheco, Paul J. (editor)

1996 *A View from the Core: A Synthesis of Ohio Hopewell Archaeology.* Ohio Archaeological Council, Columbus.

Pacheco, Paul J., Jarrod Burks, and DeeAnne Wymer

2006 Investigating Ohio Hopewell Settlement Patterns in Central Ohio: A Preliminary Report of Archaeology at Brown's Bottom #1 (33Ro21). Electronic document, http://www.ohioarchaeology.org/joomla/index.php?option=com_content&task=view&id=103&Itemid=32/; accessed March 4, May 11, 2006.

Pacheco, Paul J., and William S. Dancey

2006 Integrating Mortuary and Settlement Data on Ohio Hopewell Society. In *Recreating Hopewell,* edited by Douglas K. Charles and Jane E. Buikstra, pp. 3–25. University Press of Florida, Gainesville.

Palmer, Richard

1969 *Hermeneutics*. Northwestern University Press, Evanston, Ill.

Park, Samuel

1890 *Notes of the Early History of Union Township, Licking County, Ohio*. O. J. Smith, Terre-Haute, Ind.

Parmalee, Paul

1965 The Vertebrate Fauna. In *The McGraw Site: A Study in Hopewellian Dynamics*, edited by Olaf H. Prufer, pp. 115–118. Cleveland Museum of Natural History, Scientific Publications 4 (1). Cleveland, Ohio.

Parry, William J., and Robert Kelly

1987 Expedient Core Technology and Sedentism. In *The Organization of Core Technology*, edited by J. Johnson and C. Morrow, pp. 285–304. Westview Press, Boulder, Colo.

Patterson, Thomas C.

2003 *Marx's Ghost: Conversations with Archaeologists*. Berg, Oxford.

Patton, Michael Q.

2002 *Qualitative Research and Evaluation Methods*. Sage, Thousand Oaks, Calif.

Pederson, Jennifer, and Jarrod Burks

2002 Detecting the Shriver Circle Earthwork, Ross County, Ohio. *Hopewell Archaeology: The Newsletter of Hopewell Archaeology in the Ohio River Valley* 5 (1): 14–17.

Pederson, Jennifer, Jarrod Burks, and William S. Dancey

2001 Hopewell Mound Group: Data Collection at the Hopewell Type Site, 2001. Paper presented at the 47th Midwest Archaeological Conference, La Crosse, Wisc.

Peirce, Charles S.

1931 *Collected Papers*. Edited by Charles Hartshorne and Paul Weiss. Harvard University Press, Cambridge.

Penney, David W.

1985 Continuities of Imagery and Symbolism in the Art of the Woodlands. In *Ancient Art of the American Woodland Indians*, edited by David S. Brose, James A. Brown, and David W. Penney, pp. 147–198. Harry N. Abrams, New York.

Perez-Gomez, Alberto, and Stephen Parcell (editors)

1994 *Chora 1: Intervals in the Philosophy of Architecture*. McGill-Queens University Press, Montreal.

Perino, Gregory H.

1968 The Pete Klunk Mound Group, Calhoun County, Illinois: The Archaic and Woodland Occupations (with an Appendix on the Gibson Mound Group). In *Hopewell and Woodland Site Archaeology in Illinois*, pp. 9–124. Bulletin 6. Illinois Archaeological Survey, Urbana.

2006 *Illinois Hopewell and Late Woodland Mounds: The Excavations of Gregory Perino, 1950–1975*. Assembled and edited by Kenneth B. Farnsworth and Michael D. Wiant. Illinois Transportation Archaeological Research Program, Studies in Archaeology No. 4. University of Illinois, Urbana.

Pickard, William H.

1996 Excavations at Capitolium Mound (33WN13), Marietta, Washington County, Ohio: A Working Evaluation. In *A View from the Core: A Synthesis of Ohio Hopewell Archaeology*, edited by Paul J. Pacheco, pp. 274–285. Ohio Archaeological Council, Columbus.

Pickard, William H., and Laurie A. Gray Pahdopony

1995 Paradise Regained and Lost Again: The Anderson Earthwork, Ross County, Ohio (33RO551). *Hopewell Archeology: The Newsletter of Hopewell Archeology in the Ohio River Valley* 1 (2): 3–6.

Popper, Karl

1963 *Science: Conjectures and Refutations.* Harper and Row, New York.

Preston, James J.

1992 Spiritual Magnetism: An Organizing Principle for the Study of Pilgrimage. In *Sacred Journeys: The Anthropology of Pilgrimage*, edited by Alan Morinis, pp. 31–46. Greenwood Press, Westport, Conn.

Prufer, Olaf H.

1964 The Hopewell Complex of Ohio. In *Hopewellian Studies*, edited by J. Caldwell and R. Hall, pp. 35–83. Illinois State Museum Scientific Papers No. 12 (2). Springfield.

1967 The Scioto Valley Archaeological Survey. In *Studies in Ohio Archaeology*, edited by O. Prufer and D. Mackenzie, pp. 267–328. Kent State University Press, Kent, Ohio.

1997a How to Construct a Model: A Personal Memoir. In *Ohio Hopewell Community Organization*, edited by William S. Dancey and Paul J. Pacheco, pp. 105–128. Kent State University Press, Kent, Ohio.

1997b Fort Hill 1964: New Data and Reflections on Hopewell. In *Ohio Hopewell Community Organization*, edited by William S. Dancey and Paul J. Pacheco, 311–327. Kent State University Press, Kent, Ohio.

Prufer, Olaf H. (editor)

1965 *The McGraw Site: A Study in Hopewellian Dynamics.* Scientific Publications of the Cleveland Museum of Natural History New Series 4 (1). Cleveland, Ohio.

Putnam, Frederick W.

1885 Explorations of the Harness Mounds in the Scioto Valley, Ohio. 18th and 19th Annual Reports of the Peabody Museum, 1884–1885. *Peabody Museum Reports* 3: 405–407.

1886 Explorations in Ohio: The Marriott Mound, No. 1 and Its Contents. 18th and 19th Annual Reports of the Peabody Museum, 1884–1885. *Peabody Museum Reports* 3: 449–466.

Quine, Willard V. O.

1960 *Word and Object.* MIT Press, Cambridge, Mass.

2000 I, You, and It: An Epistemological Triangle. In *Knowledge, Language and Logic: Questions for Quine*, edited by A. Orenstein and P. Kotatko, pp. 1–6. Boston Studies in the Philosophy of Science, Vol. 210. Kluwer, Dordrecht.

Quinn, M. J., and R. P. Goldthwait
1985 *Glacial Geology of Ross County, Ohio*. Department of Natural Resources, Columbus, Ohio.

Rafferty, Janet E.
1985 The Archaeological Record on Sedentariness: Recognition, Development, and Implications. In *Advances in Archaeological Method and Theory*, vol. 8, edited by Michael Schiffer, pp. 113–156. Academic Press, New York.

Railey, Jimmy A.
1991 Woodland Settlement Trends and Symbolic Architecture in the Kentucky Bluegrass. In *The Human Landscape in Kentucky's Past*, edited by C. Stout and C. K. Hensley, pp. 56–77. Kentucky Heritage Council, Frankfort.

Rappaport, Roy A.
1968 *Pigs for the Ancestors: Ritual in the Ecology of a New Guinea People*. Yale University Press, New Haven.
1969 Ritual Regulation of Environmental Relations Among a New Guinea People. In *Environment and Cultural Behavior: Ecological Studies in Cultural Anthropology*, edited by Andrew P. Vayda, pp. 181–201. Natural History Press, Garden City, N.Y.
1971 Ritual, Sanctity, and Cybernetics. *American Anthropologist* 73: 59–76.

Redman, Charles L.
1991 Distinguished Lecture in Archaeology: In Defense of the Seventies—The Adolescence of New Archaeology. *American Anthropologist* 93: 295–307.

Reeves, Dache. M.
1930s. Aerial Photographs in the Dache M. Reeves Collection. Division of Archaeology, National Anthropological Archives, United States National Museum of Natural History, Smithsonian Institution, Washington, D.C.
1936 A Newly Discovered Extension of the Newark Works. *Ohio Archaeological and Historical Quarterly* 14: 189–193.

Reilly, F. Kent, III
2004 People of Earth, People of Sky: Visualizing the Sacred in Native American Art. In *Hero, Hawk, and Open Hand: American Indian Art of the Ancient Midwest and South*, edited by Richard V. Townsend and Robert V. Sharp, pp. 124–137. Art Institute of Chicago and Yale University Press, New Haven.

Renfrew, Colin
1989 Comments on Archaeology into the 1990s. *Norwegian Archaeological Review* 22: 33–41.
2001 Production and Consumption in a Sacred Economy: The Material Correlates of High Devotional Expression at Chaco Canyon. *American Antiquity* 66: 14–25.

Renfrew, Colin, and Paul Bahn
1991 *Archaeology, Theories, Methods, and Practice*. Thames and Hudson, New York.

Reustle, Crystal L.
1993 The Paleoethnobotanical Record of the Munson's Spring Site (33Li251): Plant

Utilization of Ceremonial and Habitation Contexts. *Ohio Archaeologist* 43 (4): 37–40.

Richmond, Michael D., and Jonathan P. Keer

2005 Middle Woodland Ritualism in the Central Bluegrass: Evidence from the Amburgey Site, Montgomery County, Kentucky. In *Woodland Period Systematics in the Middle Ohio Valley*, edited by Darlene Applegate and Robert Mainfort Jr., pp. 76–93. University of Alabama Press, Tuscaloosa.

Ridley, Matt

2002 Crop Circle Confession. *Scientific American* 287: 25.

Riordan, Robert V.

1995 A Construction Sequence for a Middle Woodland Hilltop Enclosure. *Midcontinental Journal of Archaeology* 20: 62–104.

1996 The Enclosed Hilltops of Southern Ohio. In *A View from the Core: A Synthesis of Ohio Hopewell Archaeology*, edited by Paul J. Pacheco, pp. 242–256. Ohio Archaeological Council, Columbus.

1998 Boundaries, Resistance, and Control: Enclosing the Hilltops in Middle Woodland Ohio. In *Ancient Earthen Enclosures of the Eastern Woodlands*, edited by Robert C. Mainfort Jr. and Lynne P. Sullivan, pp. 68–84. University Press of Florida, Gainesville.

2006 Altering a Middle Woodland Enclosure: Questions of Design and Environment. In *Recreating Hopewell*, edited by Douglas K. Charles and Jane E. Buikstra, pp. 146–157. University Press of Florida, Gainesville.

Roberts, John

1999 Trickster. *Oxford Art Journal* 22: 83–101

Rohde, Douglas L., Steve Olson, and Joseph T. Chang

2004 Modeling the Recent Common Ancestry of All Living Humans. *Nature* 431: 562–566.

Romain, William F.

1992 Hopewell Inter-Site Relationships and Astronomical Alignments. *Ohio Archaeologist* 42: 4–5.

1994 Hopewell Geometric Enclosures: Symbols of an Ancient World View. *Ohio Archaeologist* 44: 37–43.

1996 Hopewellian Geometry: Forms at the Interface of Time and Eternity. In *A View from the Core: A Synthesis of Ohio Hopewell Archaeology*, edited by Paul J. Pacheco, pp. 194–209. Ohio Archaeological Council, Columbus.

2000 *Mysteries of the Hopewell: Astronomers, Geometers, and Magicians of the Eastern Woodlands*. University of Akron Press, Akron.

2004a Hopewell Geometric Enclosures: Gatherings of the Fourfold. Ph.D. dissertation, School of Archaeology and Ancient History, University of Leicester.

2004b Journey to the Center of the World: Astronomy, Geometry, and Cosmology of the Fort Ancient Enclosure. In *The Fort Ancient Earthworks: Prehistoric Lifeways of the Hopewell Culture in Southwestern Ohio*, edited by R. P. Connolly and B. T. Lepper, pp. 66–83. Ohio Historical Society, Columbus.

2004c Summary Report on the Orientations and Alignments of the Ohio Hopewell Geometric Enclosures. In *Gathering Hopewell: Society, Ritual, and Ritual Interaction*, edited by Christopher Carr and Troy Case, Appendix 3. Kluwer, New York.

2005a Newark Earthwork Cosmology: This Island Earth. *Hopewell Archaeology: The Newsletter of Hopewell Archeology in the Ohio River Valley* 6 (2): 1–8.

2005b Design and Layout of the Newark Earthworks Complex. *Hopewell Archaeology: The Newsletter of Hopewell Archeology in the Ohio River Valley* 6 (2): 9–21.

Rubey, William W.

1952 Geology and Mineral Sources of the Hardin and Brussels Quadrangles (in Illinois). *Professional Paper 218, United States Geological Survey*. Washington, D.C.

Ruby, Bret J.

1997a Current Research at Hopewell Culture National Historical Park. *Hopewell Archeology: The Newsletter of Hopewell Archeology in the Ohio River Valley* 2 (2): 1–6.

1997b The Mann Phase: Hopewellian Subsistence and Settlement Adaptations in the Wabash Lowlands in Southeastern Indiana. Ph.D. dissertation, Department of Anthropology, Indiana University.

Ruby, Bret J., Christopher Carr, and Douglas K. Charles

2005 Community Organizations in the Scioto, Mann and Havana Hopewellian Regions: A Comparative Perspective. In *Gathering Hopewell: Society, Ritual, and Ritual Interaction*, edited by Christopher Carr and D. Troy Case, pp. 119–176. Kluwer, New York.

Ruby, Bret J., and Christine M. Shriner

2005 Ceramic Vessel Compositions and Styles as Evidence of the Local and Nonlocal Social Affiliations of Ritual Participants at the Mann Site, Indiana. In *Gathering Hopewell: Society, Ritual, and Ritual Interactions*, edited by Christopher Carr and D. Troy Case, pp. 480–532. Kluwer, New York.

Ruhl, Katharine C.

1992 Copper Earspools from Ohio Hopewell Sites. *Midcontinental Journal of Archaeology* 17: 46–79.

1996 Copper Earspools in the Hopewell Interaction Sphere: The Temporal and Social Implications. Master's thesis, Department of Anthropology, Kent State University, Kent, Ohio.

2005 Hopewellian Copper Earspools from Eastern North America: The Social, Ritual and Symbolic Significance of Their Contexts and Distribution. In *Gathering Hopewell: Society, Ritual, and Ritual Interactions*, edited by Christopher Carr and D. Troy Case, pp. 696–713. Kluwer, New York.

Ruhl, Katharine C., and Mark F. Seeman

1998 The Temporal and Social Implications of Ohio Hopewell Copper Earspool Design. *American Antiquity* 63: 651–662.

Sackett, James R.

1990 Style and Ethnicity in Archaeology: The Case for Isochrestism. In *Uses of Style in Archaeology*, edited by Margaret Conkey and Christine Hastorf, pp. 32–43. Cambridge University Press, Cambridge.

Sagan, Carl

1996 *The Demon-Haunted World: Science as a Candle in the Dark*. Random House, New York.

Salhqvist, Leif

2001 Territorial Behaviour and Communication in a Ritual Landscape. *Geografiska Annaler* 83B (2): 79–102.

Salisbury, James H., and Charles B. Salisbury

1862 Accurate Surveys & Descriptions of the Ancient Earthworks at Newark, Ohio. Manuscript on file. American Antiquarian Society, Worcester, Mass.

Sallnow, Michael J.

1981 Communitas Reconsidered: The Sociology of Andean Pilgrimage. *Man* 16: 163–182.

Salmon, Merrilee, John Earman, Clark Glymour, James G. Lennox, Peter Machamer, J. E. McGuire, John D. Norton, Wesley C. Salmon, and Kenneth F. Schaffner

1992 *Introduction to the Philosophy of Science*. Prentice Hall, Englewood Cliffs, N.J.

Sauer, Carl

1925 The Morphology of Landscape. *University of California, Publications in Geography* 2 (2): 19–53.

Saunders, Joe W., and Rolfe D. Mandel, Rodger T. Saucier, E. Thurman Allen, C. T. Hallmark, Jay K. Johnson, Edwin H. Jackson, Charles M. Allen, Gary. L. Stringer, Douglas S. Frink, James. K. Feathers, Stephen Williams, Kristen J. Gremillion, Malcolm F. Vidrine, and Reca Jones

1997 A Mound Complex in Louisiana at 5400–5000 Years Before the Present. *Science* 277: 1796–1799.

Schnabel, Jim

1994a Puck in the Laboratory: The Construction and Deconstruction of Hoaxlike Deception in Science. *Science, Technology, and Human Values* 19: 459–492.

1994b *Round in Circles*. Prometheus Books, Amherst, Mass.

Schwarz, Frederick A., and J. Scott Raymond

1996 Formative Settlement Patterns in the Valdivia Valley, SW Coastal Ecuador. *Journal of Field Archaeology* 23: 205–224.

Searle, John R.

1983 *Intentionality*. Cambridge University Press, Cambridge.

Seeman, Mark F.

1977 *The Hopewell Interaction Sphere: Evidence for Interregional Trade and Structural Complexity*. Ph.D. dissertation, Department of Anthropology, Indiana University. University Microfilms International, Ann Arbor.

1979 *The Hopewell Interaction Sphere: The Evidence for Interregional Trade and*

Structural Complexity. Prehistory Research Series 5. Indiana Historical Society, Indianapolis.

1995 When Words Are Not Enough: Hopewell Interregionalism and the Use of Material Symbols at the GE Mound. In *Native American Interactions: Multiscalar Analyses and Interpretations in the Eastern Woodlands*, edited by Michael S. Nassaney and Kenneth E. Sassaman, pp. 122–143. University of Tennessee Press, Knoxville.

1996 The Ohio Hopewell Core and Its Many Margins: Deconstructing Upland and Hinterland Relations. In *A View from the Core: A Synthesis of Ohio Hopewell Archaeology*, edited by Paul J. Pacheco, pp. 304–315. Ohio Archaeological Council, Columbus.

2004 Hopewell Art in Hopewell Places. In *Hero, Hawk, and Open Hand: American Indian Art of the Ancient Midwest and South*, edited by Richard V. Townsend and Robert V. Sharp, pp. 56–71. Art Institute of Chicago and Yale University Press, New Haven.

Seeman, Mark F., and James L. Branch

2006 The Mounded Landscapes of Ohio: Hopewell Patterns and Placements. In *Recreating Hopewell*, edited by Douglas K. Charles and Jane E. Buikstra, pp. 106–121. University Press of Florida, Gainesville.

Seeman, Mark F., and Ann C. Cramer

1982 The Manring Mounds: A Hopewell Center in the Mad River Drainage, Clark County, Ohio. *Ohio Journal of Science* 82: 151–161.

Seeman, Mark F., and N'omi B. Greber

1991 Flames of Reverence: Variations in the Use of Prepared Clay Basins Within Ohio Hopewell. Paper presented at 37th annual meeting of the Midwest Archaeological Conference, LaCrosse, Wisc.

Shanks, Michael, and Christopher Tilley

1987a *Reconstructing Archaeology*. Cambridge University Press, Cambridge.

1987b *Social Theory and Archaeology*. University of New Mexico Press, Albuquerque.

1989 Archaeology in the 1990s. *Norwegian Archaeological Review* 22: 1–12.

Shaw, Justine M.

2001 Maya *Sacbeob*: Form and Function. *Ancient Mesoamerica* 12: 261–272.

Sheets, Payson D., and Guy R. Muto

1972 Pressure Blades and Total Cutting Edge: An Experiment in Lithic Technology. *Science* 175: 632–634.

Sherratt, Andrew

1990 The Genesis of Megaliths: Monumentality, Ethnicity, and Social Complexity in Neolithic North-West Europe. *World Archaeology* 22: 147–167.

Shetrone, Henry C.

1926 Exploration of the Hopewell Group of Prehistoric Earthworks. *Ohio Archaeological and Historical Quarterly* 35: 1–227.

Shetrone, Henry C., and Emerson F. Greenman

1931 Explorations of the Seip Group of Prehistoric Earthworks. *Ohio Archaeological and Historical Society Quarterly* 40: 343–509.

Sieg, Lauren E., and R. Eric Hollinger
2005 Learning from the Past: The History of Ohio Hopewell Taxonomy and Its Implications for Archaeological Practice. In *Woodland Period Systematics in the Middle Ohio Valley*, edited by Darlene Applegate and Robert C. Mainfort Jr., pp. 120–133. University of Alabama Press, Tuscaloosa.

Silva, Freddy
2002 *Secrets in the Fields: The Science and Mysticism of Crop Circles.* Hampton Roads Publishing, Charlottesville, Va.

Silverman, Helaine
1988 Cahuachi: Non-Urban Cultural Complexity on the South Coast of Peru. *Journal of Field Archaeology* 15: 403–430.
1994 The Archaeological Identification of an Ancient Peruvian Pilgrimage Center. *World Archaeology* 26: 1–18.
2002 *Ancient Nasca Settlement and Society.* University of Iowa Press, Iowa City.

Skinner, Shaune M.
1985 Preliminary Results of the 1983 Excavation of the Connett Mounds #3 and #4, the Wolf Plains National Register District, Athens County, Ohio. *Archaeology of Eastern North America* 13: 138–152

Smith, Bruce D.
1989 Origins of Agriculture in Eastern North America. *Science* 246: 1566–1571.
1992 Hopewellian Farmers of Eastern North America. In *Rivers of Change: Essays on Early Agriculture in Eastern North America*, edited by Bruce D. Smith, pp. 201–248. Smithsonian Institution Press, Washington, D.C.
2001 Low-Level Food Production. *Journal of Archaeological Research* 9: 1–43.
2006 Household, Community, and Subsistence in Hopewell Research. In *Recreating Hopewell*, edited by Douglas K. Charles and Jane E. Buikstra, pp. 491–509. University Press of Florida, Gainesville.

Smith, Michael E.
1992 Braudel's Temporal Rhythms and Chronology Theory in Archaeology. In *Archaeology, Annales, and Ethnohistory*, edited by A. Bernard Knapp, pp. 23–34. Cambridge University Press, Cambridge.

Snyder, John F.
2004 A Group of Illinois Mounds. In *Early Hopewell Mound Explorations: The First Fifty Years in the Illinois River Valley*, edited by Kenneth B. Farnsworth, pp. 179–183. Studies in Archaeology 3. Illinois Transportation Archaeological Research Program, University of Illinois, Urbana. Originally published in 1885. *Archaeologist* 3 (4): 109–113.

Sofaer, Anna
1997 The Primary Architecture of the Chacoan Culture: A Cosmological Expression. In *Anasazi Architecture and American Design*, edited by B. H. Morrow and V. B. Price, pp. 88–132. University of New Mexico Press, Albuquerque.

Sosis, Richard, and Candace Alcorta
2003 Signaling, Solidarity, and the Sacred: The Evolution of Religious Behavior. *Evolutionary Anthropology* 12: 264–274.

Speck, Frank G.

1915 *Myths and Folk-lore or the Timiskaming Algonquin and Timagami Ojibwa.* Canada Department of Mines, Geological Survey, Memoir 71. Anthropological Series No. 9. Ottawa.

1931 *A Study of the Delaware Indian Big House Ceremony.* Pennsylvania Historical Commission, Harrisburg.

Speck, Frank G., and Jesse Moses

1945 *The Celestial Bear Comes Down to Earth: The Bear Sacrifice Ceremony of the Munsee-Mahican in Canada as Related by Nekatcit.* Reading Public Museum and Art Gallery Scientific Publications 7. Reading, Pennsylvania.

Spence, Michael W., and Brian J. Fryer

2005 Hopewellian Silver and Silver Artifacts from Eastern North America: Their Sources, Procurement, Distribution, and Meanings. In *Gathering Hopewell: Society, Ritual, and Ritual Interactions*, edited by Christopher Carr and D. Troy Case, pp. 714–733. Kluwer, New York.

Spriggs, Matthew (editor)

1984 *Marxist Perspectives in Archaeology.* Cambridge University Press, Cambridge.

Squier, Ephraim, and Edwin H. Davis

1848 [1998] *Ancient Monuments of the Mississippi Valley.* Smithsonian Institution Press, Washington, D.C. Reprinted. *Classics in Smithsonian Anthropology*, with introduction by David J. Meltzer. Smithsonian Institution Press, Washington, D.C., 1998.

n.d. The Papers of Ephraim Squier. Microfilm. Series IV, Vol. 9, Shelf No: DM15, 116, Reel No. 12 of 14. On file, Library of Congress, Washington, D.C.

Stafford, Barbara D., and Mark B. Sant (editors)

1985 *Smiling Dan: Structure and Function at a Middle Woodland Settlement in the Illinois Valley.* Kampsville Archeological Center Research Series, Vol. 2. Center for American Archeology, Kampsville, Ill.

Stein, John R., Judith E. Suiter, and Dabney Ford

1997 High Noon in Old Bonito: Sun, Shadow, and the Geometry of the Chaco Complex. In *Anasazi Architecture and American Design*, edited by Baker H. Morrow and V. B. Price, pp. 133–147. University of New Mexico Press, Albuquerque.

Stoltman, James B., and Richard E. Hughes

2004 Obsidian in Early Woodland Contexts in the Upper Mississippi Valley. *American Antiquity* 69: 751–759.

Struever, Stuart, and Gail L. Houart

1972 An Analysis of the Hopewell Interaction Sphere. In *Social Exchange and Interaction, Museum of Anthropology*, edited by Edwin N. Wilmsen, pp. 47–79. Anthropological Papers No. 46. Museum of Anthropology, University of Michigan, Ann Arbor.

Styles, Bonnie W.

1981 *Faunal Exploitation and Resource Selection: Early Late Woodland Subsistence in the Lower Illinois Valley*. Scientific Papers No. 3. Northwestern University Archeological Program, Evanston, Ill.

Styles, Thomas R.

1985 *Holocene and Late Pleistocene Geology of the Napoleon Hollow Site in the Lower Illinois Valley*. Kampsville Archeological Center Research Series, Vol. 5. Center for American Archaeology, Kampsville, Ill.

Sunyer, Oriol P.

1965 Lithic Industries at McGraw. In *The McGraw Site: A Study in Hopewellian Dynamics*, edited by Olaf H. Prufer, pp. 60–89. Cleveland Museum of Natural History, Scientific Publications 4 (1). Cleveland, Ohio.

Suskind, Ron

2004 Without a Doubt. *New York Times Magazine*, October 17. Also available as electronic document, http://www.lexisnexis.com/.

Swartz, B. K. (editor)

1971 *Adena: The Seeking of an Identity*. Ball State University Press, Muncie, Ind.

Taubs, Gary

1993 *Bad Science: The Short Life and Weird Times of Cold Fusion*. Random House, New York.

Tax, Sol

1937 The Municipios of the Midwestern Highlands of Guatemala. *American Anthropologist* 39: 423–444.

Thomas, Cyrus

1894 [1985] Report on the Mound Explorations of the Bureau of Ethnology. *Twelfth Annual Report, 1890–1891*. Bureau of American Ethnology. Reprinted. Smithsonian Institution Press, Washington, D.C., 1985.

1889 *The Circular, Square, and Octagonal Earthworks of Ohio*. Bureau of American Ethnology, Bulletin No. 10. Smithsonian Institution, Washington, D.C.

Thomas, Julian

2004 *Archaeology and Modernity*. Routledge, London.

Tilley, Christopher

1994 *A Phenomenology of Landscape: Places, Paths and Monuments*. Berg, Oxford.

1998 Archaeology as Socio-Political Action in the Present. In *Reader in Archaeological Theory: Post-Processual and Cognitive Approaches*, edited by David S. Whitley, pp. 305–330. Routledge, London. Original published in 1989 in *Critical Traditions in Contemporary Archaeology: Essays in Philosophy, History and Socio-Politics of Archaeology*, edited by V. Pinsky and A. Wylie, pp. 104–115.

Tozzer, Alfred M.

1941. *Landa's Relación de las Cosas de Yucatán: A Translation*. Papers of the Peabody Museum of American Archaeology and Ethnology, Vol. 18. Harvard University, Cambridge.

Trigger, Bruce G.

1989 *A History of Archaeological Thought*. Cambridge University Press, Cambridge.

Trombold, Charles D. (editor)

1991 *Ancient Road Networks and Settlement Hierarchies in the New World*. Cambridge University Press, Cambridge.

Turner, Victor

1974 *Dramas, Fields, and Metaphors: Symbolic Action in Human Society*. Cornell University, Ithaca, N.Y.

Ucko, Peter J., and Robert Layton (editors)

1999 *The Archaeology and Anthropology of Landscape: Shaping Your Landscape*. Routledge, London.

Unzicker, Joseph S.

1860 Map of the Newark Earthworks. Manuscript on file. No. 4373. Joseph S. Unzicker Papers, 1849–1869. Western Reserve Historical Society, Cleveland, Ohio.

van Dommelen, Peter

1999 Exploring Everyday Places and Cosmologies. In *Archaeologies of Landscape: Contemporary Perspectives*, edited by Wendy Ashmore and A. Bernard Knapp, pp. 277–285. Blackwell, Malden, Mass.

Van Dyke, Ruth M.

2004a Chaco's Sacred Geography. In *Search of Chaco: New Approaches to an Archaeological Enigma*, edited by David G. Noble, pp. 78–85. School of American Research, Santa Fe, N.M.

2004b Memory, Meaning, and Masonry: The Late Bonito Chacoan Landscape. *American Antiquity* 69: 413–431.

Van Gilder, C. L., and Douglas K. Charles

2003 Archaeology as Cultural Encounter: The Legacy of Hopewell. In *Theory, Method, and Practice in Modern Archaeology*, edited by R. M. Jeske and D. K. Charles, pp. 114–129. Praeger, Westport, Conn.

Van Nest, Julieanne

1997 Late Quaternary Geology, Archeology, and Vegetation in West-Central Illinois: A Study in Geoarchaeology. Ph.D. dissertation, Department of Geology, University of Iowa, Iowa City.

2006 Rediscovering This Earth: Some Ethnogeological Aspects of the Illinois Valley Hopewell Mounds. In *Recreating Hopewell*, edited by Douglas K. Charles and Jane E. Buikstra, pp. 402–426. University Press of Florida, Gainesville.

Varien, Mark

1999 *Sedentism and Mobility in a Social Landscape*. University of Arizona Press, Tucson.

Vecsey, Christopher

1983 *Traditional Ojibwa Religion and Its Historical Changes*. American Philosophical Society Memoir, Vol. 152. Philadelphia.

Vickery, Kent D.

1996 Flint Raw Material Use in Ohio Hopewell. In *A View from the Core: A Synthesis of Ohio Hopewell Archaeology*, edited by Paul J. Pacheco, pp. 108–127. Ohio Archaeological Council, Columbus.

Vogt, Evon Z.

1961 Some Aspects of Zinacantan Settlement Patterns and Ceremonial Organization. *Estudias Cultura Maya* 1: 131–146.

1964 Some Implications of Zinacantan Social Structure for the Study of the Ancient Maya. *Proceedings of the 35th International Congress of the Americas* 1: 307–319.

1969 *Zinacantan: A Maya Community in the Highlands of Chiapas.* Harvard University Press, Cambridge.

Volker, John

2004 The Geometry of the Newark Earthworks. Unpublished manuscript on file. Bradley Lepper, Ohio Historical Society, Columbus.

Waldron, John, and Elliott M. Abrams

1999 Adena Burial Mounds and Inter-Hamlet Visibility: A GIS Approach. *Midcontinental Journal of Archaeology* 24: 97–111.

Walthall, John A.

1979 Hopewell and the Southern Heartland. In *Hopewell Archaeology: The Chillicothe Conference*, edited by David S. Brose and N'omi B. Greber, pp. 200–208. Kent State University Press, Kent, Ohio.

Watson, Aaron

2001 Composing Avebury. *World Archaeology* 33: 296–314.

Watson, Patty Jo

1985 The Impact of Early Horticulture in the Upland Drainages of the Midwest and Midsouth. In *Prehistoric Food Production in North America*, edited by Richard Ford, pp. 99–147. Anthropological Papers No. 75. Museum of Anthropology, University of Michigan, Ann Arbor.

Webb, William S., and Raymond S. Baby

1957 *The Adena People, No. 2.* Ohio Historical Society, Columbus.

Webb, William S., and Charles E. Snow

1945 *The Adena People.* Reports in Anthropology and Archaeology 6. University of Kentucky, Lexington.

Weinberger, Jennifer Pederson

2006 Ohio Hopewell Earthworks: An Examination of Site Use from Non-Mound Space at the Hopewell Site. Ph.D. dissertation, Department of Anthropology, Ohio State University.

Weller Von Molsdorff, R. J.

1998 A Phase I Cultural Resource Management Survey for the Proposed 16 ha (40 a.) Raccoon Valley Park in Granville Township, Licking County, Ohio. APPLIED Archaeological Services, Inc. Submitted to the Granville Township Trustees, Granville, Ohio.

Wenke, Robert J.

1999 *Patterns in Prehistory: Humankind's First Three Million Years.* Oxford University Press, New York.

Whiteley, Peter M.

2002 Archaeology and Oral Tradition: The Scientific Importance of Dialogue. *American Antiquity* 67: 405–415.

Whittaker, Martin

2000 College Keen to Make Hay out of Crop Circles. *Times Educational Supplement* 4394: 37.

Whittlesey, Charles C.

1852 *Descriptions of Ancient Works in Ohio*. Smithsonian Contributions to Knowledge 3. Smithsonian Institution, Washington, D.C.

1922 *The Turner Group of Earthworks, Hamilton County, Ohio*. Papers of the Peabody Museum of American Archaeology and Ethnology, Vol. 8, No. 3. Harvard University, Cambridge.

Wiant, Michael D., and Charles R. McGimsey (editors)

19868 *Woodland Period Occupations of the Napoleon Hollow Site in the Lower Illinois Valley*. Kampsville Archeological Center Research Series, Vol. 6. Center for American Archeology, Kampsville, Ill.

Wiessner, Polly

1983 Style and Social Information in Kalahari San Projectile Points. *American Antiquity* 48: 253–276.

Wilden, Anthony

1980 *System and Structure*. Tavistock, Boston.

Wilford, Lloyd A.

1970 *Burial Mounds of the Red River Headwaters*. Minnesota Historical Society, St. Paul.

Wilford, Lloyd A., Elden Johnson, and Joan Vicinus

1969 *Burial Mounds of Central Minnesota: Excavation Reports*. Minnesota Historical Society, St. Paul.

Willey, Gordon R.

1953 *Prehistoric Settlement Patterns in the Virú Valley, Peru*. Bureau of American Ethnology, Bulletin No. 155. Smithsonian Institution, Washington, D.C.

1956 Problems Concerning Prehistoric Settlement Patterns in the Maya Lowlands. In *Prehistoric Settlement Patterns in the New World*, edited by Gordon R. Willey, pp. 107–114. Viking Fund Publications in Anthropology, No. 23. New York.

Willey, Gordon R., and Philip Phillips

1958 *Method and Theory in American Archaeology*. University of Chicago Press, Chicago.

Willoughby, Charles C., and Earnest A. Hooton

1922 *The Turner Group of Earthworks, Hamilton County, Ohio*. Papers of the Peabody Museum of American Archaeology and Ethnology, Vol. 8, No. 3. Harvard University, Cambridge.

Wobst, Martin H.

1977 Stylistic Behavior and Information Exchange. In *For the Director: Research Essays in Honor of James B. Griffin*, edited by Charles E. Cleland, pp. 317–342. Anthropological Papers No. 61. Museum of Anthropology, University of Michigan, Ann Arbor.

1978 The Archaeo-Ethnology of Hunter-Gatherers, or the Tyranny of the Ethnographic Record in Archaeology. *American Antiquity* 43: 303–309.

Wylie, Alison

1978 The Archaeo-Ethnology of Hunter-Gatherers, or the Tyranny of the Ethnographic Record in Archaeology. *American Antiquity* 43: 303–309.

1992 The Interplay of Evidential Constraints and Political Interests: Recent Archaeological Research on Gender. *American Antiquity* 57: 15–34.

1999 Rethinking Unity as a "Working Hypothesis" for Philosophy of Science: How Archaeologists Exploit the Disunities of Science. *Perspectives on Science* 7: 293–317.

2002 The Reaction against Analogy. In *Thinking from Things*, edited by Alison Wylie, pp. 136–153. University of California Press, Berkeley.

Wymer, DeeAnne

1987 The Middle Woodland–Late Woodland Interface in Central Ohio: Subsistence Continuity Amid Cultural Change. In *Emergent Horticultural Economies of the Eastern Woodlands*, edited by William F. Keegan, pp. 201–216. Center for Archaeological Investigations, Occasional Paper No. 7. Southern Illinois University Press, Carbondale.

1992 Trends and Disparities: The Woodland Paleoethnobotanical Record of the Mid-Ohio Valley. In *Cultural Variability in Context: Woodland Settlements of the Mid-Ohio Valley*, edited by Mark F. Seeman, pp. 65–76. Midcontinental Journal of Archaeology Special Paper No. 7. Kent State University Press, Kent, Ohio.

1993 Cultural Change and Subsistence: The Middle and Late Woodland Transition in the Mid-Ohio Valley. In *Plant Production and Social Relations*, edited by C. Margaret Scarry, pp. 138–156. University Press of Florida, Gainesville.

1996 The Ohio Hopewell Econiche: Human Land Interaction in the Core Area. In *A View from the Core: A Synthesis of Ohio Hopewell Archaeology*, edited by Paul J. Pacheco, pp. 36–52. Ohio Archaeological Council, Columbus.

1997 Paleoethnobotany in the Licking River Valley, Ohio: Implications for Understanding Ohio Hopewell. In *Ohio Hopewell Community Organization*, edited by William S. Dancey and Paul J. Pacheco, pp. 153–171. Kent State University Press, Kent, Ohio.

2001 Organic Preservation on Ohio Hopewell Copper Artifacts: New Insights into Middle Woodland Ritual. Paper presented at the 66th annual meeting of the Society for American Archaeology, New Orleans.

2002a Growing the World in Their Image: The Evolutionary Trajectory of Hopewell Plant Utilization. Paper presented at the 48th annual meeting of the Midwestern Archaeological Conference, Ohio State University.

2002b The Value of Archival Collections: Organic Preservation on Hopewell Copper Artifacts. Paper presented at the 46th annual meeting, plenary session, for the Midwestern Archaeological Conference, Ohio State University.

2004 Organic Preservation on Prehistoric Copper Artifacts of the Ohio Hopewell. In *Perishable Material Culture in the Northeast*, edited by Penelope B. Drooker, pp.

45–68. New York State Museum Bulletin 300. University of the State of New York, Albany.

2006 Organic Material on Hopewell Copper: The Field Museum's Hopewell Site Collection. Paper presented at the 52nd Midwestern Archaeological Conference, "Plants and Technology" symposium, Urbana, Ill.

Wyrick, David

1866 Ancient Works Near Newark, Licking County, O. Drawn by D. Wyrick, 1860. In *Atlas of Licking County, Ohio*. Beers, Soule, New York.

Yerkes, Richard W.

1990 Using Microwear Analysis to Investigate Domestic Activities and Craft Specialization at the Murphy Site, a Small Hopewell Settlement in Licking County, Ohio. In *The Interpretive Possibilities of Microwear Studies*, edited by B. Gräslund, H. Knutsson, K. Knutsson, and J. Taffinder, pp. 167–76. *Aun* 14, Societas Archaeologica Upsaliensis, Uppsala, Sweden.

1994 A Consideration of the Function of Ohio Hopewell Bladelets. *Lithic Technology* 19: 109–127.

2002 Hopewell Tribes: A Study of Middle Woodland Social Organization in the Ohio Valley. In *The Archaeology of Tribal Societies*, edited by William A. Parkinson, pp. 227–245. International Monographs in Prehistory, Archaeological Series 15. Ann Arbor, Mich.

2005 Bone Chemistry, Body Parts, and Growth Marks: Evaluating Ohio Hopewell and Cahokia Mississippian Seasonality, Subsistence, Ritual and Feasting. *American Antiquity* 70: 241–265.

2006 Middle Woodland Settlements and Social Organizations in the Central Ohio Valley: Were the Hopewell Really Farmers? In *Recreating Hopewell*, edited by D. Charles and J. Buikstra, pp. 50–61. University Press of Florida, Gainesville.

Zawacki, April A., and Glen Hausfater

1969 *Early Vegetation of the Lower Illinois Valley*. Reports of Investigations No. 17. Illinois State Museum, Springfield.

Zedeño, Maria N.

1997 Landscapes, Land Use, and the History of Territory Formation: An Example from the Puebloan Southwest. *Journal of Archaeological Method and Theory* 4: 67–103.

Contributors

Jarrod Burks is director of archaeological geophysics at Ohio Valley Archaeology, Inc., a small cultural resource management firm based in Columbus, Ohio. He received his doctorate in anthropology from the Ohio State University in 2004, with a dissertation focused on studying Middle Woodland period households at the Strait site in central Ohio. In his day job, Jarrod conducts geophysical surveys on all manner of archaeology sites, primarily in Ohio and surrounding states. Rediscovering Ohio's earthworks and Hopewell domestic sites using geophysics occupies most of Jarrod's research efforts.

A. Martin Byers received his Ph.D. in anthropology from the State University of New York at Albany (1987). He is retired from teaching anthropology at Vanier College in Montreal and currently is a research associate with the Department of Anthropology of McGill University. He has published two books, one on Ohio Hopewell, *The Ohio Hopewell Episode: Paradigm Lost and Paradigm Gained* (2004), and the other on Cahokia of the Mississippian period, *Cahokia: A World Renewal Cult Heterarchy* (2006), as well as having had several articles published in *Current Anthropology* and *American Antiquity* on the evolution of hominid communication and the symbolic pragmatic meaning of material culture. He is currently writing a second book on Ohio Hopewell and hopes to publish a book on the Mississippianization of the Midwest and Southeast regions of the Eastern Woodlands.

Douglas K. Charles is professor of anthropology and archaeology at Wesleyan University in Middletown, Connecticut, and is the director of collections for the Archaeology Program. His recent publications include *Recreating Hopewell* (edited with J. E. Buikstra) (2006) and *Theory, Method, and Practice in Modern Archaeology* (edited with R. M. Jeske) (2003). Current research interests include the origins of the Hopewell phenomenon and concepts of time in archaeological interpretation.

Warren DeBoer received his Ph.D. in anthropology from the University of California at Berkeley (1972) and is currently professor of anthropology at Queens College of the City University of New York. He is recipient of the Society for American Archaeology Excellence in Ceramic Studies Award

(1999) and has published over fifty monographs and articles dealing with the prehistory of lowland South America, ceramic ethnoarchaeology, and, most recently, Ohio Hopewell.

N'omi B. Greber is curator of archaeology at the Cleveland Museum of Natural History and adjunct associate professor in the Department of Anthropology, Case Western Reserve University. She has focused on Middle and Early Woodland period sites, particularly in southern Ohio, by studying archived collections and directing fieldwork that frequently combines geophysical surveys and more traditional archaeological field methods. She has edited and contributed to publications from *Hopewell Archaeology: The Chillicothe Conference* (1979) to "Re-interpretation of a Group of Low Mounds and Structures, Seip Earthworks, Ross County, Ohio," *Midcontinental Journal of Archaeology* 34:1 (2009).

John E. Hancock holds degrees from the University of Nebraska and McGill University and has taught architectural design, theory, and history at the University of Cincinnati since 1978. His essays on architectural history and interpretation have been published internationally, his media productions and exhibits on ancient architecture and landscapes have been honored widely, and his former students have assumed leadership positions in architectural theory and education throughout the world.

Ray M. Hively received his Ph.D. in physics from Harvard University in 1972. He is currently a professor of physics and astronomy at Earlham College in Richmond, Indiana. He has taught computer science, history of science, and mathematics in addition to physics and astronomy. His research interests have included theoretical astrophysics (the origin of the microwave background and the physics of active galactic nuclei) and archaeoastronomy (the study of Hopewell earthworks). He and his colleague Bob Horn have published a number of articles on the astronomical and geometrical interpretation of the Newark Earthworks and are currently working on a paper providing a similar interpretation of the High Bank Earthworks near Chillicothe, Ohio.

Robert Horn is Professor of Philosophy Emeritus at Earlham College in Richmond, Indiana. He earned the doctorate in theology and the philosophy of religion at Union Theological Seminary in New York City. He has taught at Haverford College in Pennsylvania and Union Theological Seminary in New York. At Earlham College he taught courses in the history of philosophy, concentrating on classical Greece and German philosophy from Kant to Hegel. In

2007 he published *Positivity and Dialectic: A Study of the Theological Method of Hans Lassen Martensen,* an examination of aspects of Hegel's influence in Golden Age Denmark. His research and publication on Hopewell began in 1974 with a course in the history of cosmology that he taught with Ray Hively.

Bradley T. Lepper is a curator of archaeology with the Ohio Historical Society in Columbus. In addition, he is an occasional visiting professor in the Department of Sociology and Anthropology at Denison University in Granville, Ohio. Much of his research in recent years has been focused on the Newark Earthworks and the archaeology of the Raccoon Creek valley. He is the author of *Ohio Archaeology: An Illustrated Chronicle of Ohio's Ancient American Indian Cultures* (2005).

Paul J. Pacheco is associate professor of anthropology, State University of New York at Geneseo. He is the editor of *View from the Core: A Synthesis of Ohio Hopewell Archaeology* (1996) and coeditor with W. S. Dancey of *Ohio Hopewell Community Organization* (1997). His current research is on Ohio Hopewell settlements in the central Scioto Valley, particularly working on a multistage project involving geophysical survey, excavation, and materials analyses. This project is codirected by Jarrod Burks and DeeAnne Wymer.

Robert V. Riordan is professor of anthropology and chair of the Department of Sociology and Anthropology at Wright State University in Dayton, Ohio. He has been conducting field research in Ohio since 1977, primarily at the Pollock Works and Fort Ancient sites. He is currently investigating a large circular feature dubbed the Moorehead Circle in the North Fort at the Fort Ancient Earthworks.

Lauren Sieg is a doctoral candidate at the University of Illinois, Urbana-Champaign. Her doctoral research explores patterns in Hopewell iconography. She has conducted field research at the Fort Ancient site and studied the Hopewell collections at museums in the eastern United States as well as at the British Museum. She has published research on Fort Ancient, Hopewell taxonomy, and repatriation.

DeeAnne Wymer received her Ph.D. from the Ohio State University (1987) and is currently a professor in the Department of Anthropology at Bloomsburg University in Pennsylvania. Her major research focus has been on the paleoethnobotany of the Ohio Hopewell moundbuilders and she has published extensively on their crop system and human-land interaction. She also has investigated the ritual utilization of plants by Hopewell populations, including the analysis of extant organic materials on the surface of ceremonial copper objects. She is currently codirecting (with Paul J. Pacheco and Jarrod Burks) field excavations of Hopewell communities in the Chillicothe, Ohio, region, as well as serving as a staff member and director of the paleoethnobotanical laboratory for the Akhenaten Temple Project (Mendes site) in the Nile Delta, Egypt.

Index

Page numbers in italics refer to illustrations.